Ethnic Minorities in Nineteenth and Twentieth Century Germany

THEMES IN MODERN
GERMAN HISTORY SERIES

General Editor: Panikos Panayi

Published books:

Social Democracy and the Working Class in Nineteenth and
Twentieth Century Germany

STEFAN BERGER

Ethnic Minorities in Nineteenth and Twentieth Century
Germany: Jews, Gypsies, Poles, Turks and Others

PANIKOS PANAYI

Ethnic Minorities in Nineteenth and Twentieth Century Germany

Jews, Gypsies, Poles, Turks and Others

PANIKOS PANAYI

An imprint of **Pearson Education**

Harlow, England · London · New York · Reading, Massachusetts · San Francisco · Toronto · Don Mills, Ontario · Sydney
Tokyo · Singapore · Hong Kong · Seoul · Taipei · Cape Town · Madrid · Mexico City · Amsterdam · Munich · Paris · Milan

Pearson Education Limited
Edinburgh Gate
Harlow
Essex CM20 2JE
England

and Associated Companies throughout the world

Visit us on the World Wide Web at:
www.pearsoneduc.com

First published 2000

ISBN 0–582–26760–9 PPR
ISBN 0–582–26771–4 CSD

British Library Cataloguing-in-Publication Data
A catalogue record for this book is available from the British Library

Library of Congress Cataloging-in-Publication Data
Panayi, Panikos.
    Ethnic minorities in nineteenth and twentieth century Germany : Jews, gypsies, Poles,
Turks and others / Panikos Panayi.
        p.   cm. — (Themes in modern German history series)
    Includes bibliographical references and index.
    ISBN 0–582–26760–9 (PPR) — ISBN 0–582–26771–6 (CSD)
    1. Germany—Ethnic relations.   2. Minorities—Germany—History—19th century.   3.
Minorities—Germany—History—20th century.   I. Title.   II. Series.

DD74.P27 2001
305.8′00943—dc21   00–038443

Set in 11/13½ pt Columbus MT by 35
Produced by Pearson Education Asia Pte Ltd.
Printed in Singapore

CONTENTS

CONTENTS

LIST OF MAPS

LIST OF TABLES

PREFACE

The idea for this book originates in the academic year 1991–2 which I spent in Germany researching for another volume on *German Immigrants in Britain during the Nineteenth Century, 1815–1914* (Oxford, 1995). As a scholar working on the history of minorities I found events around me just as interesting as the information I discovered in the archives. My first two months in Bremen, September and October 1991, where I took a Goethe Institute language course, had a profound impact upon me. I observed three things in particular. First, although I had previously spent two weeks in Germany researching at the Bundesarchiv in Koblenz for my PhD thesis in the summer of 1987, I had not noticed the ubiquity of foreigners in the country, which especially struck me in the autumn in 1991. I also noticed their concentration in jobs at the lower end of the social scale and their absence from any sort of state employment, the latter representing a contrast with immigrants in Britain. The second thing which struck me was the presence of a group of people from eastern Europe in my German class, mostly from the former USSR and Poland. Two of those from the former, about my age, had actually fought in the Soviet Army in Afghanistan and had scars to show for it in the form of amputated arms. I soon learnt from them and the others that they had moved to Germany because they claimed German ethnicity, which surprised me because they spoke either excellent Polish or Russian, but had the same command of German as I did. I would gradually find out about the Aussiedler, as well as the hostility which they faced, which manifested itself in an argument between one of the students and the German teacher in one lesson. But it was a third aspect of German ethnic life which had the deepest impact upon me. Arriving in a foreign country for the purpose of spending any length of time proves a difficult experience under any circumstances. Moving to Germany in the autumn of 1991 was especially trying. On 17

September, less than three weeks after I landed in Bremen, a race riot broke out in the East German town of Hoyerswerda. Although this did not disturb me at first, I quickly became frightened, along with many of my fellow students, at the speed with which racial attacks spread to the West. By the beginning of October, when I still had eleven months to live in Germany, I simply turned on the radio every morning to be greeted with a list of the racial attacks which had occurred on the previous night. This worried me further because of my Greek appearance and my heavily accented German. If some skinheads approached me in the street they would instantly recognize me as a foreigner. In fact on one night in Bremen, as I neared the student hostel where I lived, a tall native German speaker approached me and asked: '*Bist du Nazi?*' ('Are you Nazi?'). I was not sure of the correct answer but, luckily, some other people walked by which allowed me to disappear into the hostel. The fact that I had written about racist violence in Britain made me very conscious of the events around me. I therefore did not enjoy the first few months of my stay in Germany, even though, in the longer term, my attitude towards the country changed completely.

While the events around me terrified me, they also proved absolutely fascinating and I really knew fairly instantaneously that I had to write about them. I collected material for an article on the racist violence and during the first few months in Bremen and Osnabrück I became interested in the continuities in the racial history of Germany, an issue pursued by the media, which eventually resulted in the evolution of the present study.

This book falls into the series I am editing on 'Themes in Modern German History', which aims to examine developments in Germany over the last two centuries. The volumes use both secondary and illustrative contemporary material, as I have done here. My book represents the first to tackle the history of all ethnic groups in Germany during the nineteenth and twentieth centuries and should interest students, academics and the general reader.

Various organizations and individuals have offered support during the evolution of this volume. I owe a great debt to the Alexander von Humboldt Foundation. It not only financed my first year in Germany between 1991 and 1992, which gave birth to my interest in minorities in German history, but also paid for two eight-week trips to carry out the bulk of the research in Germany in the summers of 1997 and 1998. The Humboldt Foundation has played a central role in my intellectual and career development. In addition, I would also like to acknowledge the funding I received from the Department of Historical and International Studies at De Montfort University and the

Nuffield Foundation which allowed me to make two separate journeys of a fortnight each to Frankfurt at Christmas 1993 and Easter 1994, when I gathered much of the information on the post-war period.

I would also like to thank the staffs of the numerous libraries I used in Germany and England. In the former the locations were: in Osnabrück the University Library and the library of the Institut für Migrationsforschung und Interkulturelle Studien; in Berlin, the Staatsbibliothek in Unter den Linden and Potsdamer Strasse as well as the Zentrum für Antisemistismusforschung; in Frankfurt the Deutsche Bibliothek; in Göttingen the Niedersächsisches Staats- und Universitätsbibliothek; in Munich the Bayerische Staatsbibliothek and the Institut für Zeitgeschichte; and in Münster the Universitätsbibliothek. I would also like to thank the staffs of the following libraries in England: in Leicester De Montfort University Library and Leicester University Library; and in London the German Historical Institute, the British Library (St Pancras) and the British Library of Political and Economic Science.

I am also grateful to numerous individuals. In Osnabrück, from where I carried out most of the German research, I am extremely grateful to Klaus J. Bade, for making me a fellow of the Institut für Migrationsforschung und Interkulturelle Studien, allowing me to use its facilities, and for his support in my academic endeavours over a decade. I would also like to express my gratitude to the administrative staff at the Institute. They make me feel like a highly privileged scholar whenever I return there: these are Peter Marschalck, Sigrid Pusch, Ingrid Sambeth, Frank Stefan and Jutta Tiemeyer. I would also like to thank others at the Institute including Jochen Oltmar, Johannes-Dieter Steinert, Patrick Wuster and Andreas Demuth.

In England I am grateful to several of my past and present De Montfort colleagues including Gurharpal Singh, John Martin, Mark Sandle, Nick Carter, Matt Taylor, David Ryan and Jason MacDonald. I would also like to express thanks to John Solomos and Richard Overy outside De Montfort. Many students made teaching and life enjoyable during the research for this book including Rebecca Axten, Paul Bridge, Glenford Xavier, Lindsay Garrat and Nasima Ravat. I am also deeply grateful to Andrew MacLennan who commissioned this volume and the series of which it forms a part for Longman. I would also like to thank his successor Emma Mitchell. I would like to dedicate the book to my sisters, Myllia and Rodothea, who have always had complete faith in me and have always taken pride in my achievements.

PUBLISHER'S ACKNOWLEDGEMENTS

We are grateful to the following for permission to reproduce copyright material:

A poem translated by May Ayim: 'grenzenlos und unverschämt' ('borderless and brazen'), in *blues in schwarz welss*, 3rd ed. Berlin: Orlanda, 1996, reproduced by permission of Orlanda Verlag; Map 1 and Map 3 from *A History of Germany 1815–1945*, 2nd edition, by William Carr (1979) reproduced by permission of Edward Arnold (Publishers) Ltd; Map 2 from *Germany 1866–1945* by Gordon Craig (1981) reproduced by permission of Oxford University Press, © Gordon Craig 1978, 1981; Map 4 from *Nazi Germany at War* by Martin Kitchen (Longman, 1995), reproduced by permission of Pearson Education Ltd; Map 5 from *A Concise History of Germany, 1990* by Mary Fulbrook (1990) reproduced by permission of Cambridge University Press; Table 1 from *Juden in Oldenburg, 1930–1938* by Dieter Goetz (1988) reproduced by permission of Isensee Verlag; Table 3 from *A History of Foreign Labour in Germany, 1880–1980: Seasonal Workers/Forced Labourers/Guest Workers* by Ulrich Herbert (1990) reproduced by permission of University of Michigan Press.

While every effort has been made to trace the owners of copyright material, in a few cases this has proved impossible and we take this opportunity to offer our apologies to any copyright holders whose rights we have unwittingly infringed.

GLOSSARY AND ABBREVIATIONS

Amt für Fragen der Heimatvertriebenen	Office for Questions Regarding the Homeland Expellees
Antisemitische Deutschsoziale Partei	Antisemitic German Social Party
Antisemitische Volkspartei	Antisemitic People's Party
Arbeiterzentrale	Central Office of Employees
Asylant	person granted asylum
Asylbewerber	asylum applicant
Asylsuchender	asylum seeker
Ausländer	foreigners
Ausländerfeindlichkeit	hostility towards foreigners
Aussiedler	ethnic Germans living in Eastern Europe after 1949
BDF	Bund Deutscher Frauen (Federation of German women)
BfA	Bundesanstalt für Arbeit (Federal Institute for Labour)
Bildungsbürgertum	educated bourgeoisie
Bund der Heimatvertriebenen und Entrechteten	Confederation of Homeland Expellees and Disenfranchised
Bund Deutscher Mädel	League of German Girls
Bundesverband Jüdischer Studenten	Federal Association of Jewish Students
Bundesvertriebenen-gesetz	Federal Expellee Law
Bursenschaften	student fraternities
CDU	Christlich-Demokratische Union (Christian Democratic Union)
CSU	Christlich-Soziale Union (Christian Social Union)
Deutsch-Afrikanische Gesellschaft	German African Society

[xiv]

Deutsch-Israelitischer Gemeindebund	German-Israelite Parish Federation
Deutsche Nationale Volkspartei	German National People's Party
Deutscher Volksbund	German People's Confederation
Deutscher Verein für das nördliche Schleswig	German Society for the North of Schleswig
Deutscher Volksverein	German People's Society
DM	Deutsche Mark
DP	Displaced Person
DSTB	*Deutschvölkischer Schutz und-Trutz Bund* (German National Protection and Defiance League)
DVU	Deutsche Volksunion (German People's Union)
Einsatzgruppen	task forces
EU	European Union
Europa-Afrika-Kulturzentrum	Europe African Cultural Centre
FAP	Freiheitliche Deutsche Arbeiterpartei (Free German Workers' Party)
Feldarbeiterzentrale	Central Office for Field Workers
Flottenverein	Navy League
Flüchtling	refugee
Freiheitlicher deutsch-türkischer Freundschaftsverein	Liberal German-Turkish Friendship Society
Freikorps	volunteer corps
FRG	Federal Republic of Germany
Gaststätte	restaurant
GDR	German Democratic Republic
Gymnasium	grammar school
Hauptschule	high school
Historikerstreit	'historians quarrel'
Hochdeutsch	standardized German
Israelitischer Verein zur Kolonisierung von Palästina	Israelite Society for the Colonization of Palestine
Judenrein	cleansed of Jews
Das Jüdische Komitee vom 1 Dezember 1880	The Jewish Committe of 1 December 1880
Jüdische Winterhilfe	Jewish Winter Help
Jüdischer Frauenbund	Jewish Women's Federation
jus solis	law of the soil
Kaiserreich	German Empire of 1871–1918

KGB	Komitet Gosudarstvennoy Bezopasnosti (Committee for State Security)	[xv]
Komitee für den Osten	Committee for the East	
Komitee zur Abwehr Antisemitischer Angriffe in Berlin	Committe for Defence Against Antisemitic Attacks in Berlin	
KPD	Kommunistische Partei Deutschlands (Communist Party of Germany)	
Kristallnacht	Crystal night	
Landmannschaften	Land Organizations	
Kulturkampf	cultural struggle	
Mission für Südosteuropa	Mission for South East Europe	
Mittelstand	middle class	
National-jüdische Vereinigung	National Jewish Union	
Nationalrevolutionäre Arbeiterfront	National Revolutionary Workers' Front	
NATO	North Atlantic Treaty Organization	
NPD	Nationale Demokratische Partei Deutschlands (National Democratic Party of Germany)	
NSDAP	National-Sozialistische Deutsche Arbeiterpartei (German National Socialist Workers' Party)	
Ossis	Easterners	
Ostjuden	Eastern European Jews	
Ostmarkverein	Society for the Eastern Marches	
Panta Koina	All Together	
Paulskirche	St Paul's Church in Frankfurt; where the 1848 Parliament met	
PKK	Partiya Karkaren Kurdistan (Kurdish Communist Party)	
Polonia	Poland	
Preussischer Landesverband Jüdischer Gemeinden	Prussian Land Association of Jewish Parishes	
Realschule	non-classical secondary school	
Reichstag	Lower House of German Parliament, 1871–1933	
Reichvertretung der deutschen Juden	Imperial Delegation of German Jews	
Republikaner	Republicans	
RM	Reichsmark	
SA	*Sturmabteilung* (storm troops)	
SPD	Sozialdemokratische Partei Deutschlands (Social Democratic Party of Germany)	
SS	*Schutz-Staffel*	

Stasi	East German secret police
TRT-International	Türkiye Radio-Televizyon International (Turkish Radio-Television Corporation International)
UN	United Nations
UNHCR	United Nations High Commission for Refugees
UNITA	Uniao Nacional para Indepencia Total de Angola (National Union for the Total Independence of Angola)
USSR	Union of Soviet Socialist Republics
Verband der deutscher Juden	Association of German Jews
Verband der Landmannschaften	Association of Land Organizations
Verein zur Abwehr des Antisemitismus	Association for Defence Against Antisemitism
Vereinigte ostdeutsche Landmannschaften	United East German Land Organizations
Vertriebener	expellees
Volk	people
völkisch	racial/nationalist
Volksgemeinschaft	people's community
Vormärz	period before the 1848 revolutions
WDR	Westdeutscher Rundfunk (West German Broadcasting Corporation)
Wessis	Westerners
Wiedergutmachung	reparation
Zentralrat der Juden in Deutschland	Central Council of Jews in Germany
Zentralstelle zur Beschaffung deutscher Ansiedler und Feldarbeiter	Central Office for Obtaining German Settlers and Field Workers
Zentralverein deutscher Staatsbürger Jüdischen Glaubens	Central Organization of German Citizens of Jewish Faith
Zionistische Vereinigung für Deutschland	Zionist Organization of Germany
Zollverein	Customs Union
ZVF	Zionistischer Verein für Deutschland (Zionist Association of Germany)
ZwiUzaek Polaków w Niemczech	League of Poles in Germany
ZZP	Zjednoczenie Zawodowe Polskie (Polish Occupational Union)

CHAPTER 1

Majorities and Minorities in German History

During the course of the nineteenth and twentieth centuries the core German-speaking areas of Europe underwent a series of transformations. The predominantly agrarian small states under the control of local rulers unified to create the leading economic and political power in continental Europe by the end of the nineteenth century. During the course of the following hundred years the new state would attempt to take over the whole of Europe on two occasions and face humiliating defeat, to emerge, once more, from the 1950s, as the powerhouse of Europe. The dramatic transformations of German Europe over the course of the past two hundred years, typical of much of the rest of the continent, depended upon underlying economic, social, political and intellectual developments. The main victims and beneficiaries of the above developments consisted of the people who lived in the areas controlled by the various German states which have existed. All ethnic groups, whether German or minority, experienced both losses and benefits from the upheavals of recent German history.

However, the German nation state which emerged from the smaller units existing at the start of the nineteenth century, would, by the 1940s, perfect racial intolerance, so that the function of the Nazi state consisted, above all, of eliminating racial enemies for the benefit of those regarded as ethnically perfect. Nazism represented the central period in the history of modern German persecution, as the events of the Second World War had to have very deep roots, as well as a legacy. This certainly does not mean that Nazism was an inevitability in 1800, or that it still influences Germany. But it casts a shadow across both modern German and modern European history.

The present book tackles the Nazi period as just one in the history of modern Germany, although, in view of the above observations, it represents a central period. The volume is the first to examine the history of all types of German minorities during the nineteenth and twentieth centuries. For those interested

[2] in the history of ethnic groups, Germany since 1800 represents the perfect case study. During this period the different German regimes have controlled and imported all types of minorities[1] within their borders. Germany has also progressed through all types of government which have existed in Europe during the past two centuries in the form of monarchy, autocracy, fascism, communism and liberal democracy. Consequently, the country represents the perfect testing ground to examine how the position of differing types of ethnic minorities fluctuates from one type of regime to another. The book will demonstrate that, while the levels of intolerance have varied from one system of government to another, ethnic minorities have always remained outsiders in the German body politic.

Nationalism, racism, immigration and ethnicity

Before progressing any further, we need to clear up the jargon used throughout this book to avoid future confusion. Underlying all other developments which have taken place in German, European and world history during the nineteenth and twentieth centuries has been the emergence of the ideology of nationalism and its political construct the nation state. Once again, Germany represents the classic example of this process, as the unified state of 1871 emerged from the 39 different German units which existed after the Napoleonic Wars in 1815.

However, while Germany (along with Italy) may have represented the perfect example of nation state creation during the nineteenth century, nationalism is clearly not in itself bound up with Germany, but with transformations which took place in Europe from the eighteenth century. In medieval Europe the concept of nationalism may have existed, but it remained essentially confined to élites rather than to uneducated peasants, whose main form of faith and consciousness consisted of their belief in their God. This would have remained the case under the all-embracing Catholic ideology before the rise of Protestant religions and despite, in the German case, the existence of the Holy Roman Empire, which contained both German and other minorities within its borders.

The Reformation certainly made a difference, especially in German-speaking Europe, because of the translation of the Bible from Latin into the vernacular. Nevertheless, this did not prevent Germans from killing each other during the Thirty Years War (1618–48), where the driving ideology consisted of religion rather than nation. The only country in which national-ism may have emerged during the seventeenth century was England, where the people became sovereign during the English Revolution.

However, the concept of the sovereign populace essentially takes off during the French Revolution, the real starting-point for nationalism. The Revolutionary and Napoleonic armies, moving eastward, took with them the concept of liberation from autocratic monarchy and the divine right of kings. In its place would come rule by the people, linked together by a common bond, in the case of the Germans their language. Nationalism infected German-speaking Europe almost instantly and, like a disease, the whole continent had caught it by the end of the nineteenth century.

The ideology of nationalism encouraged the educated middle classes of Europe, increasing in numbers against the background of industrialization, to eliminate their rulers, usually through some form of revolutionary activity, reaching a peak in the events of 1848, which, however, proved universally unsuccessful. Nevertheless, the genie had escaped and, over the following eighty years, nation states replaced the Habsburg and Ottoman Empires which dominated central and eastern Europe in 1848. In many cases, notably Germany, the ruling élites survived and adopted nationalism to perpetuate their existence, while allowing members of the rising middle classes into government, and introducing universal manhood suffrage.[2]

However, while nationalism may represent a unifying force for those with the correct ethnic credentials, it automatically excludes those who do not possess them. Nation states which have dominated European political organ-ization since the end of the nineteenth century inevitably operate, like all state structures, on the principle of insiders and outsiders. The German nation state, like all others, has therefore practised exclusion and persecution of minorities in all of its varying guises, although, as we shall see, the methods vary from autocracy to liberal democracy. Persecution of minorities does not originate with the nation state as Jews and Gypsies endured extreme hostility through-out their years of residence in both Germany and the whole of Europe. Never-theless, the nation state guarantees exclusion on ethnic grounds and even creates new minorities within national borders where they had not previ-ously existed.

Nationalism in itself has resulted in some of the most intolerant acts of the twentieth century, above all in the form of ethnic cleansing, essentially born with the Armenian genocide of 1915 and continuing until the close of the twentieth century in Kosovo.[3] In the German case, the manifestations of persecution as a result of nationalism working upon its own have remained

[4]   relatively mild. However, when racism superimposed itself upon the already existing exclusionary structures under the Nazis, this resulted in the worst acts of ethnic persecution during the twentieth century. Outside the years 1933–45, Germany may therefore be said to represent a fairly 'normal' nation state in terms of the relationship between ethnic minorities and majorities. This poses the question of whether we should distinguish between nationalism and racism, because, like all ideologies, both are essentially exclusionary.

Nationalism springs from a favoured group called the nation, bound together by one or more of the factors of similar appearance and a shared language and/or religion. From these raw materials evolve cultures and state structures. Those with the most perfect ethnic credentials receive the most favoured treatment. In late nineteenth-century Germany, such a person would consist of a Protestant (as against a Catholic or a Jewish) ethnic German (in opposition to a Pole or a Jew, for instance). Throughout the nineteenth and twentieth centuries ethnic Germans have received the greatest privileges.

Defining and explaining race and racism proves difficult. For the Nazis, the above characteristics of their favoured group (the Germans) represented the basis of a race (the Aryans). The concept of racism in English usage has, by the end of the twentieth century, come essentially to refer to the practice of discrimination by a dominant ethnic grouping against minorities living in the same nation state.

The idea of race circulated in Europe from the medieval period[4] and had entered the German language by the seventeenth century.[5] Immanuel Kant distinguished between different races of people, although he did not think that a hierarchy existed.[6] Racial theories circulated in both Europe and North America during the early nineteenth century, but a change of direction occurred following the publication of Charles Darwin's *On The Origin of the Species by Natural Selection, or the Preservation of Favoured Races in the Struggle for Life*. Although Darwin had nothing to do with the application of his ideas to human beings, there emerged the concept of Social Darwinism, which applied his ideas of natural selection of species of animals to natural selection of races of human beings, developing into a hierarchy of different races. The encounter of Europeans with Africa and its inhabitants as a consequence of imperial expansion appeared to reinforce ideas of a hierarchy of races.[7] Concepts of racial superiority also focused upon the differences between European peoples. As we shall see, by the start of the twentieth century extreme German nationalists looked eastward towards lands which they wanted the newly created German state to annex and where there lived, what they viewed as, inferior Slavic races.

These expansionist Pan-Germans displayed just as much concern for Jews, which meant that, during the course of the late nineteenth century the traditional medieval Christian hostility towards this minority developed into a racial ideology, which began to view Jews as an unassimilable part of the body politic in the new German nation state. In essence antisemitism, which took off throughout late nineteenth-century Europe, emerged and found legitimation in Germany from the newly created German nation state. Against the background of the racial theories circulating after 1860 the Jews became, in the German case, the main racial enemy for extreme ideologues, including, before 1914, Houston Stewart Chamberlain and Lanz von Liebenfels, both of whom influenced Adolf Hitler. *Mein Kampf,* first published in 1924, brought together the German racist ideas which had emerged over the previous century, distinguishing between German Aryans, Slavs and Jews, in terms of their descending order of importance in his racial hierarchy, which his Nazi party implemented upon coming to power and intensified after the outbreak of the racial Second World War.

Nazi Germany, while remaining a nation state, also became a racial state because of the overt way in which the Nazis practised their belief in racial difference. Post-war Germany offers an example of a state in which ethnic origin determines success and failure, but to describe it as racist proves problematic because of the heavily weighted meaning of the word in view of the brutal practices of the Nazis. While academic and popular discourse in Britain and America has relatively few problems in using the phrase racism to apply to most forms of ethnic discrimination, especially against Black people, a reluctance exists to use the term in Germany. This is not only because of the experience of Nazism, but also because the majority of post-war immigrants have consisted of Europeans. In Britain racism essentially relates to discrimination faced by Blacks and Asians, rather than the largest immigrant group, the Irish, even though this group has faced much prejudice. In Germany 'safer' terms have come into existence to describe animosity towards post-war immigrants and their offspring, the most widely used of which consists of *Ausländerfeindlichkeit,* literally, hostility towards foreigners, which does not have any clear connections with Nazism and applies to negative feeling towards immigrants of all nationalities.

Therefore, the use of the terms race and racism, while complicated enough when used in any situation, proves especially problematic in the German case. Similar assertions apply to the term immigration. Historically, population movements have taken place throughout the European continent, so that every European people can ultimately trace its origins from outside its present area

[6]   of concentration. Nevertheless, many of these population movements would have taken place before the existence of organized states, which meant that newcomers inhabited essentially uncontrolled and uninhabited land. Once organized states came into existence, people who subsequently moved into them became immigrants, rather than migrants, although the former term usually works on the understanding that newcomers have a desire to remain permanently, which people most commonly decide after they have lived some-where for some length of time.

In the German case the main non-German immigrants before the nineteenth century included Jews, who first arrived under the Roman Empire, and Gypsies, who made their first appearance in the fifteenth century. In addition, German states also attracted Protestant refugees during the Reformation. For most of the nineteenth century, Germany represented a country of mass emigra-tion, but, by the 1880s, because of the pace of industrialization, Germany had a need for foreign labour and established the pattern which would char-acterize the next hundred years: newcomers received short-term labour con-tracts, varying from months to years, after which time they would have to return home. Those labourers who moved to Germany between c.1880 and 1945 did, in the vast majority of cases, return, and the best description for most of them consists of migrant labourers. However, some of the for-eign workers in Germany during the Second World War had little choice in their residence and employment because the Nazis introduced labour con-scription programmes in the territories which they invaded, so that people affected in this way are often called forced or slave labourers. The term immi-grants seems inappropriate in such cases, although some of those who moved into Nazi Germany did so voluntarily.

The Federal Republic also imported foreign labour, again by issuing short-term contracts, so that it would appear that the term migrants would apply to the post-war newcomers. Nevertheless, many of those who moved into the country between the 1950s and 1970s still live in Germany at the start of the twenty-first century. In addition, they have also subsequently brought their families with them and have had further offspring within the Federal Republic. Such people can only be described as immigrants, although the differences between migrants and immigrants are not that clear cut, especially in the case of the post-war newcomers to Germany, who do not make instant decisions about their long-term future. The definition of the children and grandchildren of immigrants born in Germany proves even more problem-atic. In German discourse, the catch-all term of *Ausländer* (foreigners) covers everybody, whereas in English second and third generation immigrants would be the standard jargon. German nationality laws, which, until 2000, did not grant citizenship to people of foreign parentage born within Germany, have complicated the situation.

One other group which has the characteristics of immigrants consists of the late nineteenth-century *Ostjuden*, who arrived uninvited in the *Kaiserreich* and remained within Germany until the genocidal policies of Hitler eliminated them. They also have much in common with refugees, in the sense that they partly moved to escape persecution in Russia and Poland. But the use of the term refugees also creates problems in the German case, as the word *Flüchtling* most commonly applies to ethnic Germans expelled from the territories lost at the end of the Second World War, who made their way to the FRG and the GDR. Such people have also attracted the phrase *Vertriebener* (expellees). *Flüchtling* further applies to refugees from the GDR who moved to the FRG.[8] By the time of the collapse of the Berlin Wall ethnic Germans who continued to live outside the borders of the Federal Republic but who moved towards it, under a right of residence granted by Article 116 of the 1949 Constitution, attracted the name of *Aussiedler*.

In addition to these ethnic German refugees, non-Germans also moved to the post-war Federal Republic in large numbers for political reasons and would, like the Germans described above, fit into the United Nations definition of a refugee as defined in the 1951 UN Geneva Convention on the Status of Refugees, which covered any person who would not return to their own country 'owing to a well-founded fear of being persecuted for reasons of race, religion, nationality, membership of a particular social group or political opinion'.[9] In the case of the Federal Republic, Article 16 of the 1949 Constitution also provided a right of asylum. The commonly used phrase for non-German refugees who moved to the Federal Republic consists of *Asylant* (literally a person granted asylum) or, if waiting for the granting of refugee status *Asylsuchende* (asylum seeker) or *Asylbewerber* (asylum applicant).

But the above terms overlap. Legalistic definitions of refugees and asylum seekers, aimed at preventing the entry of as many people as possible under new German legislation of the 1990s, hide the fact that most people migrate for a combination of reasons, both economic and political. Furthermore, few if any people have had much certainty about their length of stay once they have moved to Germany during the nineteenth and twentieth centuries, even those on short-term contracts. Immigration represents a catch-all term covering the movement of both Germans and non-Germans to Germany for any length of time for a combination of reasons.[10]

Ethnicity proves more straightforward to define, as few German complications exist with regard to the phrase. The origin of the word ethnicity lies in the Greek word, *ethnos*, which simply means nation. The full significance of

[8] this fact is that no difference exists between an ethnic group and a nation, in the true sense of the meaning of the latter word, applying to a group of people with shared characteristics. These characteristics cover one or more of the following areas: appearance, language and religion. Any combination of these factors can distinguish an ethnic minority from a majority.

In the German case appearance has played a fundamental role in distinguishing numerous minorities. Gypsies looked different upon their first arrival in the fifteenth century because of their darker skins, and continued to dress differently until the twentieth century. Jews wore distinct clothing until the assimilation process got under way. Meanwhile many post-war immigrants from southern Europe, but more especially Turkey and Africa, look different from most Germans and have also brought with them distinct ways of dressing, especially Muslim women, as well as their own foods.

Language has played a role in distinguishing virtually all ethnic minorities in German history, a factor stressed by the fact that the use of German represents the only true glue which holds Germans together, although even here, different types of the language have existed historically and continue to do so, despite standardization consequent upon mass education. While ethnic minorities also use German, their own language has usually survived. Jews and Gypsies used Romany and Yiddish, while those peripheral groupings such as Poles and Danes incorporated during the period of Prussian expansion in the eighteenth and nineteenth centuries, also had their own languages. Finally, post-war immigrants have brought in numerous new languages into Germany.

Religion has also played a role in distinguishing ethnic minorities in German history, although this proves problematic because, after the Reformation, it also played a major role in dividing German states. However, the ethnicity of the longest standing minority in Germany, the Jews, has revolved around religion. Similarly, the Roman Catholicism of the Polish minority in the *Kaiserreich* played a large role in stressing their distinctiveness. In the post-war period immigrants have brought new religions with them, including Orthodox Christianity and, more especially, Islam, the religion of millions of newcomers.

During the course of the nineteenth and twentieth centuries, both the majority and the minority populations in Germany have had a strong ethnic consciousness, particularly under the Nazis, whose system revolved around ethnic difference constructed into race. Jews have always recognized their difference because of the constant persecution which they faced through all systems of government, which reinforced their desire to hold on to their religion. Similarly, Prussian policies in Poland strengthened the ethnic consciousness of Poles. Because of the already existing state structures, immigrants moving into post-war Germany instantly recognized their difference.

Ethnicity represents a two-way process. On the one hand, the state, especially the nation state which developed after 1871, forced people into a consciousness of their difference. But, at the same time, ethnic minorities, as a reaction against nationalism, racism or religious persecution, have organized their own structures throughout German history. This has involved the construction of places of worship at a most basic level, but also the evolution of minority cultures, the setting up of local or nationwide organizations and the establishment of newspapers and, more recently, other media. Such processes have affected nearly all minorities in German history. Gypsies represent an exception because of their lack of literacy.

Within ethnic minorities, which are ultimately constructs, individuals have had some measure of choice regarding the level to which they maintain their difference, even under the Nazis in the case of Danes and Sorbs, who could lose their ethnicity and assimilate into Germanness. In fact, most ethnic groupings have had the choice of some sort of assimilation, an option which only became impossible for Jews, Gypsies and Slavs under the Third Reich. Apart from these populations in this period all members of ethnic groupings have had some choice in choosing their identity. During the nineteenth century, assimilation for Jews represented part of the emancipation contract, a path which some chose either through changing their religion or marrying a gentile. Poles also underwent similar processes, especially those who migrated to the Ruhr, although for those remaining in Prussia, living in heavy ethnic concentrations whipped up by Polish nationalists, loss of Polishness remained difficult. Post-war immigrants can lose their original identification by living away from an ethnic settlement, through marriage with a German, or by adopting German nationality and dispensing with the passport of their homeland.

Germans and minorities

The existence of minorities means the presence of a majority. Throughout the history of Germany, the majority has clearly consisted of Germans. Defining this entity proves problematic, especially before 1871. Differing types of minorities have existed in modern German history consisting of: dispersed Jews and Gypsies, both present for centuries by 1871; peripheral

[10] people, notably Poles, who represent victims of Prussian expansion; and differing types of immigrants, who have existed in large numbers in Germany
throughout the period since 1871.

Because of the absence of a unitary German state before 1871, defining a
German also proves problematic, a difficulty which would exist in designat-
ing any ethnic group before the evolution of a nation state in their name.
Attempting to define Germans before this time proves especially difficult.
Selecting a geographical area or particular states may seem attractive but proves
unsatisfactory for two reasons. First, while some of the smaller states which
existed before 1871 may have had unitary German-speaking populations,
the larger ones, i.e. Austria-Hungary and Prussia, had significant minorities,
especially the former which controlled much of central Europe and the
Balkans, areas which had an extraordinary variety of peoples in an age before
nationalism and ethnic cleansing. Second, because of patterns of medieval and
early modern migration, significant German populations lived outside even
the massive area of Austria-Hungary, Prussia and the German Confederation
in 1815, notably in parts of Russia.

Defining a German by linking the dominant people in the contemporary nation state with historical ancestors proves extremely complex and even
dangerous, as it would give succour to nativist anti-immigration racists. While
the peoples of central Europe may have maintained their distinctiveness from
each other, intermixing clearly took place. 'There are no clear and direct
connections between the tribes who arrived on Rome's northern borders and
modern Germans.'[11] Walter Schmidt has claimed that: 'The German people
were formed as a qualitatively new ethnic and social unit through the integration and assimilation of ethnically distinguishable and older population
groups – above all Germanic tribes, Celts and Slavs – during the early Middle
Ages.'[12] While this proves effective in dispelling the myth of continuity from
Tacitus to the present, the statement is equally vague.

The only 'logical' way of defining Germans consists of language. 'Germany
is probably unique among modern European states in having a name derived
not from a tribe or territory, but from a spoken language.'[13] The use of their
own language would have represented the way in which Germans distinguished themselves from the populations which surrounded them in central
Europe in the age before nation states. But language offers us only a partial
solution to our problem because so many different varieties of German
existed, some of which continue to survive even in the late twentieth-century
standardised nation state. As James J. Sheehan has recognized, 'The lines
between the speakers of Dutch and *Plattdeutsch* are hard to draw; the distance

between the dialects of Hamburg and Swabia is surely no less significant.'[14] Before 1871, while 'national identification' was 'strongly linguistic', no more than a 'small minority' used the 'national language for everyday purposes'. The majority of Germans 'spoke various and often mutually incomprehensible idioms'.[15] Language standardization through the education system and the media during the nineteenth and twentieth centuries have solved these problems. However, native command of German does not automatically turn a person into a German, as the children of post-war immigrants have discovered.

The above discussion illustrates the complexity of ethnic and national definitions of Germans. With the formation of the German nation state in 1871, the 1913 Nationality Law, the 1935 Nuremberg Law and Article 116 of the 1949 Constitution of the Federal Republic, Germans become easier to define, simply because they become a legal category. Essentially, language forms the basis of all of these categorizations, although the Nazis displayed an obsession with 'blood' in their attempts to exclude Jews.

Like all nation states during the nineteenth and twentieth centuries, the German ones which have existed since 1871 have also made efforts to standardize their citizens through the education system and through the propaganda machines of the Nazis, the GDR and the FRG. 'Mass schooling and literacy meant Germans increasingly read and experienced the same things.'[16] In addition, the Germans also invented traditions about themselves under the *Kaiserreich*, and reinvented their nation under the Nazis, and once again under the FRG and the GDR.[17] As an idea, German nationalism crystallized in the emerging romantic movement of the late eighteenth and early nineteenth centuries and then, like similar ideologies throughout Europe, became irresistible to political and economic élites, eventually spreading downwards to affect all classes by 1900.

Since 1800, and especially after 1871, Germans have had a good idea who they are, especially under the influence of the all-embracing nation state. Just as importantly, they have also recognized the different types of ethnic minorities which have existed within their midst, distinguished by varying combinations of appearance, language and religion. The state has clearly played a central role in creating outsiders, through, for instance, citizenship laws, propaganda, the use of German as the language of education, the use of residence permits for immigrants and the implementation of a wide range of measures, especially under the Nazis, to define and exclude minorities. However, even when the state has accepted some ethnic minorities, notably Jews under the *Kaiserreich* and the Weimar Republic, racist political parties have stigmatized them.

[12]   Consequently, just as Germans know who fits into their group and who falls outside it, minorities also realize their status as such. This does not simply result from the attitude of the state and the dominant population, but also from personal choice and, perhaps more importantly, the views of the élites who control the minorities and who have a vested interest in creating organized ethnic groups. Polish leaders in the *Kaiserreich* found the idea of assimilating into the dominant German population anathema. Some Jewish organizations also felt the same way, although the internal history of modern German Jewry essentially represents the struggle between maintaining Jewishness and assimilating into the surrounding population: the ideal solution, which became increasingly difficult as a result of rising antisemitism, represented remaining both German and Jewish.

As we have previously mentioned, during the course of the nineteenth and twentieth centuries the various German states which have existed have contained three types of minorities within their boundaries. The first consist of dispersed groupings, i.e. Jews and Gypsies whose status as minorities predates the birth of German nationalism. These two peoples found themselves not only spread throughout Germany, but all over the European continent by 1800. A second type of German minorities consists of localized populations, particularly Slavs, but also, after the expansion of Prussia and the creation of the Reich in 1871, Alsatians and Lorrainers until 1918, and Danes, in varying numbers, until the present. Such people, notably the Sorbs, existed before the rise of nationalism within German territories, but the creation of the nation state, its increasing control and the rise of nationalism throughout Europe, gave Poles, Sorbs, Danes, Alsatians and Lorrainers a national consciousness when they may previously not have progressed to an advanced concept of their ethnicity. The third group of minorities residing in Germany since 1871 consists of various types of migrants. While most of those entering the country before 1945 may have consisted of people on short-term contracts and may, therefore, not have developed ethnic organizations, they certainly stood out as different from Germans and clearly had consciousness of their difference. In contrast, the economic migrants and refugees who moved to the Federal Republic after 1945 have brought their families with them and have established their own ethnic organizations, clearly representing immigrant ethnic minorities of the type resident throughout Europe, despite the reluctance of the German state to recognize them as such.

All of the above groups, as minorities, have had four things in common. First, they have counted smaller numbers than the dominant German population, although they may have outnumbered Germans in particular locations, as the example of Poles in parts of nineteenth-century Prussia or urban immigrant concentrations after 1945 would indicate. Geographical concentration actually represents the second factor which all minorities have had in common, allowing the development of ethnicity on a local level. Some members of minorities, particularly those with a limited interest in continuing their ethnicity, have chosen not to live in ethnic concentrations. Third, all minorities have differed from Germans in terms of any combination of appearance, language or religion. Finally, minorities have had limited political power. While they may have established advanced ethnic organizations in the areas in which they concentrate, as the example of nineteenth-century Poles would suggest and, while some Jews have held senior political positions, German ethnicity has been essential for holding power in modern Germany.

The varying types of minorities in Germany have, collectively, evolved as such entities over the course of periods of time varying from decades to centuries. The oldest of all, existing as a people millennia before Germans developed concepts of nationhood, consist of the Jews. The entire history of Jewish life in Germany, from the Roman to the Nazi Empires, consists of one in which persecution, of the most ruthless kind, occurred on a regular basis. The first recorded Jews within the boundaries of contemporary Germany lived in Cologne in the fourth century, gradually making their way there following the Roman destruction of Jerusalem in AD 70. After the fall of the Roman Empire this minority seems to have disappeared.[18] Jewish communities reappeared and developed again from the ninth century, particularly along the Rhine and Moselle valleys, but also further afield in Regensburg, Merseburg and Magdeburg. The first instance of mass murder of the German Jews occurred during the First Crusade of 1096, when as many as five thousand may have died in the fanatical Christian atmosphere engendered by this Holy War.[19] The Jewish communities of the Rhine built themselves up again fairly rapidly, and new ones appeared further east. By the fourteenth century a well-developed ethnicity existed, which meant, for instance, the construction of synagogues as well as the evolution of a distinct Jewish language on the Rhine in the form of Yiddish, which combined elements of Latin, German and Hebrew.[20] However, animosity towards Jews remained constant throughout a medieval western Europe ideologically controlled by the Roman Catholic Church. This hostility manifested itself in the regular circulation of ritual murder stories, such as that in Fulda in 1235, when the gentile population accused the local Jews of burning to death five members of one family, resulting in a pogrom against them.[21] Medieval antisemitism peaked once again in 1349, as the Black Death ravaged Europe, for which the Jews faced the blame.

[14]   Within Germany there 'were massacres of Jews in 350 towns, and in 210 of these, every single Jew was murdered'.[22] The majority of those who remained would face expulsion during the fourteenth and fifteenth centuries, mostly moving eastward towards Poland.[23]

However, Jews did not completely disappear from Germany and began to return again after the Thirty Years War (1618–48), many of them fleeing a new outbreak of antisemitism in Poland.[24] The Berlin Jewish community, which counted about 3,500 souls by the end of the eighteenth century, dates its modern foundation from 1671 when the Elector Friedrich Wilhelm of Brandenburg allowed fifty families expelled from Vienna to settle in the city.[25] Germany as a whole contained about 270,000 Jews by the early nineteenth century, making up 1.9 per cent of the population.[26] Jews at the start of our period therefore represented a noticeable rather than a large minority within German states. The legacy of medieval antisemitism, manifesting itself most clearly in the continued restrictions which Jews faced, made them even more conspicuous. Official controls forced them to concentrate in particular areas of towns and cities and also dictated their dress.[27] Large areas of Germany, which had expelled their Jewish populations in previous centuries remained *Judenrein.* Concentrations around 1800 included the historical areas on the rivers Rhine and Main.[28] By this time German Jewry had begun to experience significant developments which would characterize its history for the following century. The Enlightenment, which facilitated the rise of an integrated Jewish intelligentsia, and the French Revolution began the process of emancipation, which reached its conclusion with the foundation of the *Kaiserreich* in 1871.

The history of German Jewry during the entire course of the nineteenth and twentieth centuries, as in the periods before, represents the struggle for full rights against the background of endemic antisemitism, which would eliminate the vast majority of this population after the Nazis came to power. By 1933 about 500,000 Jews lived in Germany,[29] consisting of the descendants of those who lived in the country at the start of the nineteenth century, augmented by newcomers from Russia and Poland at its end. Only about 28,000 Jews survived the Holocaust in Germany and Austria by going underground.[30] Some of these moved to Israel but German Jewry took off again, following a series of influxes, mostly from further east, to total around 50,000 at the end of the twentieth century.[31]

Resembling the Jews in terms of their dispersed nature, as well as their pre-modern origins, are the German Gypsies. Their first recording on German soil occurred considerably later than that of the first Jews, in 1407 in

Hildesheim, having originated in northern India, from where they began migrating in the fifth century, reaching Europe at the end of the first millennium. By 1417, about 300 Gypsies lived in the Hanseatic towns on the North and Baltic Sea coasts. Again, like the Jews, they have faced constant persecution since that time, which has remained strong after 1945. During the fifteenth century stereotypes circulated about them as spies, magicians, thieves and disease carriers.[32] They experienced especially severe persecution after 1700, when they became victims of hunting, torture, enslavement and murder. At the end of the eighteenth century stories about Gypsies as cannibals had also surfaced.[33]

Despite the attention which they have received, tiny numbers of Gypsies have lived in Germany during its history, totalling just 2,000 at the end of the nineteenth century. The figure had increased to 14,000 by 1926 largely as a result of further immigration from the Balkans.[34] Although Nazi persecution eliminated the majority of German Gypsies, new ones entered the country after the Second World War, mostly from Eastern Europe so that over 100,000 lived in the country at the end of the twentieth century.[35]

While Jews and Gypsies have much in common, notably their dispersed nature and the fact that they existed as minorities before the nineteenth century, a fundamental difference exists between the two groups after 1800. The former represented a successful grouping, whose members constantly became assimilated into the rising bourgeoisie, which aped and influenced German Jewry. In contrast, poverty and distance from the ethnic German population characterized Gypsies within the country during the nineteenth and twentieth centuries.

Nevertheless, Jews and Gypsies remain bound together because their presence as minorities predates the nation state. In contrast, the minorities living just inside German borders from the end of the eighteenth century essentially represent victims of nationalism, manifesting itself especially in Prussian annexation between 1772 and 1871, which brought in parts of Denmark, Poland and France. In addition, the age of nationalism gave rise to ethnic consciousness amongst a group long present in German territory in the form of the Sorbs.

Poles represent the most significant localized minority in Germany between 1772 and 1945. During the Middle Ages German settlers had increasingly moved eastward, especially under the leadership of the missionary Christian Teutonic Knights as well as the commercial Hanseatic League. While the Polish Kingdom nevertheless remained a dominant power in the area for much of the medieval period, the emerging Prussian state took over more and more of

[16]   its territory from the seventeenth century, culminating in the partitions of Poland of 1772, 1792 and 1795, which involved Prussia, the Habsburg Empire and Russia.[36] After losing some of the territory which it had gained at the Congress of Vienna in 1815, Prussia still counted 1.5 million Poles in its territories of Posen, Silesia and East and West Prussia.[37] The nineteenth century resulted in the rise of Polish nationalism both within Prussia and throughout the territories which formerly constituted the Polish Kingdom. After 1871 the Polish issue became central in German politics due to attempts to assimilate the Poles in the east, which had the opposite effect of increasing national consciousness. By 1890, as a result of demographic growth, about 3 million Poles lived in Prussia.[38] At the outbreak of the First World War about 450,000 Poles lived in the Ruhr, to which they had migrated to work in coal mining and heavy industry.[39] A series of ethnic organizations stressing nationalism, working-class solidarity and the Roman Catholic religion united them with their brethren in the east. The peace settlement of 1919, meaning the reconstitution of Poland, using land lost at the end of the eighteenth century, resulted in a reduction in the number of people in Germany claiming Polish as their native language to 200,000 while around 400,000 used both German and Polish.[40] The Polish minority had disappeared by the end of the Second World War due to both assimilatory pressures upon Ruhr Poles during the Nazi period and the loss of further German territory to Poland in 1945. Polish ethnicity before the Second World War was a complicated phenomenon, because of the existence of subgroups such as Masurians[41] and Kashubians.[42]

The Sorbs of Lusatia represent another Slavic group still living in eastern Germany quite distinct from the Poles. Some authorities see Lusatia, situated next to contemporary south-eastern Germany's borders with Poland and Czechoslovakia, as part of the original homeland of the Slavs, from the third millennium BC.[43] Others believe that Slavs arrived in Lusatia during the sixth and seventh centuries AD.[44] Whatever the true situation, Germans did not move into the area until the tenth century and, since 1300, Lusatia has been subject to some sort of Germanic control, with German rulers settling their own subjects in the area. Sorbian consciousness, as manifested in language use, declined during the early modern period as a result of pressure from the Saxon and Prussian authorities which controlled the area, but the age of nationalism gave a boost to the Sorbs with cultural organizations and student societies developing in the early nineteenth century. The newly created German state viewed the group as a threat in the late nineteenth century, although the national organizations continued to survive. The Nazis denied the existence of a Sorb minority and placed some of its leaders in concentration camps.

The German Democratic Republic recognized the Sorbs as an independent minority, which meant that they developed a rich ethnicity revolving around numerous cultural activities, although this ethnicity came under threat in the free-market economy and less ethnically conscious policies of the Federal Republic. At the end of the twentieth century as many as 80,000 people may have used the Sorbian language.[45]

Sorbs remain different from Poles, Alsatians, Lorrainers and Danes in the sense that they represent a purely localized minority with no concrete connection to a population beyond German borders. In addition, they also predate not only the German state, but also the presence of Germans in their area, representing a minority to invading and colonizing Germans who expelled and Christianized them,[46] although they did not represent a symbolic eternal outgroup experiencing brutal persecution in the same category as the Jews and Gypsies. Their concentration means that they have more in common with other localized minorities than with the dispersed groupings.

The annexation of Schleswig-Holstein by Bismarck in 1864 created a new minority problem in the evolving German state by bringing into its boundaries a Danish-speaking population, which remains until the present, despite border changes at the end of the First World War, which reduced the number of Danish speakers in Germany. At the end of the twentieth century about 50,000 still lived in the country.[47] Nevertheless, a German minority also existed in Denmark after the boundary changes at the end of the First World War, pointing to the insolubility of minority problems in border areas with mixed populations. Before the age of nationalism the two groups could remain fairly anonymous, but the German nation state which came into existence in 1871 made efforts to assimilate Danes. Nevertheless, because of the fact that German racists never focused upon them, as they did not view them as different enough, this minority grouping did not endure the brutal persecution experienced by Slavs, Jews and Gypsies.

Alsace and Lorraine represents a similar area to Schleswig-Holstein in the sense that it had a mixed linguistic population, in this case speaking either French or German. Whether the two provinces fell into a German or French nation state, some of the population would feel themselves minorities. These areas remained under German control from 1870 to 1918 and again briefly during the Second World War. Like the Danes, French-speaking Alsatians and Lorrainers did not have to endure the extreme treatment faced by those minorities most hated by the German racists.

While the status of Jews and Gypsies as minorities predates the German nation state and while the emergence of localized groups as minorities corresponds with its foundation, immigrants came after its formation. Whether

[18]   they entered the country at the end of the nineteenth century during the harvest season or whether they moved to the Federal Republic on a more permanent basis during the 1960s and 1970s, newcomers to Germany since 1871 display the four characteristics of ethnic minorities already outlined in terms of smaller numbers than the German population, geographical concentration, ethnic distinctiveness and lack of political power.

Although Germany represented a country of emigration for much of the nineteenth century, by the beginning of the twentieth the new state had begun to import foreign labour to feed the ravenous expansion of the German economy. Many of the sojourners, especially Dutch and Italians, worked in industry in both Prussia and the Ruhr, but the majority of Poles from Russia and Austria found employment in Prussian agriculture due to a labour shortage caused by internal migration to the Ruhr. In 1907 a total of 924,946 foreigners worked in the Reich, making up 6.4 per cent of the total workforce.[48] The First World War saw a decline in the numbers of foreign workers, which stood at 715,770 in 1918, although many of these were actually forced to labour for Germany, including a new element from invaded Belgium.[49]

Because of the economic crisis that was Weimar, this period represented the most untypical in the immigration history of modern Germany because the small numbers of foreign workers living in the country never exceeded a quarter of a million, again with a significant percentage of Poles, employed largely in agriculture.[50] The numbers of migrant labourers started to increase as the Nazi economy began to experience labour shortages at the end of the 1930s, reaching a figure of 435,903 in the last year of peace, originating mainly in Poland, Italy, Yugoslavia, Bulgaria and Hungary.[51]

With the outbreak of the Second World War, the Nazi economy entered a period which involved the massive exploitation of foreign workers reaching a peak of 7,126,000 in 1944, making up 19.9 per cent of all workers employed by the German economy. While the majority consisted of Poles and Russians conscripted in the areas invaded by the Nazis, the figure included over a million French people and hundreds of thousands of Belgians, Italians and Dutch, some of whom had moved to Germany voluntarily.[52] Many eastern Europeans worked in camps in the most hideous conditions, while others lived amongst German civilians, with whom they could have little contact.

At the end of the war foreign workers returned to their homes and for the following fifteen years Germany became flooded with ethnic Germans from further east, especially the Federal Republic, which also took in refugees from the GDR. Although both of these groups essentially formed part of the dominant German population, the former certainly displayed characteristics of minority populations in terms of geographical concentration and, in the short run at least, lack of power. Close to twelve million people actually moved from their homes as a result of the ethnic cleansing which took place at the end of the war due to the Soviet advance and the loss of German territory.[53]

By the end of the 1950s, and especially following the construction of the Berlin Wall in 1961, preventing citizens of East Germany from escaping their regime, the Federal Republic returned to the traditions of labour importation employed by the *Kaiserreich* and the Nazis. It signed contracts with a series of states on the Mediterranean periphery of Europe, as its traditional labour sources in Poland and Russia remained closed. The new countries which now fed the German economy included Italy, from 1955, followed, during the course of the 1960s, by Spain, Greece, Portugal, Turkey, Morocco, Tunisia and Yugoslavia so that by 1974, the Federal Republic contained over four million non-German residents, making up five per cent of its population, which had increased further to 4,845,882 by 1989, largely due to the fact that, rather than returning home, the post-war immigrants also brought their families with them. By this time the Federal Republic had also begun to witness an influx of asylum seekers, largely from the increasingly intolerant Eastern European regimes in their final years.[54] Meanwhile, the GDR had also imported foreign workers from the 1950s, mostly from other Soviet Bloc states, including Bulgaria, Poland, Czechoslovakia, Hungary, Cuba, Mozambique and Vietnam, although on a far smaller scale than the Federal Republic, totalling less than 250,000 in 1990.[55]

Immediately after reunification, an increase occurred in the number of asylum seekers entering the new Germany as a result of the nationalist hatreds exploding in eastern Europe, particularly Yugoslavia, at the end of the Cold War. The country actually took in 887,366 asylum seekers and 849,606 ethnic Germans between 1990 and 1992.[56] The latter could now leave states which had previously tried to keep them in including the USSR, Romania, Hungary and Poland.

At the end of the twentieth century Germany therefore had a demographic complexity typical of most other western European states, with an ethnically privileged population, among whom resided Jews, Gypsies, Sorbs, Danes and large numbers of post-war immigrants and refugees, who arrived from all over the world. Apart from newcomers from European states, Germany also attracted refugees from other parts of the globe during the 1980s and 1990s because of a generous asylum policy, which, however, faced tightening up during the middle of the latter decade. The new controls, together with a

[20] decline in the number of international conflicts, meant a decrease in the volume of refugees making their way to Germany. However, they still continued, together with illegal immigrants, working especially in the Berlin construction industry in the rebuilding boom following reunification.

Continuities and breaks in German history

Germany offers a perfect case study for testing out ideas about the treatment of minorities in different systems of government during the nineteenth and twentieth centuries. In these two hundred years Germany changed from a series of small monarchical and city states, to become a nation state in 1871 which went through further phases during the following century in the form of: autocracy between 1871 and 1918; liberal democracy from 1919 to 1933 and since 1949; Fascist dictatorship from 1933 to 1945; and Communist state between 1949 and 1989. Some authorities may question the idea of comparing the persecution practised by the Nazis with the mild levels of exclusion characteristic of the Federal Republic, but certain clear lines of development link all periods of German ethnic history between 1800 and 2000 together. The commonalities also mean that, while the minorities may have changed, policies towards the post-war immigrant groupings have clear similarities with those which affected nineteenth-century Jews. At least one minority, the Gypsies, have experienced constant persecution throughout the nineteenth and twentieth centuries, which simply intensified under the Nazis.

Nazism may represent a problem here, because of its apparent uniqueness, especially with regard to the treatment of minorities. Even after the revisions to German historiography caused by the *Historikerstreit* of the 1980s, which reassessed the centrality of Nazism to German development, the Third Reich continues to cast a shadow over modern German history. One way of approaching our subject is to see the period 1933–45 as an earthquake with fore- and after-shocks, although this approach would have to focus upon levels of persecution. In this way the Hep-Hep riots of 1819 would serve as a warning of what would come over a century later, while the attacks on foreigners in the early 1990s would represent German extreme nationalism and racism rearing its ugly head again. Obviously, a clear line links the gowth of the antisemitic parties of the *Kaiserreich* with the rise of the Nazis.

But an approach revolving around the Third Reich seems unhelpful. Apart from the fact that the Nazi seizure of power did not become inevitable until 1933, it proves more instructive to have German nationalism and the

German nation state as the core of the study. Even before 1871, unification represented the central issue in German politics from the Napoleonic period. While attitudes towards minorities before the *Kaiserreich* may represent a legacy of the medieval period, the emancipation of the Jews was an act typical of a modernizing state, as was the continued existence of hostility towards the Jews, which intensified after 1871. After 1871, we can simply see the different incarnations of the German state as masks which it has worn, behind which always stands German nationalism with its ideology including all Germans and excluding all others. The methods of exclusion may have changed dramatically between 1800 and 2000, but the fact of exclusion has not. Before 1871 the pre-modern states also operated in this way, although on a more localized basis, because the German Confederation established in 1815 did not institute a standardized citizenship, meaning, for instance, that Bavarians were technically foreigners in Prussia. Nevertheless, there was no intolerant Prussian ideology, which specifically targeted Bavarians. Nationalism represented the rising force.

To return to the Nazi period, this represents the real break in the history of minorities under German control because of the levels and methods of persecution. Ethnic minority creation and exclusion is inevitable in all organized modern states, but their physical murder is not. While the Nazis may not represent the only twentieth-century regime which has systematically eliminated ethnic minorities,[57] it is the only one in modern Germany which has pursued such policies. Even the numerous other modern regimes throughout the world which have carried out ethnic cleansing have not used the factory methods employed by the Nazis in the death camps, making Nazism unique in the organization of its racism, although not in terms of its brutality, as contemporaneous Stalinism carried out equally thorough campaigns against its social opponents.[58]

The other regimes in modern Germany have practised milder forms of exclusion, some of which link the periods before 1933 and after 1949 closely together – for example, citizenship and civil rights. In this sense the German Jews before full emancipation in 1871 have much in common with the disenfranchised foreign citizens living in the Federal Republic, whose lack of civil rights arise from the fact that their parents or grandparents migrated to Germany several decades previously. Such people face the same choices of deciding between assimilation, acculturation and distinctiveness as nineteenth- and early twentieth-century Jews. They have to choose between becoming fully German and retaining their original ethnicity under pressure from their family, ethnic organizations and, in the case of some post-war newcomers and their offspring, their original homeland. In reality, many of the post-war

[22] newcomers, like their nineteenth-century Jewish predecessors, decide upon acculturation, so that they are both ethnic and German, culturally if not legally.

Another straight path from 1871 to 1974 consists of the processes of labour importation. While the two wartime regimes may have used force, the links throughout this century seem striking. In the first place most migrants have entered the German economy to carry out manual employment. This has meant that they have always found themselves at the bottom end of the social scale. Furthermore, migrants have always entered on short-term contracts and have simply represented an economic commodity, whether under the *Kaiserreich*, the Nazis or the Federal Republic.

During the course of the previous two centuries, Germany has always contained ethnic minorities, whether they represent remnants of its medieval past or creations of the age of nationalism. While the Nazi period may be unique in the levels of persecution, both Germans and others have had little doubt about their ethnicity and status throughout the past two hundred years.

Notes

1. The different types of ethnic minorities are explained below.

2. The major works on the meaning and spread of nationalism include: Benedict Anderson, *Imagined Communities: Reflections on the Origin and Spread of Nationalism* (London, 1991); Ernest Gellner, *Nations and Nationalism* (Oxford, 1983); Eric Hobsbawm, *Nations and Nationalism Since 1780: Programme, Myth, Reality* 2nd edn (Cambridge, 1992); Eric Hobsbawm and Terence Ranger, eds, *The Invention of Tradition* (Cambridge, 1983).

3. For the inextricable connection between nationalism, the nation state and minority exclusion and persecution in modern Europe see my *Outsiders: A History of European Minorities* (London, 1999).

4. Imanuel Geiss, *Geschichte des Rassismus* (Frankfurt am Main, 1988), p. 16.

5. Michael Burleigh and Wolfgang Wippermann, *The Racial State: Germany 1933–1945* (Cambridge, 1991), p. 23.

6. Ibid.

7. Michael Banton, *Racial Theories* 2nd edn (Cambridge, 1998), pp. 17–116.

8. For a discussion about these terms see, for instance, Volker Ackermann, *Der 'echte' Flüchtling: Deutsche Vertriebene und Flüchtlinge aus der DDR, 1945–1961* (Osnabrück, 1995).

9. Quoted in Daniéle Joly, *Refugees: Asylum in Europe?* (London, 1992), p. 11.

10. For a detailed discussion of all of the above terminological complications see [23] Klaus J. Bade, *Ausländer, Aussiedler, Asyl: Eine Bestandsaufnahme* (Munich, 1994).

11. James J. Sheehan, *German History, 1770–1866* (Oxford, 1989), p. 4.

12. Walter Schmidt, 'The Nation in German History', in Mikuláš Teich and Roy Porter, eds, *The National Question in Europe in Historical Context* (Cambridge, 1993), p. 151.

13. Mary Fulbrook, *A Concise History of Germany* (Cambridge, 1992), p. 13.

14. Sheehan, *German History, 1770–1866*, p. 4.

15. Hobsbawm, *Nations and Nationalism*, pp. 37–8.

16. John Breuilly, 'The National Idea in Modern German History', in Mary Fulbrook, ed., *German History Since 1800* (London, 1998), p. 569.

17. See contributions to John Breuilly, ed., *The State of Germany: The National Idea in the Making, Unmaking and Remaking of a Modern Nation State* (London, 1992).

18. Wolfgang Wippermann, *Geschichte der deutschen Juden: Darstellung und Dokumente* (Berlin, 1994), p. 14; Ruth Gay, *The Jews of Germany: A Historical Portrait* (London, 1992), pp. 3–5.

19. Gay, ibid., pp. 6–12.

20. Ibid., pp. 12–22.

21. Wippermann, *Geschichte der Juden*, pp. 21–2.

22. Gay, *Jews of Germany*, p. 28.

23. Wanda Kampmann, *Deutsche und Juden: Die Geschichte der Juden in Deutschland vom Mittelalter bis zum Beginn des Ersten Weltkrieges* 3rd edn (Frankfurt, 1994), pp. 27–34.

24. Werner J. Cahnman, *German Jewry: Its History and Sociology* (New Brunswick, NJ, 1989), p. 5.

25. Steven M. Lowenstein, *The Berlin Jewish Community: Enlightenment, Family and Crisis, 1770–1830* (New York, 1994), pp. 3, 10.

26. This is the figure given by H. G. Adler, *The Jews in Germany: From Enlightenment to National Socialism* (Notre Dame, IN, 1969), p. 4, for the year 1829. He seems to be referring to Germany according to the boundaries of 1871.

27. Stefi Jersch-Wenzel, 'Die Juden im Zeitalter der Aufklärung', in Dirk Blasius and Dan Diner, eds, *Zerbrochene Geschichte: Leben und Selbstverständnis der Juden in Deutschland* (Frankfurt, 1991), pp. 53–63.

28. Cahnman, *German Jewry*, p. 6.

29. Lucy Dawidowicz, *The War Against the Jews, 1933–45* (Harmondsworth, 1990), p. 216.

[24] 30. Ibid., p. 448.

31. Y. Michael Bodemann, 'A Reemergence of German Jewry?', in Sander L. Gilman and Karen Remmler, eds, *Reemerging Jewish Culture in Germany: Life and Literature Since 1989* (New York, 1994), pp. 48–9.

32. Rainer Hehemann, '"... Jederzeit gottlose böse Leute": Sinti und Roma zwischen Duldung und Vernichtung', in Klaus J. Bade, ed., *Deutsche im Ausland, Fremde in Deutschland: Migration in Geschichte und Gegenwart* (Munich, 1992), p. 272; Carl Hopf, *Die Einwanderung der Zigeuner in Europa* (Gotha, 1870), p. 3. For brief details on the origins of the Gypsies and their arrival in Europe see Panayi, *Outsiders*, pp. 20–2.

33. Joachim S. Hohmann, *Geschichte der Zigeunerverfolgung in Deutschland* 3rd edn (Frankfurt, 1988), pp. 27, 44.

34. Ibid., p. 67.

35. Susan Tebbutt, 'Sinti and Roma: From Scapegoats and Stereotypes to Self-Assertion', in Tebbutt, ed., *Sinti and Roma: Gypsies in German-Speaking Society and Literature* (Oxford, 1998), p. xiv.

36. Outlines of medieval Prussian Polish relations include: Gerard Labuda, 'The Territorial, Ethnical and Demographic Aspects of Polish-German Relations in the Past (X–XX Centuries)', *Polish Western Affairs* 3 (1962), pp. 223–41; Bernhard Stasiewski, 'Zur Geschichte deutsch-polnischer Nachbarschaft', in Herbert Czaja and Gustav E. Kafka, eds, *Deutsche und Polen: Probleme einer Nachbarschaft* (Recklinghausen, 1960), pp. 7–34; and Wolfgang Wippermann, *Geschichte der deutsch-polnischen Beziehungen* (Berlin, 1992), pp. 9–19.

37. Martin Broszat, *Zweihundert Jahre deutsche Polenpolitk* 2nd edn (Frankfurt, 1972), p. 86.

38. Harry Kenneth Rosenthal, *German and Pole: National Conflict and Modern Myth* (Gainesville, FL, 1976), p. 62, n. 1.

39. Christoph Kleßmann, 'Long-Distance Migration, Integration and Segregation of an Ethnic Minority in Industrial Germany: The Case of the "Ruhr-Poles"', in Klaus J. Bade, ed., *Population, Labour and Migration in 19th- and 20th-Century Germany* (Oxford, 1987), p. 104.

40. Labuda, 'Polish-German Relations', p. 250.

41. Kleßmann, 'Long-Distance Migration', pp. 103–4.

42. Burleigh and Wippermann, *Racial State*, pp. 130–1.

43. See: Roger Portal, *The Slavs* (London, 1969), pp. 1–25; and Marija Gimbutas, *The Slavs* (London, 1971).

44. Gerald Stone, *The Smallest Slavonic Nation: The Sorbs of Lusatia* (London, 1972), [25]
p. 9.

45. See: ibid., *passim*; Elke Gemkow, Marco Heinz and Stefan Neumann, 'Die
Sorben in der Lausitz', in Heinz and Neumann, eds, *Ethnische Minderheiten in
Westeuropa* (Bonn, 1996), pp. 103–21; Burleigh and Wippermann, *Racial State*,
pp. 131–5; Leoš Šatava, 'The Lusatian Sorbs in Eastern Germany', in Minor-
ity Rights Group and TWEEC, eds, *Minorities in Central and Eastern Europe*
(London, 1993), p. 33.

46. Gemkow, Heinz and Neumann, ibid., pp. 105–10.

47. Felipe Fernández-Armesto, ed., *The Times Guide to the Peoples of Europe* (London,
1994), p. 31.

48. Ulrich Herbert, *A History of Foreign Labour in Germany, 1880–1980: Seasonal
Workers/Forced Labourers/Guest Workers* (Ann Arbor, MI, 1990), p. 55.

49. Ibid., pp. 87–119.

50. Johann Woydt, *Ausländische Arbeitskräfte in Deutschland: Vom Kaiserreich bis zur
Bundesrepublik* (Heilbronn, 1987), p. 54.

51. Karl Liedke, '. . . *aber politisch unerwünscht': Arbeitskräfte aus Osteuropa im Land
Braunschweig 1880 bis 1939* (Braunschweig, 1993), pp. 138–42.

52. Herbert, *History of Foreign Labour*, pp. 154, 156.

53. Hans W. Schoenberg, *Germans from the East: A Study of Their Migration, Resettlement and Subsequent Group History Since 1945* (The Hague, 1970), p. 32.

54. Panikos Panayi, 'Race in the Federal Republic of Germany: Immigration,
Ethnicity and Racism since the Second World War', in Klaus Larres and
Panikos Panayi, eds, *The Federal Republic of Germany Since 1949: Politics, Society
and Economy before and after Unification* (London, 1996), pp. 196–200.

55. Dirk Jasper, 'Ausländerbeschäftigung in der DDR', in Marianne Krüger-
Portratz, ed., *Anderssein gab es nicht: Ausländer und Minderheiten in der DDR*
(Münster, 1991), pp. 151–71.

56. Cornelia Schmalz-Jacobsen, Holger Hinte and Georgios Tsapanos, *Einwanderung und dann: Perspektiven einer neuen Ausländerpolitik* (Munich, 1993), p. 314.

57. The Ottoman elimination of its Armenian population represents the other
classic genocide of the first half of the twentieth century, for which see: Vahakn
Dadrian, *The History of the Armenian Genocide* (Oxford, 1995); and Richard G.
Hovanissian, ed., *The Armenian Genocide* (London, 1992).

58. For similarities between the two regimes see: Ian Kershaw and Moshe Lewin,
eds, *Stalinism and Nazism: Dictatorships in Comparison* (Cambridge, 1997).

CHAPTER 2

The Emergence of the German Nation State and the Position of Ethnic Minorities, c.1800–70

I n the first part of the nineteenth century the move towards German unification dominated politics in Central Europe until it became a reality in 1871. It did so due to a combination of ideological, economic, social and political factors. The idea of the nation began to spread as a result of the intellectual ferment caused by the eighteenth-century Enlightenment which served as the background to the French Revolution. This event brought to fruition the idea of a sovereign people for the first time in continental European history. As the Revolutionary and Napoleonic armies moved eastward they carried such ideas with them and found a receptive audience in the form of a growing and increasingly self-confident middle class, especially in Germany, which began its path towards industrialization. For much of the early nineteenth century the various strands of the German bourgeoisie had the ideological upper hand which, in the early days of the 1848 Revolutions, led to the Frankfurt Parliament which looked as though it might achieve unification from below. However, after the defeat and failure of the Frankfurt Parliament by the forces of reaction, unification seemed less likely until the rise of Bismarck, who achieved this action as Chancellor of Prussia by conquering and defeating surrounding territories and setting the pattern for the following eighty years of German history. The rising middle classes, with expanding business interests, felt comfortable with unification achieved in this manner.

The German states of the years leading up to unification, like all political units in the age before nationalism, did not by any means contain homogeneous populations. Apart from the linguistic variations from one part of Germany to another, there existed two sizeable ethnic minorities, in the form of Poles and Jews, and a small group, the Gypsies, which received considerable attention, despite its small size. The Jews and Gypsies had experienced centuries of persecution. The new age of liberal nationalism promised them a better deal, which had concrete manifestations for the Jews, who gained full civil rights in many states. But the medieval hatreds did not disappear and began to transform themselves into an ideological hostility, especially towards the Jews, whom many early nineteenth-century writers viewed as the blot on the perfect ethnic German landscape. Before 1871 the Poles did not receive such negative attention and, in fact, many liberals had sympathy for them as a people, which, like the Germans, wanted to move towards self-determination.

The Germany of the years 1800–70 underwent a series of economic, social and political transformations, which form the background for the ethnic history of this period. In economic terms, these years witnessed the beginnings of the industrialization process, or 'take off' to use the words of the economic historian W. W. Rostow. Such events occurred against an increase in the German population from 23,520,000 in 1816 to 39,231,000 by 1870,[1] which provided some of the labour power for emerging industries, although these could not mop up all the excess population streaming from the land, which meant that Germany represented a net exporter of people until the last decade of the nineteenth century.[2] Nevertheless, much change had taken place in the German economy by 1871 which meant that over 50 per cent of people found employment in the secondary and tertiary sectors in that year.[3] While some industrial growth had taken place before the 1848 revolutions, especially in textiles, it intensified more especially during the 1850s and 1860s, when sectors such as coal mining and iron and steel production also took off. Such developments went hand in hand with an increasing ease of communication, as a result of the growth of railways from the 1830s and the use of steamships on Germany's major rivers. In addition, the establishment of the *Zollverein* in 1834 meant the disappearance of tariff barriers between the eighteen states which joined it and led to the emergence of a national German market.[4]

Against these economic changes came social ones, which played a significant role in the ideological and political developments of the nineteenth century. Population growth and migration to the cities meant a change in the class composition of Germany. In the first place the bourgeoisie grew in both size and self-confidence. This group consisted of a variety of occupations, divided into the industrial middle classes, whose number increased as the century progressed, and the *Bildungsbürgertum*, essentially professionals, including academics and lawyers, who played a major role in the ideological and political changes of the years leading up to 1871.[5] The industrialization process also meant a growth in the size of the working classes, so that Berlin contained 100,000 workers by 1848.[6]

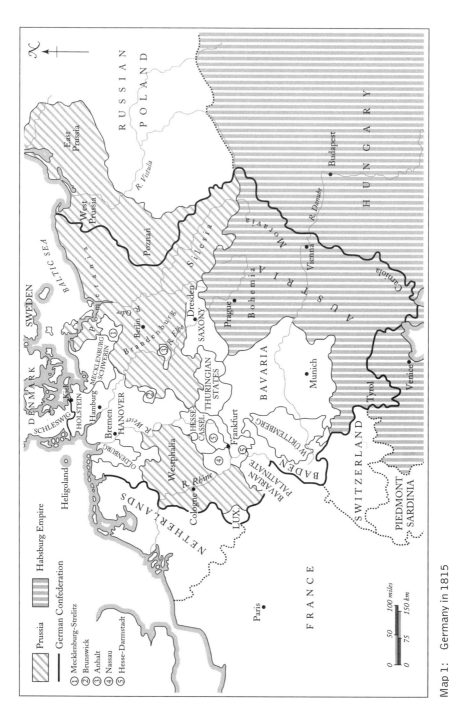

Map 1: Germany in 1815

Source: William Carr, *A History of Germany, 1815–1945*, 2nd edn (London: Arnold, 1979) p. xii.

The above changes went hand in hand with the political transformations taking place in early nineteenth-century Germany which, retrospectively, all seem to point directly to unification in 1871. The revolutionary armies which moved into German states in 1792 changed the course of the development of Europe east of the Rhine. The 300 German territories which had existed during the eighteenth century had declined to 39 by 1817, as a result of changes during the Revolutionary and Napoleonic period. These states came together in 1815 in 'a loose association of independent sovereign entities'[7] called the German Confederation. We can see this as an important precursor to the evolution of the German nation state, even though, in many ways, it represented a reactionary force controlled by the largest monarchical states of Austria and Prussia. Nevertheless, the genie of nationalism had escaped and the years leading up to the 1848 revolutions witnessed many concrete manifestations of German nationalism against the background of a spread of nationalist ideas and the existence of some sort of representative institutions in many of the states which emerged from the Napoleonic period. The waves of protest which characterized the *Vormärz* period came to a crescendo in the revolutionary outbreaks of 1848 which gave rise to a national parliament in Frankfurt wishing to see a united Germany. However, the forces of reaction had gained the upper hand by the beginning of 1849 and, not for the last time in German history, reform from below had failed. Consequently, there followed unification from above, led by the Prussian Prime Minister Otto von Bismarck, who annexed Schleswig-Holstein in 1863 and defeated Austria in 1866 and France in 1871, leading to the formation of a unitary German nation state, with a dominant Prussia, in 1871.[8]

The crystallization of ideological nationalism and the birth of racism

Elie Kedourie recognized that 'Nationalism is a doctrine invented in Europe at the beginning of the nineteenth century'.[9] However, it has deeper origins in the German case which many scholars rightly take back to Luther and the Reformation. Walter Schmidt has written: 'The term German nation was widely employed from the Reformation onwards as an expression of common aims and interests of the Germans'.[10] The translation of the Bible into German represented one of the main achievements of the Reformation, forming the basis of a literary language.

[30]   Nevertheless, the eighteenth-century Enlightenment represents a more concrete ideological foundation for the nationalism which would emerge in Germany by the 1820s. Kedourie places great weight on the intellectual changes which took place during the Enlightenment, especially the work of the Königsberg Professor Immanuel Kant, which pointed the way forward for the free-thinking individual and, by implication, led the way to national self-determination.[11] Simultaneously, and fundamentally important for the development of the national idea, the eighteenth century saw the emergence of a German literature through the works of writers such as Friedrich Gottlieb Klopstock, Gotthold Lessing, Friedrich Schiller and, above all, Johann Wolfgang von Goethe. Consequently, German gained increasing respectability by replacing Latin as the language of instruction at German universities.[12] The eighteenth century also saw a great flowering of German music especially through the works of Johann Sebastian Bach, Georg Friedrich Handel, Joseph Haydn, Wolfgang Amadeus Mozart and Ludwig van Beethoven.

Against this intellectual and artistic background the Enlightenment witnessed the emergence of a more concrete political nationalism: the key figure here was Johann Gottfried Herder. He played a central role in the perpetuation of a linguistic nationalism, by focusing upon the richness of the German literary tradition, and pointing to the fact that it rivalled that of many other European languages.[13] Perhaps, most importantly, for someone who placed so much stress upon language, he created the important concept of a German *Volk*, or people, which subsequent generations of political thinkers and politicians would turn into a racial concept to exclude Jews. Herder actually put more stress on the cultural rather than the political manifestations of the *Volk*.[14] However, Herder also drew a link between the ancient Germans and the modern ones and admired their 'tall, strong, and beautiful bodies', their 'enormous blue eyes filled with the spirit of restraint and loyalty', and their 'heroic cast of mind and great physical strength'.[15] Significantly, Herder viewed the Jews negatively, believing them too alien and distinct to become Germans.[16]

Nevertheless, while eighteenth-century enlightened thinkers may have laid the foundations for the racist and nationalist ideologues who perverted their ideas, the Enlightenment, just as importantly, released the other great modern ideology in the form of liberalism, as the intellectual changes of these years represented, as much as anything else, a reaction against despotism and the superstition inherent in 'irrational' and unscientific religion. The emancipation of the Jews emerged as a central objective of German liberals. An early request for the toleration of this group came from Gotthold Lessing, especially in his play *The Jews* of the 1750s, 'of no particular literary merit in itself, but unique in German letters at the time for putting forward a strong plea for toleration towards the Jews'.[17] The first significant work specifically calling for emancipation appeared in 1781 when the Prussian administrator Christian Wilhelm von Dohm published his book on *The Civil Improvement of Jews*. This applied the ideas of the Enlightenment, the American War of Independence and the views of Adam Smith to the position of Jews, which he linked with the emancipation of the middle classes and other ethnic groups such as Gypsies and Huguenots.[18]

The arrival of the invading French armies with their liberating ideas had a series of contradictory long-term effects upon the evolution of German political thought, assisting both liberal ideas and helping in the emergence of extreme nationalist and racist views. The Revolution initially excited enthusiastic responses from German intellectuals, but, by the end of the 1790s, many of its early supporters had turned against its consequences. During this decade German Romanticism emerged as a cultural movement which laid great stress upon art as the highest value. Politically, the Romantics turned against the individualism inherent in the Revolution and wanted, instead, to link the individual with community, which also meant looking back to the Middle Ages.[19] These ideas fed into the emerging nationalism of the first two decades of the nineteenth century, which received further impetus by the creation of external and internal enemies in the forms of the occupying French and the ubiquitous Jews.

Johann Gottlieb Fichte, often called the father of German nationalism, began as a supporter of the French Revolution, but turned against it following the seizure of power by Napoleon. His experience of watching the sack of Berlin by Bonaparte in 1807 made him intensely anti-French and led to his *Addresses to the German Nation*, which he delivered at the Berlin Academy in the winter of 1807–8.[20] He stated that he simply wanted education for the Germans, whom he described in his fourth lecture as 'a branch of the Teutonic race' and placed strong emphasis upon language as the central binding and distinguishing feature of the Germans. He claimed that 'the German spirit is an eagle, whose mighty body thrusts itself on high and soars on strong and well-practised wings'. He continued that, with the exception of some parts of Italy, German cities represented the only civilized parts of medieval Europe. But whereas wars and constant change characterized the history of Italy, 'the spirit of piety, of honour, of modesty and of the sense of community', had existed in Germany. Fichte's fourteenth and final lecture was a rousing call to incite patriotism in the fatherland among all Germans, both those present

[32]   and those beyond the lecture hall, although his vision of the future remained abstract and did not focus upon the formation of a state. He feared that, if Germans did not act, they could be 'swallowed up' by other peoples.[21]

Ernst Moritz Arndt wrote at the same time as Fichte using equally rousing language and attempted 'to create a national concept that fused culture and politics', uniting the *Volk* and the state.[22] He devoted much attention to the French enemies who controlled German soil. In a situation where no unitary German state existed he focused especially upon the concept of language as the binding force of Germans, most famously in the following verse:

> Where is the German Fatherland?
> Name me at length that mighty land!
> 'Where'er resounds the German tongue,
> Where'er its hymns to God are sung.'
> Be this the land,
> Brave German, this thy Fatherland.[23]

In proto-racist language, using concepts which appear again and again in the following two centuries, Arndt spoke about the purity of Germans 'who have not been bastardized by foreign nations'.[24]

Friedrich Ludwig Jahn wrote at the same time as both Arndt and Fichte and put forward similar concepts. He held a Chair at the University of Berlin and founded the fraternity movement (*Bursenschaften*) for the purpose of propagating German culture and encouraging physical exercise with a view to preparing Germans to fight for the unity of their country, policies which the Nazis would subsequently adopt. Similarly, in 1817 the *Bursenschaften* gathered together by the medieval Wartburg castle for the purpose of burning foreign books which had poisoned the true culture of the *Volk*.[25] Jahn's *Deutsches Volkstum* of 1810 provided a meticulous vision of a future German state. The volume went into great detail about how citizens should behave in all aspects of their public and private lives. Jahn also outlined the institutions which a German state should establish. His book divided humanity into different peoples (*Völker*) and called for a renaissance of the Germans independent of foreign teachers. Like Arndt and Fichte, Jahn layed great stress on the use of German. 'Every person has just one mother and therefore needs just one mother tongue.' Elsewhere he wrote that all Germans should learn *Hochdeutsch* as their patriotic duty.[26]

The nationalistic vision put forward so vehemently by Fichte, Arndt, Jahn and others of their contemporaries, inevitably created outgroups. Apart from the French, the Jews also surfaced as natural enemies in the first bloom of modern antisemitism, which would develop into a full-blown ideology over the next century. In fact, hostility towards Jews took off from the late eighteenth century so that even Kant viewed the Jews negatively as a group who practised an obsolete religion and as a nation of traders devoted to money, and consequently scared of freedom.[27]

Fichte is regarded as a major figure in the emergence of modern German antisemitism. In a pamphlet which he published in 1793 he singled out the Jews because they lived as a separate state, which hated the entire human race, throughout almost all European countries. He wanted to give them human rights 'even though they do not concede them to us', because this offered the only practical solution to the Jewish problem 'other than that of some night cutting off their heads, and attaching in their stead others in which there is not a single Jewish idea', although in the long run in order to 'protect ourselves against them' he saw 'no way than of conquering for them their promised land and of sending them all to it'.[28] In fact the concept of a state within a state, which would represent a fundamental antisemitic tenet until the Nazi period, had begun to circulate from the 1780s as used by Johann Heinrich Schulz.[29] More radical statements came from Arndt in 1814 and 1815 who viewed the French, the Poles and the Jews as the curse of Germany and called for purity of race and the prevention of cross breeding. Nevertheless, he was prepared to grant Jews civil rights as long as they displayed a willingness to assimilate.[30]

The Restoration period resulted in a further outburst of antisemitism, culminating in the Hep-Hep riots of 1819, in which the lower classes used the most direct form of discourse, violence, to reveal their feelings towards the Jews. But urban workers acted against a background of widespread published hostility towards the Jews. One of the most virulent works consisted of a pamphlet by Friedrich Rühs published in 1815, *On the Claims of the Jews to Civil Rights in Germany*, which the author denied on the basis that Jews consisted of a different people with a different religion who had previously turned down the opportunity to assimilate.[31] On a more popular basis the *Bursenschaften* began to practise antisemitism. Many of these banned Jews from membership, which became a principle of the constitution of the national organization following a conference in Dresden in 1820 because Jews 'have no Fatherland and no interest in ours'.[32] One of the most bigoted and irrational attacks upon Jews in the early Restoration period came from H. Hundt-Radowsky, who, in a pamphlet from 1819 stated that people throughout the world use phrases

[34] such as evil, cowardly, superstitious, thieving and profiteering to describe Jews. He saw no point in granting them citizenship because their allegiance lay to Canaan in the Orient. He wanted to see the elimination of the Jews and suggested sending them to locations throughout the British Empire.[33]

While, on the one hand the growing antisemitism of the first decades of the nineteenth century received its impetus from rising nationalism, it also represented a reaction against the first stages of the emancipation of the Jews from the medieval restrictions which they had faced in locations throughout Germany. This again establishes a pattern for the future: the greater the level of 'mainstream' and state tolerance, the more virulent becomes the popular hostility towards Jews. Consequently, both the *Kaiserreich* and the Weimar Republic are, for the Jews, positive and negative periods. This almost suggests that the medieval antisemitism was so deeply ingrained in German political and religious consciousness, that any attempt to exorcise it failed as an even more sinister demon took its place.

Clearly, an important impetus for Jewish emancipation came from the French Revolution with its liberal and egalitarian ideas. In the early years of the 1790s German Jacobin clubs came into existence as did political organizations which had both German and Jewish members. Nevertheless, while a few of those writing on the issue of emancipation did not require anything in return from the Jews, the vast majority, in keeping with the ideas of Fichte, really spoke in terms of a social contract, in which the granting of full citizenship meant the ditching of some aspects of Jewishness, which could include religion and names.[34] Most of the emancipation decrees in the following decades worked upon this pattern, forcing Jews to make choices about their ethnicity.

The years leading to the 1848 revolutions reveal similar patterns in the evolving German nationalism, liberalism, racism and antisemitism. During the 1820s, 1830s and 1840s the restored order, personified in the figure of the Austrian Prince Metternich, attempted to suppress the national and liberal ideologies which had surfaced between 1789 and 1815, by the introduction of repressive measures on several occasions forbidding freedom of speech and association. However, these proved only partially successful as outbreaks of nationalistic fervour occurred in 1820, 1830 and 1832. In May 1832 about 25,000 people gathered in Hambach in the Palatinate to participate in a festival of nationalism.[35] Intellectually the most important advances in the evolution of German national consciousness came through the work of Georg Wilhelm Friedrich Hegel, Professor of Philosophy at the University of Berlin from 1818, who brought forward the ideas of Arndt and Jahn by linking the nation and the state.[36]

The *Vormärz* period also saw the surfacing of new racist and antisemitic ideas, and a recycling of old ones, especially those demanding that Jews shed their religion in order to move forward. Such views were advocated by radicals such as Ludwig Feuerbach, Bruno Bauer and Karl Marx, taking their lead from Hegel who believed that Jews had to be liberated from an unfree psyche by German philosophy. Much of the hostility of this group writing in the 1830s and 1840s came from the animosity towards all religion. However, Marx also drew the link between capitalism and the Jews.[37] This financial hostility also helped antisemitism to spread amongst the petty bourgeoisie who, under threat from emerging factories, linked big business with the Jews. In addition to these forms of liberal and radical antisemitism, there also existed in the *Vormärz* period a hatred of the Jews from German Christian conservatives, who viewed the social and political movements of the early nineteenth century, sparked off by industrialization, as a threat to the traditional German Christian way of life. They saw the Jews as financially benefiting from the economic transformations taking place and also, as 'Christ killers', playing a central role in the decline of traditional society. They opposed liberal concepts of emancipation as Jewish and as an attack upon God's natural order and creations. The Conservatives further had a concept of a Christian German nation and, still with a view to the past, saw the solution to the Jewish problem in Baptism, which still allowed a traditional 'get-out clause' which later and modern antisemitism did not. The *volkisch* nationalism, which continued to develop during the *Vormärz* period, carried forward by people such as Heinrich Leo, saw no place for the Jews in the German people's state, although, unlike their Nazi successors, they were not, at this stage, advocating extermination, although some did suggest expulsion, while others spoke of a mixing of blood between Jews and Germans, with the aim of eliminating the former.[38] At the same time as antisemitism developed, the Poles also began to receive negative attention from authors such as Moritz Wilhelm Heffter, and Heinrich Wuttke, who began to speak of a struggle between Germans and Slavs.[39]

Nevertheless, until 1848 the Poles represented a progressive cause for many German liberals, because they also fought for liberation from an autocratic regime and the restoration of Poland according to the borders of 1772. This meant opposing Prussian, Austrian and Russian tyranny alike.[40] For many liberals, the emancipation of the Jews remained the central symbolic issue of their cause. For instance, in the case of one publicist in the *Vormärz* period, Johann Jacoby, his 'commitment to political reform was inseparable from his desire to complete the emancipation of the Jews'.[41] Similarly, a deputation of

[36] representatives of the state parliament of Saxony in 1834 devised a core of their liberal ideology in which they stated that: 'The issue of the emancipation of the Jews is the issue of the forward moving enlightenment, the issue of growing freedom.' Even so, for most liberals, emancipation continued to require something in return in the form of the shedding of Jewish ethnicity for the gaining of German citizenship, which, essentially, meant assimilation.[42]

The revolutions of 1848 and the debates in the Frankfurt Parliament solved many of the anomalies of the *Vormärz* period. In the previous year a united Prussian Diet had met and discussed the question of Jewish emancipation. During the debate the regime had declared Prussia a Christian state in which non-Christians could not have political rights and could not be trusted with office.[43] This conservative reaction represented an omen of events which would take place in 1849. Following revolutionary outbreaks in France, similar developments occurred throughout Germany and Austria, beginning in Baden and Württemberg and quickly spreading. The Frankfurt Parliament which met in May 1848, initially seemed as if it had brought the progressive liberal policies, which would, above all, benefit the liberal middle-class deputies, to reality. For instance, it introduced a declaration of the Basic Rights of the German People, following the French and American models.[44] On the question of minorities, the Parliament also initially appeared progressive, so that article 5 of the Basic Rights of the German People declared that the civil and political rights of citizens were neither dependant upon nor restricted by religious belief.[45] Jewish and Christian students even stood side by side as members of *Burschenschaften* on the barricades of Berlin and Vienna.[46] Nevertheless, the revolutions of 1848 in both Germany and elsewhere were national liberal revolutions, which meant that, while liberal values came to the fore, so did national ones. The Frankfurt Parliament, which also represented Austria, included ethnic minorities other than Jews in the form of Czechs, Slovaks, Poles and Danes, who got short shrift from the dominant ethnic Germans, despite the rhetoric of the *Vormärz* period. While, on the one hand, the Parliament granted national groupings within Germany linguistic and cultural rights, together with self-government, it wanted to hold on to the parts of Germany where these peoples lived rather than allow independence.[47] Ultimately, the wishes of the 1848 liberal and national revolutionaries proved irrelevant because the forces of reaction triumphed as the old order reimposed itself. While the insurrectionists did not have their aim of a unitary German state fulfilled, the triumph of nationalism over liberalism seemed inevitable because the two ideologies essentially contradict each other: the former works for the benefit of a mythical constructed group, while the latter, in its purest form, concerns itself with the rights of the individual. This is an ideological issue, repeated throughout the world over the following 150 years, rather than a purely German one. The failure of the 1848 revolutions may represent a turning point in German history, but would success have prevented the virulent aggressive nationalism which became dominant at the end of the nineteenth century?

The 1850s and 1860s did not mean an eradication of the gains made by the 1848 revolutionaries, as many states moved forward in constitutional terms and retained Jewish emancipation. The progress towards 'unification from above', which finally occurred under Bismarck in 1871, meant that Liberals who remained in Germany after 1848 or returned after a period of exile had fewer and fewer problems as they could see no way in which they could achieve their aim from below, which would have meant allying with the more dangerous working-class movements. The annexation of Schleswig-Holstein in 1864 resulted in nationalistic jubilation throughout Germany. Finally, in 1871, any remaining doubters within Germany joined together in the formation of the first German nation state.[48]

The drowning of liberalism by nationalism after 1848 meant a decreasing concern for the position of ethnic minorities, a new outbreak of antisemitism, which, however, generally remained relatively dormant until the 1870s, and the surfacing of racial ideas, which would become widespread by the end of the nineteenth century. A Frenchman, Arthur de Gobineau, wrote the most important racist work, *The Inequality of Human Races*, originally published between 1853 and 1855, which created the myth of the superior Aryan race. While he accepted that mixing of blood between different races could prove beneficial, although he never defined race, he drew up a racial hierarchy in which non-Europeans came near the bottom. In 1859 there followed Charles Darwin's *On the Origin of Natural Selection or the Preservation of Favoured Races in the Struggle for Life*. Although Darwin himself was not a racist, subsequent authors, many of them German, not least Hitler, applied his ideas of natural selection of species to the survival of the fittest human beings, so that a Social Darwinist thought developed.[49]

Antisemitism did remain fairly tame during the 1850s and 1860s, compared with the outbreaks which would occur from the 1870s and which would remain unremitting until 1945. The explanation for this may lie in the fact that revolutionary ideologies had burnt themselves out in 1848, remaining dormant in the reactionary atmosphere of the 1850s and 1860s. At the same time, the Jews did not make dramatic political advances and the issue of Jewish emancipation remained on the back burner in terms of the political

[38] agenda until this minority did finally receive full civil and political rights throughout Germany in 1871, after which there followed the massive expansion of agitation from the 1870s. In addition, the two decades immediately after the 1848 revolutions witnessed stable economic growth in contrast to the 1840s and the 1870s, which witnessed dramatic downturns.

However, antisemitism did make some advances during the 1850s, with Richard Wagner representing the major figure in its development. His hostility combined a mixture of personal, artistic, liberal, socialist, nationalistic and racist elements and the major antisemitic work of the 1850s and 1860s consisted of his *Das Judentum in der Musik*, originally published anonymously in 1850 (and reissued under his name in 1869), although he did comment on the Jews in other publications. His music of these years also reveals his ideas about the superiority of Germans over other 'racial' groups.

Before the 1848 revolutions Wagner had mixed in radical liberal nationalist circles and 'had absorbed the structural antisemitism implicit in Young German and Young Hegelian revolutionary thinking, which equated money-egoism with Jews'.[50] However, until 1848 he had many Jewish acquaintances and friends in the various cities in which he had lived, some of whom he kept after this time, even though he developed a paranoid belief that Jews held responsibility for all the failures in his professional and personal life after 1850.[51] He disliked the Jewish composers Felix Mendelssohn and Giacomo Meyerbeer, because he believed they could not produce truly German music,[52] which he saw as part of the move towards the unification of the German *Volk*.[53] While 'Wagner's declared intention in *Judaism in Music* was to demonstrate the destructive effect of Jewish participation in artistic endeavours',[54] this work focused upon more than just music and the arts, and resembles a conspiracy theory of the type which would become widespread later in the century. He claimed that: 'In the present state of affairs the Jew is really more than emancipated: he rules, and will continue to do so as long as money controls power.' Wagner also believed that 'the Jew' remained an outsider because he 'speaks the language of the nation, in which he lives from one generation to another, but always speaks it as a foreigner'. Because of this 'the Jew' could not write national poetry and had essentially remained an outsider in the development of European culture, which he essentially imitated.[55] The Jews as outsiders in European culture and music essentially represent the central focus of Wagner's pamphlet. However, his 'antisemitic vision' combined race, music and politics, and, like other modern German nationalists and racists, he perpetuated the view of a pure *Volk* threatened by Jews.

Jewish emancipation and Jewish persecution [39]

The contradictory ideological developments of the century before 1870 inevitably had mixed consequences for the position of German Jewry. In the first place much social mobility occurred out of the ghetto, assisted by the process of emancipation, which eventually allowed Jews to live wherever they wished. In fact, the liberation of the Jews from the medieval restrictions which they had faced represents the central development of these years. But as ideological antisemitism began to develop, manifestations of Jew hatred occurred on a daily basis, often resulting in violence, most notably in the Hep-Hep riots of 1819.

Before emancipation took place most Jews lived in an unenviable position:

> Every Jew living in the empire in the period around 1780 was the subject of restrictive exceptional laws that weighed most heavily on the mass of the group. But even the few Jews whose lives were easier by virtue of wealth or fame were greatly limited in their personal freedom. In general the Jew was an object of scorn. In the common view they were a race of beggars, peddlars, usurers; they were unlikable, deeply superstitious, uneducated, and grotesque in appearance and behaviour.[56]

While this quote specifically refers to areas within the Holy Roman Empire, it would also apply to territories throughout Germany.

By the end of the nineteenth century, Jews had become overwhelmingly concentrated in cities, but one hundred years earlier, they overwhelmingly resided, like the rest of the population of Germany, in the countryside in villages and small towns. In southern and western Germany they concentrated in villages with less than 1,000 inhabitants, where they often made up between 10 and 25 per cent of the population. In some of the towns of the newly acquired Polish territories of Prussia, Jews could constitute up to a third of the population, and sometimes formed a majority, although they made up just 67,500 out of a total population of 1,335,000 in these areas as a whole. Wherever they lived, Jews concentrated together,[57] due to a combination of reasons, including a legal obligation to do so, ethnic solidarity against an overwhelmingly hostile environment and the requirement to walk to the synagogue on the sabbath.

Nevertheless, some Jews had always lived in cities which, by the start of the nineteenth century, included Berlin, Hamburg and Frankfurt. Berlin Jewry represented one of the most developed communities in Germany. From its beginnings in the late seventeenth century this minority, which never concentrated in the ghetto, had a reputation for its wealth and, a hundred years

[40] later, it held much of the non-landed assets of the city, having done very well out of the Seven Years War of 1756–63. This wealth played a large role in the hedonistic and fashionable lifestyle which came to characterize the Berlin Jewish élite after 1750, a time during which many Jewish salons opened and were attended by both Jews and gentiles, allowing integration of the two communities as well as encouraging an escape from Jewish traditional mores and dress and facilitating a wave of conversions to Christianity. The Jewish philosopher Moses Mendelssohn played a key role in the modernization of Judaism from his arrival in Berlin in 1743 until his death in 1786, representing a key figure in the Jewish Enlightenment (*Haskala*). His legacy was perpetuated by figures who included David Friedlander and the salon hostesses, notably Henriette Herz, Rahel Vanhargen and Dorothea Schlegel. In addition to Jewish high society in Berlin, whose existence and integration played a large role in the movement for emancipation, there also existed a poorer Jewish community in the city, although the Prussian authorities restricted its size by controlling immigration.[58]

The history of Jewry in Hamburg and Altona had begun to develop from the end of the sixteenth century as Jews moved northwards from other parts of Germany. The following two hundred years witnessed the building of synagogues and schools in this city. By the beginning of the nineteenth century, at which time restrictions on residence still operated, seven different congregations of German and Portuguese Jews lived in Hamburg, Altona and Wandsbek, centred upon Altona. The 6,300 Jews residing in the city at this time made it the largest community in Germany. Major Jewish occupations included the buying and selling of second-hand clothes, as well as the retailing of coffee, tea, tobacco and food, especially meat and milk. When Napoleon's armies held Hamburg citizens prisoner, Jews made up 10 of the 41 contributors to the ransom of half a million francs.[59]

The much smaller Westfalian town of Minden counted just 21 Jewish families in 1815 meaning a total of only 112 souls: the majority of breadwinners worked as merchants.[60] In fact trading of some sort represented a significant occupation for Jews throughout Germany around 1800. 'The bulk of the German-Jewish economic élite of the nineteenth century emerged progressively from a mass of petty provincial traders.'[61] A total of 83 per cent of Jews residing in Lower Franconia in 1803, with one of the heaviest concentrations of this minority in Germany, made their living from some sort of trading including hawking.[62] One such person was Isaac Thannhäuser, born in Altenstadt in Bavarian Swabia in 1774, who, during much of the 1790s found himself employed in door to door selling. He described one such period:

I was a wandering pedlar. Every week I went with my bundle on my back to [41]
Dornstadt, Tomerdingen, and Westerstetten . . .

   I staggered on in this most degrading condition for two years, and saw nothing ahead that could have been useful or advantageous for my future. Instead, I
remained a wretched pack-bearer and hawker to peasants.[63]

The most dramatic development in the history of German Jewry during
the late eighteenth and early nineteenth centuries consisted of the granting of
emancipation in many territories. As we have seen, positive attitudes towards
the Jews partly rested upon the anticlericalism inherent in the new ideas of
the late eighteenth century but, while on the one hand the ideas followed an
escape from the endemic medieval Jew hatred, they prepared the way for the
emergence of racial antisemitism.[64]

Under the influence of Dohm's publication of 1781, the first important German step for the emancipation of the Jews came from the Austrian
Enlightened Despot, Joseph II, who, in 1782, issued a *Toleranzpatent*, in
which he envisaged the removal of controls upon Jews.[65] Much of the pre-
Revolutionary debate about Jewish emancipation actually took place in
Berlin because of the presence of a successful and 'enlightened' community,
which began presenting petitions asking for an improvement in its position
to King Frederick William II immediately after his accession to the Prussian
throne in 1786.[66]

The importation of the Revolution into Germany by the invading French
armies forced the pace of reform, because the new rulers of many parts
of western Germany simply imposed emancipation. The French National
Assembly had discussed the question of freeing the Jews, inherent in the
catchwords 'Liberty, Fraternity, Equality', from 1789 and two years later
French Jews had obtained full emancipation. Napoleonic rule in Germany
from 1800 resulted in the introduction of measures improving the position
of the minority in many French controlled territories. The legislation varied
from one area to another. In Hamburg, ruled by Napoleon from 1810 to 1814,
the Jews obtained full equality and political rights, although rights entailed
duties so that Jews, like all other citizens, had to partake in civil activities, including military service.[67] The newly founded Kingdom of Westfalia
granted Jewish subjects the same rights as the rest of the population in
1807.[68] Some territories allowed Jews to settle for the first time since the
Middle Ages, including Cologne. In Frankfurt, Jews could not go out on
Sundays and public holidays until 1798.[69]

While never actually fully controlled by Napoleon, the defeat of 1806,
the measures introduced in other parts of Germany, and the emancipation

[42] movement which began before 1789 eventually led to a legal improvement in the position of Jews in Prussia. In 1801 Frederick William III established a commission to examine thoroughly the position of the Jews within his domains and to make recommendations to improve their position.[70] However, as well as positive moves towards the improvement of the position of the minority, the years 1803–5 saw the publication of many antisemitic pamphlets.[71] The move towards emancipation intensified after the defeat at Jena, due to both external pressure upon the autocracy from the Jews themselves, and to the desire of the Prussian bureaucracy for reform, especially under the influence of Wilhelm von Humboldt, who took over responsibility for culture and education in the new Prussian regime, and Prince Karl August von Hardenberg who became chancellor in 1809. Three years later there followed the Prussian Emancipation Law, whose 39 paragraphs granted Jews the same rights as Christians, including freedom of residence and occupation. Jews no longer had to pay any special taxes and could secure a teaching, but no other government, post. Nevertheless, as elsewhere, they could not get something for nothing and had to serve in the army, receive a secular education, use government courts and employ German in business transactions.[72]

While Jews in many parts of Germany witnessed an improvement in their position under the impact of the French Revolution and Napoleon, little change took place in some regions. Saxony simply abolished the head tax on Jews, while the 1813 Bavarian Edict on Jews did not allow for a further increase in its Jewish population. Relatively few reforms took place in Freiburg im Breisgau until 1809 when the Jews obtained the right to residence: consequently the daughter of Heinrich Weil, born in the town in 1810, became the first native Freiburg Jew since 1442.[73]

Even those limited reforms passed between 1792 and 1815 came under threat in the reactionary, but also nationalistic years of the early Restoration, culminating in the Hep-Hep Riots of 1819. At the Congress of Vienna in 1815 the leading members of the German Confederation discussed the position of the Jews and made positive noises. Eventually, all states came to a compromise solution aimed at preventing a repeal of the measures passed in the previous 23 years and working towards further improvement in the position of the Jews, although even this proved unacceptable to some states, which eventually meant that individual rulers could decide their own policies towards Jews.[74] In Hamburg the freedoms granted by Napoleon underwent some revision in favour of wealthier Jews and against poorer ones.[75]

At the same time as official attitudes towards Jewish rights went backwards, popular hatred of the minority intensified into a frenzy. The virulent German

nationalism and antisemitism personified by Arndt, Jahn and Rühs, clearly
forms the background against which everyday hostility towards Jews reached
peaks in the early Restoration period. These years appear to represent a popular
reaction against the granting of full civil rights to the Jews. As the minority
came under the spotlight, resentments against it grew from both the middle
and working classes. Once outbreaks of violence started, simply the act of
their reporting in local newspapers played a role in the spread of the disturbances because anti-Jewish events in one location legitimized similar
occurrences in another.

Social and economic factors played a significant role in the outbreak of
disturbances. The first years of the Restoration witnessed severe economic
hardship, including famine in 1816, which some commentators blamed upon
the Jews. The fact that some Jews had experienced a significant increase in
income and social mobility during the Napoleonic Wars made all members
of this minority more conspicuous, even though most Jews remained poor.
The rising Judeophobia of these years received a boost from the Wartburg
Festival in 1817. The year 1819, when the Hep-Hep riots occurred, witnessed
increased repression which affected the popular nationalism of these years
and again fed into the antisemitism.

The disturbances of 1819 represented the first time since the Middle
Ages that violence had spread from just one location or region to affect
Jewish communities in several parts of Germany, even eventually moving
into Scandinavia. The disturbances began in Würzburg in August, spread to
other Bavarian towns and villages, subsequently progressing southwards to
Württemberg and Baden and then northwards towards Frankfurt, Heidelberg,
Hamburg and Copenhagen. In addition, further riots occurred in small settle-
ments in the Rhineland and Westfalia in the autumn.

The violence in Würzburg broke out on 2 August 1819, when some students greeted Professor Behr, who had recently spoken in favour of the Jews at
a meeting of the Bavarian diet, with the call '*Hep-Hep, Jud' verreck*' ('hep-hep,
die Jew'), which would subsequently be used to spark off riots elsewhere in
Germany. Disorder reigned until 5 August when the military restored order.
During this time the severity of the attacks forced the local Jews to take
refuge outside the town, but they returned under armed guard on 8 August.
The disorder quickly spread to Frankfurt, where Jewish emancipation had
also become an issue during the summer. The violence reached its peak here
on 10 August: during daylight youths had forced Jews to leave the public
promenade and during the evening as many as 6,000 men may have attacked
the Jewish quarter, smashing windows and attacking people on the street. A

report from the *Neue Speyerer Zeitung* of 28 August 1819 described events in Heidelberg in the following way:

> After several weeks in which the catch phrase 'Hep Hep' has been heard throughout the town, a Jewish girl was insulted by a local citizen two days ago . . . During the course of the day rumours circulated about an attack on the Jews in the evening, which were not widely believed. But between seven and eight in the evening bands of Hep men moved towards Jewish homes armed with axes, iron bars and similarly subtle instruments, and for almost three hours smashed doors, windows and shops, entered houses and began plundering.[76]

The Hep Hep riots meant another blow to any further hopes of immediate improvement in the position of the Jews. In the context of nineteenth- and twentieth-century German racism it is tempting to see them as a clarion call for the future, representing an outbreak of racist violence which would not reach such a peak again until the rise of the Nazis, especially in the *Kristallnacht* pogrom of 1938, which, in a far more organized state, lasted for just one night, but really was nationwide and much more destructive. On that occasion while the Nazis may not have directly participated in the disturbances, their antisemitic measures caused them. In 1819, the widespread antisemitic debate played a similar role as the background.

Although 1819 and 1938 represent high points in the history of antisemitic racial violence in Germany, Jews faced regular attacks during the years in between, especially in the rest of the Restoration period. In Coblenz in 1824, for instance, a Jewish funeral procession came under attack on the way to the cemetery, although this fits into Christian contempt for the Jewish dead, as some gentiles often allowed their animals to graze in Jewish graveyards, while others drove their carts through them as a short cut. Jews then came under attack in several locations during 1830, when revolutionary outbreaks occurred. There followed a surfacing of ritual murder accusations and con-sequent riots in the Rhineland during 1834.[77]

The violence of these years simply represented the peak of antisemitic manifestations, in a situation in which medieval traditions of Jew hatred remained alive. In Minden in 1843, for instance, a pamphlet by a senior sol-dier led to a discussion about the position of the Jews, but did not end up in violence.[78] Throughout the nineteenth century societies wishing to convert the Jews to Christianity continued to exist. One of the most significant of these, the Berlin Society for the Promotion of Christianity Among the Jews, established in 1822, opened auxiliary groupings throughout Prussia during the 1830s.[79] In addition, restrictions continued to exist in some locations (and in some cases were reintroduced) upon the choice of names used by

Jews.[80] This indicates that the halting of emancipation resulted in continued [45] official discrimination against the Jews. In Prussia one of Hegel's students found that he could not become an academic until he became a Christian.[81] Nevertheless, not all Jews faced hostility in the Restoration period. Saloman Kauffmann, who recalled his childhood experiences of the late 1830s, claimed that antisemitism remained confined to the lower orders and that the educated classes, especially school teachers, remained free from prejudice against Jews.[82]

This statement points to the fact that Jews made some social progress between 1815 and 1848, although we could not say that the middle classes as a whole were tolerant towards Jews, as the literary Judeophobia and nationalism revolved around them. The middle of the nineteenth century witnessed a slight increase in the Jewish population of the German Confederation (excluding the Habsburg lands) from 410,000 in 1847 to 470,000 in 1867, although their percentage of the German population as a whole remained at 1.23 per cent. Jews continued to live largely in rural communities, so that in 1852 only 9 per cent of them resided in towns with over 50,000 inhabitants.[83] In Bavaria, the number of Jews increased from 53,203 in 1818 to 56,033 in 1852, although their percentage of the overall population decreased from 1.46 to 1.23. Only 14 per cent lived in cities in 1840, slightly higher than the 11 per cent of all inhabitants. Largely as a result of exclusionary policies and the desire of Jews to live with their brethren for religious reasons and the principle of safety in numbers some Bavarian towns counted very small numbers of Jews in 1840 including Nuremberg, with just 6. For the same reasons Fürth's 2,535 Jews in 1840 represented the largest Jewish community in Bavaria.[84] Elsewhere the number of Jews in Freiburg had only increased to twenty by 1846.[85] By the middle of the 1830s Jews in Prussia had begun to concentrate in small and medium-sized towns. Such settlements already counted 80 per cent of Jews, compared with 30 per cent of gentiles.[86]

Some changes took place in the economic position of the Jews after 1815 as industrialization began to take off in Germany, but traditional patterns were not erased. Avraham Barkai has recognized four trends in the social and economic history of German Jewry between 1835 and 1860: first, regular commercial activity increasingly replaced pawnbroking and peddling; second, a temporary increase in Jewish craftsmen; third, the disappearance of Jewish beggars and a decline in the number of servants and day labourers; and, fourth, an increase in the number of professionals.[87] Most of these changes would continue beyond 1860 as German Jewry became increasingly bourgeois. The middle of the century witnessed some spectacular Jewish economic success

[46]   stories, including that of Hirsch Oppenheimer born in Gronau near Hanover in 1805. He began working as a second-hand clothes dealer but by 1848, had established a highly successful insurance, metal and banking firm.[88]

The small town of Landau in the Palatinate, with a population of 5,000, including 150 Jews, in 1816, demonstrated some of the above patterns. A survey from 1808 revealed Jewish second-hand goods dealers, pedlars, and animal traders, but by 1833 wholesale merchants and craftsmen outnumbered them. In this year about ten per cent of the Jewish population consisted of beggars, but these had virtually disappeared by the end of the 1850s.[89] Bavaria also witnessed a decrease in the number of Jewish hawkers, as well as a growth in Jewish craftsmen. In this Kingdom Jews actually moved into agriculture on a significant scale, with the percentage of all Jews working in farming growing from 2.4 per cent in 1822 to 8.1 per cent by 1848.[90] In Hamburg 63.9 per cent of all Jews engaged in some sort of trading activity in 1815, often on a small scale, but to a much greater extent than gentiles. The next three decades actually witnessed an increase in the number of Jews receiving help from Jewish charities. A growth took place in the percentage of all Jews involved in industry and crafts between 1815 and 1851, while day labourers decreased. Trading remained the major occupation. During this period, while some Jews continued to live just above the poverty line, Hamburg Jewry as a whole had witnessed social mobility, which made it more prosperous as a group than the total population of the city.[91]

As well as a change in occupation patterns, caused partly by the early emancipation legislation, the Restoration period also witnessed an increasing modernization in religion, continuing the process begun during the eighteenth-century Jewish Enlightenment and influenced by the new freedom and increasing desire to ape bourgeois gentile norms. Nevertheless, these developments apply particularly to the more visible wealthy Jews, rather than the mass of poorer ones.

Several changes occurred in the religious and cultural history of German Jewry in the Restoration period, some of which would only reach fruition later in the century. In the first place, some Jews became baptized into Christianity, totalling as many as 1,600 in Berlin between 1770 and 1830, which, however, works out to just 27 per year. This development tended to affect the wealthiest Jews, and also particular families.[92]

Despite the relatively small scale of conversions, they created something of a crisis in Berlin Jewry, which represented the background for the evolution of a more modern Jewish religious practice, which used German, allowed women and men to sit together, shortened the length of the service and

permitted women to sing in the choir. In 1814 Reform services began to
take place in the house of Israel Jacobson, and attracted up to 400 people.
Nevertheless, following a schism in Berlin Jewry, the Prussian government
forbade Reform Jews from holding services in 1823, and did not allow them
to do so for another fifteen years. Meanwhile, a Reform temple had opened in
Hamburg in 1818, which maintained the separation of men and women,
printed the first reform prayer book and used an organ. Changes also took
place in other parts of Germany. At the same time as these developments
occurred, there also emerged a Neo-Orthodox movement, which also wanted
changes.[93]

By the 1820s Jews had also begun to emerge out of their status as a religious minority into that of a modern ethnic grouping. This is partly linked to
a rise in apostasy, but it is also connected with the birth of European nationalism, which began similar stirrings amongst Jews. Furthermore, the unsuccessful attempts of some Jews to enter middle-class gentile organizations, threw
them back on to their own ethnicity. As early as 1840 an article in a Jewish
weekly in Constance called on the Jews to think about returning to their homeland, citing hatred towards them as a reason for this.[94] Nevertheless, Zionism
only took root towards the end of the nineteenth century. At this stage an
essentially cultural Jewishness developed. In 1819 three young Jewish men
in Berlin founded the Society for the Culture and Science of the Jews, which
organized lectures and meetings and also published the *Periodical for the
Science of Judaism*.[95] Similar groupings developed all over Germany. By the
beginning of the 1840s sixty Jewish associations existed in the Berlin Jewish
community of just nine thousand, although the majority of these consisted
of philanthropic bodies.[96] In this sphere as in much else, developments in
German Jewry paralleled changes in mainstream society.

The 1848 revolutions, which again brought Jews to public attention, had
both positive and negative manifestations for them in both the short and longer
term. Jews played a role in the revolutionary events in the streets of Berlin,
Vienna and other cities and seven became representatives in the Frankfurt
Parliament, while others gained seats in the assemblies established throughout Germany. In Hamburg Jews made up 14 out of the 188 elected members
of the local parliament in 1848.[97]

As we have seen the revolutions released both progressive and reactionary
movements, a dichotomy which also affected Jews. On the one hand, both
the Frankfurt and local Parliaments introduced measures to further emancipation, most of which disappeared in the reaction. At the same time, the 1848
revolutions witnessed another peak of popular antisemitism, manifesting

[48] itself most visibly in further riots against Jews. The background social and economic causes of the revolutions in the form of harvest failures and a general economic slow down, meant that rioters picked upon targets which they viewed as responsible for their misfortune, whether those in authority or Jews. Between 1848 and 1849 a total of 93 attacks took place against Jews. The greatest concentration of violence occurred in Baden, with 33 different locations affected.[98]

Milder forms of anti-Jewish hostility also occurred. In Freiburg, for instance, a decision by a citizens' committee to accept a Jew as one of their number on 7 March 1849 led to a campaign involving the publication of leaflets against this action.[99] A more spectacular agitation occurred against Jews in Bavaria in the following year when the lower house of the national Parliament passed an act for the full emancipation of the Jews. This measure led to a wave of petitions against it which attracted a total of 86,795 signatures. The petitions focused upon the religious, economic and political activity of the Jews. Consequently, the upper house of the Bavarian Parliament rejected the legislation.[100]

The revolutions of 1848 meant a limited improvement in the position of Jews throughout Germany as a whole, although the situation varied from one location to another depending on the attitudes of local rulers and assemblies. As many as 20 per cent of German Jews living in fifteen states enjoyed either full political rights or a significant amelioration in their legal status after 1848, although the vast majority witnessed a return to their pre-revolutionary status. Those states which took backward steps included Hanover, Prussia and Württemberg.[101]

The era between the 1848 revolutions and the establishment of the North German Confederation in 1867 'was for the Jews of Germany a period of general advancement toward complete emancipation marked by a number of setbacks'.[102] On the positive side they made significant breakthroughs in employment and public life. For instance, the number of Jews sitting in state parliaments and municipalities between 1858 and 1866 doubled in comparison with the number of the previous decade.[103]

As the 1850s and 1860s progressed many states began to introduce emancipation legislation, so that by 1867 Jews enjoyed equality in Baden, Württemberg, Hessen-Darmstadt, Homburg, Frankfurt am Main, Nassau, Brunswick, Hamburg, Lübeck, Oldenburg and Waldeck, but, significantly, still faced some restrictions in the larger states of Bavaria and Prussia. The incorporation of Hanover, Holstein, Kassel, Nassau and Frankfurt into Prussia, as a result of the war against Austria in 1867 consequently created an anomaly,

which the Parliament of the North German Confederation tried to rectify, [49]
leading to several years of debate on Jewish emancipation which reached a
final conclusion in 1869 when an edict removed all restrictions on civil and
political rights as a consequence of religion.[104] This end result, extended to
all the territories of the newly formed German Empire two years later, had as
much to do with economics and Jewish assimilation as rising liberalism. Since
the late eighteenth century, when Jews had begun to gain equality, they had
to sacrifice something in the form of their Jewishness, which many clearly
had done, as evidenced by their increasing acculturation, illustrated by the
modernization of religion and the move out of occupations at the bottom
of the social scale. The two processes, emancipation and acculturation,
therefore went hand in hand. Having refused to allow rights to the Jew for
centuries, the changing German attitudes since the French Revolution may
have had as much to do with the economic need of German rulers to make
use of this dynamic and entrepreneurial minority, as it had to do with the
spread of enlightened liberal ideas through Germany.[105] More than a century
after the legislation of 1869 and 1871 the migrant workers imported during
the 1950s and 1960s find themselves with limited civil rights, as their economic function has consisted of carrying out jobs at the bottom end of the
social scale.

An examination of the continuing economic, social, cultural and religious
transformations of Germany Jewry after 1848 demonstrates how the group
became increasingly attuned with gentile behaviour, and, in the economic
sphere, began to move ahead of it in terms of wealth. In purely demographic
terms the rise in the Jewish population from 410,000 in 1848 to 470,000 in
1867 included a net intake of about 4,500 Jews moving from areas east of
Germany,[106] even though much Jewish emigration also took place at this
time.[107]

In fact population movement, whether internally within Germany from
rural to urban environments, or externally, especially to the USA, became a
major characteristic of the history of German Jewry in the second half of the
nineteenth century.[108] The evolution of Jews as an urban group had certainly
taken off by the 1850s and 1860s, although this phenomenon affected some
cities more than others. Thus Berlin witnessed an increase in its Jews from
9,955 in 1852 to 36,000 by the end of the 1860s. In the same period Breslau
Jewry grew from 7,436 to around 13,000. In Poznań, Fürth and Frankfurt
am Main Jews made up more than ten per cent of the population. Some cities
continued to count small Jewish populations, including Munich, with less
than 3,000 at the end of the 1860s.[109] But even this location had witnessed a

[50]   significant rise in the number of Jews it held. Until 1861 the Bavarian system of registration meant that only 'a select number of Jews' could settle in
Munich, including bankers and financiers, as well as some merchants and
factory owners. After 1861 Munich witnessed an influx of Jews from villages
and small towns in Swabia, Franconia, the Palatinate, Württemberg and
further afield. The early migrants included craftsmen, merchants, bankers and
factory owners.[110]

As the nineteenth century progressed, Jews increasingly broke out of their
medieval ghettoes, as indicated both by their changing residence patterns
and by their continuing move into gentile organizations. By the 1820s
all the medieval restrictions confining Jews to particular areas of cities had
disappeared. Consequently, the number of Frankfurt Jews residing in or near
the city's old ghetto declined from 84.7 per cent in 1823 to 58.7 per cent
by 1858.[111] By this time most German Jews had a circle of gentile friends
and some gave lectures to Christian audiences, while much cultural activity catered for both Christians and Jews, including choruses and singing
societies.[112] Jews made up a significant percentage of the concert-going
public by the 1860s.[113] Such developments did not mean that everyday
hostility towards Jews had disappeared, as indicated by the fact that businessmen in Breslau during the 1860s tried to prevent the entry of Jews into their
organizations.[114]

At the same time as Jewish integration took place, so did the evolution
of a secular Jewish ethnicity. In 1860 the Zionist Israelitischer Verein zur
Kolonisierung von Palästina came into existence in Frankfurt an der Oder,
although it had disappeared by 1865. The publication of the multi-volumed
History of the Jewish People by Heinrich Graetz between 1853 and 1876 provided an indication of the evolution of a Jewish culture within Germany.[115]

Dramatic transformations had therefore taken place in the position of
German Jews in the century leading up to the formation of the German Empire
in 1871. In 1789 most Jews, eking out a meagre existence in rural locations,
remained a hated and largely untouchable group with few civil rights, a
situation which, however, would have applied to the vast majority of the
population of Germany before the rise of liberal and democratic ideas. The
earlier nineteenth century meant the disappearance of the legal restrictions
on Jewish activity, a movement into towns and cities, a shedding of traditional Jewish mores and economic improvement, processes which would continue after 1871. Nevertheless, below the surface, with regular manifestations,
there lurked, like one of Wagner's recurring themes, the evil of antisemitism,
which would become a full-blown political movement in the *Kaiserreich*.

The romanticized and hated Gypsies [51]

At the start of the nineteenth century Gypsies in Germany resembled Jews in the sense that they remained a group apart from the mainstream ethnic German population, excluded by a variety of laws and working in generally lowly occupations. However, while Jews broke out of the ghetto with the help of the emancipation legislation, Gypsies continued to remain complete outsiders, generally ignored by mainstream liberal thinkers and by the various German states, which could not see any economic benefits in improving their position. They did receive some positive attention, which romanticized them as a wandering group, while some of the most draconian legislation against them disappeared.

The eighteenth-century Enlightenment did release more positive attitudes towards the Gypsies amongst some thinkers, who pointed to the error of the brutal treatment which this group had endured. A book published in 1782 by Johann Rüdigers on the language and origin of the Gypsies called for their emancipation and pointed to their different concepts of freedom and independence. But for some state authorities, the new Enlightened attitude meant an attempt to educate the Gypsies.[116] Although this represented a milder form of intolerance than the brutality practised during the medieval period, it meant an attempt to assimilate the minority, which inevitably involved an attack on their way of life, especially as forced settlement often played a role in the change of attitude. The Enlightened Despot, Maria Theresa of Austria, had established a Gypsy settlement in Burgenland as early as 1761.[117] In 1771 the Count of Wittgenstein opened a similar camp in Saßmannshausen and, four years later, Frederick II of Prussia made efforts to settle Gypsies permanently in a colony in Friedrichslohra in Saxony, intended as the first of many camps.[118]

Friedrichslohra remained in existence into the nineteenth century and, in 1828, the Evangelical Mission Society of Naumburg and District took over the camp. In the following year Wilhelm Blankenburg arrived as a teacher of the fifty Gypsies present and, by 1835, the numbers increased to around one hundred, including thirty children, eight of whom lived in the same school house as Blankenburg and his wife. Nevertheless, the authorities in Magdeburg, which had responsibility for running the camp, withdrew their support from this sort of 'enlightened' and painless persecution in 1837, which meant that the adults went to workhouses and the children found themselves in orphanages. A similar settlement in Moordorf in Oldenburg also faced closure.[119] While this may have brought 'an end to the most striking example

[52]   in Germany of the policy of attempting to assimilate the Gypsies'[120] and, while the later actions of the Nazis may have had a less enlightened aim, the concentration of Gypsies in settlements has clear resonances in events which would take place in the 1930s. Similar statements apply to the treatment of Gypsies in Württemberg between 1835 and 1838, where attempts to educate Gypsy children often involved separation from their families. Children under 14 could not travel with their parents and their mothers had to remain in fixed accommodation to look after them.[121]

After the closure of Friedrichslohra the Gypsies received relatively little state attention until the foundation of the *Kaiserreich*. Nevertheless, a Prussian measure of 1842, followed by others passed by the North German Confederation in 1866 and 1867, concerned with registration, passports and state charity, increasingly forced Gypsies to take up German nationality. Those who did so, after further measures following the foundation of the Empire in 1871, counted as 'inlanders' while those who did not remained foreigners. By 1868 the Prussian state had the power to deport foreign Gypsies. In fact the legislation of 1842 had meant that local authorities regularly expelled Gypsies, because they had to take responsibility for offering local groups charity if they were either born within their areas or had lived there for a long time.[122]

As well as receiving relatively little attention from German states before 1871, Gypsies did not often impinge on the popular imagination. When they did, images of them tended to remain negative, as evidenced by many nineteenth-century fairy tales. In most of these they remained outsiders, and common stereotypes included Gypsies as witches, thieves and devils, which meant their 'increasingly striking marginalisation'.[123] Some of those who wrote about the group produced diatribes against them. Theodor Tetzner, the author of *Geschichte der Zigeuner* in 1835, used extremely negative language in some passages, including the following:

> The character of these people is the quintessence of badness, recklessness, gossiping, cowardice – which means that they make bad soldiers – vengeance, gluttony, laughable pride, duplicity and a laziness, from which many more vices spring.[124]

Nevertheless, Gypsies also attracted positive attention. Some of the children's literature of the nineteenth century, which may always have pointed to the Gypsies as different and therefore always created suspicion, also presented romantic views of them, a trend also apparent in adult literature, both fictional and 'serious'. Writers concentrated upon the free, natural, uncontrolled life of the Gypsies.[125] Some contemporary accounts, written by individuals who did not hate the Gypsies, provide useful insights into their life, which like that of [53] much of the population before 1871, remained fairly basic and wretched. Such books always represent an example of describing the life of the 'other'. Carl von Heister recounted his meeting with a family of Gypsies in the coastal village of Labaginien in East Prussia, which may have contained 18 Gypsy families, with 140 members, on 10 August 1842. He first met a young man of about twenty who was working in the fields with his son. He took Heister to his home, where he saw a 'very pretty young woman' suckling a baby. She also greeted Heister positively, when he said he wanted to get to know a Gypsy family. But in order to find a seat in the room Heister had to expel a sow. He wrote that, although the house was dirty, it was well ordered and the adults were well dressed. Heister also mentioned meeting 64 year old Christian Anton, born in Königsberg, who had been married twice and had fathered twelve children of whom six survived. His second wife came from Upper Silesia. Heister wrote that the East Prussian Gypsies, who were Roman Catholics, only worked out of necessity, and their activities included rag selling and horse dealing, especially at the horse markets of Wehlau, Tilsit and Labiau. Some Gypsies also lived by begging, while others may have stolen horses. Between 1836 and 1842 a total of 40 Gypsies of both sexes found themselves in the correction house in Tapiau.[126]

Another account, by Richard Lieblich, appeared in 1863. This author claimed that the German gypsies divided into three groups in the form of the Old Prussian (from Silesia and Poland), the New Prussian and the Hanoverian. In addition to horse trading, occupations included wood carving, music playing and fortune telling. Lieblich devoted attention to the criminal activity of the Gypsies, claiming that they lived by begging, deception and theft, which dictated that they moved around in bands. The author also commented on the fact that Gypsies did not always have correct identity papers, which would allow them to wander.[127]

The rise of Polish nationalism

Poles represented the third major minority in German territory, concentrated entirely in eastern Prussia during the decades leading up to the foundation of the *Kaiserreich*. In terms of their relative economic and social backwardness they have much in common with both Jews and Gypsies at the start of the nineteenth century. In addition, like both of these groups, they did not focus

[54] simply upon Germany, but also counted numbers elsewhere, in this case in the Russian and Habsburg Empires. However, unlike the Jews and Gypsies, who represent dispersed minorities, the Poles were a highly concentrated grouping still living in their historical homeland. Their concentration, together with the previous existence of a Polish monarchical state, meant that educated Poles lapped up the rising ideology of nationalism to the same degree as the German intelligentsia, which resulted in the emergence of a Polish question in Prussia, as well as Austria and Russia, before 1871.

The late eighteenth-century partitions of Poland represent major turning points in the evolution of the Polish minority in Prussia. In 1772 Frederick II obtained territories in West Prussia. The partition of 1793 meant the annexation of land further south, including the city of Poznań, while, two years later, the Polish monarchical state disappeared from the map of Europe, with Frederick William II gaining 'New East Prussia', including Warsaw and Białystok. As a result of the events of 1772–95 Prussia almost doubled in size and counted 3 million Poles in a total population of 8 million.[128] The newly gained territories faced a policy of repressive Prussianization, which included a change in the bureaucracy and a weakening of the rights of the Polish nobles, as well as an expulsion of Poles and Jews from West Prussia. An insurrection of 1794 faced repression.[129] A further uprising by the Polish nobility in 1806–7, coupled with defeat by Napoleon, meant a loss of territory gained by Prussia in 1793, which went to the newly established French satellite state of the Grand Duchy of Warsaw.[130] In Prussian public opinion the actions of the Prussian state found both supporters and opponents. The latter included Friedrich Schiller, who, in his play *Demetrius*, portrayed the Poles as a people with the qualities of wisdom and courage. On the other hand, most official documents produced by individuals from Frederick the Great downwards, reveal contempt for the Poles, a common theme over the following 150 years. In 1807 the Prussian Chief Minister, Baron von Stein, wrote a critical memorandum on the Polish people, in which he accused them of 'fecklessness, frivolity, sensuality and intemperance'. Nevertheless, he did think that the Poles had some ability to govern themselves.[131]

As a result of a loss of territory during the Napoleonic Wars and their aftermath the Polish population of Poznań, Silesia and East and West Prussia had declined to 1.5 million out of a total population of 10 million.[132] Austria, Prussia and Russia agreed at the Treaty of Vienna that the Poles should have some sort of representation, a development which Prussia and Russia recognized in a separate agreement. Prussia's chunk of the Grand Duchy of Warsaw became known as the Grand Duchy of Poznań. It used its own red

and white flag, previously employed by the old Polish Empire and, during [55]
the next fifteen years, Prussia employed a conciliatory approach to govern-
ing this territory, when it essentially worked with the Polish nobility in the
absence of a significant Polish middle class.[133]

In 1815 Frederick William III had recognized that the Poles had a fatherland within Prussia and promised the Grand Duchy the same rights as the
rest of his provinces, including a constitution, the protection of the Roman
Catholic religion and guaranteed use of the Polish language in all public documents. The Polish language in Poznań received further guarantees in a law
of 1822, which allowed its use in education as well as administration and
religion. Frederick William appointed a Pole as Governor in the form of Prince
Anton Radziwiłł, who was closely connected to him as he had married a Prussian princess. Nevertheless, essentially he was a figurehead and real power
lay in the hands of Zerboni di Sposetti, a Polish landowner. The agreement
to protect Polish rights reached in Vienna did not apply to West Prussia, where
the head of the administration, Theodor von Schön, viewed Polish priests
and nobles as enemies and simply implemented German as the language of
administration and education. The explanation for the varying treatment of
the different parts of Poland lies not just in the limited scope of the Vienna
Treaty but also in the distribution of Polish and German speakers in different
parts of Prussia. In 1825 Germans made up 68 per cent of the population of
West Prussia, whereas, ten years later, they constituted just 40 per cent of the
population of Poznań. East Prussia had a German population of 80 per cent
in 1825. The non-German populations of East and West Prussia also included
members of the slavic minorities of Masurians in the former and Kashubians
in the latter.[134] The precise ethnicity of these groups, *vis-à-vis* Germans and
Poles, would become a major bone of contention later in the century.

Although the Polish nobility of Poznań could work in the service of the
Prussian state, many preferred not to do so and demonstrated more concern
in conspiracies to re-establish the Polish state. Such movements found support in Polish academic circles and among Polish students at German universities. One of the earliest Polish student organizations consisted of the Panta
Koina in Berlin, which came into existence in the autumn of 1819 and represented a branch of a body with its headquarters in Warsaw. There followed
further Polish nationalist groupings including Polonia which counted 70
out of the 207 Polish students in Berlin, and had branches in other German
cities, including Breslau. These bodies faced closure in the repressive 1820s,
which meant that members could face imprisonment. For instance, a court in
Breslau jailed two members of Polonia in 1823.[135]

[56]   The years 1830–1 represent a significant landmark in the history of Poland and the Polish minority of Prussia. Following outbreaks of revolutionary disorder in France and Belgium in the spring of 1830, the upheaval spread to the Polish part of Russia and resulted in a full-scale war which lasted until the following year when the Russian Army finally suppressed the rebellion, after conquering Warsaw in September, having received assistance from Prussia during the course of the conflict. Prussian Poland actually remained calm, but about 2,500 people crossed the border, unhindered by the Prussian local officials (who were Polish) to assist their brethren. Many of the defeated revolutionaries left (Russian) Congress Poland and fled west. A large number made their way to Paris, but some also moved to German towns, where, during the 1830s, liberal committees celebrated the Polish refugees and sang Polish songs, so that many Germans saw the struggle of both themselves and the Poles for a homeland as identical, a view which would change in the nationalistic cold light of day in 1848. One German, August Wirth, writing in 1832, stated that the Austrian, Prussian and Russian autocracies prevented the peoples of both Poland and Germany from reaching their full potential as nation states.[136]

Despite the fact that revolutionary upheaval had not taken place in the Grand Duchy of Poznań, the Prussian autocracy turned against its Polish population before the more idealistic German liberals did so in 1848, so that the 1830s represent a period of repression, reversing many of the progressive policies of the years 1815–30. In fact the Prussian state took measures against its Polish population as soon as revolution occurred in 1830. For instance, it replaced Radziwiłł as Governor of the Duchy of Poznań with a Prussian, Edward Flotwell, who would retain his position until 1841. At the same time, Prussian officials replaced Polish ones and would continue to do so into the 1830s and beyond. In fact the period of Flotwell's rule essentially represents one in which Germanization became Prussian policy. This involved attempting to reduce the influence of the Polish priests and nobles, increasing the use of the German language, importing Germans into the area, developing closer connections between Poznań and Prussia, but also improving the position of Poles and Jews. Flotwell achieved most of these aims. When his term in office came to an end in 1841 Flotwell stated that he had extended the material and spiritual elements of German life in Poland.[137]

Flotwell left his position following Frederick William IV's accession to the Prussian throne in 1840, which meant another reversal in the attitudes of the autocracy towards its Polish subjects as the new King believed that respecting their national rights represented a more effective policy than suppressing them. Consequently, the rebels of 1830 obtained an amnesty, persecution of the Roman Catholic Church ceased and a Polish majority once again became dominant in the Poznań assembly.[138]

Nevertheless, neither the policies of the 1830s nor those of the 1840s extinguished Polish nationalism. Just like everywhere else in nineteenth- and twentieth-century Europe, once a population kindled the flame of nation state-hood, it proved impossible to put it out until the people achieved its ultimate aim, which, in this case, did not occur until 1918, when the powers contain-ing Polish populations all collapsed. Economic and social developments during the 1830s and 1840s, such as the spread of literacy, transportation improvements and migration to the city of Poznań assisted rather than hindered the spread of Polish nationalism. During the 1830s, for instance, the road system joined Poznań with Silesia and Berlin,[139] which helped the spread of people and ideas. The same applies to the increase in literacy, which sig-nificantly grew as the percentage of people attending school went from 22 to 70 in the years between 1816 and 1846. Most Polish children obtained instruction in both their own language as well as German in both the Grand Duchy of Poznań and West Prussia, although conflicts developed over which language should dominate.[140] At the same time, while Poles had made some economic progress, their position remained below that of the German popu-lation, which could only further fuel nationalistic resentments. Although the number of Polish businessmen in Poznań increased slightly between 1822 and 1837, their percentage of all businessmen decreased from eleven to six per cent. For much of the nineteenth century, especially its first half, Poles remained closely tied to the land.[141] Demographically, the Polish-speaking population of the Grand Duchy of Poznań increased from 603,334 in 1831 to 681,531 in 1846, while, during the same period, German speakers declined from 443,106 to 380,085, despite the efforts of the Prussian autocracy.[142]

Polish nationalism in the 1830s and 1840s had various manifestations. In the first place, educational and cultural activities took place, so that, for instance, Polish leaders gathered enough money to set up the Association for Education Assistance, which granted scholarships. At the same time, many of the most prominent Polish authors had their work translated into German to bring them to the attention of the German-speaking public. Polish exiles in Paris also hatched a plan for an uprising in all three parts of divided Poland. In Poznań this amounted to nothing, because the Prussian police nipped the rebellion in the bud when they arrested 254 people in 1846. In the following year the conspirators faced trial in Berlin, during which six people received death sentences and 109 faced imprisonment. Nevertheless, the King did not allow the executions to take place.

[58]   These events raised further sympathy for the Poles among German progressive circles[143] and did not prevent Poles from participating in the events of 1848. In fact, during the early days of the 'People's Spring' most German revolutionaries continued to view the causes of Polish and German nationalism as intertwined, symbolized by the fact that agitators freed the jailed Poles of 1847 when revolution broke out in Berlin in March 1848. In Poznań the Polish nobility, bourgeoisie and intelligentsia established a Polish National Committee headed by Ludwik Mierosławski, which aimed at the independence of the whole of Poland. Mierosławski managed to recruit a Polish Army of 10,000 men in the Grand Duchy of Poznań and, in the spring of 1848, with the Prussian state in turmoil, it looked as if he might achieve some success, even if this did not mean the creation of a unitary Polish state, as Russia and the Austrian part of Poland remained fairly calm. But even in these early days the impossibilities of reconciling two opposing nationalisms became apparent as committees for the protection of German interests in the Grand Duchy and West Prussia came into existence. Similarly, on 18 April about 3,000 Germans in the city of Poznań petitioned the Prussian Government to keep them within Prussia. Jews also did not view the establishment of a Polish state positively. Urged on by this opposition to the Poles Frederick William IV sent in troops to suppress the Polish rebellion, which had occurred by 9 May. While delegates at the Frankfurt Parliament and liberals in other parts of Germany also initially supported Polish independence, this situation also changed by 1849, when backing for a free Polish state disappeared, to be replaced by a constitution guaranteeing minority rights. The spring of the peoples had become the winter of the old order by the middle of 1849 as the Prussian autocracy suppressed first the National Assembly in Berlin in November 1848 and then the Frankfurt Parliament in the following spring. The authorities also dissolved the Polish League which had come into existence at the end of 1848 and had counted 35,000 members. Many prominent individuals such as Arndt and Bismarck, who at this stage did not hold high office, had opposed the Polish cause all along, using derogatory language, with strong racial undertones, to describe them, as did Friedrich Engels in 1851.[144] Polonophobia would seize the initiative once Bismarck came to power, especially in the *Kaiserreich*, and remain in command of much German thinking towards eastern Europe until the demise of the Nazis in 1945.

     In fact, hostility towards Poles in Prussian and German circles circulated widely throughout the 1850s and 1860s, as concepts of Germanization developed. Prominent figures such as the historian Heinrich von Treitschke could describe the Poles as disloyal, politically incompetent and intolerant towards foreigners. One senior Prussian official, Eugen von Puttkamer, even,

very ominously, raised the possibility of exterminating the Poles, although [59]
he ultimately rejected such a policy.[145]

Such hostility gained strength from the perceived threat of Poles in both
demographic and political terms, because a Polish population explosion and
a Polish nationalist movement emerged at the same time as German unification neared conclusion, meaning that this minority appeared to represent a
threat to these processes. The number of people speaking Polish, Masurian
or Kashubian on Prussian soil increased from 2,095,816 in 1858 to 2,436,800
by 1867,[146] although increases also took place in the German-speaking
population.[147] Concerns about differences in growth rates between Poles and
Germans would further intensify under the *Kaiserreich*, leading to attempts at
settling Germans in Polish areas as part of a Germanization process.

Conflict also took place over purely political issues. The settlement reached
after the 1848 revolutions meant that Poles could have representation.
Until 1855 the Polish faction in the Prussian Diet counted between 11 and
15 members, although, following dubious electoral changes, the size of this
group declined and became basically irrelevant after 1855.[148] Nevertheless,
other organizations of an educational and economic nature preserved Polish
ethnicity. Furthermore, while Polish virtually disappeared as an official language, it continued in schools.[149]

The first decades of the nineteenth century leading up to the foundation
of the *Kaiserreich* essentially represent a link between the medieval attitudes
towards minorities and the evolution of the even more intolerant modern
ones. Thus the Hep-Hep Riots of 1819 have as much of the character of
a medieval pogrom as they do of a modern one, so that they seem as close
to 1349 as they do to 1938. The period 1800–70 also represents the birth
of modern concepts of ethnicity and nationalism, among both the majority
German population and the minority Jews and Poles. Even before 1871,
in the works of Enlightenment thinkers, the policies of the Prussian state,
and the debates in the Paulskirche, it had become clear that minority and
majority ethnicities could not reconcile themselves. The years after 1870 would
bring such conflicts to further fruition.

Notes

1. Peter Marschalck, *Bevölkerungsgeschichte Deutschlands im 19. und 20. Jahrhundert*
    (Frankfurt am Main, 1984), p. 145. These figures refer to the borders of 1871,
    excluding Alsace and Lorraine.

[60]

2. Ibid., p. 178.

3. Robert Lee, ' "Relative Backwardness" and Long-Run Development: Economic, Demographic and Social Changes', in Mary Fulbrook, ed., *German History Since 1800* (London, 1997), p. 65.

4. Martin Kitchen, *The Political Economy of Germany, 1815–1914* (London, 1978), pp. 9–131; W. O. Henderson, *The Zollverein* (London, 1984).

5. See: the relevant contributions to David Blackbourn and Richard J. Evans, eds, *The German Bourgeoisie: Essays on the Social History of the German Middle Class from the Late Eighteenth to the Early Twentieth Centuries* (London, 1991); and Thomas Nipperday, *Germany from Napoleon to Bismarck* (Dublin, 1996), pp. 223–36.

6. This figure is from William Carr, *A History of Germany, 1815–1945* 2nd edn (London, 1979), p. 62.

7. Christopher Clark, 'Germany 1815–1848: Restoration or Pre-March', in Fulbrook, *German History*, p. 39.

8. Otto Pflanze, *Bismarck and the Development of Germany: The Period of Unification, 1815–1871* (Princeton, NJ, 1963).

9. Elie Kedourie, *Nationalism* 4th edn (Oxford, 1992), p. 1.

10. Walter Schmidt, 'The Nation in German History', in Mikuláš Teich and Roy Porter, eds, *The National Question in Europe in Historical Context* (Cambridge, 1993), p. 153.

11. Kedourie, *Nationalism*, pp. 12–24.

12. James J. Sheehan, *German History, 1770–1866* (Oxford, 1989), pp. 160–74.

13. Johann Gottfried Herder, *Von deutscher Art und Kunst* (originally Hamburg, 1773; Stuttgart, 1983), pp. 9–62.

14. Sheehan, *German History, 1770–1866*, pp. 165–6.

15. These phrases are quoted in Michael Burleigh and Wolfgang Wippermann, *The Racial State: Germany, 1933–1945* (Cambridge, 1994), p. 25.

16. Paul Lawrence Rose, *Revolutionary Antisemitism in Germany from Kant to Wagner* (Princeton, NJ, 1990), p. 107.

17. H. I. Bach, *The German Jew: A Synthesis of Judaism and Western Civilization, 1730–1930* (Oxford, 1984), p. 54.

18. Rose, *Revolutionary Antisemitism*, p. 70; H. D. Schmidt, 'The Terms of Emancipation, 1781–1812: The Public Debate in Germany and its Effects on the Mentality and Ideas of German Jewry', *Leo Baeck Institute Year Book* 1 (1956), p. 28.

19. H. S. Reiss, *The Political Thought of the German Romantics* (Oxford, 1955),   [61]
pp. 1–11; Frederick C. Beiser, *The Early Political Writings of the German
Romantics* (Cambridge, 1996), pp. vii–xxix.

20. Sheehan, *German History, 1770–1866*, pp. 376–7.

21. Johann Gottlieb Fichte, *Addresses to the German Nation* (New York, 1968). The
quotes come from pp. 45, 73, 90, 225. The original German title *Rede an die
deutsche Nation* first appeared in print in 1808.

22. Sheehan, *German History, 1770–1866*, p. 380.

23. Quoted in Louis L. Snyder, *Roots of German Nationalism* (Bloomington, IN,
1978), pp. 60–1.

24. Quoted in Sheehan, *German History, 1770–1866*, p. 381.

25. George L. Mosse, *The Crisis of German Ideology: Intellectual Origins of the Third
Reich* (New York, 1981), p. 5.

26. Friedrich Ludwig Jahn, *Deutsches Volkstum* (originally 1810; Berlin, 1936).

27. Rose, *Revolutionary Antisemitism*, pp. 96–7.

28. E. L. Schaub, 'J. G. Fichte and Antisemitism', *Philosophical Review* 49 (1940),
pp. 40–2.

29. Jacob Katz, *From Prejudice to Destruction: Antisemitism, 1700–1933* (Cambridge,
MA, 1980), p. 58.

30. Rose, *Revolutionary Antisemitism*, pp. 127–8.

31. Katz, *Prejudice*, pp. 76–81.

32. O. F. Scheuer, *Bursenschaft und Judenfrage: Der Rassenantisemitismus in der
deutschen Studentschaft* (Berlin, 1927), p. 26.

33. H. Hundt-Radowsky, *Judenspiegel: Ein Schand-und Sittengemälde alter und neuer
Zeit* (Würzburg, 1819).

34. Schmidt, 'Terms of Emancipation', pp. 36–9; Walter Grab, *Der deutsche
Weg der Judenemanzipation, 1789–1938* (Munich, 1991), pp. 41–72.

35. Briefly described by Sheehan, *German History, 1770–1866*, p. 610.

36. Snyder, *Roots of German Nationalism*, pp. 240–1.

37. For a fuller discussion of the antisemitism of these authors see: Rose, *Revolutionary Antisemitism*, pp. 109, 296–305; and Katz, *Prejudice*, pp. 159–74.

38. Eleonore Sterling, *Er ist wie Du: Aus der Frühgeschichte des Antisemitismus in
Deutschland (1815–1850)* (Munich, 1956), pp. 118–43.

39. Burleigh and Wippermann, *Racial State*, pp. 26–7.

[62]

40. William W. Hagen, *Germans, Poles and Jews: The Nationality Conflict in the Prussian East, 1772–1914* (Chicago, IL, 1980), pp. 105–6.

41. James J. Sheehan, *German Liberalism in the Nineteenth Century* (London, 1982), p. 20.

42. Dieter Langwiesche, 'Liberalismus und Judenemanzipation in Deutschland im 19. Jahrhundert', in Peter Freimark, Alice Jankowski and Ina S. Lorenz, eds, *Juden in Deutschland: Emanzipation, Integration, Verfolgung und Vernichtung* (Hamburg, 1991), pp. 148–63.

43. Wanda Kampmann, *Deutsche und Juden: Die Geschichte der Juden in Deutschland vom Mittelalter bis zum Beginn des Ersten Weltkrieges* 3rd edn (Frankfurt, 1994), pp. 191–4.

44. Snyder, *Roots of German Nationalism*, pp. 63–4.

45. Wolfgang Wippermann, *Geschichte der deutschen Juden: Darstellung und Dokumente* (Berlin, 1994), p. 49.

46. Scheuer, *Bursenschaft*, p. 37.

47. Hagen, *Germans, Poles and Jews*, pp. 110–11; Heinrich August Winkler, 'Nationalism and Nation-State in Germany', in Teich and Porter, *National Question in Europe*, p. 183.

48. Winkler, 'Nationalism and Nation-State', pp. 183–5; Snyder, *Roots of German Nationalism*, pp. 67–73.

49. Michael Banton, *Racial Theories* 2nd edn (Cambridge, 1998), pp. 62–8, 80–116.

50. Rose, *Revolutionary Antisemitism*, p. 359.

51. Jacob Katz, *The Darker Side of Genius: Richard Wagner's Antisemitism* (Hanover, New England, 1986), pp. 29–62.

52. Marc A. Weiner, *Richard Wagner and the Antisemitic Imagination* (London, 1995), p. 64.

53. Rose, *Revolutionary Antisemitism*, pp. 362, 370–1.

54. Katz, *Darker Side*, p. 33.

55. Richard Wagner, *Das Judentum in der Musik* (Leipzig, 1914 edn), pp. 3, 5, 6. The above and all subsequent quotations from German sources are my own translations.

56. H. G. Adler, *The Jews in Germany: From the Enlightenment to National Socialism* (Notre Dame, IN, 1969), p. 17.

57. Steven M. Lowestein, 'Jewish Residential Concentration in Post-Emancipation Germany', *Leo Baeck Institute Year Book* 28 (1983), p. 472; Hagen, *Germans, Poles and Jews*, p. 14.

58. Steven M. Lowenstein, *The Berlin Jewish Community: Enlightenment, Family and* [63]
Crisis, 1770–1830 (New York, 1994), especially pp. 16, 33, 55–9, 104–11,
120–33; Deborah Hertz, *Jewish High Society in Old Regime Berlin* (London,
1988), especially pp. 36, 92, 229; Ruth Gay, *The Jews of Germany: A Historical
Portrait* (London, 1992), pp. 98–117.

59. Miriam Gillis-Carlebach, 'Aus der Vorgeschichte der Hochdeutschen-
Israelitischen Gemeindschule zu Altona, ca. 1583–1843: Thesen – Dokumente
– Zusammenhänge', in Freimark, Jankowski and Lorenz, *Juden in Deutschland*,
pp. 15–17; Helga Krohn, *Die Juden in Hamburg, 1800–1850: Ihre soziale,
kulturelle und politische Entwicklung während der Emanzipationszeit* (Frankfurt am
Main, 1967), pp. 9, 10, 11, 17.

60. Hans Nordsiek, *Juden in Minden: Dokumente und Bilder Jüdischen Lebens vom
Mittelalter bis zum 20. Jahrhundert* (Minden, 1988), p. 38.

61. W. E. Mosse, *The German-Jewish Economic Élite, 1820–1935: A Socio-cultural
Profile* (Oxford, 1989), p. 9.

62. Trude Maurer, *Die Entwicklung der jüdischen Minderheit in Deutschland (1780–
1933)* (Tübingen, 1992), p. 74.

63. Quoted in Monika Richarz, ed., *Jewish Life in Germany: Memories from Three
Centuries* (Bloomington, IN, 1991), p. 68.

64. Rewin Reisner, *Die Juden und das Deutsche Reich* (Stuttgart, 1966), p. 160.

65. Bach, *German Jew*, pp. 73–4.

66. Lowenstein, *Berlin Jewish Community*, pp. 77–83.

67. Krohn, *Juden in Hamburg*, pp. 15, 17.

68. Nordsiek, *Juden in Minden*, p. 38.

69. Kampmann, *Deutsche und Juden*, pp. 127, 129.

70. C. W. Spiker, *Über die ehemalige und jetzige Lage der Juden in Deutschland* (Halle,
1809), p. 267.

71. Lowenstein, *Berlin Jewish Community*, p. 83.

72. Ibid., pp. 84–5; Kampmann, *Deutsche und Juden*, pp. 133–7.

73. Adler, *Jews in Germany*, pp. 33–4; Adolf Lewin, *Juden in Freiburg im Breisgau*
(Trier, 1890), p. 101.

74. Adler, *Jews in Germany*, pp. 38–40; Kampmann, *Deutsche und Juden*, pp. 140–
5; David Sorkin, *The Transformation of German Jewry, 1780–1840* (New York,
1987), pp. 33–4.

75. Krohn, *Juden in Hamburg*, p. 21.

[64]

76. The above account of the Hep Hep riots is based upon: Jacob Katz, *Die Hep-Hep Verfolgungen des Jahres 1819* (Berlin, 1994); Eleonore Sterling, 'Anti-Jewish Riots in Germany in 1819: A Displacement Theory of Social Protest', *Historica Judaica* 12 (1950), pp. 105–42; and Stefan Rohrbacher, *Gewalt in Biedermeier: Antijüdische Ausschreitungen in Vormärz und Revolution (1815–1848/49)* (Frankfurt am Main, 1993), pp. 94–127.

77. Rohrbacher, ibid., pp. 45–6, 62–84, 175–80.

78. Nordsiek, *Juden in Minden*, pp. 51–5.

79. Christopher M. Clark, *The Politics of Conversion: Missionary Protestantism and the Jews in Prussia, 1728–1941* (Oxford, 1995), pp. 125, 136.

80. Dietz Bering, *The Stigma of Names: Antisemitism in German Daily Life, 1812–1933* (Cambridge, 1992), pp. 27, 79.

81. Hans Liebeschütz, 'Judentum und deutsche Umwelt im Zeitalter der Restauration', in Hans Liebeschütz and Arnold Paucker, eds, *Das Judentum in der deutschen Umwelt, 1800–1850: Studien zur Frühgeschichte der Emanzipation* (Tübingen, 1977), p. 17.

82. Mosse, *German Jewish Economic Élite*, pp. 138–9.

83. Avraham Barkai, 'German Jews at the Start of Industrialisation: Structural Change and Mobility, 1835–1860', in Werner E. Mosse, Arnold Paucker and Reinhard Rürup, eds, *Revolution and Evolution: 1848 in German-Jewish History* (Tübingen, 1981), p. 124.

84. James F. Harris, *The People Speak! Antisemitism and Emancipation in Nineteenth Century Bavaria* (Ann Arbor, MI, 1994), pp. 13–17.

85. Lewin, *Juden in Freiburg*, p. 101.

86. Barkai, 'German Jews at the Start of Industrialisation', p. 125.

87. Ibid., pp. 130–2.

88. Richarz, *Jewish Life in Germany*, p. 77.

89. Werner J. Cahnman, *German Jewry: Its History and Sociology* (New Brunswick, NJ, 1989), p. 49.

90. Harris, *The People Speak!*, p. 33.

91. Krohn, *Juden in Hamburg*, pp. 35–51.

92. Lowenstein, *Berlin Jewish Community*, pp. 120–33.

93. Ibid, pp. 134–47; Bach, *German Jews*, pp. 81–102; Gay, *Jews of Germany*, pp. 152–6.

94. See Yehuda Eloni, *Zionismus in Deutschland: Von den Anfängen bis 1914* (Gerlingen, 1987), p. 18.

95. Bach, *German Jews*, p. 85.

96. Sorkin, *Transformation*, pp. 121–2.

97. Adler, *Jews in Germany*, p. 59; Peter Pulzer, *Jews and the German State: The Political History of a Minority* (Oxford, 1992), p. 84; Krohn, *Juden in Hamburg*, p. 72.

98. Rohrbacher, *Gewalt in Biedermeier*, pp. 221–2.

99. Lewin, *Juden in Freiburg*, p. 101.

100. Harris, *The People Speak!*, pp. 80, 123, 132–4, 189.

101. Werner E. Mosse, 'The Revolution of 1848: Jewish Emancipation in Germany and Its Limits', in Mosse, Paucker and Rürup, *Revolution and Evolution*, pp. 392–3; Jacob Toury, *Soziale und politische Geschichte der Juden in Deutschland, 1848–1871: Zwischen Revolution, Reaktion und Emanzipation* (Düsseldorf, 1977), pp. 300, 301, 307.

102. Adler, *Jews in Germany*, p. 65.

103. Pulzer, *Jews and the German State*, p. 85.

104. Toury, *Soziale und politische Geschichte*, pp. 313–61.

105. A discussion of the reasons for Jewish emancipation can be found in Mosse, 'Revolution of 1848', pp. 389–401.

106. Toury, *Soziale und politische Geschichte*, pp. 9, 28.

107. See Avraham Barkai, 'German-Jewish Migrations in the Nineteenth Century', *Leo Baeck Year Book* 30 (1985), pp. 304–11.

108. Ismar Elbogen and Eleonore Sterling, *Die Geschichte der Juden in Deutschland* (Frankfurt, 1988), p. 242.

109. Toury, *Soziale und politische Geschichte*, pp. 34–5.

110. Cahnman, *German Jewry*, p. 97.

111. Lowenstein, 'Jewish Residential Concentration', pp. 473, 476.

112. Toury, *Soziale und politische Geschichte*, pp. 125, 126, 129.

113. Jacob Katz, 'German Culture and the Jews', in Jehuda Reinharz and Walter Schatzberg, eds, *The Jewish Response to German Culture: From the Enlightenment to the Second Reich* (Hanover, NE, 1985), pp. 88–9.

114. Toury, *Soziale und politische Geschichte*, p. 128.

115. Eloni, *Zionismus in Deutschland*, pp. 23, 28; Bach, *German Jew*, p. 112.

116. Wolfgang Wippermann, *Geschichte der Sinti und Roma in Deutschland: Darstellung und Dokumente* (Berlin, 1993), pp. 19–20.

117. Ibid., p. 20.

[66] 118. Rainer Hehemann, *Die 'Bekämpfung des Zigeunerwesens' im Wilhelminischen Deutschland und in der Weimarer Republik, 1871–1933* (Frankfurt, 1987), p. 81; Susan Tebbutt, 'Piecing Together the Jigsaw: The History of the Sinti and Roma in Germany', in Tebbutt, ed., *Sinti and Roma: Gypsies in German-Speaking Society and Literature* (Oxford, 1998), p. 3.

119. Tebbutt, ibid., p. 4; Joachim S. Hohmann, *Geschichte der Zigeunerverfolgung in Deutschland* 2nd edn (Frankfurt, 1988), pp. 52–3; Martin Block, *Zigeuner: Ihr Leben und ihre Seele* (Leipzig, 1936), p. 42.

120. Tebbutt, ibid., p. 4.

121. Mareile Krause, *Verfolgung durch Erziehung: Eine Untersuchung über die jahrhundertlange Kontinuität staatlicher Erziehungsmaßnahmen im Dienste der Vernichtung kultureller Identität von Roma und Sinti* (Ammersbek, 1989), p. 70.

122. Hohmann, *Geschichte der Zigeunerverfolgung*, p. 55; Katrin Reemtsma, *Sinti und Roma: Geschichte, Kultur, Gegenwart* (Munich, 1996), pp. 46–7.

123. Wilhelm Solms, 'On the Demonising of Jews and Gypsies in Fairy Tales', in Tebbutt, *Sinti and Roma*, pp. 91–104.

124. Theodor Tetzner, *Geschichte der Zigeuner: Ihre Herkunft, Natur und Art* (Weimar, 1835), p. 105.

125. Sols, 'Demonising', p. 99; Wippermann, *Geschichte der Sinti und Roma*, p. 23.

126. Carl von Heiter, *Ethnographische und geschichtliche Notizen über die Zigeuner* (Königsberg, 1842), pp. 144, 145, 147, 149, 150, 151.

127. Richard Lieblich, *Die Zigeuner in ihrem Wesen und in ihrer Sprache* (Leipzig, 1863), pp. 38, 58, 63, 68, 69, 103–13.

128. Wolfgang Wippermann, *Geschichte der deutsch-polnischen Beziehungen: Darstellung und Dokumente* (Berlin, 1992), pp. 17–18.

129. Martin Broszat, *Zweihundert Jahre deutsche Polenpolitik* 2nd edn (Frankfurt, 1972), pp. 69–72.

130. Hagen, *Germans, Poles and Jews*, pp. 67, 76.

131. Harry Kenneth Rosenthal, *German and Pole: National Conflict and Modern Myth* (Gainesville, FL, 1976), pp. 9–11.

132. Broszat, *Zwei Hundert Jahre deutsche Polenpolitik*, p. 86.

133. Hagen, *Germans, Poles and Jews*, pp. 78–9; Enno Meyer, 'Die Polen im Preussischen Staat von 1815 bis 1914', in Helmuth Fechner, ed., *Deutschland und Polen, 1772–1945* (Würzburg, 1964), pp. 47–8.

134. Meyer, ibid., pp. 48–51; Wippermann, *Geschichte der deutsch-polnischen Beziehungen*, p. 21; Horst Jablonowski, *Russland, Polen und Deutschland: Gesammelte Aufsätze* (Cologne, 1972), pp. 264–7.

135. Maria Wawrykowa, *Revolutionäre Demokraten in Deutschland und Polen, 1815–* [67]
1848: Ein Beitrag zur Geschichte des Vormärz (Braunschweig, 1974), pp. 13–21.

136. Rosenthal, *German and Pole*, p. 15; Meyer, 'Die Polen im preussischen Staat', pp. 51–2; Bernhard Stasiewski, 'Zur Geschichte deutsch-polnischer Nachbarschaft', in Herbert Czaja and Gustav E. Kafka, eds, *Deutsche und Polen: Probleme einer Nachbarschaft* (Recklinghausen, 1960), p. 37; Broszat, *Zweihundert Jahre deutsche Polenpolitik*, p. 97; Hans Henning Hahn, 'Deutschland und Polen in Europa: Überlegungen zur Interdependenz zwei nationaler Fragen im 19. Jahrhundert', in Dieter Storch, ed., *Polen und Deutschland: Nachbarn in Europa* (Hanover, 1996), pp. 9–10.

137. Rosenthal, ibid., p. 15–16; Wippermann, *Geschichte der deutsch-polnischen Beziehungen*, p. 7; Meyer, ibid., pp. 52–3.

138. Meyer, ibid., pp. 53–4; Rosenthal, ibid., pp. 19–20.

139. Heinrich Geffcken, *Preußen, Deutschland und die Polen seit dem Untergang des polnischen Reiches* (Berlin, 1906), p. 56.

140. Oswald Hauser, 'Polen und Dänen im Deutschen Reich', in Theodor Schieder and Ernst Deuerlin, eds, *Reichsgründung, 1870–71: Tatsachen, Kontroversen, Interpretationen* (Stuttgart, 1970), p. 295; Jablonowski, *Russland, Polen und Deutschland*, pp. 276–7.

141. Moritz Jaffé, *Die Stadt Posen unter preußischer Herrschaft: Ein Beitrag zur Geschichte des deutschen Ostens* (Leipzig, 1909), pp. 152–3.

142. Eugen von Bergmann, *Zur Geschichte der Entwicklung deutscher, polnischer und jüdischer Bevölkerung in der Provinz Posen seit 1824* (Tübingen, 1883), pp. 29, 31.

143. Stasiewski, 'Zur Geschichte Deutsch-Polnischer Nachbarschaft', p. 38; Meyer, 'Die Polen im Preussischen Staat', pp. 54–5; Rosenthal, *German and Pole*, p. 20.

144. Hagen, *Germans, Poles and Jews*, pp. 104–13; Geffcken, *Preußen, Deutschland und die Polen*, p. 70; Rosenthal, ibid., pp. 21–4; Meyer, ibid., pp. 55–7.

145. Rosenthal, ibid., p. 25; Hagen, ibid, p. 121.

146. A. Freiherr von Fircks, 'Die preußische Bevölkerung nach ihrer Muttersprache und Abstammung' *Zeitschrift des königlich-preußischen statistischen Bureaus* 33 (1893), p. 193.

147. See Bergmann, *Provinz Posen Seit 1824*, pp. 43–63.

148. Broszat, *Zweihundert Jahre deutsche Polenpolitik*, p. 118.

149. Meyer, 'Polen im preussischen Staat', pp. 57–8; Hagen, *Germans, Poles and Jews*, pp. 139–41.

CHAPTER 3

The *Kaiserreich*, 1871–1918: Prejudice, Exploitation and Full Emancipation

The German nation state which came into existence in 1871 evolved from the economic, social and political transformations taking place in central Europe during the nineteenth century. In the period leading up to the First World War and the defeat which followed, the new political entity continued to experience many of the developments which characterized the decades leading to its formation. In addition, those in power attempted to mould the new state, although they often faced popular opposition from a series of movements from both the left and the right.

The German nation state revealed itself as the most powerful on the European continent. The basis of this position lay in concrete geographic, economic and social facts. Although smaller in size than the massive area controlled by the Russian autocracy, as well as the crumbling Ottoman Empire, it rivalled or surpassed the other large European states of France, Great Britain, the declining Habsburg Empire, the largely irrelevant and distant Spain, and the equally new Italy. In addition, the first German nation state had the advantages of a growing population, which would surpass the size of many of its rivals by the outbreak of the First World War. Expanding at a yearly average of more than ten per cent, the number of people living within the German Empire grew from 40,995,000 in 1875 to 64,568,000 by 1910.[1] In this year, Germany represented the second most populous state on the continent, way behind Russia's 160.7 million inhabitants, but considerably ahead of the UK with 40.8 million residents.[2]

In economic and social terms Germany has far more in common with Britain than Russia, as the process of industrialization, which had begun to take off earlier in the century, really reached fruition after 1871. Therefore, by the outbreak of the First World War, Germany had become a predominantly, but by no means exclusively, industrial state, which rivalled Britain, 'the workshop of the world' during the middle of the nineteenth century. Thus,

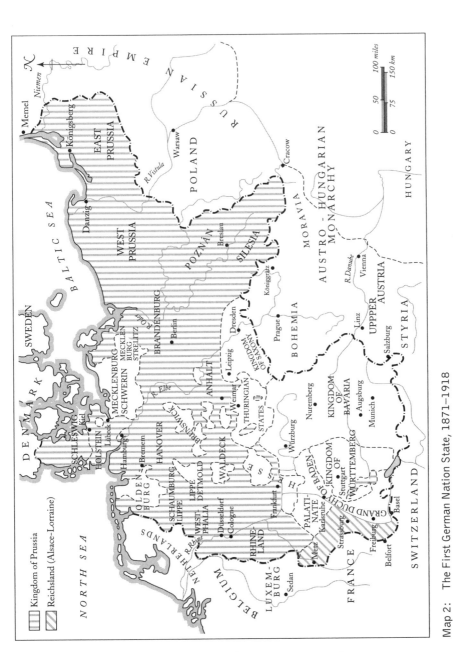

Map 2: The First German Nation State, 1871–1918

Source: Gordon Graig, *Germany, 1866–1945* (Oxford: Oxford University Press, 1981) p. vi.

the share of agriculture in the German GNP remained at between 35 and 40 per cent until the 1880s but fell back to stand at 25 per cent by the outbreak of the First World War, when industry's share had increased to 45 per cent, while the commercial and service sector made up the remaining 30 per cent.[3] The transformation took place in the heavy industries of coal, iron, steel, and railway building, which had also formed a major basis of British growth, as well as the new area of chemicals, where Germany reigned supreme because of the strength of her university science departments. By 1914 the new state produced more iron and coal than Britain.[4]

The economic transformation of Germany meant significant changes in society, above all in residence patterns and social structure. As industrialization always goes together with urbanization, the late nineteenth century witnessed a rush away from the land, which could not absorb the rapid population growth. Although this continued a trend begun earlier in the century, the excess population which had previously moved to the USA now fed the German industrialization process, especially in the Ruhr, rich in coal and iron, to which millions of people moved. Thus the town of Dortmund witnessed an increase in its population from 57,752 in 1875 to 214,226 by 1910, a growth of 271 per cent. In the country as a whole the proportion of people living in settlements of less than 2,000 decreased from two thirds in 1871 to two fifths by 1910,[5] indicating that, while significant transformation took place, the *Kaiserreich* continued to have a strong rural population base. Nevertheless, an increase took place in the size of the urban working classes at the expense of the peasantry, so that by 1907 over half of German employees belonged to the industrial proletariat, meaning an increase from 12.4 million workers in 1882 to 19.6 by 1907.[6] The middle-class occupations of businessmen, professionals and bureaucrats also saw significant expansion in the same period.[7] However, at the same time as the peasantry survived, so did the Prussian aristocracy.

The social structure of Germany before the First World War had a profound impact upon its political developments. The constitutional bodies established in 1871, while overtly representative, witnessed most clearly by the introduction of universal manhood suffrage, essentially formed part of an autocracy, because the balance of power heavily favoured the executive, in the form of Kaiser and Chancellor, at the expense of the legislature (the Reichstag) particularly because the former could dissolve parliament almost at will.[8] Thus the Prussian aristocracy had undue influence at the expense of the middle classes, especially the lower strands, and the proletariat. Nevertheless, as popular democracy certainly existed during the *Kaiserreich* mass parties could emerge, most notably the SPD, and have a profound impact upon political development. While the SPD may have represented the largest and strongest party by 1914, other popular movements also emerged, including antisemitic and patriotic ones, whose aims had more in common with those in power than the ideologically Marxist SPD.[9]

As in all nation states, the economic and social structure of Germany in the late nineteenth century impacted not simply upon its internal political development, but also upon its diplomacy. Although the 1871 Bismarckian settlement of Europe remained basically intact for the following two decades, the period from 1890 witnessed the aggressive German foreign policy which would result in the outbreak of the First World War. The basis of this may ultimately have rested in German industrialization, but the constitutional structures, which failed to meet all of the demands of the working classes, meant that an expansionist foreign policy represented a way of buying off the workers by focusing attention upon the external foe in the form of Russia, France and England, which the patriotic organizations detested to varying degrees.[10]

As well as an external ethnic enemy, there also existed internal ones, above all, to the German patriots of the late nineteenth century, Poles and Jews. The hostility towards the latter group, which, as we have seen, evolved in the intellectual turmoil created by the Enlightenment and the French Revolution, became increasingly modern and viewed Jews as disloyal, un-German, unassimilable and, increasingly, as a separate race. During the course of the 1880s, a full-blown antisemitic political movement evolved which would last until 1914. The extreme German patriots of the *Kaiserreich* also focused attention upon other minorities, although none received quite the same amount of animosity. Nevertheless, Poles faced increasing hostility, particularly as they represented a threat to many Pan-Germans looking to expansion and conquest in eastern Europe. Furthermore, while the *Kaiserreich* fully emancipated the Jews, it denied Poles many basic rights, especially in the use of their language and the practice of their religion.

Late nineteenth-century German nationalism and racism did not eliminate minorities in the way in which these ideologies would do during the 1930s and 1940s. But Jews in Bismarckian and Wilhelmine Germany could not ignore the milder manifestations of antisemitism which meant that they inevitably remained conscious of their ethnicity. The animosity could not prevent the continuing rise of Jewish economic strength, which, however, further fuelled antisemitism. Similarly, potent hostility towards both those Poles who remained in their historical areas of residence and those who

[72]   migrated to the Ruhr to take up the economic opportunities available there, could not prevent the growth of a well-developed Polish nationalism by the outbreak of the First World War. Similarly, other peripheral groupings, including Danes, also retained a sense of ethnicity. The *Kaiserreich* further witnessed the first importation of foreign workers, from eastern and southern Europe, and thus began a process which all subsequent German regimes would follow. These newcomers, on short-term contracts, remained more marginalized than any of the above groupings, because their residence status meant that they had difficulty developing any sort of political ethnicity. The other long-established minority group, the Gypsies, whose numbers increased due to immigration from eastern Europe before the First World War, faced similar levels of hostility to the other minorities within Germany but, because of a lack of literacy and low social and economic status, did not manage to organize themselves in the way that Jews and Poles could.

The flowering of nationalism, racism and antisemitism

Although the liberal ideas which had surfaced in late eighteenth-century Germany and reached their zenith in 1848 still existed in the first German nation state, as parties which put forward such ideas continued to play a role in the political process, tolerance does not represent the first word which springs to mind in any history of the new German Empire. Something of a polarization took place, which would continue to characterize German politics until the Nazis finally seized power in 1933. On the one hand the parties of the mainstream right controlled political power by the 1880s, but even farther to the right of them there existed all manner of patriotic, antisemitic, Polonophobic, eastward-looking individuals and groups, obsessed with both internal and external enemies. Although this section of German public opinion never actually held power, it influenced and reflected mainstream ideology. A group such as the Flottenverein played a large role in the building of the German navy as it had such close links with Admiral von Tirpitz, head of the Imperial Naval Office, and German steel producers. At the other end of the political spectrum lay the SPD, which, throughout the period 1871–1914, essentially remained an ideologically Marxist party, a situation which changed at the outbreak of the First World War when this group as a whole also bought the nationalist message and supported German expansionism, although the SPD would subsequently split in 1916 when an antiwar wing emerged.[11] Our primary concern lies with the ideologies of the extreme right and the way in which they perceived internal and external outgroups.

The foundation of the German Empire in 1871 may, superficially, appear to have realized and satisfied the dreams of all the German nationalists who had looked towards this goal from the early nineteenth century. Nevertheless, when we recall the fact that many of the early nationalist ideologues, including Herder, Fichte and Arndt had based their concept of German nationhood upon language, it should come as no surprise that their successors remained unsatisfied with the extent of German borders, as German speakers lived beyond them further east, as a result of migratory processes which had begun hundreds of years previously.[12] The new German nation state essentially legitimized nationalism and allowed extremists to look at further expansion, a view which gained mainstream support as foreign policy became increasingly aggressive from the 1890s. We must also remember the antisemitic content of the seeds of German nationalism sown by Herder, Fichte, Arndt and Jahn, which, once again, meant that when German nationalism fully flowered, it would produce poisonous fruit. Like their early nineteenth-century predecessors, the resentment of the Jew haters of the *Kaiserreich* intensified as a result of the full emancipation and economic success of the object of their negative views. The greater the level of Jewish success and integration, the stronger the level of antisemitism. However, the traditional Judeophobia of the medieval period, while it continued to manifest itself, especially in ritual murder accusations, became increasingly modern so that the concept of the Jews as a state within a state increasingly came to the fore. In addition, the late nineteenth century also saw a full emergence of the racist ideas which would dominate Germany from 1933 to 1945.

All extremism lay firmly grounded in, and sprang from, the mainstream German political processes, whether we are referring to the structures established after 1871 or to the foreign and domestic policies pursued by the different regimes which held power from 1871 to 1918. Like all other nation states, Germany in the late nineteenth and early twentieth centuries was obviously nationalist.

The *Kaiserreich* invented traditions about itself and implemented measures which confirmed its position as a nation state. The rulers of the new creation had to manufacture the idea of a unitary entity which held together the different states which had come together in 1871. Thus, statues and monuments to the German victory over the French in 1871, to the first German Kaiser, Wilhelm I, and to Bismarck, appeared throughout Germany. The most spectacular of these monuments included the *Deutsches Eck*, on the confluence of the Moselle and Rhine in Coblenz. In addition, national days became important, including the anniversary of the defeat of France in 1871.[13]

In addition to the monuments, there emerged the Nationality Law of 1913, legally defining Germans and non-Germans and cutting through all the speculation of the earlier nineteenth century. The 1913 Law had a series of predecessors, although these essentially based citizenship upon the locality, rather than the concept of Germanness. While the Federal Act of 1815 introduced a distinction between Germans and others, 'citizenship law remained within the jurisdiction of the individual states', many of whom, in this pre-industrial and pre-standardizing age, 'did nothing much about it'.[14] The 1848 revolutions resulted in 'a short-lived law' which 'temporarily established an imperial German citizenship', although, just before the first German nation state came into existence, the individual states determined citizenship law.[15] Legislation in 1871 meant that all Germans residing within the new state had residence rights throughout Germany, as it created the concept of insiders and outsiders.[16] However, Germans continued to possess the citizenship of individual states so that 'on passports and identity cards, the bearers' citizenship appeared as either Prussian, Bavarian, Saxon, or as the case might be'.[17] Although this situation continued into the Weimar Republic, the 1913 Nationality Law meant a significant change, as it defined German nationality according to origin, rather than residence within Germany. This decision had arrived due to the conflict in Prussia between Germans and Poles, the presence of Germans beyond the boundaries of the Reich, and the importation of foreign workers. It would have a profound impact on German nationality legislation, and who was excluded from and included in this, as it lasted for the rest of the twentieth century.[18] It very much represented a core structural component of the German nation state.

In essence, these structural elements in Germany do not differentiate the country from other contemporaneous nation states. If we looked at Britain before the First World War we would find many invented traditions revolving around Empire[19] and, at the same time, the introduction of nationality and immigration legislation[20] in this modernizing state. Similarly, mainstream British politicians obviously pursued nationalistic policies, particularly as the First World War approached. The same clearly applies to Germany, as we can see by focusing upon a series of elements in the political process, which helped to give legitimacy to extremists.

In terms of control of power, during the early years of the Bismarck Chancellorship until 1878, the dominant grouping consisted of the National

Liberal Party. Thereafter, a coalition further to the Right, combining conservative and nationalistic forces, in which patriotic and antisemitic groups
played a role, controlled power until the First World War. Although the
Social Democratic Party held most seats in the Reichstag by 1914, this hardly
mattered because of the balance of power in favour of the executive.

The 'Bonapartist dictatorship' of Bismarck until 1890 and Kaiser Wilhelm
II and his succession of chancellors until 1918, ruling primarily in the interests of large industrialists and Prussian landowners, meant the pursuance of
a series of extreme nationalistic policies – for instance, Bismarck's attack
upon the Catholic Church during the 1870s. This policy had several roots,
perhaps most importantly the fear that Catholics represented a state within a
state because their ultimate allegiance lay to Rome rather than Berlin. Consequently, Bismarck viewed the Catholic Centre Party as a sectarian group.
The strength of Catholicism in the Prussian East, as well as the Polish language, also irritated the Iron Chancellor, who held deep prejudices against
Poles. The *Kulturkampf* represented an attack upon Polish nationalism and
paved the way for other Germanizing policies in Prussia from the 1880s,
supported by groups such as the Society for the Eastern Marches. Linguistic
Germanization also affected the other peripheral parts of the Reich, illustrat-
ing the way in which the modernizing, centralizing state attempts to under-
mine minorities.

Bismarck's attack upon the Poles continued for the whole of the 1870s
and resulted in the passage of a series of measures against both Church
and language, representing another negative phase in the cyclic history of
German repression of Poles, backed up, for the first time, by a German
ideology based upon a German nation state. In 1871 the School Supervision
Law put all schools under the administration of the state, which meant, for
instance, that the state appointed all school inspectors, who had hitherto
often consisted of Polish priests. Far worse followed. In 1872 German became
the sole language of instruction for all subjects in Upper Silesia. The May
Laws of 1873 meant that all holders of clerical offices had to possess German
citizenship and a German degree. Further measures in 1873 and 1874 meant
that German replaced Polish as the language of instruction in primary and
secondary schools throughout the province of Poznań. In 1879 the Prussian
Assembly passed a law which made German the only permissible language in
public administration.[21] As we shall see, such measures gave a boost to Polish
nationalism rather than eliminate Polish ethnic consciousness.

At the same time as these measures came into operation, a Germanization
process also took place in Alsace and Lorraine. When the two territories

[76]   became part of the Reich in 1871 most people used the Alsatian dialect as their everyday means of communication, while French represented the official language. Whereas 77 per cent of the population used French according to the 1875 census, the number of German speakers totalled 87 per cent by 1910. Although part of the explanation lies in the movement of French speakers out of Alsace and Lorraine, the implementation of German as the official language represents the major explanation for the change.[22]

Meanwhile, unfounded fears circulated about the growth of the Polish population in relation to the German one in the areas in which the two groups resided as neighbours, leading, in 1886, to the passage of a Settlement Law and the establishment of a Royal Prussian Colonization Commission, which survived until 1918. It would use the 100 million marks which it initially received for the purpose of buying financially insecure estates in the eastern colonies and dividing them out to German peasant settlers. It had limited success in achieving this objective even though the funding it received had increased to 500 million marks by the outbreak of the First World War. This measure, which harks forward to even more draconian policies pursued during the Second World War, represented the most significant development in another anti-Polish campaign, which also resulted in the expulsion of 25,914 people from Prussia between 1885 and 1887. In addition, further measures ensured the primacy of German language instruction in schools. The most significant of these, from 1887, meant the elimination of the teaching of the Polish language in elementary schools in Poznań (this having already disappeared everywhere else at this level). In addition, 1886 saw a German cleric, Julius Dinder, who could, however, speak fluent Polish, become head of the Roman Catholic Church in Poznań, as his Polish predecessor remained in exile in the Vatican.[23]

Germanization policies continued after the fall of Bismarck, although the Chancellorship of Caprivi from 1890 to 1894, Bismarck's immediate successor, did result in some easing of pressure upon Poles. For instance, in 1892 a Pole again became Archbishop of Poznań. Nevertheless, there then followed another Polonophobic period when Chlodwig zu Hohenlohe-Schillingsfürst became Chancellor. In 1896–97, for instance, official discussion took place about prohibiting the use of Polish in public which would have prevented nationalist organizations from holding public meetings using their language. At this stage, such a 'ludicrous' measure did not become law.[24] A further intensification of the anti-Polish campaign occurred under the Chancellorship of Prince Bernhard von Bülow, who succeeded Hohenlohe in 1900 and remained in power until 1909. By this time the nationalistic

Ostmarkverein had developed much popular support and influence within [77] government circles. There followed further educational measures in 1901 and 1906 demanding the use of German for religious education.[25] In 1907 the idea of forbidding the use of the Polish language in public meetings surfaced and in 1908, after much opposition in the Reichstag, a compromise solution was reached whereby it was only allowed for a period of twenty years in areas throughout Germany where foreign-speaking minorities formed more than sixty per cent of the population.[26]

The attitude of the new German state towards Poles clearly represents one of increasing intolerance, from which the positive phases which characterized the years before 1871 had given way to a period in which Germanization became unquestioned policy. We could take this back to the natural conclusions of the *Paulskirche* debate, which revealed German nationalism's problems with the toleration of minorities. It is worth remembering that Bismarck passed his initial measures in the 1870s at the time when he relied on support from the National Liberals. Nevertheless, while the *Kaiserreich* pursued an overwhelmingly negative Polish policy, it differs from that implemented by the Nazis, which, in a wartime situation, after 1939, backed by a ruthless racist ideology, had no respect for human life. In the First World War the German state did not implement such brutal measures just as it did not exterminate its Jewish population. National Socialism took German nationalism on to a new plane.

Another indication of state nationalism in the *Kaiserreich* is tariff policy. The *Zollverein*, established in 1834 and the economic predecessor of the German nation state, had introduced external customs barriers, although from the 1860s German states had basically pursued a policy of free trade. This policy came under serious scrutiny following the stock market crash of 1873 and the economic recession which followed, events which would have an influence on many developments in late nineteenth-century Germany. Several sectors of the economy, including iron producers and agricultural interests, found the root of their problem in the free trade policies pursued by their state and, by the end of the 1870s, had won Bismarck to their cause. The fact that the Chancellor could not persuade the liberals to follow him strongly influenced his decision to ditch them and turn to conservatives and nationalists in 1878–79. The change 'from laissez faire liberalism to economic nationalism was a natural outcome of the steadily strengthening nationalism of the 1860s and 1870s'.[27] Although Britain persevered with free trade, most other nation states in the late nineteenth century pursued the same policies as Germany.

The clearest example of the strength of German nationalism lies in its foreign policy. The new state had essentially come into existence as a result of wars of conquest and it is therefore unlikely that it would rest on its laurels, satisfied with the borders of 1871. This did actually happen under Bismarck, at least in Europe, where the Iron Chancellor attempted to maintain the status quo of 1871, although some imperial expansion occurred, with Germany seizing her share of African territories. After the fall of Bismarck, Germany embarked upon a constantly aggressive foreign policy, which would eventually lead to the outbreak of the First World War, because it threatened the vital interests of the other three Great European Powers of France, Britain and Russia.[28]

The First World War represented the high point of imperial German nationalism. During this conflict it hatched plans for the annexation of much of central Europe. In addition, popular nationalism at home reached its highest point, epitomized by Kaiser Wilhelm II's statement on the outbreak of the war that he no longer recognized parties, only Germans. Throughout the conflict propaganda aimed at maintaining the morale of the populace. German attitudes towards its eastern provinces and the territories which it invaded continued those of the pre-war period. Although they did not descend into the brutality, murder and concentration of civilians which would occur during the Second World War, exploitation of eastern labour power took place. The plans for continental domination briefly came to fruition following the defeat of the Bolsheviks in 1918, which resulted in the latter signing away much of western Russia, including Poland, to Germany in the Treaty of Brest-Litovsk.[29]

Throughout the *Kaiserreich* a symbiotic relationship existed between the state and popular nationalist, imperialist, racist and eastern expansionist movements, especially after the fall of Bismarck. While the political system weighted power heavily in the hands of the executive, the election of the legislature took place through a process of universal manhood suffrage in a state with an educated electorate. Although this situation led, on the one hand, to the emergence of the mass Social Democratic Party, it also gave birth to pressure groups at the other end of the political spectrum, whose membership consisted mostly of members of the middle classes: 'professionals, civil servants, businessmen, less frequently artisans and peasant-farmers, more rarely the big landowners'.[30] Finance came in some cases primarily from membership dues and in others from large business concerns, especially the German Navy League, which received support from the armaments manufacturer Krupp, who had a vested interest in the construction of a German fleet.[31] We therefore have a pattern in which nationalism offered a unifying ideology, which both the state and the middle classes used to their own advantage, largely as a reaction against the demands of the working-class SPD. The focus upon internal and external ethnic enemies in the form of Poles, Jews and the English (because of their navy), as well as looking at expansion in the wider world and eastern Europe, offered an escape outwards from Germany's internal problems.

The most significant of the numerous right-wing organizations included the Pan-German League, the Navy League, the Colonial Society, the Ostmarkverein and the German Army League. The largest of these consisted of the Navy League, which counted 331,493 members in 1914, while other organizations did not exceed 100,000. For instance, the Pan-German League never reached 22,000 members.[32] The German Army League, which came into existence in 1912, counted 90,000 members on the outbreak of the First World War.[33]

Despite its relatively small membership, the Pan-German League became important and many of its ideas and personnel later played a role in the Nazi party. It came into existence in 1894, publishing a weekly journal called the *Alldeutsche Blätter* and counting 7,715 members by the end of the following year.[34] The organization aimed to protect German interests throughout the world. It believed that the borders of 1871 represented a starting point for the German state. It had an essentially *völkisch* concept of ethnicity, which meant that it demanded further expansion into eastern Europe, where more Germans lived, thus indicating clear links with Nazism. In fact, it wanted growth in all directions.[35] Its handbook declared:

> 1. The Pan-German League strives for the invigoration of German national feeling, especially the awakening and cultivation of the consciousness of racial and cultural belonging of all sections of the German people.
> 2. This task means that the Pan-German League undertakes:
> 1. the preservation of German nationality in Europe and beyond and its support in areas where it is threatened;
> 2. a solution to the cultural, educational and school questions in favour of German nationals;
> 3. to fight with all its might, whatever hinders our national development;
> 4. an energetic policy for German interests throughout the world, especially a continuation of German colonialism towards practical results.[36]

The strongest areas of the Pan-German League's support lay in the great northern ports, industrial towns in the Ruhr and several cities in central Germany including Leipzig, Dresden, Halle and Kassel. Most of the leaders of the national and local organizations belonged to the *Mittelstand*, but some members of the rank and file may have come from the working classes.[37]

[80]   The Ostmarkverein provided details about its national distribution and the social make up of its members in its annual report. Not surprisingly, it counted its greatest strength in areas with Polish populations. Of the 429 local associations which existed in 1907, 92 lay in Poznań, 53 in West Prussia, 25 in Pomerania, 66 in Silesia, 43 in East Prussia, while the rest existed in western German locations. In Germany as a whole, the most significant occupations included civil servants, school teachers and smallholders. As part of the traditions of such organizations, the Society organized festivities on various national days, including Bismarck's birthday.[38]

Many of the organizations described above inevitably had an antisemitic core to their beliefs, which receives explanation from the fact that Jews had increasingly come to represent the main internal enemy for German nationalists as the nineteenth century progressed. The Pan-German League, for instance, devoted much attention to both antisemitism and more general racial ideologies in the pages of its publications.[39] Nevertheless, while hostility towards Jews appealed to most individuals and organizations on the mainstream and extreme right, it also developed a life of its own after 1871. It became an all-embracing ideology, which attracted supporters from a variety of social backgrounds, especially the petty bourgeoisie. It gave rise to a series of demagogues, pressure groups and even political parties, which counted deputies in the Reichstag for much of the period leading up to the First World War. The growth of antisemitism had a series of social, economic and political causes.

While the hatred of the Jews may have taken off significantly after 1871, it also clearly represents a continuation of the medieval and Enlightenment antisemitism. Core elements in the animosity towards Jews included resentment at their economic success, as the late nineteenth century represented the period when this minority really developed a social structure on a higher level than the rest of the population aided by their full emancipation in 1871. This social mobility contrasted with the position of many sections of German society who felt threatened by the continual changes taking place as a result of the industrialization process.[40] While the working classes could turn to their ideology of Marxism, which targeted all wealthy people as enemies, irrespective of their ethnicity, the petty bourgeoisie, with their small amounts of property, felt threatened by Marxism, and viewed hatred of Jews as an alternative ideology, especially as they wanted to reach the status of richer gentile Germans. In addition, the final creation of a unified Germany intensified the concept of the Jews as a state within a state, even though many members of the minority became increasingly assimilated, or, at least, integrated. But this process simply fuelled the developing racist views of Jews, because, unlike the medieval period, when they remained distinct because of clothing, residence and economic activity, they could now disappear into the surrounding population. But not if, by blood, they always remained distinct. The antisemites had an answer to every development as their ideology has an extraordinary ability to reinvent itself. The views which developed during the later decades of the nineteenth century therefore combined a variety of elements which had emerged before 1871 including romantic, backward-looking conservatism, economic vindictiveness at Jewish success, forward-looking utopian racism, and extreme German nationalism.[41]

Many of the antisemites of the earlier nineteenth century were still around in the 1870s, when the ideology began to take off, especially Richard Wagner. He both continued personal friendships with Jews and often spoke about them in fairly obscene terms. For instance, he wished that more of them had burned when he heard that some had died in a theatre fire in Vienna.[42] In addition, his later operas were replete with antisemitic symbols. For instance, the negatively portrayed Nibelungen in the Ring Cycle have problems with their mobility, which ties in with one mainstream view of Jews, which saw them as physically inadequate because of their supposedly badly developed feet. More generally the Ring Cycle, in which the healthy and upright triumph over deformed dwarfs, is inherently racist.[43] Because of his role as a forerunner of the antisemitism which took off in the 1870s, Wagner attracted much attention from the new Jew haters and continued to play a role in its spread at a level below the high culture of his operas. For instance, he wrote antisemitic articles in his *Bayreuther Blätter* launched in 1878.[44]

Nevertheless, Wagner died in 1883, by which time antisemitic hotbeds had developed around other individuals. The ideology operated on different levels, from academic to street corner. The stock market crash of 1873 and the ensuing depression played an important role in the spread of antisemitism during the course of the 1870s, focusing upon prominent Jewish bankers such as Gerson von Bleichröder and the Rothschild family. In 1874 a Berlin petty bourgeois magazine entitled *Die Gartenlaube* published a series of antisemitic articles by Otto Glagau, whom the 1873 crash had financially ruined, on 'The Stock Exchange and Speculation Fraud in Berlin'. There followed antisemitic pieces in the conservative Prussian *Kreuzzeitung* in 1875, again focusing upon Jewish financial interests.[45]

Just as the years 1878–79 represented a turning point in the history of the new German nation state, as Bismarck switched allies from National Liberals to Conservatives and Nationalists and introduced the Anti-Socialist Laws, these years also proved dramatic for the development of antisemitism. In 1878 Adolf

[82]   Stöcker, a Lutheran pastor, established his Christian Social Party, originally aimed at drawing the working classes away from socialism. Although Stöcker had little appeal to the workers, by the following year he had begun to attract members of the petty bourgeoisie in the form of artisans, shopkeepers and civil servants, who 'were susceptible to antisemitism'. By the end of 1879, when several other major antisemitic developments had occurred, Stöcker's party had become overtly hostile to Jews.[46] A significant turning point for Stöcker occurred at a rally on 19 September, when he delivered a speech entitled 'What We Demand of Modern Jewry', in which he asked the Jews to be more modest and tolerant, because he resented their self-confidence in their own religion. He continued the Fichtean theme of the Jews as an unassimilable 'people within a people, a state within a state', and demanded measures to decrease their power. Stöcker's views combined both secular and Christian antisemitism.[47] The following week Stöcker gave a lecture entitled 'Self-Defence Against Modern Jewry', in which he attacked newspapers and individuals who had reacted negatively towards his initial speech and called for the German people to take up Christianity once again as a means of lessening the power of the Jews.[48]

At the time of the lecture another rabble rouser had joined the fray in the form of Wilhelm Marr. In fact, Marr, from a respectable background, had gone the way of many other nineteenth-century Germans in switching from an 1848 revolutionary to a late nineteenth-century Jew hater. Despite the fact that he had initially supported Jewish emancipation, he published his first antisemitic work in 1862 in the form of *Der Judenspiegel*. This described the Jews as a state within a state and called for their assimilation, through intermarriage and baptism, which he believed they would not accept because they viewed themselves as a racially pure people. However, Marr's most famous book, *The Victory of Judaism Over Germanism* appeared in the same year as the founding of Stöcker's movement.[49] This was an extraordinary anti-Jewish polemic, in which Marr claimed that Jews had always represented outsiders throughout history because they were workshy and because they hated all other peoples. This constructed history stated that the qualities which Jews had developed over centuries of persecution had allowed them to take over Germany, as evidenced by their control of wealth, politics and culture.[50] In 1879 Marr also founded an organization called the Anti-Semitic League and launched a journal entitled *Deutsche Wacht* with the subtitle of the *Monthly of the Anti-Jewish Association*.[51] Marr seems to have coined the phrase antisemitism, but it is 'a new term for an old matter – hatred of the Jews'.[52]

A third major development of 1878–79 came from a prestigious quarter and gave antisemitism respectability when Heinrich von Treitschke, the Berlin History Professor and Reichstag deputy, published a series of articles in the *Preussische Jahrbücher* which he edited. In fact, his views essentially continued those of his predecessor as a Berlin Professor, Johann Gottlieb von Fichte, because he saw no space for Jews as a separate group within Germany and called for their assimilation.[53] In his historical work Treitschke revealed *völkisch* sentiments in his romanticization of the pre-industrial German peoples, which 'the Jew', as the bringer of modernity, had done much to destroy.[54] Paul de Lagarde, who eventually gained a Chair at Göttingen, also played a major role in the evolution of the racial concept of the German *Volk*, although, unlike most of his contemporaries, he rejected Christianity in favour of a Germanic religion, but, like Treitschke, saw the Jews as a threat to traditional German rural values. The solution he saw consisted either of assimilation or emigration of the Jews. His major work, *Deutsche Schriften*, also appeared in 1878, although he produced other works on the subject of Germans and Jews in the following decade.[55] Another History Professor, Theodor Mommsen, had replied to Treitschke's articles in the *Preussische Jahrbücher* fearing that his colleague had helped to create a bad atmosphere in political discourse, although Mommsen looked forward to a time when Jews would all convert to Christianity.[56] The fact that such prominent intellectuals wrote in such a way about Jews, indicated, once again, as had been the case during the Napoleonic and *Vormärz* period, the centrality of the Jewish question in German political thought.

The years 1878–79 simply represent a take-off point in the history of German antisemitism: during the rest of the *Kaiserreich*, especially until 1900, it remained a central issue in German political discourse as well as everyday life:

> The most virulent kind of anti-Semitism was spread throughout Germany by teachers, students, industrial and commercial employees, petty officials, professional people, and followers of cults of every variety: members of 'life reform movements', whole-rye bread dieticians, opponents of vivisection, and 'back to the future' builders of body and soul.[57]

The meetings of Stöcker continued to attract several thousand people in 1880 and 1881,[58] although the most important event of these years consisted of the circulation of an antisemitic petition organized by Bernhard Förster, Max Liebermann von Sonnenberg and Ernst Henrici, the first two of whom established the Deutscher Volksverein in 1881. The petition called

[84] for the suspension of Jewish immigration from Eastern Europe, which had become a major issue, the exclusion of Jews from public positions and the restoration of a special census. On a visit to the town of Neustettin in March 1881, Förster and Liebermann had caused an antisemitic disturbance which had resulted in the burning of the local synagogue, although violence against Jews represented an unusual occurrence in this period. The petition actually managed to secure 225,000 signatures.[59]

Despite these developments, for most of the 1880s 'political antisemitism remained in the doldrums'.[60] It received a boost following the election of the antisemitic Otto Böckel to the Reichstag in 1887. He was a librarian, who subsequently produced two significant antisemitic pamphlets. His *Quintessenz der Judenfrage* in which he attacked Jewish financial power and its control over the rest of the population, especially those living on the land, was a direct reference to the poor constituents he represented in his Marburg seat. He concluded his pamphlet by declaring that 'antisemitism is a world shattering movement; it must and shall triumph'.[61] His subsequent publication *Die Juden – Die Könige unserer Zeit!*, rehashed these views, but devoted more attention to areas other than finance, such as the press and politics, in which, like many of his contemporary antisemitic colleagues, he claimed that the Jews had too much influence.[62]

The early 1890s represented the high point of antisemitic manifestations, especially politically. In 1889 the Antisemitische Deutschsoziale Partei came into existence, under the leadership of Förster, Fritsch and Sonnenberg, while Böckel and his followers established the Antisemitische Volkspartei.[63] A leaflet published by the former grouping during the 1890 election for voters in Hesse, one of the poorest areas of Germany, used direct methods, providing what it claimed was a list of Germans expelled from their homes and a list of the Jews responsible for these actions.[64] Such tactics obviously proved effective as Hesse elected five antisemitic deputies.[65]

But the greatest political success of the Jew haters occurred in the Reichstag election of 1893, when they secured the return of 16 representatives with 342,425 votes, or 4.4 per cent of the total votes cast.[66] Other developments also occurred during the course of the 1890s including the formation of new groups such as the German Federation of Salaried Commercial Employees in 1893, which questioned the loyalty of all ethnic minorities.[67] In addition ritual murder accusations, which were resurfacing elsewhere in Europe, including Austria-Hungary, began to circulate in Germany. In fact, twelve ritual murder trials occurred in the two countries, although eleven of them collapsed, because of the absurdity of the evidence.[68] Furthermore, there were also attempts to boycott Jews and prevent them from travelling and entering shops, although such tactics proved unsuccessful.[69]

The entry of large numbers of eastern European Jews into Germany during the 1890s played a role in the success of the antisemites. These immigrants started moving into the country from Russia and Austria-Hungary at the end of the 1860s, but their numbers increased significantly during the 1890s. They received hostile attention from the state, which reduced their numbers and tried to expel them, as well as from Treitschke, who wrote about the invasion of 'multitudes of assiduous trouser-selling youths from the inexhaustible cradle of Poland'. Furthermore, the mainstream Conservative and National Liberal parties also displayed hostility towards them, as did established German Jewry, which felt the poor newcomers threatened the position they had fought for so long to establish.[70]

Political antisemitism declined in importance after 1900, as witnessed by the fall in the number of deputies with such views to 11 in 1903 and 7 in 1912.[71] Nevertheless, it certainly did not disappear and developed further in ideological terms. The overt Jew haters had an interesting relationship with the political establishment and the rest of the German parties, although, ultimately, while the *Kaiserreich* certainly represented the prelude to Nazi Germany, it never went the same way. Those who held political power accepted the realities of emancipation, however reluctantly, and did not practise the sort of overt discriminatory policies that they did towards the Poles, because, unlike Poles, Jews could not, literally, set up a state within a state. Several historians have discussed the relationship of Bismarck and Kaiser Wilhelm with the Jews and, while both may have been ambivalent, neither of them was Hitler. The instruments of the state were not poisoned with antisemitism between 1871 and 1914. Unlike 1819 and 1938, there was no year of pogroms in the *Kaiserreich*, which also contrasts with the vicious antisemitic riots which occurred in Tsarist Russia between 1881 and 1905. In fact, in late nineteenth-century Germany 'the state had proved its utter reliability by using troops to quell riots in Neustettin (1881), Xanten (1891), and Constance (1900), and by handing out stiff punishments to rioters'. We should also remember events in contemporary France where political discourse in the 1890s revolved around the Dreyfus Affair.[72]

While the Conservatives, Nationalists and National Liberals may have overtly sympathized with antisemitism, the left of the German political spectrum devoted little attention to it. Although members of the emerging Social Democratic Party had made antisemitic statements during the 1870s, by the end of that decade the group had begun to oppose the Judeophobes. A speech by August Bebel, one of the SPD leaders, at a meeting in Berlin in 1906 revealed the position of the Party, as he declared that antisemitism appealed to the lowest common denominator. Social Democrats opposed all capitalists, whether Jewish or Christian. Unlike those on the right of the political spectrum, the SPD fought a class war, not a racial one.[73]

Although the power of the antisemites may have declined by the outbreak of the First World War, it had certainly not disappeared, as the conflict gave their ideology a new lease of life, despite the fact that German Jews did more than their fair share of fighting on the frontline. Initially, the outbreak of war allowed the Jews to become a part of the German nation as they, like all sections of German society, were sucked into the national euphoria. For a short while antisemitism disappeared as an issue from mainstream public discussion. Nevertheless, some of the leading Judeophobic individuals and organizations did not remain silent for long. As early as 3 September 1914, following the death of the Jewish Deputy Ludwig Frank, the antisemitic Franz Oppenheimer declared: 'Don't raise your hopes, you are and remain the pariahs of Germany.' The hostility intensified as the conflict continued and propaganda began to perceive Jews as shirkers and profiteers. This animosity reached its high point at the end of 1916 when the Prussian War Ministry ordered an investigation into the number of Jews serving in the army. Hostility intensified further as the Allied Blockade resulted in the 'turnip winter' of 1916–17, when groups such as the Fatherland Party and the Pan-German League increased their antisemitic activity.[74] This would intensify even further in the bitterness of defeat of the post-war period.

By 1918 antisemitism had become part of a racist ideology, in which the pure German *Volk* contrasted with the impure people which threatened it, including Jews, eastern Europeans, Gypsies and unhealthy Germans, so that Hitler's ideas did not have much originality. The racist ideas which emerged by 1914 combined *völkisch* views, financial hostility towards Jews, and concepts of loyalty and disloyalty with emerging scientific ideas originating in Darwin. Many of the views actually originated in the works of writers in other countries. These included Francis Galton, who developed concepts of race and differentiated people according to physical and mental ability. He believed that healthy parents should have healthy children and has been regarded as the father of eugenics.[75] Racial ideology essentially had its birthplace in France, under the influence of Gobineau, who invented the concept of the pure Aryan race.

Although Wagner inherently shared many of his ideas, racism and eugenics really began to take off in Germany during the 1890s, especially under the influence of Houston Stewart Chamberlain, an Englishman who had moved to Germany and came under the influence of Wagner and his family (as he married one of the composer's daughters) and wrote in the language of his adopted land, producing, most importantly, his monumental two-volume *The Foundations of the Nineteenth Century*. Chamberlain stated that, 'Nothing is so convincing as the consciousness of the possession of race. The man who belongs to a distinct, pure race, never loses the sense of it.' Using terminology typical of a dog breeder, Chamberlain believed that, for a race to emerge, some mixture of blood between different groups would have to take place. He linked contemporary Germans with the Teutonic invaders of the Roman Empire, who had also protected Roman Europe from eastern invasions. Clearly, as one of the proudest of all Germanophiles, he heaped extraordinary praise upon 'the Germanic races' because they 'possess a harmony of qualities, maintaining the balance between the instinct of individual freedom, which finds its highest expression in creative art, and the instinct of public freedom which creates the state'. He even wrote, 'That the Teuton is one of the greatest, perhaps the greatest power in the history of mankind, no one can deny.' In ominous language, which seems to prepare the way for events in Europe during the Second World War, Chamberlain continued:

> No one can prove that the predominance of Teutonism is a fortunate thing for all the inhabitants of the earth; from the earliest times down to the present day we see the Teutons, to make room for themselves, slaughtering whole tribes and races, or wholly killing them by systematic demoralisation.

Chamberlain did not regard such actions negatively because of his positive view of the triumph of the Teutons. Their real enemy consisted of the Jews, as Chamberlain essentially created a dialectic between the two groups, which Hitler would later copy. Chamberlain pointed to the ancient origins of the Jews but asserted that, in contrast to Romans and Greeks, 'their intellectual horizon appears so narrow, their mental abilities so limited', although the power of their faith counterbalanced these deficiencies. Chamberlain viewed the Jews as exclusive, 'alien' and 'responsible for many a shocking historical development, for the fall of many heroic, powerful peoples'.[76]

Apart from Chamberlain, two other major figures who had an influence upon Hitler consisted of Karl Lueger and J. Lanz von Liebenfels. The former became Lord Mayor of Vienna in 1897 and retained his position until his death in 1910, preaching antisemitic rhetoric during his time in office.[77] Lanz von Liebenfels, on the other hand, was 'an eccentric occultist-racist', who published a series of pamphlets between 1907 and 1910 in which 'he depicted the struggle between the blond Aryan heroes and the dark, hairy ape-men representing the lower races', with the latter threatening the sexual purity of the former. He actually advocated that Jews and other inferior races should be eliminated.[78]

Another pamphlet published in Leipzig in 1912 by Daniel Fryman, explaining what he would do if he became the Kaiser, devoted much attention to the Jews and other minorities. In language reminiscent of Chamberlain and, later, Hitler, Fryman stated that the Jews had not earned their emancipation and that, since they had obtained it, they had enslaved Germans. Germans and Jews, he claimed, differed like fire and water. The main interests of the former included a belief in freedom and independence and a laid-back attitude to success and failure. In contrast, acquisition and possession meant everything for the Jews, who remained unfree. Fryman then went on to make the popular association of Jews with materialism, as well as focusing upon what he saw as the overwhelming power of the Jews, who had corrupted German life. He wanted Jewish influence to disappear, both by the restriction of further immigration and the curtailment of the rights of those Jews living in the country.[79]

Fryman also devoted attention to other minorities within Germany. For instance, despite the measures already in existence against the Poles, he called for even tighter ones.[80] Another pamphlet, by Kaethe Schirmacher, originally given as a lecture at the East German Women's Day, focused on 'The Eastern Danger' in the form of Poles, described as 'an aggressive and rapacious nation, living both inside and outside Germany', increasing internally both because of reproduction and the arrival of foreign workers. The author stated that the German state should stand firm against the minority and not grant it any rights.[81]

By the outbreak of the First World War the scientific racism which would lead to Nazi eugenics had also established itself in Germany. The First International Hygiene Exhibition in Dresden in 1911 opened the German Hygiene Museum. The Racial Hygiene Society, founded in Berlin in 1905, represented an organization which unified 'Pan-German Aryan ideologues' and social hygienists. The trauma and crisis of the First World War helped such ideas to gain wider circulation.[82]

Nevertheless, while extreme nationalism, antisemitism and racism may have become central in Germany by 1918, the ideas circulating during the *Kaiserreich* need not have seized power in 1933 and resulted in the nightmare of the Second World War. The humiliation of defeat in 1918 and the economic crisis of the Weimar years played an essential role in the rise of the Nazis. While we cannot deny the centrality of nationalism, racism and antisemitism

in Germany before 1918, such ideas played just as important a role in the
other major European states.

The fully emancipated Jews

As we have seen, one of the fundamental causes of the growth of antisemitism in the *Kaiserreich* consisted of the resentment engendered by the full
emancipation of the Jews, which they achieved with the foundation of the
new German nation state. The economic success of the Jews, which gave
them a superior social and economic profile to Gentiles also caused hostility,
as did ghettoization in wealthier quarters of major cities. Jews reacted to
the endemic antisemitism in various ways, including an increasing desire to
assimilate, or, at the other extreme, displaying a pride in their Jewishness and
even taking on the claims of the Jew haters.

Demographically, the Jewish population of the *Kaiserreich* experienced
some growth, but did not increase its overall proportion of the German
population. The arrival of *Ostjuden*, whose numbers remained small, made a
contribution to the overall increase in numbers. Between 1871 and 1910 the
number of Jews grew from 112,000 to 615,000, although their percentage
of the entire German population actually fell from 1.25 to 0.95. This is
despite the immigration of Eastern Jews, whose numbers grew from around
18,000 in 1880 to 70,234 in 1910, although this figure could have grown
further had the state not taken measures to expel many of the newcomers.
The expulsion affected 1,800 people resident in Berlin in 1884. The decrease
in the overall proportion of Jews amongst the whole population of Germany
had a number of causes including marriage with non-Jewish partners, which
may have accounted for a third of all weddings involving Jews. Emigration
also took place either to the USA, or, in the case of some of the newly acquired
Jews of Alsace and Lorraine, to other parts of France, so that the Jewish
population of these areas declined from 40,938 in 1871 to 39,483 in 1910.
In addition conversions to Christianity continued in Germany as a whole
while the Jewish birth rate fell by a third between 1880 and 1900, as Jews
became increasingly middle-class. In 1866 Jews in Prussia had a birth rate
of 33 per thousand, compared with 41.1 per cent for the population as a
whole, but by 1910 Jews had half as many children as other Prussians.[83]

The settlement patterns which had emerged in the earlier part of the nineteenth century continued to develop. In the first place, this meant a continued

[90] urbanization, which also increasingly affected the whole of the German population at the time when German industrialization really took off. Thus, the Jewish population of Berlin increased from 47,489 or 9.27 per cent of all German Jews in 1871 to 117,972, making up 20.1 per cent of all German Jews in 1910. In 1900 a total of 43 per cent of German Jewry lived in the 21 largest cities of the German Empire, whereas the figure for the population as whole stood at 16 per cent. Jews also followed the internal migration patterns of the rest of the German population which meant a move from east to west. Thus the number of Jews living in the provinces of East Prussia, West Prussia, Pomerania and Poznań decreased from 116,075, or 22.67 per cent of all Jews living in Germany in 1871, to 78,310, or 13.35 per cent, in 1900. Meanwhile, in the provinces of Hesse-Nassau and Rhineland, the number of Jews increased from 74,813, or 14.61 per cent, in 1871, to 100,356, or 17.10 per cent, in 1900.[84] Eastern European Jewish immigrants also moved to larger cities including Berlin, Dresden, Hanover, Leipzig and Munich.[85]

Whether native or foreign Jews, the new urban dwellers, like all ethnic minorities and like their early nineteenth-century Jewish predecessors, tended to focus upon particular parts of the cities in which they now resided for reasons of security and ethnic solidarity. In some of the cities with significant established Jewish communities, including Hamburg and Berlin, some expansion of the traditional areas of settlement took place, together with the foundation of new ethnic concentrations, often in wealthy areas. Some of the eastern immigrants established their own 'ghettoes', such as the centre of Leipzig, or the Scheunenviertel in Berlin which counted many shops selling kosher food. However, most of the immigrants lived in the same areas as the established community.[86]

Nevertheless, the two communities had quite different social and occupational patterns, although, as a whole, because of its movement to the cities and the escape from the shackles of medieval discrimination, German Jewry differed vastly from the population as a whole. Even in 1871 as much as sixty per cent of the German Jewish population was in the higher levels of the middle classes, outside the petty bourgeoisie.[87] During the *Kaiserreich* as a whole the Jewish community would provide some of the most successful German businessmen including Albert Ballin and Emil Rathenau.[88] Only about 1 per cent of Prussian Jews worked in agricultural employment throughout the Second Empire, providing one of the clearest indications of their change in status since the beginning of the nineteenth century.[89] In 1907, 51.8 per cent of Jewish women and 64.1 per cent of Jewish men worked in trade and commerce compared with just 11.5 per cent of the population as a whole. In contrast Jews were under-represented in industry, at 26 per cent for men and 27.7 per cent for women, to the 37 per cent of the population as a whole, although the figures in the professions did not show such a great variation between Jews and Germans.[90] Important middle-class areas of employment for Jews included trade, transport, catering, the insurance business and textile production. In 1907 Jews made up 6 per cent of all German doctors and 15 per cent of lawyers.[91]

However, in view of the ubiquitous antisemitism which affected all levels of the state, Jews faced strong prejudice in securing government employment, even though they did make breakthroughs.[92] In essence, Jews remained under-represented in most areas of the civil service, especially in comparison with their share of university students, which goes a long way towards explaining why they set up in business on their own, a path which immigrants to the Federal Republic would tread.

In 1895 Jews made up 10 per cent of university students, which again stresses their vast over-representation in the middle classes. However, in 1909, they only made up 2 per cent of German professors and, in contrast, 10 per cent of *Privatdozenten*, essentially qualified professors who had not obtained an established Chair. Even the Nobel prize-winning Paul Ehrlich had never secured a full time professorship at a state university. Practising Jews had the greatest difficulties. But the 'obstacles that Jews faced in universities were negligible when compared with those that they faced in schools' so that, in 1906 just 386 Jewish teachers worked in Prussian schools.[93]

Much controversy raged about Jewish service in the army, especially during the First World War when accusations about Jews as shirkers arose. Never-theless, despite prejudice, members of the minority had served at all levels of the forces in both peace and war. An investigation in 1894 revealed that Jewish participation in the Franco-Prussian War had equalled that of the rest of the population in terms of the percentage of Jewish soldiers and the pro-portion of deaths and injuries. During this conflict 100 Jews had served as officers in the Prussian Army, together with 22 in the Bavarian forces, as well as others fighting for Baden, Hesse, Brunswick and Mecklenburg. But, with the rise of antisemitism in the Second Empire, the numbers of Jewish officers declined. Nevertheless, Jews came to the service of their Fatherland between 1914 and 1918, when 84,352 participated in the armed forces, making up 15.66 per cent of all Jews counted in the census of 1910. Over 10,000 of these, making up 12 per cent of the total, died for Germany.[94] These included Lieutenant Fritz Baer, who in an ominous letter to his parents from the front, wrote:

I have already sent so many lines to you from the battlefield. How often I can still make you happy with these reports is uncertain. Everyday the war demands new victims and who knows when my hour of destiny will arrive, whereupon I will not be able to write such lines again.[95]

Although most Jews may have fallen into the middle strata of German society before 1918, a significant minority still found itself employed in working-class occupations, especially those who had recently arrived from eastern Europe. In 1910 about 20,000 eastern Jews worked in industry, construction and mining. Particular concentrations existed in the Offenbach leather industry, the Leipzig fur trade and cigarette production in Dresden and Berlin. About half of eastern European Jewish women worked in industry, twice as high as for their male counterparts. In Berlin, about 14 per cent of Eastern Jewish women actually found employment as domestic servants. Nevertheless, even the immigrants counted a significant petty bourgeoisie which set up small businesses. Jewish workers increased during the First World War, when the labour importation programmes instituted by the German armies which invaded Poland and Russia brought in about 35,000 of them.[96]

In their religious and cultural lives Jews could react to the increasing antisemitism of the years before the First World War in a number of ways, although completely ignoring it proved rather difficult in view of its widespread nature. Many Jews quickened their assimilation into the German population, through any combination of intermarriage, conversion or name changing, all of which increased significantly after 1871. For instance, the number of Jews who changed their names in Prussia rose from 27 in the years 1862–71 to 288 between 1892 and 1901.[97] Meanwhile, about 1,000 adult Berlin Jews were baptised into Christianity between 1900 and 1908.[98]

Religious activity certainly continued among Jews in the years leading up to the First World War. Despite the emergence of Reform and Neo-Orthodox Judaism earlier in the nineteenth century, few settlements actually developed two separate communities and also integrated the newly arrived Eastern Jews. But conflict certainly occurred between the different sections of German Jewry, especially in the decade before the First World War. The Deutsch-Israelitische Gemeindebund, established in Leipzig in 1872, acted as the unifying national organization for German Jewry, providing large-scale nationwide welfare activities.[99] In 1915 the Jewish community of Munich counted twenty religious or social organizations.[100] Although many Jews became increasingly indifferent to their religion as they progressed up the social ladder, for others it continued to play a major role in their life. Samuel Spiro, born in Schenklengsfeld in 1885 in Hesse-Nassau, later wrote:

I have retained especially vivid memories of the night of the Shavuot festival [93]
and the night before *Hoshana Rabba*. On these nights, the whole community
came together to 'learn', each in his own *chevre*. The 'learning' took place in
private homes. The tables were festively set and covered with all sorts of fruits
and baked goods.[101]

On a more secular basis, the Association for Jewish History and Literature
came into existence in 1892, while in 1915 Munich Jewry counted six student,
three scientific and four youth and sporting organizations.[102] We should also
mention the Jüdischer Frauenbund, which was founded in 1904 and was a
member of the German women's umbrella organization, the Bund Deutscher
Frauen (BDF). The Jüdischer Frauenbund aimed at opposing antisemitism.
Like other groups within the BDF, it was not really a feminist organization.
It had restrictive sexual attitudes, promoted motherhood, told its members
to have large families and also supported the traditional activity of women's
social work. However, the Jüdischer Frauenbund also worked through a
tactic of 'subtle subversion', which included, for instance, challenging Jewish
tradition and the monopoly of men in interpreting the law. The organization
actually counted almost 25 per cent of Jewish women as members before the
First World War.[103]

Some Jewish leaders felt that they had to stand up to the rising tide of
antisemitism. For instance, Rabbi Wilhelm Münz wrote an open letter to one
of the leaders of the antisemitic movement, Liebermann von Sonnenberg,
refuting any allegations about Jews and ritual murder.[104] In addition, numerous
organizations came into existence specifically for the purpose of combating
antisemitism. One of the first of these consisted of Das Jüdische Comite vom
1 Dezember 1880 which, however, only held a few public meetings. More
important was the Verein zur Abwehr des Antisemitismus, which was initially
established by Christians in 1891. When it held its first general assembly in
Berlin in 1893 it counted 13,338 members from 963 localities and published
its own weekly paper. One of its major activities, which reached a peak
during the First World War, consisted of a propaganda campaign against
the claims of Chamberlain. Meanwhile, in 1893 the Comite zur Abwehr
Antisemitischer Angriffe in Berlin came into existence.[105] The tactics of this
organization included the publication of pamphlets refuting the allegations
of antisemites so that in 1896 it produced a leaflet statistically breaking down
Jewish criminality rates and comparing them with those of gentiles.[106] The
most important self-defence group consisted of the Central Verein deutscher
Staatsbürger Jüdischen Glaubens, which also came into existence in 1893
and counted 40,000 members in 1916. It published a journal called *Im deutschen*

Reich, sent out free to libraries and politicians, with a circulation of 37,000 by 1912. By 1918 it counted 174 local branches. One of its major activities consisted of taking legal action against antisemites and their assertions, particularly on the basis of libel, and could count on numerous Jewish lawyers for support. The Central Verein actually established its own legal department as early as December 1893. By 1902 this handled about a hundred cases per year. In addition, like its sister organizations, it also issued propaganda portraying Jews positively against the claims of the antisemites, a tactic which some historians have viewed as defensive and apologetic.[107] A final self-defence group we can mention is the Verband der Deutscher Juden, established in 1904. This launched attacks on the state, pointing to the discrimination of the bureaucracy and calling for its end, while also criticizing the literary images of Jews, especially those perpetuated by academics.[108]

Zionism also developed in Germany during the *Kaiserreich*. The major organization came into existence in 1897 when a body called the National-jüdische Vereinigung joined together with ten other groups in August 1897, the same month as the first Zionist Congress met in Basel, to establish the Zionistische Vereinigung für Deutschland (ZVF). But Zionism remained relatively weak in Germany and tended to attract Eastern Jews more than those born in Germany. Indeed, some of the latter displayed open hostility towards Zionism, stressing instead their German nationality. Zionism, in one sense, appeared like a surrender to the antisemites. Nevertheless, by 1913 the ZVF counted 8,964 members. From 1902 it published a newspaper called the *Jüdische Rundschau*, which had the third largest Jewish circulation in Germany, printing 9,000 copies at the end of the First World War. Although the ZVF had initially fudged the issue of a return to Palestine, a conference held at Poznań in 1912 passed a resolution which obliged 'every Zionist – in the first place the economically independent – to incorporate settling in Palestine into his life's programme'. This especially alienated the integrationist Central Verein, which still had faith in the German Fatherland, and led to conflict, which meant that some Zionists left the Central Verein's ranks, although the two groups worked together during the First World War to establish the Komitee für den Osten.[109]

By the end of the First World War, German Jewry had emerged from decades of antisemitism battered, bruised, traumatized, but very much still standing and as self-confident as ever. Having finally achieved full emancipation in 1871, it had become the victim of vicious, constant antisemitic attacks, led by all manner of individuals, with all manner of justifications for hating Jews. The minority had no choice but to react to the slurs. But, despite the

experiences of the years 1871–1918, the trauma of 1933–45 would simply   [95]
have been inconceivable at the end of the First World War.

The legal exclusion of Gypsies

In contrast to the Jews the Gypsy population of the *Kaiserreich* did not have
the ability to stand up for itself, both because of its tiny size and its social
status. It has more in common with the Polish minority in the sense that it
endured both unofficial hostility and increasingly tight state restrictions. The
link between the persecution of the Gypsies carried out from the *Kaiserreich*
through the Weimar Republic and into the Nazi years, seems even clearer in
this case than it does in the case of antisemitism, because the state did not
practise persecution of the Jews between 1871 and 1933.

At the start of the twentieth century about 2,000 Gypsies lived in Germany, a figure which increased to approximately 8,000 by 1906 as a result of
migration from the Balkans.[110] Although industrialization, state intervention
and missionary activity increasingly controlled the lives of the Gypsies, they
still managed to pursue their traditional way of life. They could, for instance,
still travel for most of the year, although, like their brethren elsewhere, tended
to settle in winter quarters. The south German Gypsies, for instance, remained
in villages near Karlsruhe and Stuttgart, and especially in Alsace where
they hired outhouses, although their stay only lasted for a short period
around Christmas.[111] During this time, much of their activity revolved around
preparations for Yuletide festivities, including the catching of hares. They
heartily celebrated Christmas and New Year and stayed put for a few weeks
afterwards, but looked forward to the opportunity to start roaming again.[112]
For this they needed their caravans, which they still possessed, and in which
they carried out tasks dictated by their taboo system. Thus, Gypsy women
could not give birth in them. When they travelled in small groups they tended
to stick to particular routes.[113]

The Gypsies still tried to carry on with their traditional economic activities, despite the fact that industrialization undermined some of these. Consequently, many Gypsies sank into the subproletariat, although they have
essentially remained distinct from traditional class structures. Occupations
which declined during the course of the nineteenth century included metal
work, basket making and horse trading. Nevertheless, some gypsy trades
flourished including jewellery, textile and carpet selling, while musicians also

did well, as Gypsy music became popular.[114] One of the best known musicians was a blind violinist called J. Reinhardt, who even achieved fame amongst other Gypsies. But despite their technical ability, Gypsy musicians often had to work with poor-quality instruments.[115]

The taboo system still operated in Gypsy life, as it has done and still does for members of this minority all over the world.

> Besides criminals . . . those who consume the flesh of dogs, horses, or cats, or even simply eat out of a pot or dish in which such meat has been kept or cooked, become *bale čido* in a less serious sense. So does a man who eats or drinks out of a vessel which a Gypsy woman has touched with her dress, or grazed, as, for instance, by stepping over it. Such objects must be destroyed immediately, even if they are brand new, and of course anything that is being cooked in them. Speaking ill of one's dead relatives, or one's own wife, admits of no defence . . . A man who has connection with his wife during menstruation, and in general all who commit offences against chastity, whether in or out of marriage (for example visiting prostitutes, onanism, etc., serious crimes which sometimes involve exclusion from society for ever), are outlawed and scorned. Similarly with breaches of morality, unnatural lust, infanticide, etc.[116]

In terms of organization, the German Gypsies had their own elected leader,[117] but by the end of the nineteenth century, 'philanthropic' bodies and the state increasingly controlled their activities. The groups which concerned themselves with the Gypsies included the Mission für Südosteuropa, based in Silesia. Another mission also opened in Berlin in 1908,[118] which provided schooling for the children of Gypsies camped in the city. The people who worked for such organizations had standardization as the goal of their work as they commented negatively on the living conditions and perceived wretchedness of the local Gypsies,[119] despite the strict taboo system, which covers all aspects of Gypsy life, including, as we have seen, cleanliness. One commentator, surveying a settlement in Berlin, whose residents he described as his 'friends', carried out precise measurements of the subjects he studied, a practice which would become commonplace during the Nazi period. Thus he listed seven men and eleven women separately and provided the dimensions of their heads, face and feet, accompanied by comments such as: 'A true Gypsy; upright carriage'.[120]

Such attitudes simply reflected the view of both the populace and the state towards the Gypsies. One Romany wrote that: 'It is notable that the German Gypsies are contemptuously handled and humiliated by all other people', especially those who lived on the land.[121] This tied in with the attitudes of the state. The issue of the 'Gypsy plague' received attention in Reichstag debates,

as well as in discussions of local assemblies.[122] The police displayed particular
hostility towards the Gypsies, especially in Bavaria, where a special office
came into existence to deal with them.[123] Its head, Alfred Dillmann, produced
a *Zigeuner-Buch* in 1905, with a 310-page list of Gypsies who had passed
through Bavaria, prefaced by a negative account of the Gypsies, which essentially resented the freedom that they had to wander between the German,
Swiss, French and Austrian boundaries. Dillmann also focused upon the
ways in which Gypsies made a living, paying particular attention to begging.
He used the word 'plague' liberally. Dillmann further listed the numerous
regulations which existed against Gypsies in Bavaria, before then giving
details of individual Romanies. Some of the entries could contain detailed
information, as the following indicates:

> Amberger Elizabeth (allegedly), Gypsy, as an estimation born in approximately
> 1885, birth date, place of birth, country of origin, nationality unknown . . . She
> was heading towards the district office in Beilingries on 30.6.1903 and then had
> two children of approximate age 1½ and 7 months old with her.

The entry then went on to describe how she had a further six children
with her, who belonged to another couple, at a different location on
10 August 1904.[124]

Not surprisingly, in view of the sort of paranoia about Gypsies indicated
by Dillmann's book, despite their small numbers, new legislation came into
operation under the *Kaiserreich*, especially in those states in the south, particularly Bavaria, which witnessed an influx of foreign Gypsies.[125] This is
despite the fact, again as indicated by Dillmann's book, that previous measures meant that the Gypsies were already a tightly controlled group. The
explanation for this situation includes not only their inability to stand up for
themselves, in contrast to the Jews, but also the fact that many of those after
1900 had foreign nationality. Furthermore, the foundation of the *Kaiserreich*,
as we have seen, intensified concepts of Germans and others, with the Gypsies
representing a social, ethnic and racial outgroup. In addition, while some
people still found the Gypsy way of life romantic and free, both reactionaries
and liberals wanted to change it: the former did not like the difference and
freedom of the Gypsies, while the liberals essentially wanted to improve their
living conditions and bring them to the standards of mainstream society.

Therefore, we should not be surprised to learn that a measure from 1899
required Gypsy children to attend school, otherwise they could be taken away
from their parents.[126] A Prussian measure from 1901 meant that the state could
separate children from their parents and place them in a boarding school.[127]

[98] Another law from 1907 required Gypsies to have a fixed address to obtain a licence for trading.[128] Such measures meant that Gypsies increasingly had to think of becoming sedentary, an underlying aim of all anti-Gypsy legislation through the ages. Therefore, fixed settlements began to appear in Frankfurt, Berlin and Hamburg.[129] Some of the measures passed had more direct aims, particularly the expulsion of foreign Gypsies. Prussia began such a policy in 1906 against those Romanies who could not, beyond doubt, prove their German nationality.[130]

Peripheral minorities: Poles and others

If Gypsies represented the smallest minority in Germany before 1918, the largest included those which lived on the German borders, namely Poles, Alsatians and Lorrainers, and Danes, together with a few smaller Slavic groups. As we have seen, these groups, especially the Poles, received more attention than the Gypsies, largely due to their size, and faced controls of a different type to the smallest minority in Germany, concerned largely with changing their language of communication to German. Such methods essentially represented an obvious way of assimilating the minorities concerned, which we might see as the pre-Nazi German nationalist method of elimination, which would simply turn to the use of force between 1939 and 1945. Nevertheless, far from eradicating its peripheral groupings, the policy of the *Kaiserreich* actually proved counter-productive, because it fuelled the growth of nationalism, especially amongst the Poles. In addition, the existence of foreign protecting states, in the case of Danes, Alsatians and Lorrainers (for those who felt French and did not migrate), as well as the presence of Poles beyond German borders, also gave a boost to peripheral minority nationalism within Germany. Finally, size obviously mattered, particularly in the case of the Poles, although, in the case of Alsace and Lorraine, migration to other parts of France undermined the French-speaking minority and helped the spread of the German language.

Population movement, in the form of an internal migration towards the Ruhr, also affected the Polish minority of Germany. This formed part of the more general east-west movement of all ethnic groups in late nineteenth-century Germany away from under-developed Prussia and towards the industrializing West. Thus, by the outbreak of the First World War, the 'Polish problem' of the early nineteenth century had two foci, which nationalist leaders of the Poles used to their advantage in order to prevent assimilation.

The repressive policies of Bismarck and his successors, particularly the language legislation and the establishment of the Settlement Commission, took place against the background of a fairly obsessive concern with the growth of the Polish population, which resulted in the appearance of numerous publications on the subject. The German population in the province of Poznań had previously grown at a faster rate than the Polish one, meaning that the Germans had reached their 'demographic high point' in 1871,[131] after which Poles maintained their share of the population, both here and elsewhere, due to a combination of emigration patterns and, more significantly, fertility rates. Thus, despite the controls on the official use of the Polish language, the number of Polish speakers actually increased in Poznań from 905,607 out of 1,583,843, making up a percentage of 57 per cent in 1871, to 1,209,119, making up 61 per cent, in 1905, while, in the same period, the German speakers increased from 678,236 to 777,518.[132] A similar picture emerges in Silesia where the number of Poles grew from 973,554 in 1890 to 1,221,268 in 1905, or a percentage increase from 35.21 to 37.72.[133] Meanwhile, in West Prussia, the number of Poles actually fell from 109,553 (18.6 per cent) to 102,080 (13.74 per cent) between 1890 and 1905.[134] Similarly, the Polish-speaking population of East Prussia also declined, quite significantly, from 216,009 (11.02 per cent) in 1890 to just 81,147 in 1910 (3.93 per cent).[135] Nevertheless, for the whole of Prussia, the number of Poles grew from 2,765,101 in 1890 to 3,325,717 in 1905, an increase of over half a million in fifteen years.[136] The census of 1910 revealed that Prussia counted a Polish population of 3,500,621, of which 3,072,118 lived in the four eastern provinces, while the vast majority of the rest resided in the Ruhr.[137]

The above figures reveal some contradictions and require some explanation. It is obvious that Poles increasingly focused upon particular parts of Prussia, intensifying already existing patterns. This growing concentration occurred within the individual eastern Prussian provinces. Thus, in Silesia, Poles found themselves overwhelmingly focused around the eastern town of Oppeln, and largely absent from Breslau further west.[138] In Poznań, meanwhile, Poles dominated the central area, while Germans found themselves focused further north in Bromberg. Similarly, in West Prussia, Poles counted largest numbers around Marienwerder and very much formed a minority around Danzig.[139] The other significant development in the population distribution lay in increasing urbanization within the Prussian East, so that the proportion of urban to rural population in Poznań changed from 29 to 71 in 1890 to 35 to 65 by 1910.[140]

At the same time as these developments occurred, and connected with them through the same underlying demographic and migratory factors, there also evolved the westward movement of Poles towards the Ruhr, which meant that the Polish population of Rhineland Westfalia grew from just 39,846 in 1880 to 497,471 in 1910. Significantly, in view of demographic developments in the eastern provinces, the largest number, 218,269, came from East Prussia while 153,187 originated in Poznań, 94,714 in West Prussia and 31,301 in Oppeln. Moving to work primarily in coal mining, they formed between ten and twenty per cent of the population in some of the areas and towns in which they settled.[141] In Bottrop, for instance, the Polish population increased from just 2,000 in the early 1880s to make up a third of the population by 1906.[142] Concentration in particular areas allowed the formation of ethnic communities, important for the survival of Polishness. Thus, those Poles who moved towards the town of Gelsenkirchen found themselves concentrated in the area of Sophienau, where they made up one third of the inhabitants. Such developments took place against the background of massive expansion of Ruhr towns, whether the influx of population consisted of eastern Poles or Germans. For instance, the population of Gelsenkirchen grew from just 505 in 1818 to 41,716 by 1910.[143]

The statistics from the eastern provinces clearly reveal two separate but linked developments in both the Polish and the German population of the area. The first consists of the purely demographic increase in the numbers of both groups, caused essentially by the decline in mortality and the rise in fertility which affected the whole of Germany during the nineteenth century. The decline in mortality had become a permanent peacetime fixture, while fertility did not begin to fall until the start of the twentieth century.[144]

Equally clearly, the late nineteenth and early twentieth centuries saw a significant migration out of the eastern provinces towards the industrially expanding Ruhr. Between 1850 and 1910, a total of 3,964,200 people left east Elbian Germany.[145] Many of these people actually moved to the USA as part of the mass emigration of people out of Germany which had taken place during the course of the nineteenth century, beginning initially in the south west and gradually spreading to Prussia. A series of push factors caused this movement out of Prussia. In the first place, the demographic growth in itself played a role because it resulted in overpopulation. This combined with the fact that the size of the holdings of the smaller landholders grew even smaller while those of junkers grew larger, resulting in the emergence of unprofitable smaller farming units and an increase in landless labourers. Furthermore, the importation of foreign Polish seasonal migrants from Russia and Austria by the large Prussian landowners to work on their fields for low wages caused resentment on the part of native Poles and Germans. They decided, instead, to move to the higher wages, although equally bad working conditions, of the Ruhr coalfields, where many of them obtained better housing. Over the course of time, attractive ethnic communities developed leading to the emergence of chain migration.[146] Thus push and pull factors combined to force the westward migration out of the Prussian provinces during the Second Empire.

In social and economic terms the Poles of the *Kaiserreich*, whether they remained in the east or moved west, differed from both the Jews and Gypsies. Unlike the former, they did not have anything like the same level of economic success and, in contrast to the latter, they remained very much within the mainstream social and economic structure, concentrated towards the bottom of it, but with characteristics which resembled the mainstream German population.

Those who stayed in the eastern provinces faced a series of contradictory processes. The work of the Settlement Commission established by Bismarck had some influence on patterns of landownership, although not as much as he and his successors would have liked, above all because the proportion of Germans to Poles in the eastern provinces did not drastically change. Nevertheless, the Settlement Commission managed to purchase 126,690 hectares, or 4.85 per cent of land in West Prussia, together with a further 270,708 hectares, or 9.35 per cent of land, in Poznań, although in some areas it bought as much as 25 per cent of available acreage. This clearly worked in favour of the German-speaking element, because Poles could not buy this property back.[147] By the end of 1890 the Settlement Commission had actually spent 30,281,211 marks on the purchase of land, although it had only settled 1,000 German families.[148] Furthermore, much of the land purchased was not in a very good condition and needed improvement. In some cases this necessitated the construction of new buildings so that, in 1890, the Commission had built 132, which it either leased or sold to the settlers.[149] In opposition to the activities of the Settlement Commission, Polish activists established the Polish Land Bank in 1889 for the purpose of refinancing the debts of the Polish gentry, whose land the Settlement Commission purchased and then parcelled out. Although the Land Bank had achieved little in the short run, in the long term it played a role in land redistribution similar to that of the Settlement Commission. Therefore, between 1886 and 1914, while the Settlement Commission established 21,714 new farms in Poznań, Polish private finance initiatives had set up 25,000 new ones.[150] 'On the eve of the war, the nationalities were deadlocked in their competition for landowning primacy, neither one clearly winning or losing.'[151]

At the same time as the changes on the land occurred, industrialization in the Prussian East also began, with both Poles and Germans establishing themselves as businessmen. Figures for Poznań from 1907 reveal that Germans owned 52.7 per cent of industrial concerns, while Poles possessed 46.5 per cent: in total, this meant 23,421 German concerns and 20,797 Polish ones. Most of these firms employed small numbers of people and produced traditional goods such as leather and wood products, together with clothing and foodstuffs.[152] An increase in the number of professionals also took place in the province.[153] The above statistics suggest that the Prussian state had relatively little success in its attempts to Germanize its eastern provinces.

Those Poles who made their way towards the Ruhr coalfields and industry did so as an urban proletariat, typical of international migrations in late nineteenth- and twentieth-century Europe, as revealed in their employment, living and housing conditions. Their ethnic concentration and organization certainly points to patterns similar to those established by people moving across national boundaries. However, while their social and economic patterns may also suggest this pattern, their working and living conditions further reflected that of Germans migrating from East to West.

As the Polish immigrants in the Ruhr moved primarily for the purpose of working and improving their economic position, they consisted, in demographic terms, overwhelmingly of people between the ages of 14 and 40. In 1900 a total of 68.5 per cent of Polish men and 52.3 per cent of Polish women in the Ruhr fell into these age groups.[154] Although Polish men outnumbered Polish women, the discrepancy was noticeable but not overwhelming. Thus the 25,539 men of 1890 had increased to 171,892 by 1910 while the figures for women grew from 10,145 to 131,930.[155]

The vast majority of Poles who moved into the Ruhr laboured in coal mining, so that a sort of chain migration developed, initiated, in the case of Bottrop, by an agent employed by one of the local mines who journeyed east to Rybnik in Upper Silesia in January 1871 and returned with 25 employees. In the next few years agents for other mines also made their way east towards other parts of Upper Silesia and returned with Polish workers.[156] By 1907 over 70 per cent of male employees in the Ruhr with origins in the eastern Provinces actually worked in coal mining, with a further 9 per cent employed in the metal industry, as well as 7 per cent in construction. For Poles, the concentration in coal mining was over 90 per cent during the 1890s. Women, meanwhile, found themselves working primarily in the textile and clothing industries. The overwhelming majority of the newcomers laboured as employees, as very few could accumulate the capital to set up in business in a

short time, a fact which applied to both Germans and Poles.[157] However, people [103]
did change their occupations, especially by the start of the twentieth century,
when many migrants had become established in the area. This is indicated by
the decline in the percentage of Polish males employed in mining and steel
production to 81.5 per cent by 1905.[158]

Employment and living conditions in late nineteenth-century working-
class occupations in the Ruhr were hardly comfortable, but they proved
preferable to those which the Poles had left behind in the East. While the
average annual salary for miners in Upper Silesia totalled 1,204 marks in 1913,
the figure for the Ruhr stood at 1,755. For other occupations in the east,
including farming, earnings would have been less secure. The migrants clearly
took risks, because of the inherent dangers involved in mining. Between 1891
and 1910 a total of 1,779 miners lost their lives as a result of fatal accidents
in the Ruhr. In addition, about two thirds of miners from the East suffered
from illness between 1907 and 1914. Between 1903 and 1905 an epidemic
of intestinal worms spread through the Ruhr coalfields. If one could remain
healthy, the working hours were certainly tolerable in this age when trade
unions reached one of the high points of their strength, because, following
a strike in 1889, hours had gone down to eight per day.[159] Many mining
companies provided their own newly constructed housing at a decent standard. In Gelsenkirchen at the turn of the century, the employees could live in
two to five room houses, which cost between 75 and 155 marks, meaning
that miners only had to spend between five and ten per cent of their annual
salary on rent. A total of 89.9 per cent of the homes actually came with a
garden and stables.[160] The migrants therefore appear to have had an overall
improvement in their living conditions.

By the beginning of the twentieth century both eastern and western Poles
had various choices to make about their ethnicity, which they could ultimately
decide independently under pressure from both German and Polish circles.
On the one hand the Prussian state developed an obsession with the assimilation of Polish speakers. On the other hand all manner of Polish nationalist,
trade unionist and Roman Catholic organizations, concentrating their attention on either eastern or western Poles, and in many cases both, aimed at
persuading Polish speakers to hold on to their original ethnicity, the definition of which meant different things to different pressure groups. Nevertheless, at its most basic Polishness would include some combination of the
command of the Polish language and connection to the Roman Catholic
Church. The central decisions which individuals made therefore included the
language which they used, the marriage partners whom they chose, the length

[104] of time they held on to their original Polish names and the organizations which they joined.

As we have seen, the attempts to eliminate the Polish language from the Prussian east proved unsuccessful, as the number of people who used it remained relatively stable in relation to the proportion of people who spoke German. This was partly because the various measures introduced had not completely eliminated the use of Polish in teaching.[161] This might have changed in the longer run, if no Polish state had come into existence. The move into the Ruhr proved more of a threat in the short run because of a complete absence of Polish institutions there, although these subsequently came into existence. In the longer term, however, the continued absence of Polish schools and the lack of its availability in German schools meant that linguistic assimilation became inevitable in the second and subsequent generations.[162] A marriage between a Pole and a German, either in the East or the West, also increased the chances of the disappearance of Polish language use because of the unlikelihood of the German parent having command of anything other than their mother tongue in the repressive linguistic atmosphere of the *Kaiserreich*. Of children born from such marriages who lived in Poznań counted in the 1910 census, 52 per cent used German, 42 per cent Polish and 6 per cent both languages.[163] In the Ruhr a survey carried out in 1893 demonstrated that 4,563 out of 20,494 Polish-speaking male miners had actually married a German woman, giving a percentage of 40.2 per cent of all married Polish men in the area. However, this figure went down drastically as Polish women began to arrive so that in 1910 only 3.8 per cent of Polish males had German wives.[164] In Bottrop, 14.7 per cent of Polish marriages had involved partners of different ethnic groups, although this figure includes the second generation which always feels more at home with its birthplace and the local population.[165] Name changing by Poles in the Ruhr did not really start until after the First World War.[166]

In addition to language, religion remained just as important an indicator of Polish ethnicity, although the existence of Catholic Germans and Evangelical Polish speakers in both East and West complicated this issue. Thus in the Province of Silesia in 1905 there were nearly 1.5 million German Roman Catholics who made up 29.5 per cent of the population, together with nearly 46,000 Evangelical Poles, who constituted 1 per cent.[167] Nevertheless, the Polish Roman Catholic Church put much effort into retaining its flock once it had moved to the Ruhr, where the migrants would probably have had more of a need for religion during their absence from their homes and where a service in their own language would have been preferable to one in German. The first Polish Church organization in the Ruhr came into existence in

Bochum in 1877 and by the First World War the number of these associ- ations had increased to around 250.[168]

The religious bodies established by the Poles in the Ruhr represented part of a highly developed organizational culture which encompassed all manner of societies. By the outbreak of the First World War these included: 100 singing groups with about 4,000 members; 110 women's organizations, with 8,000 members; and 125 gymnastic societies, with a membership up to 4,700. There were also music, lottery and businessmen's societies. By 1912 a total of 875 Polish organizations in the Ruhr counted 81,532 members. In view of the vast number and variety of Polish societies a series of umbrella organizations came into existence to keep them together. The most important of these consisted of the Związek Polaków w Niemczech, founded in Bochum in 1894.[169] Organizational activity had also taken off in the eastern provinces. In the town of Danzig, for instance, with a Polish minority, a total of 127 Polish societies existed in 1911.[170]

Numerous Polish newspapers reflected the interests of the groups which backed them. The most important of those in the Ruhr included the national-ist *Wiarus Polski*, established in 1890 by a cleric, Franziskus Liss, and with a circulation of 9,000 in 1911. The largest circulation newspaper of all, the *Głos Górnika*, printed 30,000 copies in 1911.[171] Numerous newspapers existed in the eastern provinces. Those in Danzig, for instance, included the *Gazeta Gdańska*, with a circulation of 3,500 in 1913.[172]

The largest Polish trade union in the Ruhr, the Zjednoczenie Zawadowe Polksie (ZZP), owned *Głos Górnika*. Established in 1902, the ZZP counted 75,171 members by 1912.[173] This represented the largest of several Ruhr Polish trade unions before 1918, which participated in several strikes, nota-bly in the early 1890s, 1895, 1899 and 1912. The SPD and their trade unions had attempted to attract Poles into their membership, but this policy had limited success, although cooperation did take place between German and Polish workers' organizations.[174]

When it came to participation in elections, the Polish populations of both east and west had several choices. Many of those in the Ruhr voted for the SPD: candidates of this party were returned in constituencies with heavy Polish populations on several occasions before 1914. Others, especially in the early days of settlement, chose the Catholic Centre Party. In fact, the conflict between the Centre and the SPD, reflected the pressure upon the migrant Poles from clerics and socialists.[175]

In the east, Polish nationalist groupings came to prominence in the final decades of the *Kaiserreich* as an obvious reaction against official Polonophobia. Although the ZZP had branches in the east, socialist candidates did badly. In the Reichstag election of 1912 the population of Poznań cast 343,000 votes for Polish nationalist, and German conservative, liberal and clerical candidates, but only 13,000 for socialists, although they had greater support in the more industrially advanced Upper Silesia. One of the most dramatic political developments before 1914 consisted of school strikes against the language of instruction, which reached their high point in 1906.[176]

The First World War largely solved the Polish problem in the east if not in the west of Germany. In the former it initially created a situation in which Poles would potentially face each other fighting for either Russia or the Central Powers of Austria and Germany. Tsar Nicholas II had promised the creation of a Polish state if he won the war, which meant that the central powers had to respond to the offer. Germany did so officially in November 1916 when it declared the establishment of the Kingdom of Poland. However, this consisted of territory seized by German armies in Russia and did not solve the problem of Poles in Prussia. It caused doubts over loyalty to Germany in the minds of the Ruhr Poles, accentuated by continuing hostility towards them in many circles, as well as the fact that there was little easing of official restrictions towards the rights of Poles in eastern Germany. Polish leaders became further alienated following the arrest of Jósef Piłsudski, because of his demands for Polish independence. Revolution broke out in Poznań at the end of the war, by which time German defeat and the fact that the creation of a Polish state represented one of President Wilson's Fourteen Points, gave birth to a Polish state, out of the parts of it which had fallen to Russia, Prussia and Austria during the eighteenth century. Nevertheless, the new Poland, whose borders took several years to resolve fully, had massive minority problems, not the least of which consisted of the presence of a significant German population.[177] The acrimonious history of Polish–German relations had not ended and would reach its nadir in the Second World War.

Before 1918, in addition to the Poles, there also existed several other Slavic minorities in Germany, two of which had connections with the Poles and whose ethnicity caused much dispute between Polish and German nationalists. The most sizeable group consisted of the Masurians originating in the south of East Prussia, who spoke an old dialect of Polish, practised the Evangelical religion, remained loyal to the Prussian state and may have counted up to a third of the Polish population of the Ruhr, although this represents the highest possible figure.[178] In any case, their ethnic consciousness remained relatively undeveloped, although they did establish their own religious societies in the Ruhr.[179] In contrast to the Masurians there also existed the Kashubians, a non-Polish Slavic Roman Catholic group living in West Prussia,

which also had a fairly primitive sense of their own ethnicity and, like the [107]
Masurians, remained caught between Poles and Germans.[180] Unfortunately
for historians the censuses of the Second Empire did not distinguish between
Kashubians, Masurians and Poles but, instead, lumped them all together. The
1890 count in Prussia also revealed several other groupings including the
Slavic Sorbs (67,967) and Lithuanians (121,345).

In addition, 139,400 Danes also lived in Prussia in 1890, concentrated in
North Schleswig, having remained after the annexation of Schleswig Holstein
by Bismarck in 1864.[181] Since that time some emigration of Danes had taken
place, especially towards the USA. The main development after 1864 consisted of the Germanization of the province in linguistic terms through education laws, as well as through the influence of German political parties, who
came to dominate the scene. In addition, the German nationalistic pressure
groups also took root, including the Deutscher Verein für das nördliche
Schleswig. Nevertheless, Danish ethnicity did not disappear as seen, for
example, by the existence of eight Danish newspapers in 1896 with 9,400
subscribers. Furthermore, like the Poles, the Danish minority established a
network of clubs, revolving around all manner of social and sporting activity.
Much attention focused upon the language issue, leading to the setting up of
several organizations to preserve its use, as well as the circulation of a petition with this aim in mind in 1884. In political terms, however, support for
Danish nationalist parties declined as the mainstream German ones, especially the SPD, increased their influence. In the Reichstag election of 1871,
the Danish Nationalists had obtained 19.8 per cent of the votes cast, while the
Social Democrats had gained 12.2, yet by the 1912 election the two groups
secured 5.5 and 40.4 per cent of votes respectively. When the First World
War broke out the leading Danish nationalists faced arrest and internment.
The end of the conflict resulted in a decline in the number of Danes due to a
plebiscite which changed the border between Germany and Denmark.[182]

Alsace-Lorraine represented another important minority area, in this case
annexed following the German victory over France in 1871. Like Schleswig
and Poznań it contained a mixed population, which, as we have seen, the
new masters of the area successfully Germanized, due to their language policy,
assisted by the fact that emigration took place to France. Nevertheless, traces
of French nationalism certainly survived in the two provinces and this historically disputed area went back to France at the end of the First World War
despite the Germanization of the population which had taken place, destined
for German re-annexation in 1940. Between 1871 and 1918 it had experienced several constitutional changes.[183]

[108] The first example of labour importation

By the end of the nineteenth century Germany had begun to import foreign workers from eastern, southern and western Europe. This process would continue, with short breaks, until 1973. Immigration had certainly taken place into Germany before the 1880s, as the examples of Gypsies, Protestant refugees and Italian craftsmen arriving in the early modern period would testify.[184] Nevertheless, for most of the nineteenth century Germany experienced mass emigration, mostly to the USA. The underlying reason consisted of population growth: this caused pressure on land resources which became increasingly incapable of sustaining the excess people, especially in areas where inheritance laws meant plots of land faced division. The other major factor causing emigration consisted of the pull of the US economy, which had more ability to absorb the excess German population than the German economy did until the end of the nineteenth century. Beginning in south west Germany before 1848, the emigration craze spread gradually north and east to affect the whole country by the 1880s. Between 1816 and 1914 a total of 5.5 million Germans migrated to the USA, while several hundred thousand others made their way to other locations, especially in Europe and South America.

Nevertheless, by the end of the nineteenth century emigration had declined as a factor in German demographic development, so that the last peak occurred between 1880 and 1893.[185] Instead, the economic growth rates of the country caused by the industrial expansion meant that it could now absorb its surplus population, which, in the first place, resulted in internal migration replacing emigration, indicated most clearly by the mass movement of Germans and Poles from East to West. Nevertheless, during the 1880s the number of foreigners in Germany had begun to increase dramatically from the 206,775, mostly westerners, present in 1871,[186] a process which would continue until the end of the First World War.

The underlying cause of the change in German population movements lies in the strength of the domestic economy: industrial growth rates averaged out at 4.5 per cent per annum between 1882 and 1896 and 3.1 per cent from 1896 to 1913.[187] Nevertheless, this only offers a partial explanation, and the full picture needs to take into account a series of other pull factors, as well as the push factors which led people to seek work away from their place of birth, especially Austrian and Russian Poland and Italy.

A large percentage of foreigners employed in Germany actually worked in Prussian agriculture, which means we need to analyse the factors which caused people to work in this sector. In the first place we need to link the arrival of foreigners with the migration of the local population to the USA and then to western Germany. The disappearance of about two million people just to internal migration during the *Kaiserreich*[188] clearly created something of a labour shortage, despite continuing population growth, some of which, however, would have also migrated within Prussia to Berlin and Upper Silesia. Nevertheless, as previously indicated, something of a self-perpetuating process occurred because one of the reasons for the movement of native Poles and Germans out of East Prussia consisted precisely of the fact that Austrian and Russian Poles moved into the area on a seasonal basis to work for cheaper wages.

This brings in the issue of the desire of the large Prussian landowners to use foreign Poles and the efforts which they put into recruiting them, a process which eventually incorporated the state. Initially, recruitment took place directly, involving individuals working on farms or in factories in the case of industrial workers, who liaised with carriers in Prussia or Austria who brought the migrants to the border, from where they were taken to their place of work, a process resembling the export of African slaves. By the 1890s agents had become involved in the process in the countries of recruitment where they placed adverts.[189]

The state became increasingly involved in immigration, thus establishing the importation patterns which would last until the late twentieth century. In fact, the initial intervention of the Prussian state occurred because of its concern with the presence of foreign Poles on its soil during the anti-Polish campaign of the middle of the 1880s, an issue which was whipped up further by the press, which feared increasing Polonization of Prussia as a result of the influx. Consequently, around 40,000 Poles faced deportation between 1885 and 1887, a process which was accompanied by a ban on recruitment. This lasted until 1890 when the large landowners persuaded the government to allow importation to begin again on condition that the workers would only obtain short-term summer contracts which meant that they had to return home during the winter.[190]

After 1890 recruitment became increasingly organized by employers and the state. By 1903 the Ostmarkverein and the Pan-German League, concerned about the influx of foreign Poles, had become involved in the process by establishing the Centralstelle zur Beschaffung deutscher Ansiedler und Feldarbeiter, which, in 1905, became the *Feldarbeiterzentrale* under the Prussian Ministry of Agriculture. This subsequently became the Arbeiterzentrale and had responsibility for issuing permits to both agricultural and industrial

[110]   employees who wanted to work in either the east or the west. The system in which local agents recruited in Russian and Austrian Poland continued.[191]

The outbreak of the First World War, which meant that over three million Germans had to do military service in August 1914, made the demand for foreign labour in all sectors of the economy even more necessary. This was partly met by the use of over 2.5 million prisoners of war during the course of the conflict. Most were Russians but the figure included soldiers from the other states at war with Germany. In addition, unemployment in Belgium and Russia, which the German army invaded, also resulted in the willingness of some of the local population to move to employment in Germany, when recruitment began in 1915. Nevertheless, the outbreak of war also resulted in the decision to hold on to all Polish workers already present in the country, beginning another twentieth-century German phenomenon to be repeated in the Second World War, of using forced labour. By the end of 1916 the invading Germans had also implemented labour conscription upon the local populations of Russian Poland and Belgium.[192]

Any analysis of migration to Germany between 1880 and 1918 clearly has to recognize the primacy of pull factors and the role of the state in the process. Nevertheless, as most of the migrants originated in particular areas, above all Russian and Austrian Poland, push factors also played a role. These resembled those which affected the eastern territories of Prussia in the form of a growing population together with a consolidation of estates by large landholders at the expense of smaller ones. In Russia peasant emancipation intensified this process, because the newly liberated serfs could not afford to pay off the debts which they had taken on to purchase their land and therefore had to sell it. In addition a population growth of 117 per cent occurred in the three partitioned parts of Poland between 1860 and 1910 (compared with a European average of 70 per cent). These factors combined to create a large landless rural proletariat, many of whom went to the USA, but others of which crossed the border into Germany, where, despite the fact that their pay tended to remain lower than that of the local population, it exceeded what they could earn if they remained stationary. Whereas a field worker could earn 15 marks per month if he stayed in Galicia and about 22 in Russian Poland, the figure could increase to 30 marks if the person carried out the same work in Prussia. Apart from these economic considerations, other factors also operated so that, for instance, some women would have moved to escape control of their husbands and fathers.[193]

A similar set of circumstances caused people to emigrate from Italy, again mostly to the USA, but also to Germany. In the first place population growth took off in the late nineteenth and early twentieth centuries, especially in [111] the north eastern provinces which sent large numbers of people to Germany, including Belluno, Padova, Rovigo, Treviso, Udine and Venice. Their population increased from 2,814,000 in 1881 to 3,314,000 by 1901 and 3,999,000 by 1921. Consequently, the size of holdings decreased and did not provide much of a living for their owners, who had to seek alternative employments with larger landholders who bought out the smaller ones. If they became agricultural labourers, they could earn twice as much in Baden as Friulia. In addition, the Italian state also had a positive attitude towards emigration as it would relieve social tension.[194]

Between 1871 and 1918 millions of people, both men and women, made their way to Germany to work in either agriculture or industry, in the east or the west of the country, having arrived at their workplace either voluntarily or through varying degrees of force from a variety of locations. As we have mentioned, the main area of origin throughout this period consisted of eastern Europe, especially the areas of former Poland in Russia and Austria adjacent to Prussia. Thus, in 1907 out of the 882,315 foreign workers in Germany, 212,326 came from Russia while 380,393 originated in Austria-Hungary. A further 129,556 consisted of Italians.[195] Of the 5,317 foreigners in Brunswick in 1900, 66.4 per cent gave their native language as Polish.[196] During the First World War some change occurred in the national and ethnic composition of foreign workers because Belgians made up a large proportion. In the last year of the conflict, the 715,770 foreign workers included 178,911 Russians (mostly Poles) and 110,177 people from Holland and Belgium.[197]

Although the agricultural sector led the way in the importation of migrant labour, industry soon caught up. Thus, by 1907, 294,893 foreigners worked in agricultural employment, while 500,953 were employed in industry although throughout the war agriculture came to use more foreigners.[198] In fact, without foreigners the sugar and potato crop would not have been harvested in the Grand Duchy of Brunswick as early as 1914, before wartime recruitment even began.[199]

While most agricultural workers may have worked in the eastern Prussian provinces and many industrial employees may have moved towards the Rhineland, the example of Brunswick warns us against geographical generalizations. The Grand Duchy also employed over one third of its foreign workers in industry, especially in the mining of lignite, and the manufacture of textiles and bricks.[200] Those who made their way to north west Germany, between Oldenburg and Bremerhaven, before the First World War worked in a variety of occupations including ship building, textiles and the construction

[112] of dikes on the river Weser, while others found employment in peat cutting and brick making.[201] Many Italians moved to work in construction and steel and coal production in the Ruhr and found themselves concentrated particularly in Essen. Italians had come to dominate brick making south of the Danube, while others worked in mines in Lorraine. Only a small minority found employment on German farms, so that, in 1907, 121,000 out of 125,000 Italians working in Germany did so in industry.[202]

Although most of the foreign workers in Germany consisted of men, the figures also included a significant proportion of women. In 1907 a total of 176,418 foreign women laboured in Germany, making up 25 per cent of all non-German employees. The main states of origin again consisted of Russia and Austria-Hungary. Most women worked in agricultural employment, in the case of the 1907 figures, making up a total of 125,239.[203] With regard to demographic features, most of the newcomers, whether men or women, consisted of people who came alone, although they may have had families in their land of origin, in the prime of their working years, which meant that they were rarely under 15 or over 60.[204]

Foreigners labouring in Germany during the *Kaiserreich* faced unenviable working and living conditions. These sometimes represented an improvement on what they experienced in their homeland but usually meant a situation worse than that of native Germans. In terms of wages, for instance, these remained lower for early agricultural migrants in the Prussian east than they did for natives, although some improvement did take place over time. During the early 1890s Max Weber demonstrated that migrant workers, which included people who moved internally within the German east, tended to get paid in kind, which meant that their wages included food and lodging. Thus, in the areas of Stettin and Stralsund on the Baltic coast, he gave the following statistics:

> District of Kammin 2: 12 kg of potatoes per week (origin: Warthbruch, Poznań, Silesia, Russia).
> District of Regenwalde 1: Flour and potatoes (Poznań, Uckermark).
> Pyritz 1: 12 kg of potatoes per week (Warthbruch, Poznań, West Prussia).
> Pyritz 2: The same (the same and from Russia).
> Pyritz 3: 6 kg of potatoes per week (Landsberg) – higher wages, of 2 marks per day, over 7½ months.
> Pyritz 4: 12 kg of potatoes per week (Warthbruch, West Prussia, Poznań etc.) – the same.[205]

Foreign women working on the land generally earned less than German ones: this situation varied from one area to another and they could earn

more.[206] Similar patterns reveal themselves in industrial employment, with
foreign workers witnessing an increase in their wages as the First World War
approached, which meant that they often earned as much as Germans.[207] But
after 1914, Poles earned considerably less than Germans.[208]

Foreigners often had to work long hours in dangerous occupations with
sometimes brutal employers. Those employed in brick making sometimes
worked between 16 and 18 hours per day.[209] The chances of injury were
certainly high: between 1 July 1913 and 30 June 1914 a total of 1,525
Italians in Germany became victims of industrial accidents. Due to a combination of longer working hours, bad living conditions and poor diet,
Italian migrants were more susceptible to sickness than their German
colleagues.[210] Meanwhile, in the east, agricultural labourers often faced
injury due to the actions of their employers, as the following list of incidents
in Silesia in 1913 indicates:

> Werdermühle by Domnowitz, district of Trebnitz:
> The workers were without cause mistreated by their superiors.
> Konstantin Niedziela in Muchenitz in the district of Oppeln hit a 16 year old
> youth in the face and the calves with a stick . . .
> Heinrichau, district of Müsterberg:
> The manager slapped the worker Fedko Hadjuczak in the face and beat him with
> a stick because he turned up five minutes late for work.[211]

The living conditions of migrant workers attracted much attention at the
time, as well as subsequently, and clear parallels exist with the situation of
those people who arrived from the Mediterranean states during the 1960s
and 1970s. The period before the First World War saw the first use of
barracks for the housing of foreign workers establishing one tradition of
foreign worker mistreatment which linked *Kaiserreich*, Third Reich and
Federal Republic. During the 1890s all of the administrative districts of the
Grand Duchy of Brunswick contained such barracks, with the largest lignite
mining firm representing the worst offender in this sense.[212] Nevertheless,
such housing solutions existed all over Germany, including the farms of the
Prussian East, which eventually had separate rooms in some cases. In other
instances migrant agricultural workers had to sleep on the floor in stables
and barns.[213] In Bremen workers would typically initially live in 'workers
homes' provided by employers or would become lodgers with another employee and, if they got married, subsequently move out into accommodation
in immigrant districts.[214]

Foreign workers therefore lived an unenviable existence in the *Kaiserreich*.
As well as the terrible working conditions and accommodation they endured,

[114] they also faced hostility from the German working classes as well as from the trade union and SPD representatives, who essentially regarded them as undercutters. However, in order to solve this problem the representatives of the German working classes wanted to see the foreigners brought into the German labour movement and their conditions improved.[215]

Foreigners in industrial occupations went on strike themselves when the need arose, with the ZZP organizing Poles, although for those working in agriculture little unionization took place.[216] Those employed in industry, who developed a fairly settled existence, also established their own social organizations. Thus, Poles in Bremen set up, for instance, many of the types of bodies which existed amongst their countrymen in the Ruhr, including gymnastic and women's groups.[217] Italians had various groupings in Germany revolving around religion, opera, cycling and a series of other activities, although many of these counted less than 100 members.[218]

The *Kaiserreich* represented an example of a state in which intolerance, prejudice and exploitation formed part of the everyday life of the millions of members of ethnic minorities which lived within its boundaries. It proves extremely tempting to view the years before 1918 as a clear step on the way to Nazism. This may well apply to antisemitism and Polonophobia, although for these prejudices to develop further the disasters of the Weimar Republic and the killing culture of the Second World War needed to set in. On the other hand, one would have to ask how much difference exists between the treatment of Gypsies and foreign workers throughout any of the systems of German government which existed between 1871 and 1945.

Notes

1. Peter Marschalck, *Bevölkerungsgeschichte Deutschlands im 19. und 20. Jahrhundert* (Frankfurt am Main, 1984), p. 146.

2. Clive Trebilcock, *The Industrialization of the Continental Powers, 1780–1914* (London, 1981), p. 450.

3. Volker Berghahn, 'Demographic Growth, Industrialization and Social Change', in Mary Fulbrook, ed., *German History Since 1800* (London, 1997), p. 171.

4. Trebilcock, *Industrialization*, pp. 46–7.

5. Thomas Nipperday, *Deutsche Geschichte, 1866–1918*, I, *Arbeitswelt und Bürgergeist* (Munich, 1990), pp. 34–7.

6. Ibid., p. 291.

7. Ibid., p. 374.

8. The constitutional structure is well analysed by Hans-Ulrich Wehler, *The German Empire, 1871–1918* (Oxford, 1991), pp. 52–71.

9. For the SPD see Stefan Berger, *Social Democracy and the Working Class in Nineteenth and Twentieth Century Germany* (London, 2000), pp. 54–93. For the extreme right see above pp. 78–80.

10. See, for instance, contributions to Gregor Schöllgen, ed., *Escape into War: The Foreign Policy of Imperial Germany* (Oxford, 1990).

11. See Abraham Joseph Berlau, *The German Social Democratic Party, 1914–1921* (New York, 1970).

12. See contributions to Klaus J. Bade, ed., *Deutsche im Ausland: Fremde in Deutschland* (Munich, 1992), pp. 29–122.

13. Eric Hobsbawm, 'Mass-Producing Traditions: Europe, 1870–1914', in Eric Hobsbawm and Terence Ranger, eds, *The Invention of Tradition* (Cambridge, 1994 reprint), pp. 273–8.

14. Andreas Fahrmeier, 'Nineteenth Century German Citizenships: A Reconsideration', *Historical Journal* 40 (1997), p. 731.

15. William A. Barbieri Jr, *Ethics of Citizenship: Immigration and Group Rights in Germany* (London, 1998), pp. 22–3.

16. Ibid., p. 23.

17. Fahrmeier, 'Nineteenth Century German Citizenships', p. 751.

18. See Rogers Brubaker, *Citizenship and Nationhood in France and Germany* (London, 1992), especially pp. 114–37.

19. See, for instance, John M. MacKenzie, *Propaganda and Empire: The Manipulation of British Public Opinion, 1880–1960* (Manchester 1984).

20. Panikos Panayi, *Immigration, Ethnicity and Racism in Britain, 1815–1945* (Manchester, 1994), p. 105.

21. Richard Blanke, *Prussian Poland in the German Empire (1871–1900)* (Boulder, CO, 1981), pp. 20, 22; William W. Hagen, *Germans, Poles and Jews: The Nationality Conflict in the Prussian East, 1772–1914* (Chicago, 1980), pp. 127–30.

22. Eva Rimmele, *Sprachenpolitik im deutschen Kaiserreich vor 1914: Regierungspolitik und veröffentlichte Meinung in Elsaß-Lothringen und den östlichen Provinzen Preußens* (Frankfurt, 1996), pp. 17, 18, 23–41.

23. Hagen, *Germans, Poles and Jews*, p. 135; Blanke, *Prussian Poland*, pp. 60–86; Martin Broszat, *Zweihundert Jahre deutsche Polenpolitik* 2nd edn (Frankfurt am

[116]   Main, 1972), pp. 139–52; Robert Lewis Koehl, 'Colonialism Inside Germany, 1886–1918', *Journal of Modern History* 25 (1953), p. 255.

24. Broszat, ibid., p. 135; Blanke, ibid., pp. 177–202.

25. Broszat, ibid., p. 161.

26. Hans-Ulrich Wehler, 'Polenpolitk im Deutschen Kaiserreich', in *idem*, ed., *Krisenherde des Kaiserreichs, 1871–1918: Studien zur deutschen Sozial- und Verfassungsgeschichte* 2nd edn (Göttingen, 1979), p. 197.

27. Louis L. Snyder, *Roots of German Nationalism* (Bloomington, IN, 1978), p. 94.

28. See, for instance, Imanuel Geiss, *German Foreign Policy, 1871–1914* (London, 1976).

29. For German expansionism see Fritz Fischer, *Germany's Aims in the First World War* (London, 1967). Attitudes towards Poland are covered in Broszat, *Zweihundert Jahre deutsche Polenpolitik*, pp. 175–200. Propaganda is covered by Roger Chickering, *Imperial Germany and the Great War, 1914–1918* (Cambridge, 1998), pp. 13–17, 46–50, 134–40.

30. Geoff Eley, *Reshaping the German Right: Radical Nationalism and Political Change After Bismarck* (London, 1980), p. 122.

31. Ibid., pp. 140–7; Volker R. Berghahn, *Germany and the Approach of War in 1914* 2nd edn (London, 1993), p. 41.

32. Eley, ibid., p. 366.

33. Marilyn Shevin Coetzee, *The German Army League: Popular Nationalism in Wilhelmine Germany* (Oxford, 1990), p. 4.

34. Roger Chickering, *We Men Who Feel Most German: A Cultural Study of the Pan-German League, 1886–1914* (London, 1984), p. 54.

35. Ibid., pp. 74–96.

36. *Handbuch des Alldeutschen Verbandes* 17th edn (Munich, 1914), p. 7.

37. Fuller details about membership and geographical distribution can be found in Chickering, *We Men who Feel Most German*, pp. 102–18, 142–8.

38. *Jahrbuch des deutschen Ostmarkvereins, 1908* (Berlin, 1908), especially pp. 18–20.

39. Chickering, *We Men Who Feel Most German*, p. 242.

40. This point is stressed by Werner Jochmann, *Gesellschaftskrise und Judenfeindschaft in Deutschland, 1870–1945* (Hamburg, 1988), p. 30.

41. Two of the best general accounts of antisemitic ideology are: Peter Pulzer, *The Rise of Political Anti-Semitism in Germany and Austria* (London, 1964), pp. 29–73; and George L. Mosse, *The Crisis of German Ideology: Intellectual Origins of the Third Reich* (London, 1964), pp. 13–145.

42. Jacob Katz, *The Darker Side of Genius: Richard Wagner's Anti-Semitism* (Hanover, NE, 1986), pp. 92–7. [117]

43. See the extraordinary deconstruction of Wagner's artistic work in Marc A. Weiner, *Richard Wagner and the Anti-Semitic Imagination* (London, 1995). See also the brilliant essay by Patricia Vertinsky, 'Body Matters: Race, Gender and Perceptions of Physical Ability from Goethe to Weininger', in Norbert Finzsch and Dietmar Schirmer, eds, *Identity and Intolerance: Nationalism, Racism, and Xenophobia in Germany and the United States* (Cambridge, 1998), which, on pp. 354–63, has a section entitled 'The Jew's Foot'.

44. Katz, *Darker Side of Genius*, p. 106.

45. Paul W. Massing, *Rehearsal for Destruction: A Study of Political Anti-Semitism in Imperial Germany* (New York, 1949), pp. 10, 13; Pulzer, *Rise of Political Anti-Semitism*, pp. 76–89.

46. Pulzer, ibid., pp. 90–3.

47. An English translation of the speech is reprinted in Massing, *Rehearsal for Destruction*, pp. 278–87.

48. Adolf Stöcker, *Das moderne Judenthum in Deutschland, besonders in Berlin: Zwei Reden in der christlich-sozialen Arbeiterpartei* (Berlin, 1880), pp. 21–40.

49. Moshe Zimmermann, *Wilhelm Marr: The Patriarch of Antisemitism* (Oxford, 1986), pp. 8–52.

50. Wilhelm Marr, *Der Sieg des Judenthums über das Germanenthum* (Bern, 1879).

51. Zimmermann, *Wilhelm Marr*, pp. 90–1.

52. Wolfgang Wippermann, *Geschichte der deutschen Juden: Darstellung und Dokumente* (Berlin, 1994), p. 52.

53. Heinrich von Treitschke, *Ein Wort über unser Judenthum* (Berlin, 1880).

54. Mosse, *Crisis of German Ideology*, p. 201.

55. Pulzer, *Rise of Political Anti-Semitism*, pp. 82–6; Mosse, ibid., pp. 31–40.

56. Hans Liebeschütz, 'Treitschke and Mommsen on German Jewry', *Leo Baeck Institute Year Book* 7 (1962) pp. 175–7.

57. Massing, *Rehearsal for Destruction*, p. 75.

58. Ibid., p. 37.

59. Ibid., pp. 24–6; Pulzer, *Rise of Political Antisemitism*, pp. 94–6.

60. Pulzer, ibid., p. 103.

61. Otto Böckel, *Die Quintessenz der Judenfrage* (Marburg, 1889).

62. Otto Böckel, *Die Juden – die Könige unserer Zeit!* (Berlin, 1901).

[118]   63. Pulzer, *Rise of Political Antisemitism*, p. 110.

64. Deutsch-Soziale Partei, *Wie der Jude im Hessenlande 'arbeitet'* (Leipzig, 1890).

65. Pulzer, *Rise of Political Anti-Semitism*, p. 112.

66. Levy, *Downfall of the Antisemitic Political Parties*, p. 90.

67. Massing, *Rehearsal for Destruction*, p. 137.

68. Pulzer, *Rise of the Anti-Semitic Political Parties*, p. 71.

69. Massing, *Rehearsal for Destruction*, p. 113.

70. Jack Wertheimer, *Unwelcome Strangers: East European Jews in Imperial Germany* (Oxford, 1987), pp. 11–41; Steven E. Aschheim, *Brothers and Strangers: The East European Jew in German and German Jewish Consciousness* (London, 1982).

71. Massing, *Rehearsal for Destruction*, p. 113.

72. Levy, *Downfall of the Antisemitic Political Parties*, pp. 154–5. For pogroms in Tsarist Russia see John D. Klier and Schlomo Lambroza, eds, *Pogroms: Anti-Jewish Violence in Modern Russian History* (Cambridge, 1992). For antisemitism in France see Jean-Denis Bredin, *The Affair: The Case of Alfred Dreyfus* (New York, 1986).

73. Arno Herzig, 'The Role of Antisemitism in the Early Years of the German Workers' Movement', *Leo Baeck Institute Year Book* 26 (1981), pp. 248–59; Massing, *Rehearsal for Destruction*, p. 151; August Bebel, *Sozialdemokratie und Antisemitismus* (Berlin, 1906).

74. Egmont Zechlin, *Die deutsche Politik und die Juden im Ersten Weltkrieg* (Göttingen, 1969), pp. 516–52; Jochmann, *Gesellschaftskrise und Judenfeindschaft*, pp. 99–119.

75. George L. Mosse, *Towards the Final Solution: A History of European Racism* (New York, 1978), pp. 73–5.

76. Houston Stewart Chamberlain, *Foundations of the Nineteenth Century*, 2 Volumes (London, 1912), which originally appeared in German in 1900 as *Die Grundlagen des XIX. Jahrhunderts*. For a wealth of information on Chamberlain's life and work see Geoffrey G. Field, *Evangelist of Race: The Germanic Vision of Houston Stewart Chamberlain* (New York, 1981).

77. Steven Beller, *Vienna and the Jews, 1867–1938: A Cultural History* (Cambridge, 1988), pp. 193–9.

78. Lucy S. Dawidowicz, *The War Against the Jews, 1933–45* (Harmondsworth, 1987), pp. 33–4.

79. Daniel Fryman, *Wenn ich der Kaiser wär!: Politische Wahrheiten und Notwendigkeiten* (Leipzig, 1912), pp. 30–9, 74–9.

80. Ibid., pp. 81–3.

81. Kaethe Schirmacher, *Die östliche Gefahr* (Lissa, 1908).

82. See, briefly, Arnd Krüger, 'A Horse Breeder's Perspective: Scientific Racism in Germany, 1870–1933', in Finzsch and Schirmer, *Identity and Intolerance*, pp. 377–8, and, for more detail, Paul Weindling, *Health, Race and German Politics Between National Unification and Nazism, 1870–1945* (Cambridge, 1989), pp. 11–304.

83. Ismar Elbogen and Eleonore Sterling, *Die Geschichte der Juden in Deutschland* (Frankfurt, 1988), p. 249; Wertheimer, *Unwelcome Strangers*, p. 185; Helmut Neubach, *Die Ausweisungen von Polen und Juden aus Preussen, 1885/6: Ein Beitrag zu Bismarcks Polenpolitik und zur Geschichte des deutsch-polnischen Verhältnisses* (Wiesbaden, 1967), p. 20; Vicki Caron, *Between France and Germany: The Jews of Alsace-Lorraine, 1871–1918* (Stanford, CA, 1988); pp. 73–5; Marion A. Kaplan, *The Making of the Jewish Middle Class: Women, Family and Identity in Imperial Germany* (New York, 1991), p. 42.

84. Werner Habel, *Deutsch-Jüdische Geschichte am Ausgang des 19. Jahrhunderts* (Kastellaun, 1977), pp. 78–80.

85. Wertheimer, *Unwelcome Strangers*, pp. 187–9.

86. Ibid., p. 80; Steven M. Lowenstein, 'Jewish Residential Concentration in Post-Emancipation Germany', *Leo Baeck Institute Year Book* 28 (1983), pp. 479–93.

87. Ruth Gay, *The Jews of Germany: A Historical Portrait* (London, 1992), p. 180; Wippermann, *Geschichte der deutschen Juden*, p. 52.

88. Gay, ibid., pp. 169–80.

89. Habel, *Deutsch-Jüdische Geschichte*, p. 81.

90. Kaplan, *Making of the Jewish Middle Class*, p. 159.

91. Habel, *Deutsch-Jüdische Geschichte*, p. 81; Wippermann, *Geschichte der deutschen Juden*, pp. 53–4.

92. For a thorough discussion see Ernst Hamburger, *Juden im öffentlichen Leben Deutschlands: Regierungsmitglieder, Beamte und Parlamentarier in der monarchischen Zeit, 1848–1918* (Tübingen, 1960).

93. Elbogen and Sterling, *Geschichte der Juden in Deutschland*, p. 251; Wippermann, *Geschichte der deutschen Juden*, p. 54; Peter Pulzer, *Jews and the German State: The Political History of a Minority, 1848–1933* (Oxford, 1992), pp. 109–13.

94. Pulzer, ibid., pp. 114–16; Rolf Vogel, *Ein Stück von Uns: Deutsche Juden in deutschen Armeen, 1813–1926* (Mainz, 1977), pp. 35–7, 139; Jacob Segall, *Die deutschen Juden als Soldaten im Kriege, 1914–1918* (Berlin, 1921), pp. 9, 31.

[120]   95.   Reichsbund Jüdischer Frontsoldaten, ed., *Gefallene deutsche Juden: Frontbriefe, 1914–18* (Berlin, 1935), p. 8.

96.   Wertheimer, *Unwelcome Strangers*, pp. 89–102; Marie-Elisabeth Hilger, 'Probleme jüdischer Industrie-Arbeiter in Deutschland', in Peter Freimark, Alice Jankowski and Ina S. Lorenz, eds, *Juden in Deutschland: Emanzipation, Integration, Verfolgung und Vernichtung* (Hamburg, 1991), p. 308; Kaplan, *Making of the Jewish Middle Class*, pp. 160–1; S. Adler-Rudel, 'East-European Jewish Workers in Germany', *Leo Baeck Institute Year Book* 2 (1957), pp. 136–65.

97.   Dietz Bering, *The Stigma of Names: Antisemitism in German Daily Life* (Cambridge, 1992), p. 88.

98.   Richard Mun, *Die Juden in Berlin* (Leipzig, 1924), p. 109.

99.   Kurt Wilhelm, 'The Jewish Community in the Post-Emancipation Period', *Leo Baeck Year Book* 2 (1957), pp. 60–5; Wertheimer, *Unwelcome Strangers*, pp. 123–8; H. I. Bach, *The German Jew: A Synthesis of Judaism and Western Civilization, 1730–1930* (Oxford, 1984), p. 179.

100.   Hans Lamm, ed., *Von Juden in München: Ein Gedenkbuch* (Munich, 1958), p. 30.

101.   Quoted in Monika Richarz, ed., *Jewish Life in Germany: Memories from Three Centuries* (Bloomington, IN, 1991), p. 201.

102.   Bach, *German Jew*, p. 145; Lamm, *Juden in München*, p. 30.

103.   Marion A. Kaplan, *The Jewish Feminist Movement in Germany: The Campaigns of the Jüdischer Frauenbund, 1904–1938* (Westport, CT, 1979), pp. 11, 14, 44, 46, 69, 70, 73, 152.

104.   Wilhelm Münz, *Ritual, Mord und Eid* (Gleiwitz, 1902).

105.   Ismar Schorsch, *Jewish Reactions to German Anti-Semitism, 1870–1914* (London, 1972), pp. 61, 64, 80, 82, 85, 113; Erik Lindner, 'Houston Stewart Chamberlain: The Abwehrverein and the "Praeceptor Germaniae", 1914–1918', *Leo Baeck Institute Year Book* 37 (1992), pp. 213–36.

106.   Comite zur Abwehr Antisemitischer Angriffe in Berlin, *Die Kriminalität der Juden in Deutschland* (Berlin, 1896).

107.   Schorsch, *Jewish Reactions*, pp. 115, 119, 120, 122–35; Elbogen and Sterling, *Geschichte der Juden in Deutschland*, p. 275; Arnold Paucker, 'Zur Problematik einer jüdischen Abwehrstrategie in der deutschen Gesellschaft', in W. E. Mosse and Arnold Paucker, eds, *Juden im Wilhelminischen Deutschland* (Tübingen, 1976), pp. 479–548.

108.   Schorsch, ibid., pp. 157–8; *Das deutsche Judentum: Seine Parteien und Organisationen* (Berlin, 1919), pp. 47–58.

109. Schorsch, ibid., pp. 182–202; Stephen M. Poppel, *Zionism in Germany, 1897–1933* (Philadelphia, 1977), pp. xiii, 21–2, 79; *Das deutsche Judentum*, pp. 29–30.

110. Joachim S. Hohmann, *Geschichte der Zigeunerverfolgung in Deutschland* 2nd edn (Frankfurt, 1988), p. 67.

111. E. Wittich, 'The Organization of the South German Gypsies', *Journal of the Gypsy Lore Society* 4 (1911), p. 291.

112. W. Brephol, *Aus dem Winterleben der Wanderzigeuner* (Seegefeld, 1910).

113. E. Wittich, *Blicke in das Leben der Zigeuner* (Striegau, 1911), pp. 26–31.

114. Wolfgang Wippermann, *Geschichte der Sinti und Roma in Deutschland* (Berlin, 1993), p. 22.

115. Wittich, *Blicke in das Leben der Zigeuner*, p. 7.

116. Wittich, 'Organisation of South German Gypsies', p. 290. *Bale čido* seems to mean untouchable, because when a Gypsy fell into this status, decided, in the case of the German Gypsies, by a court in Alsace during the autumn, 'the offender is for a certain period, or for his lifetime, excluded from all intercourse or dealings with the rest of the Gypsies'. See *idem*, pp. 287, 290.

117. Ibid., p. 287.

118. Martin Block, *Zigeuner: Ihr Leben und ihre Seele* (Leipzig, 1936), pp. 188–9.

119. See Frieda Plinzner, *Bilder aus dem Leben der Berliner Zigeunerkinder* (Striegau, 1912).

120. Johan Miskow, 'A Recent Gypsy Settlement in Berlin', *Journal of the Gypsy Lore Society* 5 (1911), p. 16.

121. Wittich, *Blicke in das Leben der Zigeuner*, p. 31.

122. Rainer Hehemann, *Die 'Bekämpfung des Zigeunerwesens' in Wilhelminischen Deutschland und in der Weimarer Republik, 1871–1933* (Frankfurt, 1987), pp. 214–17.

123. George von Soest, *Zigeuner zwischen Verfolgung und Integration: Geschichte, Lebensbedingungen und Eingliederungsversuche* (Weinheim, 1979), p. 30.

124. Alfred Dillmann, *Zigeuner-Buch* (Munich, 1905).

125. Hehemann, *'Bekämpfung des Zigeunerwesens'*, p. 244.

126. Mareile Krause, *Verfolgung durch Erziehung: Eine Untersuchung über die jahrhundertlange Kontinuität staatlicher Erziehungsmaßnahmen im Dienste der Vernichtung kultureller Identität von Roma und Sinti* (Ammersbek, 1989), pp. 81–2.

[122]   127. Hohmann, *Geschichte der Zigeunerverfolgung*, p. 75.

128. Soest, *Zigeuner zwischen Verfolgung und Integration*, p. 30.

129. Ibid.

130. Hehemann, *'Bekämpfung des Zigeunerwesens'*, pp. 261–2.

131. Hagen, *Germans, Poles and Jews*, p. 138.

132. Broszat, *Zweihundert Jahre deutsche Polenpolitik*, p. 145.

133. Max Broesike, 'Die oberschlesischen Polen, 1905', *Zeitschrift des Königlich-Preussischen Statistischen Landesamts* 49 (1909), p. 25.

134. Waldemar Mitscherlich, *Die Ausbreitung der Polen in Preussen* (Leipzig, 1913), p. 200.

135. Ibid., p. 213.

136. Broesike, 'Die oberschlesischen Polen', p. 25.

137. Paul Weber, *Die Polen in Oberschlesien: Eine statistische Untersuchung* (Berlin, 1914), p. 1.

138. Ibid., p. 26.

139. Broszat, *Zweihundert Jahre deutsche Polenpolitik*, p. 145.

140. Hagen, *Germans, Poles and Jews*, p. 211.

141. Christoph Kleßmann, *Polnische Bergarbeiter im Ruhrgebiet, 1870–1945* (Göttingen, 1978), pp. 260, 267.

142. Richard Charles Murphy, 'Polish In-Migration in Bottrop, 1891–1933: An Ethnic Minority in a German Industrial City' (University of Iowa PhD thesis, 1977), p. 47.

143. Valentina-Maria Stefanski, *Zum Prozeß der Emanzipation und Integration von Außenseitern: Polnische Arbeitsmigranten im Ruhrgebiet* (Dortmund, 1984), pp. 34, 52.

144. For an overview see Peter Marschalck, 'The Age of Demographic Transition: Mortality and Fertility', in Klaus J. Bade, ed., *Population, Labour and Migration in 19th- and 20th- Century Germany* (Leamington Spa, 1987), pp. 15–33.

145. Gerhard Labuda, 'The Territorial, Ethnical and Demographic Aspects of Polish-German Relations in the Past (X-XX Centuries)', *Polish Western Affairs* 3 (1962), p. 247.

146. The above account is based upon Kleßmann, *Polnische Bergarbeiter*, pp. 24–9.

147. Julia Marchlewski, *Zur Polenpolitik der preussischen Regierung: Auswahl von Artikeln aus den Jahren 1897 bis 1923* (Berlin, 1957), p. 66.

148. Heinrich Geffcken, *Preußen, Deutschland und die Polen seit dem Untergang des polnischen Reiches* (Berlin, 1906), p. 114. [123]

149. M. Gehre, *Die deutsche Kolonisation in Posen und Westpreußen* (Grosenhain, 1899), pp. 29, 33.

150. Ibid., p. 49; Hagen, *Germans, Poles and Jews*, pp. 150, 209.

151. Hagen, ibid., p. 221.

152. Max Broesike, 'Deutsche und Polen der Provinz Posen im Lichte der Statistik', *Zeitschrift des preußischen statistischen Landesamts* 52 (1912), pp. 386, 388, 389.

153. Hagen, *Germans, Poles and Jews*, p. 213.

154. Krystyna Murzynowska, *Die polnischen Erwerbswanderer im Ruhrgebiet während der Jahre 1880–1914* (Dortmund, 1979), p. 39.

155. Kleßmann, *Polnische Bergarbeiter*, p. 268.

156. Murphy, 'Polish In-Migrants in Bottrop', p. 46.

157. Murzynowska, *Die polnischen Erwerbswanderer*, pp. 52–4; Kleßmann, *Polnische Bergarbeiter*, p. 69

158. Kleßmann, ibid., pp. 69–70.

159. Ibid., p. 68; Murzynowska, *Die polnischen Erwerbswanderer*, pp. 72–5, 79.

160. Stefanski, *Zum Prozeß der Emanzipation*, pp. 42–3.

161. See Rimmele, *Sprachenpolitik*, pp. 107–27.

162. Murphy, 'Polish In-Migrants in Bottrop', p. 148.

163. Broesike, 'Deutsche und Polen in der Provinz Posen', p. 385.

164. Kleßmann, *Polnische Bergarbeiter*, pp. 72–3, 280.

165. Murphy, 'Polish In-Migrants in Bottrop', p. 182.

166. Kleßmann, *Polnische Bergarbeiter*, p. 73.

167. Broesike, 'Die oberschlesischen Polen', p. 57.

168. S. Wachowiak, *Die Polen in Rheinland-Westfalen* (Leipzig, 1916), p. 61.

169. Hans Ulrich-Wehler, 'Die Polen im Ruhrgebiet bis 1918', in idem, ed., *Moderne deutsche Sozialgeschichte* (Cologne, 1966), pp. 446–7; Kleßmann, *Polnische Bergarbeiter*, p. 103.

170. Dietrich von Oppen, 'Deutsche, Polen und Kaschuben in Westpreußen', *Jahrbuch für die Geschichte Mittel- und Ostdeutschlands* 4 (1955), p. 199.

[124]   171. Kleßmann, *Polnische Bergarbeiter*, pp. 105–10, 281; Murzynowska, *Die polnischen Erwerbswanderer*, p. 94.

172. Oppen, 'Deutsche, Polen und Kaschuben', p. 202.

173. Wehler, 'Polen im Ruhrgebiet', pp. 447–9.

174. For a full account of Polish trade unions in the Ruhr and their relationship with German workers and their organizations see John J. Kulczycki, *The Foreign Worker and the German Labour Movement: Xenophobia and Solidarity in the Coal Fields of the Ruhr, 1871–1914* (Oxford, 1994).

175. Wehler, 'Polen im Ruhrgebiet', p. 451; Wachowiak, *Polen in Rheinland-Westfalen*, pp. 100–8; Stefanski, *Zum Prozeß der Emanzipation*, pp. 160–70.

176. Hagen, *Germans, Poles and Jews*, pp. 256–9; Rimmele, *Sprachenpolitik im deutschen Kaiserreich*, pp. 120–4.

177. For the emergence of the Polish state, see, for instance: Wehler, 'Polenpolitik im deutschen Kaiserreich', pp. 199–201; Konrad Mewes, 'Die Entstehung des polnischen Staates, 1916–1921', in Helmuth Fechner, ed., *Deutschland und Polen, 1772–1945* (Würzburg, 1964), pp. 68–93; and Broszat, *Zweihundert Jahre deutsche Polenpolitik*, pp. 176, 182–91. Ruhr Poles in the First World War are covered by Kleßmann, *Polnische Bergarbeiter*, pp. 145–50.

178. Christoph Kleßmann, 'Long-Distance Migration, Integration and Segregation of an Ethnic Minority in Industrial Germany: The Case of the "Ruhr Poles"', in Bade, *Population, Labour and Migration*, pp. 103–4.

179. Gau 'Ruhr und Lippe' des Alldeutschen Verbandes, *Die Polen im rheinisch-westfälischen Steinkohlen-Bezirk* (Munich, 1901), pp. 88–90.

180. See Oppen, 'Deutsche, Polen und Kaschuben', pp. 157–223.

181. A. Freiherr von Fircks, 'Die preussische Bevölkerung nach ihrer Muttersprache und Abstammung', *Zeitschrift des Königlich-Preussischen Statistischen Bureaus* 33 (1893) pp. 189–96.

182. The above is based upon: Oswald Hauser, 'Polen und Dänen im deutschen Reich', in Theodor Schieder and Ernst Deuerlin, eds, *Reichsgründung, 1870–71: Tatsachen, Kontroversen, Interpretationen* (Stuttgart, 1970), pp. 309–17; Hans Schultz Hansen, 'Demokratie oder Nationalismus: Politische Geschichte Schleswig-Holsteins, 1830–1918', in Ulrich Lange, ed., *Geschichte Schleswig-Holsteins: Von den Anfängen bis zur Gegenwart* (Neumünster, 1996), pp. 459–85; and Otto Brandt, *Geschichte Schleswig-Holsteins* 7th edn revised by Wilhelm Klüver (Kiel, 1976), pp. 279–314.

183. Hans-Ulrich Wehler, 'Das "Reichsland" Elsaß-Lothringen von 1870 bis 1918', in idem, *Krisenherde des Kaiserreichs*, pp. 23–69; Paul Smith, 'The Kiss

of France: The Republic and the Alsatians during the First World War', in
Panikos Panayi, ed., *Minorities in Wartime: National and Racial Groupings in
Europe, North America and Australia during the Two World Wars* (Oxford, 1993),
pp. 27–49.   [125]

184. See the contributions of Rainer Heheman, Heinz Durchardt and Anton
Schindling to Bade, *Deutsche im Ausland*, pp. 271–94.

185. See, for instance, Klaus J. Bade, 'Die deutsche überseeische Massenaus-
wanderung im 19. und frühen 20. Jahrhundert: Bestimmungsfaktoren und
Entwicklungsbedingungen', in Bade, ed., *Auswanderer, Wanderarbeiter, Gastarbeiter: Bevölkerung, Arbeitsmarkt und Wanderung in Deutschland seit der Mitte des
19. Jahrhunderts*, Vol. 1 (Ostfildern, 1984), pp. 255–99.

186. Ulrich Herbert, *A History of Foreign Labour in Germany: 1880–1980: Seasonal
Workers/Forced Labourers/Guest Workers* (Ann Arbor, 1990), p. 21.

187. Trebilcock, *Industrialization*, p. 46.

188. Kleßmann, 'Long-Distance Migration', p. 102.

189. Klaus J. Bade, 'Vom Auswanderungsland zum "Arbeitseinfuhrland": kon-
tinentale Zuwanderung und Ausländerbeschäftigung im späten 19. und
frühen 20. Jahrhundert', in Bade, ed., *Auswanderer, Wanderarbeiter, Gastarbeiter:
Bevölkerung, Arbeitsmarkt und Wanderung in Deutschland seit der Mitte des 19.
Jahrhunderts*, Vol. 2 (Ostfildern, 1984), pp. 445–6; Herbert, *History of Foreign
Labour*, p. 32.

190. Klaus J. Bade, '"Kulturkampf" auf dem Arbeitsmarkt: Bismarcks "Polenpolitik" 1885–1890', in Otto Pflanze, ed., *Innenpolitische Probleme des Bismarck-
Reiches* (Munich, 1985), pp. 121–42; Herbert, ibid., pp. 13–19.

191. Klaus J. Bade, ' "Billig und willig" – die "ausländischen Wanderarbeiter" im
kaiserlichen Deutschland', in Bade, *Deutsche im Ausland*, pp. 315–17; Bade,
'Vom Auswanderungsland zum "Arbeitseinfuhrland"', pp. 454–62.

192. Friedrich Zunkel, 'Die ausländischen Arbeiter in der deutschen Krieg-
wirtschaftspolitik des 1. Weltkrieges', in Gerhard A. Ritter, ed., *Entstehung
und Wandel der modernen Gesellschaft: Festschrift für Hans Rosenberg zum 65.
Geburtstag* (Berlin, 1970), pp. 280–311; Jochen Oltmar, 'Zwangsmigration
and Zwangsarbeit – Ausländische Arbeitskräfte und bäuerliche Ökonomie
im Ersten Weltkrieg', *Tel Aviver Jahrbuch für deutsche Geschichte* 27 (1998),
pp. 142–52.

193. Anton Knoke, *Ausländische Arbeiter in Deutschland* (Leipzig, 1911), pp. 26–35,
46; Ewa Morawska, 'Labour Migrations of Poles in the Atlantic World
Economy, 1880–1914', in Dirk Hoerder and Leslie Page Moch, eds, *European Migrants: Global and Local Perspectives* (Boston, 1996), p. 175; Kathrin

Roller *Frauenmigration und Ausländerpolitik im deutschen Kaiserreich: Politische Arbeitsmigrantinnen in Preußen* (Berlin, 1994), p. 25.

194. For a full discussion of the Italian causes of migration see: Adolf Wennemann, *Arbeit im Norden: Italiener im Rheinland und Westfalen des späten 19. und frühen 20. Jahrhunderts* (Osnabrück, 1997), pp. 47–67; and René Del Fabbro, *Transalpini: Italienische Arbeitswanderung nach Süddeutschland im Kaiserreich, 1870–1918* (Osnabrück, 1996), pp. 47–82.

195. Herbert, *History of Foreign Labour*, p. 23.

196. Karl Liedke, '. . . *aber politisch unerwünscht': Arbeitskräfte aus Osteuropa im Land Braunschweig 1880 bis 1939* (Brunswick, 1939), p. 23.

197. Herbert, *History of Foreign Labour*, p. 108.

198. Ibid., pp. 22, 107–8.

199. Liedke, '. . . *aber politisch unerwünscht'*, p. 83.

200. Ibid., pp. 39, 47.

201. Karl Marten Barfuss, *'Gastarbeiter' in Nordwestdeutschland, 1884–1918* (Bremen, 1986), p. 55, 61, 67, 72.

202. The full details can be found in Del Fabbro, *Transalpini*, pp. 135–203; Wennemann, *Arbeit im Norden*, pp. 111–30; and Wilhelm Stieda, 'Ausländische Arbeiter in Deutschland', *Zeitschrift für Agrarpolitik* 9 (1911), p. 360.

203. Roller, *Frauenmigration*, pp. 52–3.

204. See, for instance, the figures for Italians in the Rhineland during the early 1890s given by Wennemann, *Arbeit im Norden*, p. 42.

205. Max Weber, *Die Lage der Landarbeiter aus dem ostelbischen Deutschland* (originally 1892; Tübingen, 1984), p. 460.

206. Roller, *Frauenmigration*, p. 85.

207. Bade, ' "Billig und Willig" ', p. 318.

208. Herbert, *History of Foreign Labour*, pp. 109, 113.

209. Bade, ' "Billig und Willig" ', p. 318.

210. Wennemann, *Arbeit im Norden*, pp. 133, 139.

211. For a fuller list of incidents see Johannes Nichtweiß, *Die ausländischen Saisonarbeiter in der Landwirtschaft der östlichen und mittleren Gebiete des deutschen Reiches: Ein Beitrag zur Geschichte der preussisch-deutschen Politik von 1890–1914* (Berlin, 1959), pp. 224–8.

212. Liedke, ' . . . *aber politisch unerwünscht*', pp. 50–1.

213. Knoke, *Ausländische Wanderarbeiter*, p. 48.

214. Barfuss, *'Gastarbeiter' in Nordwestdeutschland*, pp. 145–8.

215. Herbert, *History of Foreign Labour*, pp. 69–72; Franz Laufkötter, 'Das Verhältniss zwischen den einheimischen und den fremden Arbeitern', *Sozialistische Monatshefte* 10 (1904), pp. 801–6.

216. Liedke, ' . . . *aber politisch unerwünscht*', p. 68; Roller, *Frauenmigration*, p. 124.

217. Barfuss, *'Gastarbeiter' in Nordwestdeutschland*, p. 232.

218. Del Fabbro, *Transalpini*, pp. 221–3; Wennemann, *Arbeit im Norden*, pp. 157–8; Luciano Trincia, *Migration und Diaspora: Katholische Kirche und italienische Arbeitswanderung nach Deutschland und der Schweiz vor dem Ersten Weltkrieg* (Freiburg im Breisgau, 1998).

CHAPTER 4

A Liberal Interlude? The Weimar Republic, 1919–33

Economic, social and political background

The Weimar Republic, which came into existence in the humiliation of German surrender at the end of the First World War and remained in existence until the Nazis seized power, has a series of apparently diverse characteristics. In contrast with the previous century of German evolution, the years 1919–33 represent a period in which Germany had suffered a serious reverse. After the hubris in the sunshine of August 1914, the downfall of the winter of 1918 proved particularly bitter. In the years leading up to 1914, it seemed to the German nationalists that the future belonged to them. For such people, the Weimar years, in contrast, essentially symbolized a period in which Germany had become the victim of external enemies, in the form of the British, French and Americans, who had worked in tandem with internal ones, in the form of Jews and Bolsheviks. Superficially, the Weimar years represent a period in which the aggressive nationalists who had increasingly dominated German politics as the nineteenth century progressed, appear to have lost the upper hand. Instead, the other political grouping which had increased its influence during the *Kaiserreich* in the form of the SPD, finally tasted power at the end of the First World War. In theory this should have meant that the Weimar Republic became a less nationalistic and more tolerant state than its immediate predecessor. This certainly happened in some ways, as indicated by the decadence of Weimar culture. Furthermore, politics became more fluid, as evidenced by the seizure of power by a former vagrant in 1933. While a revolution may have given birth to the Republic, those members of the SPD who seized power quickly ditched their former more extreme allies and moved into an alliance with the old order. Consequently, any notions of a progressive Weimar Republic need balancing against the fact that nationalism and reaction constantly simmered, usually above the surface. The experience of those minorities which remained within German borders after the carve up of Versailles did not differ much from that of the years before 1918, especially as the Nazis marched to power using brutal tactics, particularly against their nemesis in the form of the Jews.

Economically, Weimar was a catastrophe in comparison with both her predecessors and successors, representing a failed interlude in the forward march of German industrialization. Although some growth did take place in the period 1924–29, these years equate to a thin slice of meat in a sandwich of thick and unpalatable bread of economic disaster caused by the reparations crisis and bankruptcy of 1919–23, and the consequences of the Wall Street Crash from 1929 to 1933. In the early post-war years Germany faced problems of starvation and fiscal collapse. The neglect of agriculture during the war due to mass mobilization, and the consequences of the Allied Blockade, meant widespread food shortages in 1919. The financial burden of reparations led to the currency collapse and inflation of the early Weimar years. In addition, Germany also faced the demobilization problems of other states which had participated in the First World War.[1] Even during the recovery of 1924–29, growth remained patchy and basic structural problems had not been solved.[2] The uneven expansion of 1924–29 collapsed with the Wall Street Crash, leading to more financial disaster as German banks, dependent on US support, dropped like flies. Unemployment represented the most concrete manifestation of the 1929–33 crisis, reaching an official total of six million by the time the Nazis came to power, although the real figure may have been much higher.[3] The callous policies of the various short-lived governments of the period 1929–33 meant that, in the winter of 1932–33, there may have been 'over a million people capable of work who were without either a job or any form of support'.[4]

In social terms, perhaps the most unusual characteristic of the Weimar Republic consisted of the fact that the middle classes suffered particularly badly as a result of the inflation of the early 1920s, one of the reasons for their over-representation in support for the Nazis. Nevertheless, it could not be said that they endured the worst deprivation, as the peasantry and the working classes also became victims of the international agricultural crisis of the 1920s and the rise in unemployment respectively.[5] The Weimar Republic broke new ground in various aspects of social policy, including the guaranteeing of workers' rights. In the words of Detlev J. Peukert, it created a 'welfare state', resulting, in 1927, in the introduction of unemployment insurance, although measures introduced in the early 1920s had also attempted to help the unemployed.[6]

In political terms Weimar, born in revolution, resembles events in 1848, not only because of the uprising from below, but because the old order regained the initiative, both in the short run, in 1919, and in the long run, in 1933. The events in Germany in 1918 remained quite different from those in the Russian Empire of the previous year. The German revolution did not result in a root and branch reconstruction of society, but meant, instead, essentially a change in the nature of government, from a sham democracy to a 'real' democracy, in which the legislature had power but where the President replaced the Kaiser at the top of the executive, with the ability to act independently in times of emergency. In the context of both German and European history the Weimar Republic represents a progressive liberal democracy.

In fact, it may have been too progressive, perpetuating the plethora of parties covering all sections of the political spectrum. The system of proportional representation meant that any party could, in theory, rise from nothing to seize power, which true liberals must have viewed positively. As we know, this did actually happen, but the group which managed to succeed in this way completely despised and destroyed the free and open democracy which had allowed it to come to power.[7]

In diplomatic terms the Weimar Republic represented a pale shadow of the previous German nation state because of the consequences of the vindictive Treaty of Versailles, essentially a diktat from the victorious Allies. This meant that Germany lost territory to the north, south, east and west, which helped lessen its peripheral minority problems, but created German populations in the new Polish state (which obtained Poznań, West Prussia and Upper Silesia), Denmark (which gained north Schleswig) and Belgium (which took Eupen and Melmedy). In addition, Alsace and Lorraine went to France, while the remaining areas west of the Rhine came under Allied occupation. The new German state faced further emasculation because of limitations on the size of its naval, air and military forces. In addition, the rump German state had to pay 132 billion marks in reparations.[8]

The above terms caused deep resentment, especially amongst the extreme German nationalists, determined to reverse Versailles at any cost, a task which Hitler would eventually accomplish by force. In fact, none of the inter-war governments actually accepted Versailles; they simply did not have the self confidence to stick two fingers up to the Allies in the way that Hitler would do. Instead, people such as Gustav Stresseman, tried to reverse Versailles by diplomatic means and therefore return Germany to a place of respectability amongst the world's nation states, escaping from its position as a despised outcast.[9]

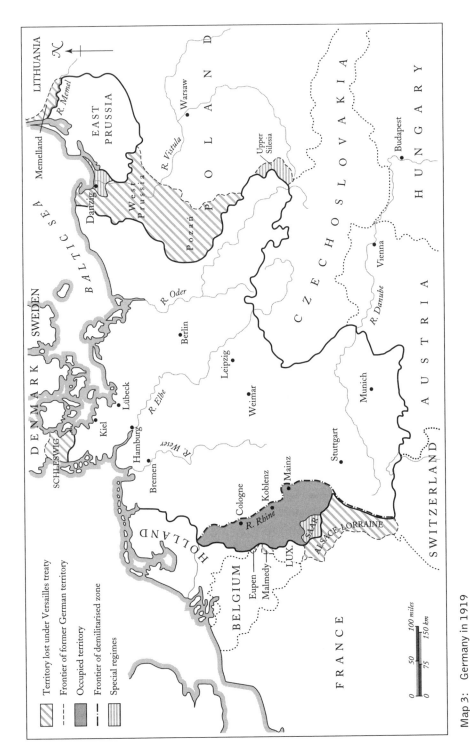

Map 3: Germany in 1919

Source: William Carr, *A History of Germany, 1815–1945*, 2nd edn (London: Arnold, 1979) p. 273.

Legend:
- Territory lost under Versailles treaty
- Frontier of former German territory
- Occupied territory
- Frontier of demilitarised zone
- Special regimes

Clearly, as Germany did not face complete destruction, nationalism within it continued to exist. On the one hand this manifested itself in the virulent views of groups such as the Deutschvölkischer Schutz und Trutz Bund (DSTB) and the rising Nazis, both of which had their origins in the Pan-German League. On the other hand the normal structures of a nation state meant that Weimar acted as such an entity always does with regard to the treatment of ethnic insiders and outsiders, as well as the preaching of the nationalist message through, for instance, the education system.[10] However, the Weimar Republic dealt with its ethnic groupings better than either its immediate predecessor or successor.

This was hardly difficult to do in comparison with the Third Reich, but Weimar did not represent an ethnic paradise. For instance, the state simply continued the traditions of its predecessors towards the Gypsies, which very much linked Wilhelmine with Nazi Germany, while those Poles who remained in the East also faced armed suppression following uprisings immediately after the war. Even if Weimar did not persecute its minorities in the same way as the Second or Third Reich, the mere presence of groups such as the NSDAP hardly made the Jews feel any more comfortable than they did before 1918, especially as the Nazis employed violent tactics, uncharacteristic of previous antisemitic groups.

In addition, many of the ideas which Hitler and his followers would put into practice had widespread credibility during the 1920s. Of the other right wing groups, the reconstituted mainstream Conservative Party, which renamed itself the Deutsche Nationale Volkspartei, adopted, as its name suggests, völkisch and antisemitic principles, with which, however, the group had flirted before 1918.[11] Furthermore, scope existed for propagation of racial ideas in the written word, especially through the publisher Julius Lehmann. During the 1920s eugenic ideas increasingly moved into the mainstream,[12] meaning that their implementation by the Nazis had immediate precedents. Weimar represented a nationalist state and an increasingly racist one, especially for Jews, whose position certainly deteriorated, either because of persecution or economic collapse.

With the exception of the GDR, the Weimar Republic represents the most ethnically pure manifestation of German statehood in the sense of the small number of ethnic groupings it counted. The explanation for this does not simply lie in the carving up of Germany at the end of the war, which largely eliminated the Danish and eastern Polish problem, as well as completely cutting away Alsace Lorraine. In addition, in contrast to the labour shortage of the *Kaiserreich* and the early decades of the Federal Republic, an over-supply

of domestic labour and consequent unemployment characterized the Weimar
Republic, meaning that the need for foreign workers remained largely absent
for much of the 1920s and early 1930s, although they did not actually disappear. Ruhr Poles certainly remained, but began to decrease, either because
of migration to the new Polish state and elsewhere, or as a result of assimilation.
Gypsies continued as a small group, but, as ever, attracted a remarkable amount
of attention considering their size.

Jewish life: success, economic disaster and antisemitism

Despite the claims of Nazi propaganda, the position of the Jews in Germany
during the 1920s had more negative than positive aspects. True, on the
one hand, they continued to represent a minority characterized by privilege,
compared with the rest of the German population, a fact which, as in
the *Kaiserreich*, provided much of the basis for the virulence of antisemitic
hatred. But the strength of opposition towards them, especially as the Nazis
neared their ultimate goal of power, made their lives increasingly difficult.
Furthermore, like the rest of the German population, they also faced the
consequences of the failed Weimar economy.

In demographic terms, in accordance with its status as an overwhelmingly
bourgeois grouping, German Jewry actually experienced a numerical decline
under the Weimar Republic, at a time when the rest of the population simply
witnessed a fall in growth rates compared with the pre-war period. Although
a Jewish increase had occurred between the 1910 figure of 539,000 to one of
568,000 in 1925, the number of German Jews fell to 503,000 by 1933, when
they made up just 0.76 per cent of the population. Some Jewish emigration
took place before 1933, whether for political or economic reasons, as a total
of 603,000 people of all religions left Germany between 1919 and 1932. At
the same time conversion and assimilation continued. But the main explanation for the decline in Jewish numbers lies in the fact that the Jewish death
rate surpassed the figure for births. Between 1880 and 1884 Jewish births
had totalled 27.9 per thousand in comparison with 17.2 deaths, but between
1930 and 1932 the figures had fallen to 7.2 and 14.4 respectively, compared
with the respective German figures of 16.2 and 11 in the latter years.[13] However, the percentage of Jews who married Gentiles also increased from 11 per
cent in 1910 to 20 per cent by 1930.[14]

Table 1:   Major Jewish urban concentrations under the Weimar Republic

	1910		1925		1933	
	Absolute number	% of city	Absolute number	% of city	Absolute number	% of city
Berlin	144,007	3.9	172,672	4.3	160,564	3.8
Frankfurt	26,228	6.3	29,385	6.3	26,158	4.7
Breslau	20,212	3.9	23,240	4.2	20,202	3.2
Hamburg	19,472	1.9	19,904	1.8	16,885	1.5
Cologne	12,393	2.0	16,093	2.3	14,816	1.9
Leipzig	9,434	1.6	12,540	1.8	11,564	1.6
Munich	11,083	1.9	10,068	1.5	9,005	1.2

Source: Dieter Goetz, *Juden in Oldenburg, 1930–1938* (Oldenburg, 1988), p. 24.

Local Jewish population figures mirror the national picture. The number of Jews in Munich fell by 9 per cent after the First World War as a result of war losses, the decline of the birth rate, an increase in emigration after the 1923 Beer Hall Putsch, and the fact that no foreign Jews from Austria or Russia moved to the city, as they had done before 1914.[15] Thus the 1925 figure of 10,068 had fallen to 9,005 by 1933. The other large Jewish communities of Berlin, Frankfurt am Main, Breslau, Hamburg, Cologne and Leipzig experienced corresponding declines. Similarly, smaller Jewish communities also witnessed a decrease in numbers, as evidenced by the Jews of Osnabrück, whose total went from a peak of 474 in 1905 to 454 in 1925 and 435 in 1933, when they made up just 0.45 per cent of the town's population.[16]

As a consequence of high mortality and low fertility, the Jews were older than the general population. In 1933, while 30.8 per cent of all Germans were less than twenty, the Jewish figure totalled just 21.5. Similarly, while 21.7 per cent of the whole population was over fifty, the Jewish figure reached 31.6, although, in both sets of figures, foreign Jews had a slightly younger age profile than native ones.[17]

The Jewish urban concentration which had evolved during the course of the nineteenth century intensified further during the Weimar Republic. In 1925, when 61.1 per cent of the entire population of Germany lived in towns with less than 20,000 inhabitants, the figure for Jews totalled just 20.8 per cent. Furthermore, 26.8 per cent of all Germans lived in cities of over 100,000 inhabitants compared with 66.8 per cent of Jews. By 1933 the Jewish figure for small towns had fallen further to 18.9 per cent, while that for large cities had reached 70.9 per cent. Of particular significance is the concentration of Jews in Berlin, which housed a third of German Jewry by 1925. Nevertheless, 1,600 synagogue communities still existed in 1933,[18] indicating a continuation of geographical dispersal, although some cities would clearly have contained more than one settlement. Berlin counted twenty different locations in which Jews made up more than 0.5 per cent of the population, from the rich suburbs, such as Halensee and Grunewald, to the poorer areas which often housed eastern European immigrants, including Dragoner- and Grenadierstrassen.[19] Nevertheless, at least two thirds of German Jewry 'lived in sophisticated, upper-middle class districts' of the large cities in which they concentrated.[20]

The settlement patterns of German Jewry reflect its social and economic status, which continued the employment divisions established under the *Kaiserreich*. Table 2 demonstrates the continuing focus upon middle class non-agricultural employment, a fact which fuelled the resentments of the antisemites. Jews had particular concentrations in specific middle class occupations. For instance, in 1930 they owned nearly 40 per cent of wholesale textile firms. In 1932, Jews accounted for 79 per cent of business carried

Table 2:   Percentage of Jews in specific economic activities during the Weimar Republic compared with the rest of the population

	1907		1925		1933	
	Jews	Whole population	Jews	Whole population	Jews	Whole population
Agriculture and Forestry	1.58	36.28	1.91	30.5	1.73	28.9
Industry and Crafts	26.54	42.0	24.24	42.1	23.14	40.4
Trade and Communication	61.35	13.0	61.32	16.4	61.27	18.4
Services	7.94	6.5	9.72	6.7	12.46	8.4
Domestic Service	2.59		2.81		1.40	

Source: Abraham Barkai, 'Die Juden als Sozio-ökonomische Minderheitsgruppe in der Weimarer Republik', in Walter Grab and Julius H. Schoeps, eds, *Juden in der Weimarer Republik* (Stuttgart, 1986), p. 333.

out by department stores, a fact to which the Nazis devoted particular attention. Furthermore, in 1933 Jews made up 11 per cent of German doctors and 16 per cent of lawyers.[21] Jews made some breakthrough into the public sector, which had tried to bar them from employment under the *Kaiserreich*, although prejudice still existed. In the judicial sphere, Jews began to obtain positions as magistrates, although they faced hostility once they had secured them. The number of practising or baptized Jewish full professors increased from 69 in 1909–10 to 114 by 1931–32, although their share of all such appointments had fallen from 6.9 to 5.6 per cent.[22]

Many Weimar Jews rose to prominence in culture and politics. 'What today we are apt to call Weimar culture was largely the creation of left-wing intellectuals, among whom there was such a disproportionate number of Jews that Weimar Culture has been called, somewhat snidely, an internal Jewish dialogue'.[23] Jews made their living as theatre directors, actors, film producers, critics, artists, composers and authors. One need only mention the names of Fritz Lang, Max Reinhardt, Arnold Zweig, Franz Kafka, Bruno Walter, Otto Klemperer, Kurt Weill and Alexander Korda.[24] Jews also made a breakthrough in politics, most famously Walther Rathenau, who became foreign minister in January 1922 but became the victim of antisemitic assassins in June of the same year. After that Jews remained largely absent from cabinet positions, with the exception of Rudolf Hilferding, who twice became finance minister, while Erich Koch-Weser and Curt Joël held the justice portfolio. In total just five people of Jewish descent held cabinet positions in the Weimar Republic, three of whom were not practising Jews. The other two consisted of Hugo Preuß and Otto Landsberg. We also need to mention Kurt Eisner, who headed the Bavarian Soviet Republic briefly established in January 1919.[25]

The economic picture for German Jews did not simply contain the bright colours of success, especially against the background of the constant economic crisis. Even if we ignore the depression, the *Ostjuden* did not have the same occupational pattern as German Jewry as a whole. An individual in this group, who made up twenty per cent of all Jews in Germany, 'was forced to eke out an existence as an industrial worker, minor artisan, or itinerant salesman'.[26] Jews as a whole suffered at least as badly as the rest of the population from both the inflation of the early Weimar years and the final economic crisis which affected Germany after 1929. The concentration of Jews in the middle classes meant that they suffered especially from the inflation, which most affected those with money, although some members of the minority managed to do well out of it. After 1929, Jewish unemployment figures paralleled those of the rest of the population. In Frankfurt young Jews under the age of 25 had a higher unemployment rate than Gentiles in 1931. Consequently, Jewish welfare agencies worked flat out to help the unemployed, poor and destitute.[27] In Prussia and Berlin the social position of Jews deteriorated, as is indicated by a decline in the number of self-employed people and a rise in manual workers.[28] While the income of self-employed people went down in real terms by 47 per cent between 1913 and 1933, that of wage earners declined by 19 per cent.[29]

The period during and after the First World War saw several developments in the ethnic and religious history of German Jewry. In the first place the practice of Judaism declined, although individuals such as Leo Baeck tried to stress the religious uniqueness of Jews against increasing secularization and stressed Judaism as a way of life.[30] Such ideas had limited impact, indicated, for instance, by the fact that the number of rabbinical students declined and by the fact that, even on the holiest Jewish days during the later 1920s, only between forty and sixty per cent of the Jews of Breslau, Frankfurt and Berlin attended synagogue.[31] Hannele Zürndorfer, born in Düsseldorf in 1925, remembered that: 'Although my father was wholeheartedly Jewish, we kept Christmas, as well as Channukah, and Easter as well as Passover.'[32] In Osnabrück Jews divided into various groupings consisting of Orthodox, Reform and, in between, Conservative.[33] Meanwhile, in Munich, the number of social and religious organizations had actually increased from 20 in 1915 to 38 by 1932.[34]

In the Weimar period, as in the years before the First World War, numerous non-religious Jewish organizations existed. Zionism, for instance, continued to hold much strength, especially among east European Jews, although the membership figure for the Zionistische Vereinigung für Deutschland had declined from around 20,000 in the early 1920s to less than 7,546 by 1932, yet it would subsequently increase dramatically as a reaction against Nazi policies. Zionism had taken ideological leaps forward through the works of individuals such as Martin Buber, who developed ideas about Jews as a racial group linked by blood, which therefore mirrored the views of many Weimar antisemites, and essentially represented a continuing reaction against them.[35] The Jewish defence organizations established during the late nineteenth century also continued to exist, notably the Central Verein, whose membership grew from 45,000 in 1918 to 64,000 by 1933. New bodies also came into existence, including the National League of Jewish Frontline Soldiers, concerned with defending the record of Jewish servicemen in the First World War against the slurs of antisemites. It became the second largest Weimar Jewish grouping, counting 30,000 members by 1932.[36] Meanwhile, the Preußische Landesverband Jüdischer Gemeinden was formed in 1922 with the aim of spiritually and financially assisting the 400,000 Jews of Prussia.[37] In Osnabrück all manner of Jewish organizations existed in addition to those of a religious and philanthropic nature. These included a Society for Jewish Literature and Culture, established in 1913, and a Jewish tennis club, which came into existence because the main tennis organization in Osnabrück refused to accept Jews as members.[38]

'Antisemitism was endemic to Weimar Germany',[39] and its manifestations countless, leaving Jews in little doubt about their status as a minority. The hostility towards this minority continued the Judeophobia which had become so widespread before 1918, but, with the rise of organizations such as the Nazis, became increasingly violent. While many Jews certainly experienced success during the 1920s, the negative gentile perception of them meant that they could not ignore the hostility which existed, even though, because of their concentration in bourgeois suburbs, few of them ever became the victims of racial attacks.[40] The Weimar Republic certainly represents a direct link between Wilhelmine and Nazi antisemitism, but 1933 certainly did not seem inevitable in 1919, or even in 1929.

Overt and virulent antisemitism existed throughout the Weimar period, even though it may have become increasingly violent and widespread after 1929 as the Nazis came ever closer to seizing power, a process which involved both the jackboot and the ballot box. At the start of the Weimar Republic there existed 400 völkish organizations together with 700 antisemitic journals.[41] The Deutscher Volksbund, for instance, wanted to see the expulsion of the Jews from Germany even if this meant the use of violence, indicating that the new post-war breed of antisemite, born in the defeat of 1918, for which Jews always held some responsibility, no longer minced his words. Judeophobia also became extremely widespread amongst the defeated army. One soldier in the Bavarian Guards sent a report to the President of Bavaria in 1920 which called for the separation, incarceration and extermination of German Jews. After the disbanding of the Army under the terms of Versailles many former soldiers joined the paramilitary and antisemitic Freikorps, which the state used for the suppression of left wing uprisings.[42]

The most important early post-war antisemitic political grouping, providing a link between the Pan-German League and the Nazis, consisted of the Deutschvölkischer Schutz und Trutz Bund, established in 1919, out of the Pan-German League. By the end of that year it counted 25,000 members and 85 branches, and, by 1922, its membership had increased to 180,000. It had a following throughout Germany, although the strongest points included

Munich, Bremen, Hamburg, Hanover and Stettin. Like the pre-war predecessors of the group and the Nazis which followed it, the DSTB attracted much of its support from the petty bourgeoisie, especially civil servants. It put much effort into recruitment in the Freikorps, as well as universities. Its ideology combined völkisch antisemitism and pan-Germanism, although it also devoted much time towards the financial power of the Jews. It only lasted until 1923, but its successor group consisted of the Nazis, with which it had contact in one of its strong points in Munich.[43]

Some of the mainstream political parties also developed an antisemitic streak in their ideology. The exception to this rule consisted of the SPD, which, as we have seen, had already turned against Judeophobia by the start of the twentieth century. During the Weimar period the party actively campaigned against the antisemitic parties and their slurs.[44] Similarly, the liberal German Democratic Party also supported the Jews, especially as it had many Jewish members and supporters, although some sections of the party resented Jewish influence. The liberal German People's Party had a more ambivalent attitude towards the Jews, while the German National People's Party was overtly antisemitic. The Catholic Centre Party also displayed hostility towards the Jews.[45] In the immediate post-war years, although the Centre Party in Düsseldorf resorted to antisemitism, it did so less viciously than its counterpart in Nuremberg in the form of the Bavarian People's Party.[46]

Against this background, popular antisemitism manifested itself in numerous ways during the first decade of the Weimar Republic. For instance, all manner of organizations had begun boycotting Jews by the early 1920s. For instance, in 1926 the annual meeting of the Munich section of the Society of Alpinists voted 'on a motion to introduce a *numerus clausus* by effectively limiting the acceptance of new Jewish members'.[47] In Minden antisemitic pamphlets published by several organizations circulated throughout the early post-war years.[48] In view of the activities of the DSTB in universities, we should not be surprised to learn that German student organizations banned Jews from becoming members in 1920.[49] Although antisemitic violence remained rare before the rise of the Nazis, it did break out. On the night of 25–26 May 1921, for instance, a fire occurred in an internment camp in Stargard in Pomerania which held Jewish refugees from eastern Europe, forbidden from entering Germany. While the mere existence of the camp points to the continuation of official hostility to *Ostjuden*, the fire itself may have occurred as a result of an arson attack and, even if it did not, the actions of those camp guards, who did nothing to help the internees to escape, suggested that they were culpable.[50] A murder of a Jew occurred in 1920, and occasional

looting took place until 1923 when, against the background of hyperinfla-
tion, serious antisemitic riots occurred on 5 and 6 November when a crowd
of 30,000 people attacked the Eastern European Jewish quarter of Berlin, the
Scheuneviertel.[51] The year 1923 also seems to represent the beginnings of a
violent development which would become increasingly widespread during
the latter years of the Weimar Republic, and would continue even after the
Nazi period, in the form of the desecration of Jewish cemeteries, indicating
the strength of contempt and hatred of Weimar antisemitism. On three separate
occasions in January and February 1923 vandals destroyed 54 headstones
in Schneidemuhl, while, at the end of November the walls, gate and graves of
the Jewish cemetery in Sandersleben in Anhalt were desecrated.[52]

Such incidents point to the future development of political antisemitism in
Germany once the violent, antisemitically obsessed Nazis seized the initiative in the future evolution of German Judeophobia. The NSDAP initially
came into existence on 5 January 1919 as the Deutsche Arbeiter Partei under
the leadership of Anton Drexler and Karl Harrer, with the aim of establishing
a völkisch state free from the foreign influence of Communists, pacifists and
Jews.[53] By the summer of 1921, when Adolf Hitler, a former tramp, failed
artist but distinguished First World War Austrian corporal, had taken control
of the party, it had become known as the National Sozialistische Deutsche
Arbeiterpartei, or Nazis, and from then on, it would steadily rise to prominence, until it came to power in the election of January 1933.

One of the earliest indications of the aims of the party came in the twenty
five point plan published by the DAP on 25 February. The first four read:

> 1. We demand the union of all Germans to form a Great Germany on the basis of
> the right of self-determination enjoyed by nations.
> 2. We demand equality of rights for the German people in its dealings with other
> nations and abolition of the peace Treaties of Versailles and Saint-Germain.
> 3. We demand land and territory (colonies) for the nourishment of our people and
> for settling our excess population.
> 4. None but members of the nation may be citizens of the state. None but those of
> German blood, whatever their creed, may be members of the nation. No Jew
> therefore may be a member of the nation.

The rest of the demands continued the Greater Germany, anti-alien and
strong racial völkisch theme, while others praised the petty bourgeoisie but
opposed big business.[54]

From the start the Nazis and their military wing, the SA, used obscene
language against the Jews, again indicating the new plane to which they had
taken hatred of the Jews. In a hark back to the Hep Hep riots the SA would

cry '*Juda, Verrecke*' ('Jews, drop dead'), while one SA marching song had a line
which ran: 'When Jewish blood drips from the knife.'[55] When the Bavarian
government threatened to deport the Austrian Hitler because of his activities,
members of his party declared that, if this happened, 'the Jews in Munich
would die by the dozen like dogs'.[56] The launch of the antisemitic *Der Stürmer*
in 1923, edited by Julius Streicher, meant the circulation of such views in a
newspaper.[57]

The Nazis impacted on German national consciousness as a result of the
failed Munich Beer Hall Putsch and the election of 1924 when they obtained
3 per cent of the vote. Nevertheless, Hitler then faced a prison sentence and,
with the Weimar economy in a stable condition, the NSDAP did not make a
real breakthrough until the election of 1930, when it became the second largest
party with 18.3 per cent of the vote,[58] continuing to rise to its peak support of
43.9 per cent of the electorate, or 17,277,000 votes following the election of
6 March 1933, which legalized the Nazi seizure of power.[59]

The Nazis ultimately came to power because of their assertiveness in what
they promised in economic and foreign policy against the background of the
chaos which existed in Germany after 1929. While they obtained support
from all social groups and all parts of the country, their strongest followers
consisted of the middle classes and the farmers, the traditional supporters
of right wing groups in Germany.[60] Antisemitism remained a core part of
Nazi rhetoric and actions, as those who voted for the party must have realized, even though the Nazis may not always have stressed this policy.[61] One
election pamphlet for farmers from 1932 declared that 'Big capitalism . . .
annihilates the independent, earth-rooted farmer, and its final aim is the
world dictatorship of Jewry.' It further declared that: 'Big capitalism and
bolshevism work hand in hand; they are born of Jewish thought and serve
the master plan of world Jewry.'[62] Another leaflet from 1931 directed towards
'Farmers! Workers! Racial Comrades!' and beginning 'Warning!' levelled
numerous accusations against the Jews and concluded that 'Without the
removal of the Jews there can be no revival, no salvation!'[63]

Against this background, the life of German Jews became increasingly
difficult between 1929 and 1933. Hannele Zürndorfer remembered the
concern of her parents as a child:

> Before I myself became aware of the tensions in the streets, I sensed that things
> were worrying my parents. I remember a great deal of talk about the *Wahltag*
> (election day). That must have been as far back as 1932. The name of Hitler was
> already very familiar and I knew that my parents dreaded his coming to power. I
> was surprised to find that some of the children with whom I played in the street,

obviously echoing their parents, expressed the opposite view. I recall great gloom in our house when the election results were announced.[64]

This author's childhood experiences were not as bad as those of others, as some schoolchildren in Nuremberg actually faced attack in the street.[65]

This reflected the increasing violence of the years after 1929. Although much of it involved fights between the paramilitary forces of the Nazis and their left wing opponents, Jews, as well as other minorities, also became victims. Attacks upon synagogues became a regular nationwide occurrence. The following happened in Bottrop in 1930:

> During the morning of 11 April a number of graves were destroyed, several gravestones knocked over, two gravestones smashed, and two others smeared with oil paint. The perpetrators had forced their way into the cemetery. Despite a reward of RM 100 offered by the Jewish community it has not been possible to establish the perpetrators.[66]

By this time attacks upon synagogues had also become a regular occurrence, as the following example from Berlin in 1930 indicates:

> On the night of 16 to 17 February the synagogue in Kottbusser Tor was defiled in a way not yet seen either in Berlin or the Reich. Twenty swastikas, one metre in size, covered the entire house of God and its doors. Outstretched over the entire width of the façade were the words 'Juda verrecke, Judas den Tod, die Rache naht.'[67]

Physical attacks upon Jews accompanied such developments, especially after Nazi meetings. Before 1930 such incidents had occurred in Chemnitz, Breslau, Essen, Bad Harzburg, Herne, Nahstätten, Plauen and Weimar. Students, who displayed considerable support for the Nazis, attacked their Jewish colleagues in Berlin on several occasions during the early 1930s.[68] In fact, eight Jews were killed in Berlin in early 1930.[69] During the summer of 1932 Jews and Jewish-owned shops in East Prussia and Silesia came under attack.[70] Economic boycotts of the Jews accompanied such actions[71] while members of the minority would face daily insults.[72] Unfortunately, the events of the final years of Weimar simply represented a prelude to the actions the Nazis would take once they seized power.

The position of the Jews clearly deteriorated during the Weimar Republic, particularly during its final years, although before 1933 they managed to hold on to the gains they had made as a result of the emancipation of the nineteenth century. Until 1933, while some instruments of the state, such as the judiciary and the army, may have had deep antisemitic prejudices, Jews did not face official discrimination; the state did not implement special measures directed against them, although it did aim to keep out further [143] influxes of *Ostjuden*. Because of their bourgeois status in a progressive liberal democracy Jews retained their positions of prominence, which faced most threat from the economic crisis.

Increasing control of the Gypsies

As throughout the whole of nineteenth- and twentieth-century German history, the Gypsies offer a direct contrast to the Jews. As we have seen, they never made the sort of gains achieved by the Jews during the nineteenth century, so that the *Kaiserreich* continued to implement new measures to control them. We might expect the progressive Weimar Republic to have moved away from the obsessive control over the Gypsies practised by its predecessor. This did not happen as the Weimar period simply meant the introduction of further measures to curtail the liberty of the Gypsies, which provided the direct link between *Kaiserreich* and Third Reich. Part of the problem lay in the continuing small numbers and underprivileged position of the Gypsies which meant that they could not really stand up for themselves. Furthermore, as an itinerant, unassimilated and unacculturated group, they remained too different from mainstream society for policy makers to regard them as 'normal' people.

It is not clear exactly how many Gypsies lived in Germany during the Weimar Republic, but further increases had occurred as a result of continuing immigration from the Balkans so that by 1926 the Munich office for the control of Gypsies had biographical information, photographs and fingerprints of 26,000 individuals. Bavaria still represented the area of Germany through which most Gypsies lived or travelled, providing support for their lifestyle which depended heavily on the land.[73] But members of this minority certainly lived elsewhere. Those in Frankfurt carried out similar work to that of the rest of the city's population and often resided in the same type of accommodation, although others lived in camps, with basic amenities.[74] In Berlin, meanwhile, missionaries continued to interfere in the lives of the Gypsies.[75]

The numerous pieces of local and national anti-Gypsy legislation introduced during the Weimar Republic received support from public opinion. At the end of the First World War Gypsy haters claimed that they had done well out of the conflict as currency and horse dealers.[76] More generally, stereotypes circulated about them as aimless wanderers who were dirty and lazy and made their living from begging, stealing and prostitution.[77] On some occasions local citizens tried to take action against Gypsies living in their area. In August 1930, for instance, 500 residents in Frankfurt sent a letter to the city authorities requesting the removal of the 'Gypsy Plague' from their neighbourhood. They followed this up with a letter to the Frankfurt magistrate with the same demand, but received a reply which said that no existing legislation allowed him to carry out such an act.[78]

Nevertheless, many anti-Gypsy measures did exist, some of them from the *Kaiserreich* but supplemented by new laws passed after 1918 concerned particularly with controlling the movement of the minority. Despite the unconstitutional nature of many of the measures, neither liberal lawyers nor politicians did anything against them,[79] as Gypsies lay outside the constituency of both. As in the pre-war period, policemen displayed particular concern with Gypsies and took the initiative in many of the new measures. In 1919, the interior ministry of Württemberg, with the perennial aim of making Gypsies sedentary, passed a law to prevent them from making stops in inhabited areas and, in 1925, made plans for the establishment of a Gypsy settlement.[80]

One of the most important of Weimar measures consisted of the 1926 Bavarian Law for the Combating of Gypsies, Travellers and the Workshy, which contained a series of articles aimed at controlling various aspects of Gypsy activity. Article 1 forbade movement without police permission; article 2 did not allow children to move with their parents unless they could provide adequate schooling. Article 5 stated:

> Gypsies and travellers may not roam about or camp in bands. The association of several single persons or several families, and the association of single persons with a family to which they do not belong, is to be regarded as constituting a band. A group of persons living together like a family is also to be regarded as a band.

Article 6 allowed Gypsies to encamp on specially designated sites, while, under article 9, Gypsies 'over sixteen years of age who are unable to prove regular employment may be sent to workhouses for up to two years by the responsible police authorities on the grounds of public security'.[81] In 1929 Hessen also adopted the Bavarian Law.[82] This particular measure seems interesting because it appears to combine straightforward ethnic prejudice with Weimar welfarism.

Further measures followed during the final few years of the Weimar Republic. In 1927 the Prussian interior ministry decided to fingerprint all itinerant persons living within its borders. As well as keeping one fingerprint for its own use, it sent another to the Gypsy police centre in Munich.[83] In 1929 this centre began coordinating the control of Gypsies on a national level.[84] Such measures laid the groundwork for the Nazis, whose policies moved from control of movement, to ethnic cleansing of German cities and eventually to genocide.

Peripheral minorities on both sides of German borders

As a result of the German defeat in 1918 and the vindictive Treaty of Versailles which followed, many of the pre-war peripheral minorities in Germany lessened in number, although only the Alsatians and Lorrainers, among the largest groups, actually disappeared. Consequently the Polish and Danish question persisted, although not on the same scale and consequence as before 1918. However, while the peace settlement may have partially solved the problems of border groupings within Germany, it also created German ones who found themselves on the wrong side of the changed boundaries.

The Polish question, which the *Kaiserreich* had dealt with clumsily and heavy handedly, represented the most irksome minority issue before 1919. It largely disappeared as an internal problem, but developed into an external one. Although the establishment of a Polish state had become inevitable even before it became one of Woodrow Wilson's Fourteen Points, the extent of its borders proved more problematic, especially those with Germany, in which complicated ethnic population distribution made the drawing of new lines on a map complicated with regard to placing Germans in Germany and Poles in Poland. The latter certainly had a better deal, as the Germans had lost the war, but plebiscites did reduce the number of Germans in Poland. The German–Polish border did not actually become finally settled until 1921.

In the immediate post-war period the new governments of Germany and Poland fought like little children over who would hold which scraps of territory which contained members of their own populations. Germany lost Poznań, West Prussia, Silesia, South East Prussia and Pomerania to Poland. The last of these had an entirely German population, while the other four all had German populations exceeding one third of the total. In addition, Danzig became a free city.[85] The consequences of the changes were fairly absurd from the point of view of having solid national boundaries because the loss of West

Prussia, Poznań and Danzig, and the retention of East Prussia, meant that
Germany was divided into two as a consequence of Versailles.

Neither the German government nor the German population of the areas
which went to Poland felt overjoyed with the loss of territory. The Germans
of South Poznań sent a document to the Allied Powers in which they
pointed out:

> These lands are not areas recently expropriated. They are inhabited by a German
> population since the earliest cultivation, for more than 300 years. These stripes
> of land have not been colonised by Germans only after the Second Partition
> of Poland (at which time this territory came to Prussia), but these districts were
> already then as German, even still more German, as nowadays.[86]

Another publication from 1919 claimed:

> West-Prussia owes everything to the German – everything that the German has
> taken over from the past, all that she possesses of historic memories and treasures.
> But also in the case of Posen, all history reports that it has been the Germans who
> economically as well as culturally fostered this province.

The same report rightly pointed out that the Polish and German nationalities
'overlap each other to such an extent that it is impossible to draw a boundary line which would separate the two nationalities with some degree of
justice.'[87] Injustice therefore became inevitable.

In an ideal world, in which nation states and the bitter resentments of 1919
did not exist, the populations of small pockets of territory would have chosen
their identity, but this would have been unworkable in the realities of the
post-war period. In fact plebiscites did take place which added Allenstein
and Marienwerder to East Prussia, although both had Polish minorities.
In March 1921 a plebiscite in Upper Silesia resulted in two thirds of the
population deciding to join Germany. In October 1921 the Council of
Ambassadors of the Allied Powers imposed the division and created a
border which 'severed' Upper Silesia's 'long-standing economic, cultural and
political unity'. The solution meant that Poland obtained part of the province
holding about 25 per cent of the territory and 44 per cent of the population.[88] In many ways the most unfair decision concerned Danzig, which,
in 1929, had a German population of 407,519 and a Polish one of 15,000.
The solution of a Free City was less unjust than if it had gone to Poland
and, although it gave the new state access to the sea, it satisfied nobody.[89]

As a result of the territorial changes at the end of the First World War,
the Polish census of 1921 found that 1,058,824 Germans lived in Poland,
making up 3.9 per cent of the population. Nevertheless, this figure declined

during the inter-war years, as Germans moved westward both for economic reasons and because of the less than favourable minority policies pursued by the Polish state, which resembled Prussian anti-Polish measures before 1918. By the 1931 census the number of Germans in Poland had declined to 741,000, making up 2.3 per cent of the total population. Those who remained maintained their ethnic identity despite the attitude of the Polish state.[90]

The presence of residual populations in Poland and other East European states (many as a result of the loss of Habsburg territory at the end of the First World War), caused much resentment in Germany and concern with them formed a central tenet of inter-war German foreign policy. Hitler solved the problem temporarily by taking over eastern Europe, but the final solution reached at the end of the Second World War in the form of ethnically cleansing millions of Germans, proved equally unjust. The German presence in eastern Europe during the twentieth century may be a specifically German problem, but it points to the problems of nationalism throughout Europe in the twentieth century, with the ultimate desire to have homogeneous populations.

The Treaty of Versailles meant that far more Germans found themselves in Poland than Poles in Germany. A total of 214,115 people who claimed Polish as their native language still lived within German borders in 1925, together with 507,721 who used both German and Polish. The Polish minority in the Weimar Republic included the Ruhr Poles. The figure increases to 802,934 if Masurians and Kasubians are added. By 1933 this gross figure had fallen to 440,168.[91]

Part of the explanation for the decline in the number of Poles lies in the emigration of members of the minority. The less than favourable policy pursued by the early Weimar governments put little effort into the maintenance of Polish minority schools. Furthermore, in 1919, 1920 and 1921 German forces put down Polish insurrections in Upper Silesia. Nevertheless, by the end of the 1920s, partly because of a desire to improve the position of the German minority in Poland, Polish schooling took off in Germany so that, by 1930 a total of 5,872 children in Germany received Polish instruction in state or private schools.[92]

Developments on the border between Denmark and Germany mirrored those which occurred on the Polish–German boundary, but on a smaller and less contentious scale. A plebiscite took place in Schleswig in 1920, in two separate zones. In the first, affecting a population of 170,000, 75,431 voted to join Denmark and 24,519 Germany, which meant that it united with Denmark, while in the more southerly region, 51,724 people decided for

[148] Germany, compared with 12,800 for Denmark, which meant that it remained part of the Weimar Republic. These decisions meant that border minorities remained, both in Denmark and Germany, despite the fact that some migration took place out of both areas.[93]

New and old migrants

Although population movement during the Weimar Republic may have taken place on a smaller scale than under any other twentieth century German regime, migration remained a factor in the development of Germany between 1919 and 1933. In the first place, as we have seen, some people left the country, and moved mostly to the USA, because of the dire economic situation. Secondly, despite the downturn, the eastern provinces still had the ability to attract agricultural labourers from further east, while industrial workers also moved to Germany. Finally, there remained the Ruhr Poles, whose numbers declined due to emigration and to the process of assimilation.

Immediately after the end of the First World War the vast majority of the two million foreign workers and prisoners of war who had laboured in Germany rushed home to Poland, France and Belgium, although some of the Poles actually migrated further into France and Belgium because of greater economic opportunities there than in Poland. The German authorities encouraged the movement out of the country in order to create opportunities for demobilized soldiers. Consequently, by 1925 the number of foreign workers in Germany had declined to 173,153.[94]

Despite the mass demobilization of German soldiers, there still remained labour shortages, caused by a number of factors. In the first place, while the urban population of Germany had increased from 37,677,704 in 1919 to 40,123,837 in 1925, the number of people living in rural areas declined from 22,734,380 to 22,224,945, meaning that the labour shortages caused by village to city migration, which had characterized the *Kaiserreich*, persisted in agriculture. In some rural areas an intensification in land use due to planting of turnips and sugar beet also occurred after the First World War.[95] Persuading Germans to work on Prussian land would have proved difficult and, at the same time, the junkers preferred to employ foreigners because they were cheaper, worked harder and complained less.[96] Foreign workers continued to find employment in industry and mining during the Weimar Republic, especially in the recovery of 1924–28. In fact, 1928 represented the peak year in the employment of foreign workers, totalling 236,870, after which the figure fell back to just 108,622 in 1932. In 1928 the division between agriculture and industry was 145,871 and 90,999 respectively.[97]

As during other periods, most foreign workers entered Germany on short-term contracts, although those who laboured in the country for a longer period could obtain more permanent permits. Similar to the years before the First World War, the large landowners managed to persuade the state to persist with foreign worker recruitment during the early 1920s because of the labour shortages which they experienced. In 1922 the Labour Exchange Act unified previously existing controls and regulations. The Imperial Labour Office gained responsibility for recruitment. In addition, the police took charge of issues such as the deportation of foreign workers where necessary.[98]

The vast majority of those who worked in agriculture originated in Poland, which would be explained by geographical proximity, traditions of migration established before 1919 and the lower level of Polish economic development. Nevertheless, the 1928 total of agricultural labourers included 5,000 ethnic Germans and 3,000 non-Germans from Yugoslavia, 3,000 Austrians, and 2,000 Germans from Czechoslovakia. Most of those who worked in industry and mining consisted of Czechs, Slovaks and Dutch people, together with a few Poles, Austrians and Yugoslavs.[99]

As we would expect, the largest numbers of foreigners laboured in the eastern provinces of Germany so that, in 1921, the employment offices which recorded heaviest concentrations lay in Pomerania, Silesia, Brandenburg, Saxony-Anhalt and Mecklenburg-Schwerin, while Bavaria had no record of any foreign worker.[100] The ratio of males to females was fairly even among Poles.[101] Like their predecessors before the First World War and those who would follow them subsequently, the foreign workers in Germany during the Weimar Republic had to endure difficult living and working conditions, particularly those employed in agriculture. Wages tended to be on a lower level than those of Germans, while a day's agricultural work could last 20 hours. Poles often lived in camps. In 1921 the area of Wolfenbüttel in Brunswick counted 37 such places. In another case, recorded in 1928, 14 women and 22 children lived in a room of 22 square metres.[102]

Those Poles who had moved to the Ruhr before the First World War did not have to endure such conditions, but faced assimilatory pressures, to which many of them increasingly succumbed, especially those in the second and third generation. The number of Ruhr Poles had fallen to 150,000 by 1929. In Herne the figure declined from 12,364 in 1925, when they made up 21.64 per cent of the population, to 491 in 1910, or just 0.73 per cent.

[150] Although many Poles moved to their newly created homeland immediately
after the end of the war, a significant proportion of them returned to the Ruhr.
About 23 per cent of the Polish population of Bottrop left the city between
1919 and 1933. Some went to Poland but others moved to Holland and the
largest percentage actually simply moved to other parts of Germany.[103]

Some Poles would have disappeared due to the classic assimilatory act
of name changing.[104] In addition, women would have lost their names by
marrying a German, as the number of unions between Germans and Poles
increased, reflecting the fact that the second generation felt far more at
ease with their German neighbours than their parents did. In Bottrop, the
percentage of Polish marriages involving a Pole and a German grew from
14.7 in 1891–1918 to 39.5 between 1930 and 1939.[105]

Like the Jewish community of the Weimar Republic, the Ruhr Poles
endured both positive and negative experiences. On the positive side, unlike
the *Kaiserreich*, the new regime recognized the minority status of individual
groups, enshrined in the constitution. Article 113 stated that the rights of
minorities could not be restricted, especially in the use of their own language
in education[106] (a clear reaction against the intolerant policies pursued before
1918) which led to the establishment of Polish schools in both the Ruhr
and Prussia. Polish ethnicity therefore continued to flourish, in some cases
unifying both eastern and western Poles. The most important body in this
respect consisted of the Union of Poles in Germany, established in Berlin in
1922, which acted as an umbrella organization for other Polish groupings.[107]
In addition, numerous other organizations existed, revolving especially around
religion and youth.[108]

But Ruhr Poles and their ethnicity had to face the endemic hostility towards
minorities which existed in the Weimar Republic. Organizations such as the
Deutschvölkische Schutz-und Trutz-Bund and the Nazis certainly did not
view Poles favourably. In addition, the German press in the Ruhr carried negative images of the local Polish population. This Polonophobic atmosphere
sometimes resulted in violence between the majority and minority communities and also affected schoolteachers, so that some pupils had negative
experiences. Sophia Kuzor remembered her teacher shouting at her: 'You
little Pollack.'[109]

Ethnic minorities therefore endured a difficult, if ultimately bearable, time
under the Weimar Republic. This temporary regime, while not overtly racist,
did not make life easy for its ethnic minorities, either because of economic
reasons, or due to the all-embracing unofficial racism which ate away at the
soul of the Republic. Racism may not actually have represented the main reason

for the Nazi success, in comparison with the economic crisis, the weakness of [151] alternative regimes and the humiliating international position of Germany. Nevertheless, Nazi voters knew what they were voting for and they should have had no surprise when the Nazis unleashed brutal policies against their ethnic and political enemies straight after they had taken control of government.

Notes

1. For the condition of German society and economy during the early Weimar years see Richard Bessel, *Germany After the First World War* (Oxford, 1993).

2. See, for instance, Theo Balderston, *The Origins and Course of the German Economic Crisis, 1923–32* (Berlin, 1993).

3. Richard J. Evans, 'Introduction: The Experience of Unemployment in the Weimar Republic', in Richard J. Evans and Dick Geary, eds, *The German Unemployed: Experiences and Consequences of Mass Unemployment from the Weimar Republic to the Third Reich* (London, 1987), pp. 1–22.

4. Ibid., pp. 7–8.

5. The experience of the middle classes is looked at by Gerald D. Feldman, *The Great Disorder: Politics, Economics and Society in the German Inflation, 1914–1924* (Oxford, 1993), pp. 527–55. For the peasantry see Harold James, *The German Slump: Politics and Economics* (Oxford, 1986), pp. 246–82. For unemployment in the Weimar Republic see contributions to Evans and Geary, *German Unemployed.*

6. See: Detlev J. Peukert, *The Weimar Republic: The Crisis of Classical Modernity* (New York, 1991), pp. 130–4; Evans, 'Introduction', pp. 1–7.

7. For the Weimar constitution see: Helmut Heiber, *The Weimar Republic* (Oxford, 1993), pp. 24–42; and Peukert, ibid., pp. 35–42.

8. John Hiden, *Germany and Europe, 1919–1939* 2nd ed (London, 1993), pp. 20–31; Niall Ferguson, 'The German Inter-War Economy: Political Choice Versus Economic Determinism', in Mary Fulbrook, ed., *German History Since 1800* (London, 1997), p. 265.

9. This is the argument of, amongst others, Hiden, ibid.

10. See H. J. Hahn, *Education and Society in Germany* (Oxford, 1998), pp. 50–70.

11. George L. Mosse, *The Crisis of German Ideology: Intellectual Origins of the Third Reich* (London, 1964), p. 238.

[152]   12. Paul Weindling, *Health, Race and German Politics Between National Unification and Nazism, 1870–1945* (Cambridge, 1989), pp. 305–439.

13. Erich Rosenthal, 'Trends of the Jewish Population in Germany, 1910–1939', *Jewish Social Studies* 6 (1944), p. 236; Abraham Barkai, 'Die Juden als sozio-ökonomische Minderheitsgruppe in der Weimarer Republik', in Walter Grab and Julius H. Schoeps, eds, *Juden in der Weimarer Republik* (Stuttgart, 1986), p. 331; Klaus J. Bade, 'Arbeitsmarkt, Bevölkerung und Wanderung in der Weimarer Republik', in Michael Stürmer, ed., *Die Weimarer Republik* (Königstein im Taunus, 1985), pp. 162–7.

14. Dieter Goetz, *Juden in Oldenburg, 1930–1938* (Oldenburg, 1988), p. 255.

15. Werner J. Cahnman, *German Jewry: Its History and Sociology* (New Brunswick, NJ, 1989), p. 98.

16. Peter Junk and Martina Sellmeyer, *Stationen auf dem Weg nach Auschwitz: Entrechtung, Vertreibung, Vernichtung: Juden in Osnabrück* (Bramsche, 1989), p. 11.

17. Rosenthal, 'Trends of the Jewish Population', p. 244.

18. Ibid., pp. 237, 239; Goetz, *Juden in Oldenburg*, p. 27; Cahnman, *German Jewry*, p. 43; Barkai, 'Die Juden als sozio-ökonomische Minderheitsgruppe', p. 331.

19. Steven M. Lowenstein, 'Jewish Residential Concentration in Post-Emancipation Germany', *Leo Baeck Year Book* 28 (1983), pp. 490–2.

20. Donald L. Niewyk, *The Jews in Weimar Germany* (Baton Rouge, LA, 1980), p. 85.

21. Ibid., pp. 13, 15.

22. Peter Pulzer, *Jews and the German State: The Political History of a Minority, 1848–1933* (Oxford, 1992), pp. 274–6.

23. George L. Mosse, *German Jews Beyond Judaism* (Bloomington, IN, 1985), p. 22.

24. Jost Hermannd, 'Juden in der Kultur der Weimarer Republik', in Grab and Schoeps, *Juden in der Weimarer Republik*, pp. 9–37.

25. Ruth Gay, *The Jews of Germany: A Historical Portrait* (London, 1922), pp. 240–4; Pulzer, *Jews and the German State*, p. 272; Ismar Elbogen and Eleonore Sterling, *Die Geschichte der Juden in Deutschland* (Frankfurt, 1988), p. 287; *Wir deutschen Juden, 321–1932* (Berlin, 1932), p. 40.

26. Niewyk, *Jews in Weimar Germany*, p. 15.

27. Donald L. Niewyk, 'The Impact of Inflation and Depression on the German Jews', *Leo Baeck Institute Year Book* 27 (1983), pp. 19–36.

28. Rosenthal, 'Trends of the Jewish Population of Germany', p. 261. [153]

29. Barkai, 'Die Juden als sozio-ökonomische Minderheitsgruppe', p. 340.

30. H. I. Bach, *The German Jew: A Synthesis of Judaism and Western Civilization, 1730–1930* (Oxford, 1984), pp. 169–75, 231–4.

31. Niewyk, *Jews in Weimar Germany*, pp. 102–3.

32. Hannele Zürndorfer, *The Ninth of November* (London, 1983), p. 29.

33. Junk and Sellmeyer, *Stationen auf dem Weg nach Auschwitz*, p. 24.

34. Hans Lamm, ed., *Vom Juden in München: Ein Gedenkbuch* (Munich, 1958), p. 30.

35. Stephen M. Poppel, *Zionism in Germany, 1897–1933: The Shaping of Jewish Identity* (Philadelphia, 1977), Table 3; Niewyk, *Jews in Weimar Germany*, pp. 125–64.

36. Niewyk, ibid., pp. 89–90.

37. Alphons Silbermann, 'Deutsche Juden oder jüdische Deutsche? Zur Identität der Juden in der Weimarer Republik', in Grab and Schoeps, *Juden in der Weimarer Republik*, p. 353.

38. Junk and Sellmeyer, *Stationen auf dem Weg nach Auschwitz*, pp. 26–7.

39. Daniel Goldhagen, *Hitler's Willing Executioners: Ordinary Germans and the Holocaust* (New York, 1996), p. 83.

40. Niewyk, *Jews in Weimar Germany*, pp. 84–5.

41. Trude Maurer, 'Die Juden in der Weimarer Republik', in Dirk Blasius and Dan Diner, eds, *Zerbrochene Geschichte: Leben und Selbstverständnis der Juden in Deutschland* (Frankfurt, 1991), p. 107.

42. Verein zur Abwehr des Antisemitismus, *Abwehr ABC* (Berlin, 1920), pp. 13, 85, 95; Klaus P. Fischer, *The History of an Obsession: German Judeophobia and the Holocaust* (London, 1998), pp. 127–8.

43. See Uwe Lohalm, *Völkischer Radikalismus: Die Geschichte des deutschvölkischen Schutz- und Trutz-Bundes, 1919–1923* (Hamburg, 1970).

44. Donald L. Niewyk, *Socialist, Anti-Semite, and Jew: German Social Democracy Confronts the Problem of Anti-Semitism, 1918–1933* (Baton Rouge, LA, 1971).

45. Pulzer, *Jews and the German State*, pp. 214–47.

46. Anthony Kaukers, *German Politics and the Jews: Düsseldorf and Nuremberg, 1910–1933* (Oxford, 1996), p. 87.

47. Cahnman, *German Jewry*, 115.

[154]

48. Hans Nordsiek, *Juden in Minden: Dokumente und Bilder jüdischen Lebens vom Mittelalter bis zum 20. Jahrhundert* (Minden, 1988), p. 56.

49. O. F. Scheuer, *Bursenschaft und Judenfrage: Der Rassenantisemitismus in der deutschen Studentenschaft* (Berlin, 1927), p. 55.

50. Mathilde Wurm, 'Kulturschande!', *Jüdische Arbeiterstimme* 15 July 1921, quoted in Ludger Heid and Julius H. Schoeps, eds, *Juden in Deutschland: Von der Aufklärung bis zur Gegenwart* (Munich, 1994), pp. 245–52.

51. Niewyk, *Jews in Weimar Germany*, p. 51.

52. Central-Verein Deutscher Staatsbürger Jüdischen Glaubens, *Friedhofsschändungen in Deutschland, 1923–32: Dokumente der politischen und kulturellen Verwilderung unserer Zeit* 5th edn (Berlin, 1932), p. 3.

53. Fischer, *History of an Obsession*, p. 133.

54. The twenty five point plan is quoted in Anton Kaes, Martin Jay and Edward Dimendberg, eds, *The Weimar Republic Sourcebook* (London, 1994), pp. 124–5.

55. George L. Mosse, *The Crisis of German Ideology: Intellectual Origins of the Third Reich* (London, 1964), p. 305.

56. Helmut Heiber, *The Weimar Republic* (Oxford, 1993), p. 97.

57. Fischer, *History of an Obsession*, p. 139.

58. Richard Bessel, *Political Violence and the Rise of Nazism: The Storm Troopers in Eastern Germany, 1925–1934* (London, 1984), p. 11.

59. William Carr, *A History of Germany, 1815–1945* 2nd edn (London, 1979), pp. 326–7.

60. For an excellent analysis of Nazi supporters see Michael H. Kater, *The Nazi Party: A Social Profile of Members and Leaders* (Oxford, 1983).

61. For a fuller discussion of the role of antisemitism in the fall of the Weimar Republic see, for instance, Werner Jochmann, *Gesellschaftskrise und Judenfeindschaft in Deutschland, 1870–1945* (Hamburg, 1988), pp. 171–94.

62. Kaes, Jay and Dimendberg, *Weimar Republic Sourcebook*, p. 142.

63. The whole leaflet, together with numerous others, is quoted in Simon Taylor, *Prelude to Genocide: Nazi Ideology and the Struggle for Power* (London, 1985), pp. 69–71.

64. Zürndorfer, *Ninth of November*, p. 45.

65. Kaukers, *German Politics and the Jews*, p. 156.

66. Zentralverein deutscher Staatsbürger jüdischen Glaubens, *Friedhofsschänd-* [155]
ungen, p. 23.

67. Ibid., p. 28. This is translated as: 'Jews drop dead, death to Jews, vengeance is approaching.'

68. Fritz Marburg, *Der Antisemitismus in der deutschen Republik* (Vienna, 1931), p. 53.

69. H. G. Adler, *The Jews in Germany: From the Enlightenment to National Socialism* (Notre Dame, IN, 1969), p. 132.

70. Bessel, *Political Violence*, p. 80.

71. Marburg, *Antisemitismus*, pp. 55–6.

72. *Jüdisches Jahrbuch* (Berlin, 1932), p. 6.

73. Joachim S. Hohmann, *Geschichte der Zigeunerverfolgung in Deutschland* 2nd edn (Frankfurt, 1988), pp. 67, 79.

74. Eva von Hase-Michalik and Doris Kreuzkamp, *Du kriegst auch einen schönen Wohnwagen: Zwangslager für Sinti und Roma während des Nationalsozialismus in Frankfurt am Main* (Frankfurt, 1990), p. 36.

75. Maria Michalsky-Knak, *Zigeuner: Und was wir mit ihnen in Berlin erlebten* (Berlin, 1935), p. 18.

76. Karin Reemstma, *Sinti und Roma: Geschichte, Kultur, Gegenwart* (Munich, 1996), p. 97.

77. Hohmann, *Geschichte der Zigeunerverfolgung*, pp. 73–7; Michael Zimmermann, *Rassenutopie und Genozid: Die nationalisozialistische 'Lösung der Zigeunerfrage'* (Hamburg, 1996), pp. 66–71.

78. Hase-Michalik and Kreuzkamp, *Du kriegst auch einen schönen Wohnwagen*, pp. 35–6.

79. Wolfgang Wippermann, *Geschichte der Sinti und Roma in Deutschland: Darstellung und Dokumente* (Berlin, 1993), p. 24.

80. Hohmann, *Geschichte der Zigeunerverfolgung*, p. 73.

81. Quoted in Michael Burleigh and Wolfgang Wippermann, *The Racial State: Germany, 1933–1945* (Cambridge, 1991), pp. 114–15.

82. Reemstma, *Sinti und Roma*, p. 97.

83. Rainer Hehemann, *Die 'Bekämpfung des Zigeunerwesens' im Wilhelminischen Deutschland und in der Weimarer Republik, 1871–1933* (Frankfurt, 1987), pp. 273–7.

84. Wippermann, *Geschichte der Sinti und Roma*, p. 25.

85. Hartmut Boockmann, *Deutsche Geschichte im Osten Europas: Ostpreussen und Westpreussen* (Berlin, 1992), p. 398.

86. Preussische Staatsbibliothek, Berlin, 'Memoir Drawn Up by the Germans of the South Posen Borderland and Presented to the Allied and Associated Powers' (1919).

87. Maurice Weiss, *Some Facts Concerning the German Element in Posen and West Prussia* (Berlin, 1919), pp. 9, 25.

88. Ibid., p. 3; Hiden, *Germany and Europe*, p. 26; Peter Herbert Rempel, 'The Geneva Convention on Upper Silesia and Germany's Diplomacy for the Rights of German Minorities' (University of Manitoba MA dissertation, 1995), p. 1; Wolfgang Jacobmeyer, 'Die deutsch-polnischen Beziehung in der Neuzeit als Konfliktgeschichte', in D. Storch, ed., *Polen und Deutschland: Nachbarn in Europa* (Hanover, 1996), p. 18.

89. Horst Jablonowski, 'Die Danziger Frage', in Erwin Hölze, ed., *Die deutschen Ostgebiete zur Zeit der Weimarer Republik* (Cologne, 1966), pp. 65–87; Franz Dettmann, *Danzig zwischen Deutschland und Polen* (Berlin, 1939).

90. Harald von Riekhoff, *German-Polish Relations, 1918–1933* (Baltimore, MD 1971), pp. 204–5; Bernhard Stasiewski, 'Zur Geschichte Deutsch-Polnischer Nachbarschaft', in Herbert Czara and Gustav E. Kaffka, eds, *Deutsche und Polen: Probleme einer Nachbarschaft* (Recklinghausen, 1960), p. 48. See also: Gotthold Rhode, 'Deutschtum in Posen und Pommerllen in der Zeit der Weimarer Republik'; and Ernst Birke, 'Schlesien', in Hölze, *Die deutschen Ostgebiete*.

91. See three sources which offer conflicting figures: Gerard Labuda, 'The Territorial, Ethnical and Demographic Aspects of Polish-German Relations in the Past (X-XX Centuries)', *Polish Western Affairs* 3 (1962), p. 250; Riekhoff, *German-Polish Relations*, p. 196; Emil Kurónski, *Die Polen in Deutschland nach den amtlichen Volkszählungen* (Berlin, 1938), p. 22.

92. Riekhoff, ibid., pp. 196–204; Wolfgang Wippermann, *Geschichte der deutschpolnischen Beziehungen* (Berlin, 1992), p. 29.

93. Otto Brandt, *Geschichte Schleswig-Holsteins* 7th edn revised by Wilhelm Klüver (Kiel, 1976), pp. 308–14; Panikos Panayi, *Outsiders: A History of European Minorities* (London, 1999), pp. 57–8, 88–9.

94. Johann Woydt, *Ausländische Arbeitskräfte in Deutschland: Vom Kaiserreich bis zur Bundesrepublik* (Heilbronn, 1987), pp. 52, 54; Ulrich Herbert, *A History of Foreign Labour in Germany, 1880–1980: Seasonal Workers/Forced Labourers/Guest Workers* (Ann Arbor, MI, 1990), p. 121.

95. F. Faas, 'Die ausländischen Wanderarbeiter in der deutschen Landwirtschaft',   [157]
Berichte über Landwirtschaft 6 (1927), pp. 115–32.

96. Herbert, *History of Foreign Labour*, p. 122; Joachim Tessarz, *Die Rolle der ausländischen landwirtschaftlichen Arbeiter in der Agrar- und Ostexpansionspolitik des deutschen Imperialismus in der Periode der Weimarer Republik (1919–1932)* (Halle, 1962), p. 52.

97. Woydt, *Ausländische Arbeitskräfte*, p. 54.

98. Ibid., p. 53; Bade, 'Arbeitsmarkt', p. 176; Herbert, *History of Foreign Labour*, p. 124; Tessarz, *Rolle der ausländischen landwirtschaftlichen Arbeiter*, p. 140.

99. Tessarz, ibid., p. 181; Lothar Elsner and Joachim Lehmann, *Ausländische Arbeiter unter dem deutschen Imperialismus, 1900 bis 1985* (Berlin, 1988) p. 102.

100. G. Gross, 'Ausländische Arbeiter in der deutschen Landwirtschaft und die Frage ihrer Ersetzbarkeit', *Landwirtschaftliche Jahrbücher* 59 (1924), p. 31.

101. Karl Liedke, '. . . *aber politisch unerwünscht': Arbeitskräfte aus Osteuropa im Land Braunschweig 1880 bis 1939* (Braunschweig, 1993), p. 123.

102. Ibid., p. 126; Woydt, *Ausländische Arbeitskräfte*, p. 58.

103. Christoph Kleßmann, *Polnische Bergarbeiter im Ruhrgebiet, 1870–1945* (Göttingen, 1978), pp. 150–68; Ralf Karl Oenning, *'Du da mitti polnischen Farben . . .': Sozialisationerfahrungen von Polen im Ruhrgebiet 1918 bis 1939* (Münster, 1991), pp. 31, 43, 44; Richard Charles Murphy, 'Polish In-Migrants in Bottrop, 1891–1933: An Ethnic Minority in a German Industrial City' (University of Iowa PhD thesis, 1977), pp. 285–6.

104. Oenning, ibid., p. 114.

105. Murphy, 'Polish In-Migrants in Bottrop', p. 182.

106. Kleßmann, *Polnische Bergarbeiter*, p. 172.

107. Wojciech Wresiński, 'The Union of Poles in Germany (1922–1939)', *Polish Western Affairs* 9 (1968), pp. 19–33.

108. Kleßmann, *Polnische Bergarbeiter*, p. 174.

109. Oenning, *'Du da mitti polnischen Farben'*, pp. 37, 57, 60–100, 109, 111.

CHAPTER 5

The Triumph of the Racists: Nazism and Its Consequences

Ideological and structural underpinnings

The Nazi seizure of power meant that the extremists who had influenced German politics since the foundation of the first nation state in 1871 now had the opportunity to put their evil plans into operation. A direct link exists between the most extreme Pan-Germans and antisemites of the period before the First World War and the Nazis who took control in 1933. Members of minorities who had lived from the 1890s to 1933 would have been horrified at the fact that one of the most extreme German parties that had ever existed now had control of power. It may be too strong an assertion to suggest that the extermination of German, and even European, Jewry became inevitable once the Nazis became the legitimate government of Germany, but, on the other hand it might not be. In view of the recent decades and even centuries of antisemitism, Slavophobia, anti-Gypsy legislation and exploitation of foreign workers, no German, of whatever ethnic group, could have had any doubt about the fact that the Nazis would implement some extremely nasty policies against their political and racial enemies, especially in view of their propaganda and tactics since their formation during the early 1920s. Here was an extraordinarily dynamic, committed and outspoken political grouping which now had control of political power.

Nazi ideology represented a continuation of the beliefs which had circulated with the Pan-Germans since the 1890s. In fact, we might say that the Nazis would finally solve the problem recognized by the Enlightenment and romantic philosophers of the presence of a state within a state, which all subsequent German nationalists had stressed. It is tempting to see Nazism and its genocidal policies as inevitable in the light of the concern with the Jews which had existed in Germany for the previous 150 years, beginning with Herder, Kant and Fichte. While none of them advocated an elimination of the Jews through brutal methods, these philosophers could not find a place for unassimilated Jews in their concept of the German nation: the elimination of Judaism, by some means or other, was, as we have seen, inherent in their nationalistic ideas. Similarly, Herder and Fichte gave birth to the concept of the German volk, united by language and physical appearance, which, by the time of the Nazis, following the birth of Social Darwinism during the nineteenth century, had become transformed into a racial concept. Nazi ideology essentially revolved around the idea of the racially pure German Aryan, who had evolved as an entity from the ideas of Gobineau, below which lay a series of inferior races, of whom Jews represented the most hated group of all. While such views may have roots in the late eighteenth century, their transformation into practical politics did not become inevitable until the Nazis seized power in 1933. 'The crisis of German ideology' pushed such ideas to the forefront by this time, but the economic and diplomatic disasters which befell Germany after 1914, as well as the campaigning tactics and charisma of Adolf Hitler and his party resulted in the seizure of power in 1933. However, we might argue that only the historical virulence of German nationalist ideas could have led to the birth of Nazism: it did not spring from nowhere and, fuelled by resentments at Germany's position during the 1920s, German nationalism transformed itself into the evil vision of Adolf Hitler. Without the deep roots stretching back as far as Herder the strong tree of German nationalism could never have born the poison fruit of Nazism, even though the short-term fertilizer may have consisted of the crises of the 1920s. Alternative scenarios may have emerged, but these would have involved the victory of liberal democratic forces in 1848 or 1871, although, as we have seen, even such groups had serious problems with Jews, Poles and Gypsies. Nazism represented the most potent and uncompromising manifestation of German nationalism and is very much rooted in the whole historical tradition of the evolution of this idea during the nineteenth and twentieth centuries.

What constituted Nazi ideology? How did it differ from other types of German nationalism? Both questions have a similar answer. Nazism essentially combined the concept of the German volk, with its origins in Herder, with the racial ideas which had emerged during the course of the nineteenth century, so that the Germans became the pure Aryan race, while other groups remained inferior. While all state manifestations of nationalism in nineteenth- and twentieth-century Germany have focused upon Germans as a distinct people, essentially because of their linguistic difference, only the Third Reich overtly displayed concern with race, resulting in the construction of a state in which those with the correct German Aryan racial characteristics had the world at their feet, as long as they obeyed, while those regarded as racially inferior became victims of discriminatory legislation and state-sanctioned violence. Thus, while the Federal Republic may practise discrimination in its national-ity laws, it is not an overtly racial state both because of its ideology, which differs from that of the Nazis, and because it does not openly persecute.

The starting point for Nazi ideology must be *Mein Kampf*, which Hitler wrote in prison in 1924 after the failed Munich Beer Hall Putsch. This essen-tially represents the Bible of Nazi Germany because all developments after 1933 appear in the ideas which Hitler put to paper as a prisoner of Weimar justice. For intentionalist interpretations of the Holocaust, as well as the conquest of eastern Europe, *Mein Kampf* appears to represent a frightening blueprint of what actually did happen after 1933 and, more especially, 1939.[1] Hitler wanted the establishment of a racial state in which physically fit German Aryans would rule and in which physical and racial inferiors would face outright persecution. An examination of the book, linked with other Nazi texts and propaganda, as well as subsequent developments, would leave us in no doubt about the central tenets of Nazi thought.

For Hitler and the Nazis everything revolved around race, so that they developed an obsession with racial purity. In *Mein Kampf* Hitler compared races of men with species of animals, stating that breeding only occurred between animals of the same type. Taking his cue from Houston Stuart Chamberlain, he claimed that, as history demonstrated, interbreeding resulted in the inferior race destroying the superior. Hitler believed that the Aryan race had produced all human advancement. Aryan tribes in the past had subjugated foreign peoples and used their labour power for their own benefit, as the Nazis would do when they conquered eastern Europe. Hitler did not define the Aryan race, but stated that its basis consisted of a combina-tion of 'the Greek mind and Teutonic technical skill'.[2]

Clearly, Hitler believed in the existence of a nation state, in which blood linked people of the same racial group together.

> The state is only a means to an end. Its end and its purpose is to preserve and promote a community of human beings who are physically as well as spiritually kindred. Above all, it must preserve the existence of the race, thereby providing the indispensable condition for the free development of all the forces dormant in this race.[3]

Hitler wanted to prevent Germans from breeding with other groups, because this would result in a decline in racial purity. In addition, putting forward ideas with origins in Turnvater Jahn, he also laid heavy stress on the physical fitness of Germans, necessary for fighting war and expanding eastward. The concern with the healthy German, also adopted from the inter-war racial hygienists, meant that Hitler desired the introduction of measures to ensure racial purity. In 1923 he told an American magazine editor that he wanted to see the isolation and sterilization of syphilitics, alcoholics and criminals, which became policy after 1933. He believed that 'The preservation of the nation is more important than the preservation of these unfortunates.'[4] In *Mein Kampf* he stated that while such measures for incurables might be 'barbaric', they were necessary. Hitler wanted to encourage a high birth rate by fighting abortion, which he made illegal, and restoring the large family to a place of honour. He even viewed it as morally reprehensible to refrain from producing healthy children.[5]

Hitler therefore wanted a pure healthy German people, which he held in the highest esteem. Clearly, in view of his obsession with purity, he believed in racial threats, above all the Jews, who represented the nemesis of the German. He attacked them using the most virulent of language for all manner of reasons which could leave nobody who read his book or heard his statements before 1933 in any doubt that he would take extremely nasty measures against them if he ever became Chancellor. Many of his views simply repeat those which his antisemitic predecessors had put forward since Wagner: the main difference between Hitler and, say, Stöcker and Chamberlain, is that Hitler became the leader of Germany. Hitler believed that: 'The Jew offers the most striking contrast to the German' and then proceeded to list what he saw as the differences, in fairly direct language. For instance, 'the Jew' had never had 'his' own civilization, but had 'always been furnished by others with a basis for his intellectual life'. Only an instinct for self-preservation held Jews together. He believed that 'the Jew' has 'always been a parasite, battening on the substance of others' and who 'from time to time was driven out by people who were tired of having their hospitality abused by such guests'. He further stated that the Jews had no idealism, working for short-term gains. Not surprisingly, he believed that the Jews had a bad influence on the German people and went on to create his own history of Jewish settlement in Germany from Roman times until the end of the First World War, so that by 1924 they controlled political power. He linked the Jews with Marxism by stating that Marxism was invented by them because its doctrine of anti-individualism and anti-race ideas would allow the Jews, who controlled the socialist movement, to seize control of power. In Russia Jews had killed thirty million people, but Hitler concluded that: 'The death of the victim is followed sooner or later by the death of the vampire.'[6] Both in *Mein Kampf* and elsewhere Hitler used

[162] extremely derogatory language to describe Jews, including terms such as 'spongers', 'parasites', 'poisonous mushrooms', 'rats', 'leeches' and 'bacilli'. The use of such words 'suggested one possible fate for the Jews, namely extermination'.[7]

Once the Nazis came to power, antisemitic propaganda remained as potent as ever. A 1937 publication from the Institute for the Study of the Jews, entitled *Die Juden in Deutschland*, indicates the way in which the Nazi state gave racism central academic respectability. The issues which the book tackled included the criminality of the Jews, an age old theme, as well as their 'racial degeneration'.[8] A volume by Paul Alexander from 1940, on the mixing of Jewish and German blood, could rejoice that: 'National socialism renewed the old divisions through the famous racial laws and taught the German people about racial thinking and how to look after their own blood.'[9] The reconstruction of German history under the Nazis meant that those writing after 1933 constantly looked backward and reinterpreted history according to the new racial order. On 21 November 1936, for instance, Wilhelm Stopel gave a lecture on the literary domination of Germany by the Jews under the Weimar Republic.[10] Assertions such as this remained quite mild compared with the contents of the pages of organs such as Julius Streicher's *Sturmer*. One of the tactics employed by this newspaper consisted of 'exposing' the activities of individual Jews.[11] Other articles used even more direct language. One from 1934, with the title of 'The World Gangster: The Genetically Gifted Criminal', began:

> Racial research has demonstrated that the Jews are nothing more than the left overs of a racial mixing dating back thousands of years. In the Jews circulates the blood of Semites, Mongols, Niggers and other long disappeared races.
> The Jew is driven by the lust of the Nigger, the cunning of the Mongol, and the criminality of all the races with which his blood had mixed. *The Jew is a born criminal.*[12]

In an antisemitic one-party state in which Jews had lost all their civil rights, the making of such unsubstantiated statements occurred daily.

Although Hitler said little about the Gypsies in *Mein Kampf,* they also represented a racial enemy and, after 1933, the Nazis devoted much 'scientific' attention and propaganda towards them. Nazi ideology regarded the Gypsies, like the Jews, as a sexual threat whose blood could corrupt that of Germans, although much of the hostility towards Gypsies lay in the historical suspicion of them as an asocial, unassimilated group, which pursued an itinerant life-style different from the majority sedentary population. A publication from

1937 by an employee of the Racial Political Office of the NSDAP, Dr Otto Finger, which appeared in a series of books edited by the Institute for Inheritance and Race in Gießen, examined the lifestyles and make up of two Gypsy 'clans', detailing, rather like Ernst Dillmann had, all the members of the two groups, which Finger claimed totalled several hundred people. Finger displayed concern about both the activities of the people he studied and their origins.[13] In fact, much of the new research of the Third Reich focused specifically on the racial make up and antecedents of the Gypsies, partly in an attempt to explain their 'asocial' behaviour. Several academics made their career in this expanding field, most notably Robert Ritter, who, in 1936, established a Racial Hygiene and Population Biology Research Unit within the Ministry of Health in Berlin, which subsequently transferred to the Central Police Headquarters. Although Ritter became the most prominent Gypsy researcher in the Third Reich, several other people who held Chairs at some of the most prestigious German universities jumped on the bandwagon, including scientists, anthropologists and sociologists. Much dispute developed over the purity of Gypsies as a racial group. Consequently, many academics carried out physical measurements of Gypsies. In 1939–40, for instance, Karl Morawek worked on a research project which involved measuring the colour of 113 Gypsies in Austria for the purpose of determining their racial characteristics. The work of these 'scientists' provided the 'evidence' for Nazi anti-Gypsy policy. During the war Ritter actually served as an adviser on whether particular individuals actually constituted Gypsies and whether they should therefore face deportation to the camp specially built for this group at Auschwitz.[14]

In accordance with their Pan-German antecedents the Nazis, and Hitler in particular, displayed much concern with eastern Europe, whose conquest represented a core tenet in Nazi ideology for several reasons. In the first place, Hitler believed that the German state was too small to make an impact upon the world stage, which necessitated expansion eastward, not only to recover the borders of 1914, but to move them as far as Russia, which would, as a consequence of conquest, be delivered from 'Jewish Bolshevism'. The expansion to the east would also allow Germans to escape the confines of their narrow borders. Once they moved into the newly conquered territories the Germans would establish themselves as the ruling class, an idea which fitted in with Hitler's view that the Aryans had previously invaded and controlled new areas and subjugated local peoples.[15] This very much prophesied Nazi actions after 1939, especially the use of eastern European labour.

Because it represented the home of Bolshevism, Nazi Slavophobia had few problems with focusing on Russia. In contrast, the party displayed caution about opposing Poland during the 1930s, because of the existence of an alliance between the two states. However, 'many Germans throughout Germany and especially in the eastern provinces sincerely believed that German achievements had given the Germans a moral right to retain and even expand their position in East Central Europe'.[16] As with attitudes towards the Gypsies, the expansion which did eventually take place in eastern Europe received legitimation from academics.[17]

Arising from the ideological division of human beings into healthy Aryans and others, the Nazis developed the concept of *Volksgemeinschaft*, or people's community, which would link those with the correct ethnic and health credentials together and exclude the rest. By creating such a community the Nazis wanted to eliminate the class differences and conflicts which had bedevilled the evolution of German industrial society. Such ideas again have their origins in the *völkisch* ideas of Herder, Fichte, Jahn and Arndt.[18] The ideal world in the eyes of Nazi ideologues also glorified people who lived on the land, as well as artisans involved in pre-industrial forms of production, both of whom remained untouched by the corrupting hand of the metropolis, where Jews congregated.[19]

In fact, the Nazis had limited success in achieving their social aims. Although they quickly eliminated unemployment, class differences continued to exist if measured in terms of relative wealth and earnings of social and occupational groups. Farmers and artisans witnessed little improvement in their economic position, because German economic recovery took place as a result of road building, mechanization and, above all, rearmament, the main driving force of the German economy from 1936 to 1945, which clearly meant large-scale industrial production.[20] On the other hand, following the elimination of political undesirables, in the form of members of the SPD and KPD, once the Nazis seized power, class consciousness lessened because the independent representatives of the working classes were replaced with organizations such as the German Labour Front, an official trade union, and the Beauty of Labour and Strength Through Joy Movements, which made employees feel good about their work and about being German by introducing limited improvements in their conditions.[21] At the same time Nazi propaganda constantly stressed the racial unity of the German people, inculcating a sense of *Volksgemeinschaft* with the Führer as its pinnacle.[22] But this propaganda also victimized unhealthy Germans in attempts to persuade those with sick relatives to allow them to die. Hitler's promises in *Mein Kampf* became reality as euthanasia and sterilization formed part of medical policy under the Third Reich. The racial hygienists who had lurked in the background of German medicine since the *Kaiserreich* now had their day.[23] The elimination of the unhealthy and 'asocials', such as homosexuals, reflected Hitler's concern with the declining birth rates of healthy Aryans which had to rise for German conquest of eastern Europe. Therefore, the Nazis offered incentives for larger families and also put mothers on a pedestal, as well as trying to force women out of the workplace. While women's rights may have deteriorated drastically, birth rates actually fell and women continued to work, if only in typical women's jobs such as manual factory employment, clerical work and nursing.[24]

If the Nazis transformed some aspects of German society, they also made significant political changes. Within the first few months of the seizure of power, Hitler and his followers had transformed Germany into a one-party state,[25] and created a personality cult to rival any other in the twentieth century.[26] These developments partly explain the relative lack of open resistance to the Nazis, in contrast to nonconformity, which existed in this, as in other regimes. The establishment of concentration camps for political enemies immediately after the Nazis came to power,[27] as well as the existence of the SS and Gestapo, who could send people into the camps without trial, cowed people into submission. These organizations set up surveillance networks to report on people who did not obey the racial order. Nevertheless, they employed relatively few informers. This leads to the conclusion that every German had some degree of responsibility for the events of 1933–45. In March 1937 the Düsseldorf Gestapo employed 291 persons, 242 of them bureaucrats, to control a population of approximately 500,000.[28] Such statistics tend to suggest that, while the terror of the Nazis may have frightened people, most Germans voluntarily accepted the new order and actively participated in it: otherwise the elimination of German Jewry, for example, would not have been possible.[29] Someone had to round people up in concentration camps, drive the trains, carry out the paperwork and, ultimately pull the trigger. On the one hand, the banal activities may find explanation in the normal functioning of twentieth-century bureaucracy because, ultimately, people were 'just doing their jobs', and were thus anaesthetized from the consequences of their actions.[30] At the same time, German soldiers acted in the service of the Fatherland, just as they had done in the wars of 1870–71 and 1914–18: all forms of nationalism dictate obedience, including Nazism, especially during war. Nevertheless, while all war ultimately means killing, ethics have sometimes controlled the activities of soldiers. Those Germans and eastern Europeans who served in the Einsatzgruppen, which shot millions of Jews, or who worked in the death camps, must have conceived the wickedness of what they were doing. Nazism was an especially evil regime and, by 1940, when the mass killing of Jews began to take place, an all-out total war raged through the whole of Europe, in a situation in which all sides dispensed with any conception of ethics.

As dictated in *Mein Kampf*, Hitler had always intended to move eastward and to expand German borders through conquest. Thus he wanted to go further than his predecessors in the Weimar Republic, who simply sought a revision of Versailles. Initially, he took fairly mild steps, such as investing in and expanding the armed forces and remilitarizing the Rhineland. However, as opposition from the signatories of Versailles remained either absent or muted, Hitler became ever bolder, resulting in the Anschluss with Austria in 1938 and the devouring of Czechoslovakia by the following year, both of which fitted in with pan-German goals, because of the German populations of these two states. Once the Second World War broke out, the Nazis quickly defeated Poland and their western neighbours and, in 1941, embarked upon the task of attempting to conquer the Soviet Union, despite the odds against the achievement of this goal.[31]

The Second World War, which Hitler had always wanted, and whose outbreak, in the context of such a dynamic regime, had an inevitability to it, brought Nazism to its logical conclusion. It meant, especially the move east, that the NSDAP could fulfil several of its goals in the form of colonizing eastern Europe, enslaving local populations, and eliminating Jews and Gypsies. Nevertheless, a regime as vigorous as Nazism knew no limits which meant that, by taking on the whole world, it had essentially pressed the self-destruct button. The barbarization which occurred between 1940 and 1945 meant not only the extermination of millions of Jews and Gypsies, but also the murder of millions of civilians throughout western Europe as a result of the bombing of urban centres and the disappearance of any war ethics regarding civilians. The Germans suffered worst out of all the western European populations, losing about five million soldiers and civilians.[32] Apart from the destruction of German cities, the post-war peace settlement, which solved the problem of German borders in the east by simply moving them further west, meant the creation of millions of German refugees, who faced one of the most systematic acts of ethnic cleansing of the twentieth century. Germany therefore became a vast refugee camp in 1945, with westward-moving ethnic Germans, eastward-migrating foreign workers and aimless Jews physically and mentally traumatized by their experiences in the Nazi camps. Hitler's vision in *Mein Kampf*, of superior Germans enslaving and exterminating eastern inferior races, therefore lay in ruins in the dust of 1945. The path to the destruction of

the late 1940s had involved the death of tens of millions of European citizens [167]
of every variety of ethnic allegiance.[33]

The exclusion and extermination of the Jews

In view of the history of antisemitism in Germany and the intensity of hatred
preached by the Nazis before 1933, the Jews became the main victims of
racism in the twelve-year Reich. They faced a combination of violence and
legislative measures immediately after the Nazis seized power in March
1933. There then followed five years of relative peace during which time,
however, they led a wretched existence as antisemitism had become official
policy. Legislation in 1933 and 1936 had turned back the clock to the
Middle Ages as all the gains of the emancipation period disappeared. The
Kristallnacht pogrom of November 1938 essentially unleashed the Holocaust,
as it displayed that the Nazis no longer had any fear about using violence
against the Jews. The outbreak of the Second World War not only meant the
destruction of German Jewry, it also allowed the Nazis to get at the great
unassimilated Yiddish populations of Poland and the Soviet Union, for
whom they set up the death camps.

The violence which had accompanied the Nazi rise to power reached its
climax immediately after the party had gained control of the state in the
spring of 1933. Although the bully boy tactics initially displayed most concern for members of the KPD and the SPD, who represented a potential
political threat,[34] the Nazis did not forget their other old enemies in the
form of the Jews. Communities of all sizes throughout the country came
under attack. In Worms, for instance, 'Jewish stores were tear-gassed' on
12 February while, on 9 March, 'several Jews were brutally beaten by contin-
gents of the local SA'. Similar incidents occurred in the town throughout
March.[35] In the Upper Silesian town of Cosel a group of Nazis actually fired
shots into the houses and businesses of Jews on 23 February. In Breslau on
13 March Jewish lawyers and judges 'were dragged from courtrooms while
cases were being heard, and some of the unfortunate victims were beaten.'[36]
Albert Einstein had his house broken into at the end of March 1933 while
he was sailing back from the USA, which caused him never to set foot on
German soil again.[37]

The early violence came to an end on boycott day, 1 April 1933. In a
centrally organized anti-Jewish action authorized by Hitler, and previously
publicized in newspapers, posters appeared outside Jewish shops all over the

[168]   country, together with SA men, who physically prevented customers from entering. Although the protests remained generally peaceful, physical attacks also occurred in, for instance, Berlin, Dortmund, Duisburg and Saxony, while arrests of Jews also took place.[38] In Osnabrück paramilitaries and policemen flooded the city centre and arrested Jewish shop owners, doctors and lawyers, who were placed in 'protective custody'.[39]

As well as using violent methods to persecute its Jewish population, the new German government introduced numerous pieces of legislation to reverse the progress made since the Enlightenment. In fact, the Nazis passed a total of 400 laws against the Jews during their twelve years of power.[40] On 7 April 1933, just a month after the Nazis had gained sole control, the Law for the Restoration of the Professional Civil Service dismissed non-Aryans, overwhelmingly Jews, from government, including academic, employment.[41] Perhaps the most important legislation for the formalization of the racial state consisted of the Nuremberg Laws passed at the end of 1935, which forbade Germans from marrying or having sexual relations with Jews, Gypsies or negroes, and also restricted citizenship to people of 'German blood'.[42] Those people who had mixed Jewish and German ancestry could claim German citizenship depending on the level of their Germanness.[43] Those who broke the Nuremberg Laws included 57 year old Konrad Rosenthal who received a prison sentence of one year for continuing sexual relations with Anna Lehmann, a 'citizen of German blood', with whom he had had a relationship since 1932.[44]

Although, after 1933, antisemitic violence declined until *Kristallnacht*, normality in peacetime Nazi Germany meant an experience of everyday discrimination and prejudice against a background in which the state increasingly controlled the activities of Jews, while, as we have seen, propagating antisemitism in all manner of ways, whether through films, newspapers or academic research. Under such a pervasive antisemitism Jews faced constant verbal abuse and the ending of long-term friendships. Some Germans in the small East Frisian town of Weener felt that they could not speak to their Jewish neighbours or old school friends in case they faced denunciation. Organizations of all types 'Nazified' themselves by excluding Jews as members. Most shockingly, a group called the German Christians also preached antisemitism. At the inaugural meeting of this group in Osnabrück in the summer of 1933 Pastor Meyer-Aurich declared: 'We must apply the racial order to the organization of the Church. Only aryans can be members of the German churches.'[45] Jews walking through the streets would notice that the walls of houses had antisemitic graffiti painted on them. In Oldenburg slogans included 'Death to Jews' and 'Jews Out'.[46] Not surprisingly, against this background, physical violence also remained an everyday occurrence, even if it did not result in the sort of nationwide explosion which occurred in 1938. Jews faced particular threat in smaller towns and villages, where they were particularly visible. On Palm Sunday 1934, for instance, two Jews were killed during a riot in Gunzenhausen in Franconia.[47] The hostility also filtered through to children especially after schools became segregated in 1935 and 1936. Hannele Zürndorfer remembered that as a child the tranquillity of her life was spoiled when a new girl, who was a member of the Bund Deutscher Mädel, the Nazi organization for girls, moved to Gerresheim, the Düsseldorf suburb where she lived. Her new neighbour 'felt it her duty to see that I was treated as a Jew ought to be', which meant that 'some of the other children became actively hostile, teasing and baiting me and pushing me about when I was on roller-skates, so that I no longer liked going out to play'.[48] In fact, even Jewish adults stopped going out, which changed their social life as they avoided attending the theatre, opera and cinema.[49]

The economic existence of Jews changed completely as a result of the violence and measures passed in the first years of the Nazi regime. Former doctors and lawyers found that they could only make a living by turning to the pre-emancipation occupation of itinerant peddling. Those Jewish businesses which survived violence employed other Jews which suited both employers, because of the attitude of Aryans towards Jews as shopkeepers and employees, although the fact that some Aryans functioned as rational human beings in consumer decisions helped Jewish shops to survive. Jewish merchants and factory owners also managed to continue. In the area of Aschaffenburg fifteen Jewish clothing factories still existed in 1938. Nevertheless, the number of Jewish businesses declined by about sixty per cent between 1933 and 1938, most of them disappearing before 1935. While some middle-class Jews did manage to find employment by accepting a drastic deterioration in their status, others had to live off Jewish welfare organizations, which spent vast amounts of money to alleviate poverty and unemployment after 1933. In most areas over twenty per cent of Jews found themselves in dire straits during 1934–35. Some of the money raised by the welfare organizations came from within German Jewish circles, but much of it also arrived from Jewish communities abroad, especially the USA. In 1936 the American Joint Distribution Committee sent nearly RM 1.2 million to the Reichsvertretung der Deutschen Juden, the centralized German Jewish welfare body founded in 1933, whose main concern actually lay in helping young German Jews to emigrate. One of the other significant organizations, Jüdische Winterhilfe, helped 82,067 people during the winter of 1936–37.[50]

A semblance of normality survived in social and religious life. Between 1933 and 1938 Jewish theatre, music, art, film and sport continued, especially in some of the larger Jewish centres, which had well-developed cultural activities.[51] However, social and religious activity did not escape the attention of the state. In Minden the synagogue, the Jewish Cultural Association, the Imperial Association of Jewish Frontline Soldiers, the Zionist Work Association and the Jewish Sports Association Helmannia, faced restriction from 1935 and closure in 1937.[52] The Jewish organizations established before 1933, including the Central Verein deutscher Staatsbürger Jüdischen Glaubens, continued to exist and still displayed some defiance.[53] Not surprisingly, in view of the level of persecution and the spiritual need it created, religious observance and synagogue attendance increased dramatically where possible, while Zionist groupings saw a growth in their numbers.[54] Other Jews took more drastic measures, including suicide. Although this phenomenon had been higher among Jews than gentiles even before the Nazi era, it 'took on the character of a mass phenomenon' after 1933.[55] Emigration represented another way out, although the Nazis attempted to make this difficult. Nevertheless, about 150,000 of the approximately 520,000 Jews living in Germany in 1933 had left by the beginning of 1938.[56] Some towns had witnessed an even more drastic decrease in their Jewish communities. The Jewish population of Worms, for instance, fell by 65 per cent from 1,104 people in 1933 to 400 by 1938,[57] while that of Munich declined from 9,005 to 6,392 in the same period.[58]

Any semblance of normality which may have remained in Jewish life between 1933 and 1937 had disappeared by the end of 1938, especially after *Kristallnacht*. Antisemitism had gained a new lease of life following the Anschluss with Austria in March, which resulted in pogroms against the Jewish communities there, and the humiliation of the most exalted Jews. 'The Chief Rabbi of Vienna was dragged out into the streets and forced to scrub pavements.'[59] The Nazis publicized the assassination of an official at the German Embassy in Paris, Ernst vom Rath, by a Polish Jew, on 7 November and, in fact, turned him into something of a martyr.[60] This led to the nationwide explosion of antisemitic violence on the night of 9–10 November, which resulted in the destruction of 7,500 shops and more than 250 synagogues, as well as at least 236 deaths.[61] One Berlin Jew subsequently wrote:

> As the war progressed I saw so many deserted towns and countless houses lying in ruins. But no destruction, no wreckage, left such a deep impression on me as the scene of the streets of demolished Jewish businesses in Berlin on 10 November 1938. Fanatical hate and systematic vandalism had wreaked havoc here.[62]

Similarly, in the city centre of Worms, 'dozens of stores, shops and offices stood empty', while 'hundreds of homes scattered throughout Worms remained almost uninhabitable, their contents smashed and hurled out of the windows into the street below'.[63] In the aftermath of the pogrom 30,000 Jews faced arrest and incarceration in the concentration camps of Dachau, Buchenwald and Sachsenhausen, a clear indication of the unleashing of the Holocaust. Although the surviving internees were released by the spring of 1939, as many as 2,500 may have died within them due to a typhus epidemic and mistreatment by their guards.[64]

In the ten months between *Kristallnacht* and the outbreak of the Second World War further measures meant that Jews had to pay for the damage caused by the Holocaust, while they faced a ban from attending public entertainment and control of their movement in the areas where they lived.[65] The final few months of peace therefore witnessed an increase in the emigration of Jews from the expanded Reich, which, by the outbreak of War, incorporated Austria and the whole of Czechoslovakia. Despite the obstacles put up by the Nazis and the reluctance of other states to accept Jews, about 115,000 left in the final ten months of peace.[66] The historian Peter Gay managed to escape with his parents when he was fifteen after months of bureaucratic wrangling by his father. The family initially sailed to Cuba and subsequently to Florida, where Peter's uncle lived.[67] In contrast many children had to make the journey out of the Third Reich on their own, leaving behind their parents whom they would never see again. These included Hannele Zürndorfer, who left Düsseldorf station for England with her sister Lotte on 3 May 1939 and later recorded her haunting experience of departure and separation:

> I can't remember whether there were other parents seeing their children off – there must have been. I do remember when the unbelievable moment of separation actually came. We were all busy with the preoccupations of finding the right coach and compartment, of stowing the luggage. Then the last clinging embrace: my face against the familiar tweed of my father's coat and the comforting feel of my mother's fur collar.
>
> Then we were on the train. We didn't cry then. We all knew we mustn't. Not mummy either. She was so brave. I think Lotte and I waved goodbye happily, still hearing their last firm assurance: 'We're coming soon . . . in a few weeks . . .'
>
> Then, as I saw their lonely figures receding as the train drew out, looking so forsaken after all they had done for us, I cried, but not for long. There were so many faces to take in, so much to think about, and then there was Lotte, weeping away beside me. 'Look after Lotte!' were their last instructions and I promised myself that I would. It was the least I could do, now we were on our own.[68]

[172]

As well as these and other Jewish children who managed to escape the Nazis, some of the most famous German, Austrian and Czech Jewish cultural and scientific figures of the interwar period also got out, many of whom made their way to Britain, which had a more favourable attitude towards refugees from Nazism than her neighbours.[69]

The peacetime antisemitic measures of the Nazis simply prepared the way for the genocidal state that would surface following the outbreak of war, especially in the areas in eastern Europe over which the Nazis gained control and which contained the vast majority of Europe's Jews. Poland, with deep antisemitic traditions of its own, became the scene of the 'Final Solution', decided upon at the Wannsee Conference of January 1942, after which the death camps came into full operation. Before then wartime Nazi antisemitism had gone through two other stages, which essentially destroyed the Jewish communities of Germany and the invaded eastern Europe. The first involved the establishment of ghettoes, which had characterized medieval European Jewish settlement, but had also begun to materialize during peacetime Nazism in Germany. When the Nazis invaded the Soviet Union, they used mobile Einsatzgruppen, German and east European troops who shot local Jewish populations in the Soviet Union.[70]

For German Jews the first years of the War meant the further elimination of any lingering traces of freedom which may have survived. In the first place, following the 1938 pogrom, new employment restrictions meant that most of those who had managed to continue practising as doctors and lawyers during the early Nazi period could no longer do so, while the 'Aryanization' of German economic life meant that other Jews whose businesses had survived the pogrom now lost them, either through forced sale or, after the outbreak of war, confiscation. In 1941 both male and female German Jews of all ages, most of them with middle-class backgrounds, became victims of conscripted labour programmes and found themselves working long hours in factories for meagre pay. In the first few years of the war, the German Jews also endured restrictions on their movement, were forced to wear the yellow star and moved to concentration camps within Germany. While some died within the German camps, others were forced to the Polish gas chambers.[71] About 28,000 Jews actually survived the Holocaust in Germany and Austria by going underground.[72] The number of Jews in Munich had declined to just 430 at the end of the war, a number which included those who had gone into hiding and those not considered 'full Jews'.[73] Smaller towns lost their Jewish communities altogether, in the case of Worms by the end of 1942.[74] The 53

Jews who lived in the East Frisian settlement of Dornum at the start of the
Second World War had all disappeared by March 1940 on their way to the
Polish death camps.[75]

Similar patterns of persecution evolved throughout Nazi Europe. The
German invasion of Poland led to direct control. This state contained three
million Jews making up ten per cent of the population[76] and provided the
ground upon which the Final Solution was implemented. The invading
Nazis came into contact with a much poorer Jewish community than that in
Germany, concentrated in particular areas of some of the largest cities. Like
their German brethren they faced a loss of civil rights, recruitment into labour
battalions as well as constant violence. In 1940 the Nazis established ghettoes
in cities with the largest Jewish populations including Warsaw and Lodz, which
took in the surrounding Jewish settlements.[77] Life in the ghetto meant humiliation, starvation and the prospect of death at any time. In the Warsaw ghetto
on the night of Friday, 17–18 April 1942, '52 Jews were shot down in the
streets like dogs'.[78] By this time the Polish ghettoes had also begun to take in
the deported Jewish populations of other invaded European states and cities.
One SS officer drew attention to the 'catastrophic conditions' in the Lodz
ghetto which 'was permanently overcrowded'.[79] By 1944, its inhabitants
suffered from 'intestinal typhus in the summer, tuberculosis in the fall, influ-
enza in the winter'.[80] In addition to forcing Jews into Polish cities the Nazis
also quickly established concentration camps in Poland, which would eventually develop into the death camps which killed most European Jews. These
consisted of: Auschwitz, Belzec, Chelmno, Majdanek, Sobibor and Treblinka.
In statistical and non-personal terms antisemitism in Second World War Poland
meant the virtual elimination of Jewish life, with one of the oldest and most
developed Yiddish traditions in eastern Europe, from Polish soil, reducing
the Jewish population to around 250,000 souls, a fall of 90 per cent.[81]

A few Polish Jews attempted to move eastward into the Soviet Union on
the outbreak of war while others were temporarily saved by the fact that they
fell into the eastern half of the country annexed by the Soviet Union, as agreed
by the Nazi-Soviet Non-Aggression Pact of August 1939. However, with
the Nazi advance into the Soviet Union after the launch of Operation
Barbarossa at the end of 1941, the Nazis soon began to implement the racial
order which they had already perfected in Poland during the preceding
two years. Local antisemitism, which had manifested itself in violence in the
Russian borderlands from the late nineteenth century until the end of the
First World War, assisted Nazi policies. The Nazis were further helped by

local anti-Soviet nationalist inhabitants in the Baltic States and the Ukraine who willingly participated in hunting down and killing Jews in the occupied lands. About a million Jews were murdered in the Soviet Union in this way during 1941 and 1942.[82] In one typical incident in the Rumbuli Forest just outside Riga on 30 November 1941 'a narrow cordon, which was formed by SS units, a contingent of the Special Task Unit Riga, and Latvian Units' shot Jews, who would then fall into prepared pits. The victims included 'over one thousand Jews from Berlin' who 'were pulled off a train, herded immediately up to the pits, and shot'.[83] As a result of the Rumbuli Forest massacres in November and December 1941, about 20,000 Riga Jews died, leaving about 7,000 survivors.[84] In Lithuania the 'intense involvement of the local population, in large numbers', meant that they 'perpetrated most of the torture and killing, generally without any German officials on the spot'.[85] Overall more than 2 million Soviet Jews were murdered either by the actions of the Einsatzgruppen, or deportation to the death camps. This meant that Jewish losses were about four times as heavy as those of the Soviet population as a whole.[86]

Large-scale murder of Jews occurred elsewhere throughout much of eastern Europe. Hungary had a strong antisemitic tradition which resulted in the passage of discriminatory legislation throughout the inter-war years and acted as a background factor to the deportation of its Jews to Poland,[87] meaning that the Jewish population shrank from about 825,000 to 255,000.[88] In Czechoslovakia, annexed by Hitler just before the outbreak of war, about 240,000 Jews were killed, leaving just 22,000 in the Czech areas and 3,500 in Slovakia.[89] Romania lost about 300,000 out of its 757,000 Jews.[90] At the outbreak of war in Greece 'there were between 70,000 and 80,000 Jews . . . of whom over 50,000 lived in the city of Salonika. Fewer than 10,000 survived, and some of the oldest Jewish communities in Europe perished as a result.'[91] Bulgaria represented the classic exception to the rule in eastern Europe and the Balkans in the fact that it saved virtually all of its Jews because the government did not hand them over to the Nazis for deportation to the death camps.[92]

In western Europe the picture varied from one country to another for similar reasons to those in the eastern half of the continent. In Scandinavia much effort went into supporting and hiding Jews within Denmark with assistance from neutral Sweden.[93] Holland deported 110,000 of its Jews to the Nazi extermination camps in Poland, meaning that only about 30,000 survived the Second World War.[94] France had one of the deepest antisemitic traditions in western Europe and passed its own racial laws under the Second World

War Vichy regime – as well as setting up its own concentration camps.
Nevertheless, about 70 per cent of the 350,000 Jews living in France in 1939
survived.[95] Italy, with a more limited antisemitic tradition, had one of the
most impressive survival rates, losing only 8,000 of its 57,000 Jews,[96] due
to a popular refusal to surrender to the Nazi will, despite the alliance of
Mussolini and Hitler.[97]

In all, Lucy Dawidowicz estimates that 5,933,900 out of 8,861,800 Jews
in the countries occupied by the Nazis were murdered, meaning a death
rate of 67 per cent.[98] The extent to which the Nazis fulfilled their aims in
individual states depended on a series of factors including the nature and
extent of German occupation and the levels of antisemitism and sympathies
of the local non-Jewish population. Areas annexed by the expanded Third
Reich or contiguous with it, passing under direct Nazi rule, also tended to be
those with the strongest antisemitic traditions and, consequently, those which
lost the highest proportion of their Jews. Those under less direct control
and with less developed traditions of antisemitism were those with the
lowest death rates, notably Italy and Bulgaria. There remains no scientific
equation which determined the rates of survival so that Greece, with less
developed traditions of modern antisemitism, nevertheless suffered significant Jewish losses.

The exclusion and partial extermination of the Gypsies

As we have seen, the ideological vision of the Nazis viewed Gypsies negatively as an asocial group which represented a racial threat to the dominant
Aryan population. The measures introduced against the group by the Nazis
before 1939 continued policies pursued by the *Kaiserreich* and the Weimar
Republic, although the level of force used and the thoroughness of the process pointed to new departures, which, after 1939, certainly intensified as the
Nazis also began to murder Gypsies on a large scale.

According to Robert Ritter the total number of Romanies in Germany had
increased to 30,000 by the beginning of 1939 as a result of the incorporation of Austria and the Sudetenland into the Reich.[99] The Nazis had begun to
introduce measures against the German Gypsy population during their first
year of power. In September 1933 the SA and SS arrested a small number of
Romanies for begging and placed them in the camps in Buchenwald, Dachau

[176] and Sachsenhausen.[100] The first year of Nazi rule also meant the extension of the 1926 Bavarian Law to cover the whole country, although several other regions introduced additional measures. Furthermore, new legislation allowed for the sterilization of Gypsies.[101]

Persecution of the Gypsies increased from 1936. In that year, in the lead up to the Olympic games, the police escorted all Berlin Gypsies with their caravans and horses to a camp established in the suburb of Marzahn, where they would remain to carry out forced labour.[102] A camp for Gypsies also came into existence in Frankfurt in 1936, which was tightly controlled by the local police and whose inhabitants became subject to examination by a Frankfurt biological research institute.[103]

By the outbreak of the Second World War, the Nazis had prepared the way for the deportations and murders of Gypsies which would take place during the conflict. The year 1938 meant an intensification of persecution for Romanies as well as Jews. The Imperial Police Office in Berlin took over the task of dealing with the Gypsies on a nationwide basis.[104] In both 1938 and 1939 the number of Romanies in concentration camps, especially Buchenwald, Dachau and Sachsenhausen, increased.[105]

Nevertheless, a degree of normality remained so that 200 Gypsies still lived in Munich at the outbreak of war, either in houses or caravans,[106] despite the history of Bavaria as the centre of Gypsy persecution in Germany. Missionary work also continued, certainly in the early years of the Nazi regime.[107] Similarly, the traditional Gypsy occupation of peddling survived until at least the late 1930s.[108] But Romanies lived in constant fear, as one of their number, who was a child at the time, later recalled:

> In the middle of the 1930s our life was haunted by the fear of persecution. My mother always reported that Gypsies would be taken to concentration camps. The streets of our own quarter were filled with stories of Gypsy families who had already been deported. Fear was spreading. My mother seemed to be indifferent about her own life but worried about me and my future. As I was often outside, she must have thought that I was in danger. When I came home in the evening her tired eyes brightened. She smiled at me when I opened the creaking door.[109]

The outbreak of the Second World War and the takeover of eastern Europe meant that, as in the case of Jews, German forces entered the European states with the highest numbers of Gypsies. These included Bulgaria (80,000), Yugoslavia (100,000), Poland (50,000), Romania (300,000), Slovakia (80,000), the Soviet Union (200,000) and Hungary (100,000).[110] While

European Gypsies endured similar racial persecution to the Jews, they had a higher survival rate.

Just after the outbreak of the war a decree prevented Gypsies from travelling within German territory and plans emerged to deport German Gypsies to Poland, a process which began in April 1940. As German troops marched into the Soviet Union at the end of 1941 the Einsatzgruppen began murdering Romanies there. By this time Gypsies also faced deportation to concentration and forced labour camps established in eastern Europe, although most of those in Germany remained to face continually deteriorating conditions. The Nazis decided upon the final solution to the Gypsy question in December 1942, which involved deportation to camps throughout Europe, including Auschwitz BIIe, which accounted for the death of 20,078 people. The deportation from Munich began on 8 March 1943 and continued for the rest of the year. Elisabeth Guttenberger remembered her arrival in the camp:

> The first impression we had of Auschwitz was shocking. We were tattooed and our hair was cut off. Our clothes, footwear and the few things we were allowed to bring with us, were taken away from us.
>
> The barracks, which were former stables, had no windows, only shutters for ventilation, called skylights. The floor was made out of clay. In one hut, which had space for perhaps 200 people, more than a thousand were put up.

Like Jews, Gypsies were worked, often to death, in the camps. The Gypsies also continued as subjects of Nazi research. Much concern focused upon their racial origin, but they also became guinea pigs in concentration camp experiments, especially in attempts to find a vaccine for spotted fever.[111]

The Nazis had an impact upon the Gypsy populations of Europe almost as dramatic as that on the Jews. While estimates of the number of Gypsies murdered by the Nazis vary, Donald Kenrick and Grattan Puxon have documented 219,700 deaths,[112] although Puxon believes that the actual number was closer to 500,000.[113] In Germany, as we might expect, Gypsy life was virtually destroyed.[114] The few thousand who remained included people who survived the concentration camps and those who managed to evade arrest by the various Nazi policing authorities.[115] Konrad H., who was born in Kitzingen in Bavaria and married Alma, born in Scheßel bei Rottenburg, managed to stay alive during the war with his children. The family faced deportation to Auschwitz from Munich on 8 March 1943. Although Alma died there, the other members of the family survived and were moved to other camps. In Ravensbrück the children all faced sterilization. At the end of the war they found themselves in different camps, hungry and diseased but still alive.[116]

Elsewhere in Europe the Nazis killed up to 35,000 Gypsies in the Soviet Union, including almost all of those in Latvia and Estonia, but, like the Jewish population of the Soviet Union, those who lived beyond the area of German occupation were protected by the Soviet authorities.[117] In Poland the Gypsies initially found themselves concentrated in ghettos. In November 1941 they were gathered in the Lodz ghetto with a view to their extermination, subsequently being sent to the death camp at Chelmno.[118] However, even in the heartland of Nazi genocide as many as 20,000 Gypsies may have survived. As the historian of Polish Gypsies writes, they:

> managed to evade the camps, gas chambers and executions. Some of them now came out of the depths of the forests where they had managed to survive; others returned from the concentration camps where they had not yet been exterminated; still others came back from the Soviet Union as repatriated persons. A very few highland Gypsies had managed to survive the war in the mountain fastnesses that their ancestors had inhabited.[119]

In Czechoslovakia persecution took place with the establishment of camps after the arrival of the Nazis, although deportation also took place to Auschwitz. Nevertheless, mass extermination did not occur because the war had ended too soon for this to happen. In addition, the establishment of an independent Slovak state had actually helped Gypsies to survive, so that the number of Gypsies in Czechoslovakia increased during the course of the Second World War.[120] Nevertheless, the Nazis killed between 36,000 and 39,000 Gypsies in Romania and 30,000 in Hungary.[121] The situation for Gypsies in Yugoslavia varied according to the fate of the area in which they lived. The highest death rate occurred in the Nazi-supported Croatian state, where over 25,000 Gypsies were killed, while 12,000 of the 60,000 Serbian Gypsies suffered a similar fate. The safest were those living in Macedonia and Slovenia.[122]

The Nazis did not destroy Gypsy settlement in Europe in the way that they eradicated Jewish communities. The main explanation for this lies in the fact that antisemitism formed a central core of Nazi ideology, whereas Gypsies remained more peripheral. This finds further explanation in the positions of power which Jews had developed during the emancipation period, which intensified the hatred towards them. Gypsies in contrast offered no economic threat, just a racial one, as well as proving irritating because of their itinerant lifestyle. Nevertheless, if the Nazis had won the Second World War, it seems likely that the Gypsies would have faced extermination, even if some may have proved difficult to track down in view of their way of life. They had no place in the new world order envisaged in *Mein Kampf*.

Persecution and exploitation of Slavs and others [179]

German Slavophobia, like antisemitism and hostility towards Gypsies, reached its zenith under the Nazis, especially during the Second World War. Those Slavic minorities already living within the German borders of 1933 did not really stand a chance of ethnic survival and had the choice of either hiding their origins or facing persecution. The invasion of eastern Europe had dire consequences for the local dominant populations, regarded with complete contempt as racial inferiors by the Nazis and, especially in the case of Poles and Soviet citizens, receiving similar treatment to that meted out to their Jewish neighbours. The move into eastern Europe also provided the Nazis with a massive supply of potential labour, which they fully exploited, as well as importing foreign workers from the west.

Once the Nazis seized power the Polish population in the Ruhr faced increasing hostility and pressure to assimilate. In keeping with their heavy handed tactics, the Nazis closed down Polish societies in the region and increasingly tightened controls over the use of the Polish language.[123] Although, the Union of Poles in Germany managed to survive until 1939, 'anti-Polish terroristic activities' had become commonplace by then.[124] Seven days after the outbreak of the Second World War all surviving Polish organizations in the Ruhr faced dissolution and, on 11 September 1939, the Nazis arrested 249 leading Polish functionaries from the Ruhr and threw them into concentration camps. Most of these were released in the spring of 1940, but at least 60 Ruhr Poles were shot, beheaded or died in concentration camps.[125] However, as a group, these western Poles, away from the eastern front, came off relatively lightly compared with Poles living in territories invaded by the Nazis.

Another persecuted Slavic group already living in Germany in 1933, with roots going back several centuries, consisted of the Sorbs, situated on the border with Czechoslovakia. Like the Germans, they had experienced a national reawakening during the nineteenth century.[126] The 1925 census revealed that 70,908 people used Wendish, the language of the Sorbs.[127] The Sorbs actually voted for the Nazis in large numbers, which meant that the new government initially treated the group quite favourably, promising it the same rights as other German citizens. Nevertheless, as early as 1934, the Nazis had already begun to close down Sorbian ethnic organizations. Persecution intensified further, especially in March 1937 when new measures prevented the main Sorbish grouping, the Domowina, from continuing with its activities. From 1938 Wendish could no longer be used as a language in schools. Persecution intensified following the outbreak of war. Sorbian leaders

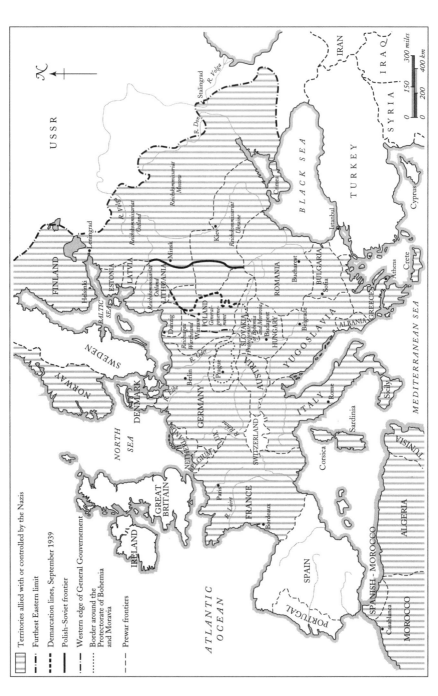

Map 4: The Height of Nazi Power in 1942.

Source: Martin Kitchen, *Nazi Germany at War*, (London: Longman, 1995) pp. 316–17.

faced incarceration while at least 23 Sorbian priests had to leave their parishes. Furthermore, any overt signs of Sorbian ethnicity disappeared.[128]

When the Germans invaded eastern Europe during the First World War they carried out some atrocities, but not on the scale in which they would during the Second, as they fought against both racial and, in the case of the Soviet Union, ideological enemies. Any animosity which existed before 1939 intensified as a result of the brutalization inevitable in wartime. Attacking enemy soldiers, killing foreign civilians, exterminating Jews, Gypsies and Slavs, as well as enslaving and exploiting these three groups all formed elements of the most brutal war ever fought on European soil.

Poland and the Soviet Union endured the worst of the Nazi scorched earth policy. Following the Nazi-Soviet Non-Aggression Pact, the Nazis took over western Poland once they invaded it in September 1939, while the USSR annexed the east. The Nazis would subsequently seize the entire country when they moved towards the invasion of the Soviet Union in 1941. The north western areas became directly annexed into the Reich, while those further south became the General Gouvernement. However, the whole of the country essentially came completely under the control of Nazis, so that Poles only carried out the most petty bureaucratic tasks. The Nazis saw Poles as a labour reserve and, for many of them, moving to Germany proved preferable to remaining within Poland, because of the way in which the invaders treated their new subjects. A racial hierarchy in the General Government meant that, while Germans could receive 2,613 calories per day, Poles obtained 699 and Jews got only 184. The Nazis closed down universities, schools and theatres. In addition, they also took away children with 'Nordic characteristics' and exported them to parents in Germany. Deportation of Poles, as well as Jews, also took place out of the incorporated territories to the General Government. Harking back to the policies pursued by the *Kaiserreich*, the Nazis particularly victimized the Polish clergy. However, while the Germans before 1914 had simply gagged priests and prevented them from teaching, the new more ruthless rulers of the Second World War had no problems with killing them. A church report of October 1941 for the diocese of Poznań-Gnesen, in the Warthegau, which the Nazis wanted for the settlement of ethnic Germans, pointed out that:

> Of 681 priests (1939) 22 are not permitted to perform their functions, 120 are in the General Government, 74 have been shot or died in concentration camps, 24 are in exile beyond the Reich borders, 12 are missing, 451 are in prison or concentration camps. Of 431 former churches and 74 chapels, only 30 churches and 1 chapel are still open.

[182] By the end of 1941 the concentration camp at Dachau contained 1,700 clergy. About 17 per cent of the population of Poland died during the war, consisting of three million Jews and three million gentiles, who, collectively, perished as a result of combat, the camps, disease and labour exploitation.[129]

Similar events occurred in the USSR, following its invasion in 1941, although losses took place on a larger scale, as the Second World War resulted in the death of 10 million Soviet civilians and 10 million soldiers.[130] Furthermore, the invading Nazis destroyed around 1,700 towns and 70,000 villages. In addition they commandeered agricultural produce, shot communists, and brutally treated prisoners of war, meaning that about 3.3 million out of the 5.7 million seized between June 1941 and May 1944 actually died, mostly due to starvation, although the SS may have executed about half a million.[131]

The Nazis also made use of the labour power of the invaded eastern territories, as well as importing workers from some of the countries occupied in the west. This certainly continued the policies of the *Kaiserreich* and provides a link with the Federal Republic. But foreign workers under the Nazis, especially those who found themselves in concentration camps, received far worse treatment than those employed in Germany before 1919 or after 1949.

In contrast to the situation following the outbreak of war, the Nazis put limited effort into the importation of foreign workers in peacetime, due largely to the desire to solve the German unemployment problem. But foreign labourers never disappeared from Germany, despite the closing of the German border to Poles in 1932. As labour shortages began to develop from about 1936, the Nazi economy increasingly utilized foreigners. Thus, the 148,455 foreign labourers in Germany in 1933 had increased to 229,374 in 1936 and 435,903 in the last year of peace, meaning that foreigners constituted 2.12 per cent of the German workforce in 1938–39, divided fairly equally between agriculture and industry. The countries of origin included Poland, whose migrants counted a 66 per cent quota of women, Italy, Yugoslavia, Bulgaria and Hungary. Economic conditions in the land of origin encouraged people to move to Germany despite long working hours, which could stretch to twelve per day. As with all sections of the German population, the Nazi state made sure it controlled its imported workers, establishing a Reich Agency Labour Exchange and passing a Foreigner Police Ordinance in 1938.[132]

The outbreak of the Second World War created a massive demand for foreign labour because of the millions of German men needed to fight wars on several fronts and police local populations and concentration camps at the same time as armaments production increased. Although the British state solved its wartime labour shortage by simply mobilizing women, the Nazis refused to follow a similar path because it 'would inflict both physical and mental harm' upon them 'and damage their psychic and emotional life and possibly their potential as mothers'.[133] Consequently, following historical precedent, the Nazis turned to the use of foreign workers and prisoners of war, which also fitted in with their ideological goals of exploiting eastern Europeans for manual labour. Total numbers increased from 301,000 in 1939 to 7,126,000 in 1944, or from 0.8 to 19.9 per cent of all workers employed in the German economy. The 1944 total counted 5,295,000 civilians and 1,831,000 prisoners of war.[134] While those in the latter category consisted almost exclusively of men, the Nazis made much use of female foreign labourers. At the end of 1943 they employed 3,631,000 males and 1,714,000 females.[135]

The people employed by the Nazis came from locations all over Europe and moved to Germany through a combination of force and, to a much smaller extent, willingness. Fritz Sauckel, who became responsible for the recruitment of foreigners in March 1942, estimated two years later, that out of the 5 million foreigners who had made their way to Germany, not even 200,000 had done so voluntarily.[136] Even if people had moved to Germany of their own free will, part of the reason for this lay in the consequences of the German invasion of their country. This applied, for instance, to Denmark, where unemployment had risen following the Nazi takeover of June 1940. Moving to Germany offered opportunities to earn more money than short-term unemployment benefit at home could provide.[137] Similarly, unemployed men from Holland migrated to Germany following an official announcement on 21 June 1940 that they should register to do so, with the promise of good pay, on the same level as Germans and regular return trips.[138]

The economic consequences of the Nazi invasion also helped French people to move to Germany for the purpose of securing employment, although force also operated. In fact, immediately after the defeat of France in the spring of 1940, the Nazis found themselves with 1,580,000 new prisoners of war, 95 per cent of whom initially worked for the Nazi war economy, although the number of French prisoners of war had sunk to 980,000 by 1943.[139] About 200,000 voluntarily transferred to civilian employment,[140] but the recruitment of new French civilian employees made up for the shortfall in numbers. By September 1944 France provided 646,421 civilian workers, making up 10.8 per cent of the total of such employees and constituting the third largest national grouping. Although the 300 recruitment offices established in France initially managed to persuade people to move to Germany voluntarily, especially against the background of the rise in unemployment caused by the German invasion, the Nazis, with the assistance of the Vichy

Table 3: Major nationalities of civilians and prisoners of war employed by the Nazi war economy, August 1944

Nationality	Civilians	POWs	Total
Belgian	203,262	50,386	253,648
French	654,782	599,967	1,254,749
Italian	158,099	427,238	585,337
Soviet	2,126,753	631,559	2,758,312
Polish	1,659,764	28,316	1,688,080
Others	919,223	192,621	1,111,844
Total	5,721,883	1,930,087	7,651,970

Source: Ulrich Herbert, *A History of Foreign Labour in Germany, 1880–1980: Seasonal Workers/Forced Labourers/Guest Workers* (Ann Arbor, MI, 1990), p. 154.

government, increasingly turned to force as the French economy had begun to absorb its surplus labour following its reorganization in the interests of the Nazis. Consequently, during the course of the war, Fritz Sauckel sent Pierre Laval, the puppet chief of state, a series of demands outlining the numbers of French civilians which he required to work in Germany. For instance, on 13 January 1943 Sauckel called for 250,000 people by 15 March, meaning 4,500 people a day. The Nazis also introduced employment conscription for people born in particular years.[141]

The invading Germans also instituted conscription in the parts of eastern Europe which they controlled, as well as, more brutally, simply transporting other individuals to work in German concentration camps. In Poland the Germans established recruitment offices immediately after they invaded the country: those in the largest cities often employed over 100 civil servants. As elsewhere, the economic consequences of the Nazi invasion encouraged people to move to employment in the country of their new masters. By the end of 1939 the Nazis had instituted conscription in Poland for both males and females which many Poles tried to avoid. The invaders simply reacted by forcibly transporting Poles to Germany.[142]

In November, 1941, for instance, 300 Polish railwaymen were taken from the repair shops and from road-work in Białystok, in order, as was explained to them, to be transferred to another working place. A few hours later they were put into a train and sent to Berlin. They had no opportunity to communicate with their families before they left.[143]

The Nazis employed similar policies in the Soviet Union. Inna Efimowna
Kulagina, born in 1925 in the Rostov region, stated that when the Nazis
entered her region they issued conscription notices. Anyone who did not
make themselves available would be shot. She left her homeland on 6 October
1942, travelled to Wuppertal on a goods train and eventually worked in the
Ford plant in Cologne.[144]

Once they arrived on German soil the new foreign employees of the Nazis
found themselves working in a variety of occupations involving differing
degrees of freedom and imprisonment. While, in accordance with Nazi ideology, people from the east experienced the worst treatment, in which many
victims simply found themselves worked to death in camps, many of those
from the west had similar experiences to German employees.

In terms of sector employment, 2,042,000 foreigners laboured in agriculture in 1944, together with 4,724,000 in other areas, overwhelmingly
industry, which counted 45 per cent of all foreigners, especially in mining,
metals, construction and transport.[145] One of the smaller national groups,
Hungarians, who reached a peak of 5,729 in 1942, worked only on the
land.[146] A few eastern European women found employment as nannies for
German families, which represented a comfortable existence compared with
the experience of people who laboured in industry, especially those who found
themselves in camps, and agriculture.[147]

As in the *Kaiserreich* and the Federal Republic, foreigners lived and worked
all over the country, wherever the needs of the economy dictated that they
should find themselves stationed. In April 1941 the areas with the highest
concentrations consisted of Lower Saxony and Pomerania, where foreign
workers made up over 13 per cent of all employees. At the other extreme,
they constituted less than 4 per cent in southwest Germany and Saxony.[148]
Many of those working in industry and mining lived in the Ruhr. The 39,388
foreigners in Essen in December 1944 made up 10.5 per cent of the entire
population of 375,179. A total of 10,612 of these worked in the Krupp
cast iron factory.[149] Elsewhere, 6,000 foreign workers found themselves in
Bremen at the end of the war, employed especially by six firms.[150] All manner
of industrial concerns used foreigners, including, for instance, the Osram
light bulb factory in Berlin, which made particular use of Russian women.[151]
German wartime capitalism, like its peacetime equivalent, simply utilized
whatever form of foreign labour the state provided and had few scruples
about the system of exploitation involved. As agriculture also employed so
many foreigners, again continuing German historical traditions, many eastern
Europeans lived and worked in tiny settlements all over the country. In the

'Lipper Land', between the Teutoberg Forest and the Weser hills, in north western Germany, agriculture became highly dependant upon foreign workers and prisoners of war by the end of 1940.[152] By the end of 1942 these two groups made up ten per cent of the population of the small town of Blomberg and the villages which surrounded it.[153]

Most of the foreigners imported into Germany during the Second World War faced bad or appalling living and working conditions. In accordance with Nazi ideology, different racial groups received varying treatment. Germans naturally stood at the top, followed by west Europeans, south Europeans, central Europeans, Poles and Russians.[154] Overall, 'for most of the eastern workers and some of the western workers, life in the Reich was one long, continual nightmare of hard work, insufficient food, inadequate quarters, personal discrimination and cruelty'.[155]

Continuing traditions established under the *Kaiserreich*, which would also resurface in the Federal Republic, the typical dwelling place of a foreign worker consisted of a barracks or a camp, whose conditions certainly varied, the worst of which would not make a reappearance after 1945. Those living and working in concentration camps controlled by the SS faced the most dreadful conditions.[156] In Ravensbrück, for instance, women slept in bunk beds three high, and a single barracks could house up to one thousand women.[157] Anna Maiboroda recalled the Schönebeck camp.

> It was surrounded by a two meter high wall covered with glass. Barbed wire. A power line of 3,800 volts. As I came in the two sisters Anja and Njura told me: there was an alarm, the current was turned off, during which time a girl tried to escape covered in her blanket. But the current was turned on and she burnt. Everyone was summoned and told: 'Whoever else considers escaping will suffer the same fate.'[158]

Nevertheless, not all foreign workers lived in camps. For instance, at the end of 1943 between 3,000 and 4,000 resided in houses in Bremen.[159]

Unsurprisingly, the foreigners imported into Germany had to endure long and difficult working conditions. During 1941 those working on the land, both natives and non-Germans, laboured over eighty hours per week. During harvest time this could increase to more than 100. Twelve-hour shifts became commonplace in factories, as the examples of the Daimler-Benz works in Berlin and the Ford plant in Cologne would indicate.[160] The wages received by the working classes in Germany varied according to ethnic group, with Germans at the top and eastern Europeans at the bottom.[161] Like the rest of the German population, foreign workers had to endure food rationing.

In Blomberg the latter received the following daily provisions: 245 grams of rye flour, 31 grams of meat, 16 grams of margarine, 13 grams of sugar, 18 grams of cereal and 660 grams of potatoes.[162] In April 1944 eastern European workers and Soviet prisoners of war actually experienced an increase in their rations, although these still remained lower than that received by either western Europeans or Germans.[163] As well as being insufficient, the food which foreign workers received was generally disgusting. Nevertheless, many individuals constantly hungered after more food. M. M. Šarovskaja later recalled: 'I dreamt about food and a quick end to the war. When my lunch stood before me, I dreamt about sunset, and I always wanted to eat.'[164]

The importation of millions of foreign workers into the German heartland potentially threatened the racial hierarchy established by the Nazis, which meant that they introduced measures to limit contact between natives and newcomers, especially Poles and Soviets, and brutally punished anyone who broke the rules. In a situation in which large numbers of German males had disappeared to the frontline 'male foreign workers became a focus of sexual interest for German women'.[165] Just in case people did not recognize Poles, they had to wear a 'P' on their clothes from April 1941.[166] In addition, the Nazis put up placards which read 'Keep Your Blood Pure'.[167] Despite the controls of the Nazis, contact did take place between Germans and foreigners, often with dire consequences. Between 18 April 1941 and 7 January 1942 a total of 9 Polish males were hanged in Baden and Alsace simply because they were seen with German women. The latter faced incarceration in a concentration camp and the shaving of their hair in public as a warning to local youth.[168] But public contact between Germans and foreigners did not always have such brutal consequences, as there were examples of humanitarian acts of the former towards the latter.[169] More commonly, however, foreigners faced constant mistreatment from their employers, the security services, or civilians.[170]

During their twelve years of terror the Nazis had exploited and murdered tens of millions of Germans, Jews, eastern and western Europeans. The defeat of 1945 meant liberation for those who had managed to survive the brutality instituted by Hitler and his followers, but it created new problems, both for the Germans of the eastern provinces and for the surviving Jews and foreign workers. But the most intolerant years in the history of German racism came to an end in 1945. While the policies implemented by the Nazis certainly left a residue in the treatment of post-War minorities, mass murder had ceased as a core element of German political history.

[188] Notes

1. See, especially, Eberhard Jäckel, *Hitler's World View: A Blueprint for Power* (Cambridge, MA, 1981).

2. Adolf Hitler, *Mein Kampf* original edn 1924, translated by James Murphy (London, 1939), pp. 252–60.

3. Ibid., p. 340.

4. Quoted in Philippe Burrin, *Hitler and the Jews: The Genesis of the Holocaust* (London, 1994), p. 26.

5. Hitler, *Mein Kampf,* pp. 350–2.

6. Ibid., pp. 261–88.

7. Michael Burleigh and Wolfgang Wippermann, *The Racial State: Germany, 1933–1945* (Cambridge, 1991), p. 42.

8. Institut zum Studium der Judenfrage, *Die Juden in Deutschland* (Munich, 1937).

9. Paul Alexander, *Jüdisch-deutsche Blutmischung: Eine sozial-biologische Untersuchung* (Berlin, 1940), p. 7.

10. Wilhelm Stopel, *Die Literarische Vorherrschaft der Juden in Deutschland 1918 bis 1933* (Hamburg, 1937).

11. See the examples in *Was soll mit den Juden geschehen? Praktische Vorschläge von Julius Streicher und Adolf Hitler* (Paris, 1936), pp. 7–11.

12. Ibid., p. 29.

13. Otto Finger, *Studien an zwei asozialen Zigeunermischlings-Sippen* (Gießen, 1937).

14. Michael Zimmermann, *Rassenutopie und Genozid: Die nationalsozialistische 'Lösung der Zigeunerfrage'* (Hamburg, 1996), pp. 129–55; Burleigh and Wippermann, *Racial State,* pp. 118, 120, 125; Joachim S. Hohmann, *Geschichte der Zigeunerverfolgung in Deutschland* (Frankfurt, 1988), p. 109.

15. Hitler, *Mein Kampf,* pp. 250–2, 546–65.

16. Harry K. Rosenthal, *German and Pole: National Conflict and Modern Myth* (Gainesville, FL, 1976), p. 84.

17. See Michael Burleigh, *Germany Turns Eastward: A Study of Ostforschung in the Third Reich* (Cambridge, 1988).

18. This is made clear in Carl Petersen and Paul Hermann Ruth, *Deutsche Volkwerdung: Sein politisches Vermächtnis an die deutsche Gegenwart* (Breslau, 1934).

19. For an introduction to *völkisch* ideas see, for example, Alfred Rosenberg,   [189]
    'The Folkish Idea of State', in Barbara Miller Lane and Leila J. Rupp, eds,
    Nazi Ideology Before 1933 (Manchester, 1978), pp. 59–74.

20. Richard J. Overy, *War and Economy in the Third Reich* (Oxford, 1994); Hartmut
    Berghoff, 'Did Hitler Create a New Society? Continuity and Change in
    German Social History Before and After 1933', in Panikos Panayi, ed.,
    Weimar and Nazi Germany: Continuities and Discontinuities (London, 2000).

21. See David Schoenbaum, *Hitler's Social Revolution: Class and Status in Nazi
    Germany, 1933–39* (London, 1967).

22. David Welch, *The Third Reich: Politics and Propaganda* (London, 1995),
    pp. 50–89.

23. Burleigh and Wippermann, *Racial State*, pp. 136–97; Paul Weindling, *Health,
    Race and German Politics Between National Unification and Nazism, 1870–1945*
    (Cambridge, 1989), pp. 489–564.

24. See: Claudia Koonz, *Mothers in the Fatherland: Women, the Family and Nazi Politics*
    (London, 1987); and Lisa Pine, *Nazi Family Policy, 1933–1945* (Oxford, 1997).

25. Karl Dietrich Bracher, *The German Dictatorship: The Origins, Structure and Con-
    sequences of National Socialism* (Harmondsworth, 1973), pp. 243–87.

26. Ian Kershaw, *The 'Hitler Myth': Image and Reality in the Third Reich* (Oxford,
    1987).

27. Wolfgang Sofsky, *The Order of Terror: The Concentration Camp* (Princeton, NJ,
    1997).

28. Robert Gellately, *The Gestapo and German Society: Enforcing Racial Policy, 1933–
    1945* (Oxford, 1990), p. 45.

29. This is, of course, the argument of Daniel John Goldhagen, *Hitler's Willing
    Executioners: Ordinary Germans and the Holocaust* (New York, 1996). Other
    books which prove responsibility of the German populace for the Holocaust
    include David Bankier, *The Germans and the Final Solution: Public Opinion Under
    Nazism* (Oxford, 1992).

30. This is the argument of Zygmunt Bauman, *Modernity and the Holocaust* (Cam-
    bridge, 1989).

31. For an outline of Nazi foreign policy see, for example, K. Hilderbrand, *The
    Foreign Policy of the Third Reich* (London, 1973).

32. Gil Eliot, *Twentieth Century Book of the Dead* (London, 1972), p. 83.

33. For more precise figures see ibid., pp. 83, 215.

[190]

34. Richard Bessel, *Political Violence and the Rise of Nazism: The Storm Troopers in Eastern Germany, 1925–1934* (London, 1984), pp. 98–105.

35. Henry R. Huttenbach, *The Destruction of the Jewish Community of Worms, 1933–1945: A Study of the Holocaust Experience in Germany* (New York, 1981), p. 14.

36. Bessel, *Political Violence*, p. 105.

37. Klaus P. Fischer, *The History of an Obsession: German Judeophobia and the Holocaust* (London, 1998), p. 235.

38. Avraham Barkai, *From Boycott to Annihilation: The Economic Struggle of German Jews, 1933–1943* (London, 1989), pp. 17–25; Wolf-Arno Kropat, 'Die hessischen Juden im Alltag der NS-Diktatur, 1933–1939', in Christiane Heinemann, ed., *Neunhundert Jahre Geschichte der Juden in Hessen: Beiträge zum politischen, wirtschaftlichen und kulturellen Leben* (Wiesbaden, 1983), pp. 412–14.

39. Karl Kühling, *Die Juden in Osnabrück* (Osnabrück, 1983), pp. 81–2.

40. Nora Levin, *The Holocaust Years* (Malabar, FL, 1990), p. 16.

41. Wolfgang Wippermann, *Geschichte der deutschen Juden: Darstellung und Dokumente* (Berlin, 1994), p. 77.

42. Burleigh and Wippermann, *Racial State*, pp. 49–50.

43. See the thorough discussion of this issue in Jeremy Noakes, 'The Development of Nazi Policy Towards the German-Jewish "Mischlinge", 1933–1945', *Leo Baeck Institute Year Book* 34 (1989), pp. 306–15.

44. Erst Noam and Wolf-Arno Kropat, *Juden vor Gericht, 1933–1945: Dokumente aus hessischen Justizakten* (Wiesbaden, 1975), pp. 118–20.

45. Marion A. Kaplan, *Between Dignity and Despair: Jewish Life in Nazi Germany* (New York, 1998), pp. 40–6; Fritz Wessels, 'Die Reichspogromnacht und das Ende der jüdischen Gemeinde in Weener', in Herbert Reger and Martin Tielke, eds, *Frisia Judaica: Beiträge zur Geschichte der Juden in Ostfriesland* (Aurich, 1988), pp. 289–90; Kühling, *Juden in Osnabrück*, p. 83.

46. Dieter Goetz, *Juden in Oldenburg, 1930–1938* (Oldenburg, 1988), p. 95.

47. Steven M. Lowenstein, 'The Struggle for Survival of Rural Jews in Germany 1933–1938: The Case of Bezirksamt Weissenberg, Mittelfranken', in Arnold Paucker, ed., *Die Juden im nationalsozialistischen Deutschland* (Tübingen, 1986), p. 117.

48. Hannele Zürndorfer, *The Ninth of November* (London, 1983), p. 46.

49. Heinemann Stein, *Warum hassen Sie uns eigentlich? Jüdisches Leben zwischen den Kriegen* (Düsseldorf, 1970), pp. 197–8.

50. Barkai, *From Boycott to Annihilation*, p. 77; Günter Plum, 'Wirtschaft und Erwerbsleben', in Wolfgang Benz, ed., *Die Juden in Deutschland, 1933–1945: Leben unter nationalsozialistischer Herrschaft* 3rd edn (Munich, 1993), pp. 292–313; David Kramer, 'Jewish Welfare Work Under the Impact of Pauperization', in Paucker, *Die Juden im nationalsozialistischen Deutschland*, pp. 173–88.

51. Volker Dahm, 'Kulturelles und geistiges Leben', in Benz, ibid., pp. 125–222.

52. Hans Nordsiek, *Juden in Minden: Dokumente und Bilder jüdischen Lebens vom Mittelalter bis zum 20. Jahrhundert* (Minden, 1988), p. 66.

53. Alfred Hirschberg, 'Der Zentralverein deutscher Staatsbürger jüdischen Glaubens', in *Wille und Weg des deutschen Judentums* (Berlin, 1935), pp. 12–29; Lucy Dawidowicz, *The War Against the Jews, 1933–45* (Harmondsworth, 1990), pp. 215–46.

54. Kaplan, *Between Dignity and Despair*, pp. 52–3.

55. Konrad Kwiet, 'The Ultimate Refuge: Suicide in the Jewish Community under the Nazis', *Leo Baeck Institute Year Book* 29 (1984), pp. 135–48.

56. Michael Marrus, *Unwanted: European Refugees in the Twentieth Century* (New York, 1985), pp. 129–30.

57. Huttenbach, *Jewish Community of Worms*, p. 16.

58. Werner Cahnman, *German Jewry: Its History and Sociology* (Brunswick, NJ, 1984), p. 83.

59. Anthony Read and David Fisher, *Kristallnacht: Unleashing the Holocaust* (London, 1991), pp. 27–30.

60. Ibid, pp. 33–72; Uwe Dietrich Adam, 'How Spontaneous Was the Pogrom?', in Walter H. Pehle, ed., *November 1938: From 'Reichskristallnacht' to Genocide* (Oxford, 1991), pp. 73–94.

61. Read and Fisher, *Kristallnacht*, pp. 73–4.

62. Quoted in Kurt Pätzold and Irene Runge, *'Kristallnacht': Zur Pogrom 1938* (Cologne, 1988), pp. 120–1.

63. Huttenbach, *Jewish Community of Worms*, p. 21.

64. Read and Fisher, *Kristallnacht*, pp. 73, 134–5; Erika Weinzierl, 'Schuld durch Gleichgültigkeit? Zur Geschichte der Novemberpogrome 1938', in Günter Gorschenck and Stephan Reimers, eds., *Offene Wunden – brennende Fragen: Juden in Deutschland von 1938 bis heute* (Frankfurt, 1989), p. 20.

65. Wippermann, *Geschichte der deutschen Juden*, p. 84.

66. Konrad Kwiet, 'To Leave or not to Leave: The German Jews at the Crossroads', in Pehle, *November 1938*, p. 146.

67. Peter Gay, *My German Question: Growing up in Nazi Berlin* (London, 1998), pp. 138–54.

68. Zürndorfer, *Ninth of November*, p. 71.

69. See Werner E. Mosse, *et al.*, *Second Chance: Two Centuries of German-Speaking Jews in the United Kingdom* (Tübingen, 1991).

70. For a general account of the years 1939–41 see Götz Ally, *'Final Solution': Nazi Population Policy and the Murder of European Jews* (London, 1999).

71. Kaplan, *Between Dignity and Despair*, pp. 145–228; Konrad Kwiet, 'Nach dem Pogrom: Stufen der Ausgrenzung', in Benz, *Die Juden in Deutschland, 1933–1945*, pp. 545–613; Barkai, *Boycott to Annihilation*, pp. 152–74.

72. Dawidowicz, *War Against the Jews*, p. 448.

73. Constantin Goschler, 'The Attitude Towards Jews in Bavaria After the Second World War', *Leo Baeck Institute Year Book* 36 (1991), p. 445.

74. Huttenbach, *Jewish Community of Worms*, pp. 38–9.

75. Horst Reichwein, 'Die Juden in nationalsozialistischer Zeit', in Reyer and Tielke, *Frisia Judaica*, pp. 275–7.

76. Arno J. Mayer, *Why Did the Heavens Not Darken: The Final Solution in History* (London, 1988), p. 69.

77. Ibid., pp. 186–92.

78. Abraham Lewin, *A Cup of Tears: A Diary of the Warsaw Ghetto* (Oxford, 1988), p. 70.

79. Hans Mommsen, *From Weimar to Auschwitz: Essays in German History* (Cambridge, 1991), p. 246.

80. Raul Hilberg, *The Destruction of the European Jews* vol. 1 (London, 1985), p. 267.

81. L. Dobroszycki, 'Restoring Jewish Life in Post-War Poland', *Soviet Jewish Affairs* 3 (1973), p. 59.

82. Burrin, *Hitler and the Jews*, p. 93; Mark Levene, 'Frontiers of Genocide: Jews in the Eastern War Zones, 1914–1920 and 1941', in Panikos Panayi, ed., *Minorities in Wartime: National and Racial Groupings in Europe, North America and Australia during the Two World Wars* (Oxford, 1993), pp. 83–117.

83. Gerald Fleming, *Hitler and the Final Solution* (Oxford, 1986), pp. 78–80.

84. Mayer, *Why?*, p. 275.

85. Dina Porat, 'The Holocaust in Lithuania: Some Unique Aspects', in David Cesarani, ed., *The Final Solution: Origins and Implementation* (London, 1994), pp. 162, 163.

86. Alec Nove and J. A. Newth, 'The Jewish Population: Demographic Trends and Occupational Patterns', in Lionel J. Kochan, ed., *The Jews in the Soviet Union Since 1917* 3rd edn (Oxford, 1978), p. 149.

87. Randolph L. Braham, *The Politics of Genocide: The Holocaust in Hungary*, vol. 1 (New York, 1981).

88. Martin L. Kovacs, 'National Minorities in Hungary, 1919–1980', in Stephan M. Horak, ed., *Eastern European National Minorities, 1919–1980* (Littleton, CO, 1985), pp. 167–8.

89. H. Renner, 'The National Minorities in Czechoslovakia After the Second World War', *Plural Societies* 7 (1976), p. 30.

90. Dawidowicz, *War Against the Jews*, pp. 458–61.

91. Mark Mazower, *Inside Hitler's Greece: The Experience of Occupation, 1941–44* (London, 1993), p. 256.

92. Estha Benbassa and Aron Rodrigue, *The Jews of the Balkans* (Oxford, 1995), pp. 173–9.

93. Myrna Goodman, 'Foundations of Resistance in German-Occupied Denmark', in Ruby Rohrlich, ed., *Resisting the Holocaust* (Oxford, 1998), pp. 213–37.

94. Richard A. Stein, 'Antisemitism in the Netherlands – Past and Present', *Patterns of Prejudice* 19 (1985), p. 19. For more detail see J. Pressner, *Ashes in the Wind: The Destruction of Dutch Jewry* (London, 1968).

95. Robert S. Wistrich, *Anti-Semitism: The Longest Hatred* (London, 1992), pp. 132–34. For more detail see, for instance, Michael R. Marrus and Robert O. Paxton, *Vichy France and the Jews* (Stanford, 1995).

96. Dawidowicz, *War Against the Jews*, pp. 441–3.

97. See Jonathan Steinberg, *All or Nothing: The Axis and the Holocaust, 1941–43* (London, 1990).

98. Dawidowicz, *War Against the Jews*, p. 480.

99. Hans Joachim Döring, *Die Zigeuner im nationalsozialistischen Staat* (Hamburg, 1964), p. 18.

100. Michael Schenk, *Rassismus gegen Sinti und Roma: Zur Kontinuität der Zigeunerverfolgung innerhalb der deutschen Gesellschaft von der Weimarer Republik bis in die Gegenwart* (Frankfurt, 1994), p. 114.

101. Sybil Milton, 'Antechamber to Birkenau: The *Zigeunerlager* After 1933', in H. Gubitz, H. Bästlein and J. Tuckel, eds, *Die Normalität des Verbrechers: Bilanz und Perspektiven der Forschung zu den nationalsozialistischen Gewaltverbrechen* (Berlin, 1994), pp. 241–3.

[194] 102. Ibid., p. 245.

103. Eva von Hase-Malik and Doris Kreuzkamp, *Du kriegst auch einen schönen Wohnwagen: Zwangslager für Sinti und Roma während des Nationalsozialismus in Frankfurt am Main* (Frankfurt, 1990), pp. 40–1, 46.

104. Milton, 'Antechamber to Birkenau', p. 249.

105. Zimmermann, *Rassenutopie*, pp. 118–24.

106. Ludwig Eiber, Eva Strauß and Michael Krausnick, *'Ich wußte, es wird schlimm': Die Verfolgung der Sinti und Roma in München, 1933–1945* (Munich, 1993), p. 30.

107. See Maria Michalsky-Knak, *Zigeuner: Und was wir mit ihnen in Berlin erlebten* (Berlin, 1935).

108. See Hans Weltzel, 'The Gypsies of Central Germany', *Journal of the Gypsy Lore Society* 17 (1938), pp. 9–24, 20–8, 73–80, 104–90.

109. Alfred Lessing, *Mein Leben im Versteck: Wie ein deutscher Sinti den Holocaust überlebte* (Düsseldorf, 1993), p. 30.

110. These approximate figures are given by Ulrich König, *Sinti und Roma unter dem Nationalsozialismus* (Bochum, 1989), pp. 44–5.

111. Ibid., pp. 80–9; Burleigh and Wippermann, *Racial State*, pp. 120–7; Bernhard Steck, 'Die nationalsozialistische Methoden zur Lösung des Zigeunerproblems', *Tribüne* 20 (1981), pp. 53–78; George von Soest, *Zigeuner zwischen Verfolgung und Integration: Geschichte, Lebensbedingungen und Eingliederungsversuche* (Weinheim, 1979), pp. 41–6; Eiber, Strauß and Krausich, *'Ich wußte, es wird schlimm'*, pp. 78–92. The experiences of Elisabeth Guttenberger can be found in Anita Geigges and Bernhard W. Wette, *Zigeuner heute: Verfolgung und Diskriminierung in der BRD* (Borheim-Merten, 1979), pp. 248–52.

112. Donald Kenrick and Grattan Puxon, *The Destiny of Europe's Gypsies* (London, 1972), pp. 183–4.

113. Grattan Puxon, 'Forgotten Victims: Plight of the Gypsies', *Patterns of Prejudice* 11 (1977), p. 26.

114. König, *Sinti und Roma*, p. 44.

115. Michael Zimmermann, '"Jetzt" und "Damals" als imaginäre Einheit: Erfahrungen in einem lebensgeschichtlichen Projekt über die nationalsozialistische Verfolgung von Sinti und Roma', *BIOS* 4 (1991), pp. 228–31.

116. Eiber, Strauß and Krausnich, *'Ich wußte, es wird schlimm'*, p. 103.

117. David M. Crowe, *A History of the Gypsies in Eastern Europe and Russia* (London, 1995), p. 186.

118. Isabel Fonseca, *Bury Me Standing: The Gypsies and their Journey* (London, 1995), pp. 265–71. [195]

119. I. Ficowski, *The Gypsies in Poland* (Warsaw, 1989), p. 49.

120. Willy Guy, 'Ways of Looking at Roms: The Case of Czechoslovakia', in Farnham Rehfisch, ed., *Gypsies, Tinkers and Other Travellers* (London, 1975), p. 215; Jiří Lípa, 'The Fate of Gypsies in Czechoslovakia Under Nazi Domination', in Michael Berenbaum, ed., *A Mosaic of Victims: Non-Jews Persecuted and Murdered by the Nazis* (London, 1990), pp. 207–15; David J. Kostelancik, 'The Gypsies of Czechoslovakia: Political and Ideological Considerations in the Development of Policy', *Studies in Comparative Communism* 22 (1989), p. 309.

121. See the relevant contributions on Hungary and Romania in David M. Crowe and I. Kolsti, eds, *The Gypsies of Eastern Europe* (Armonk, NY, 1991).

122. Crowe, *History of the Gypsies*, pp. 220–1.

123. Ralf Karl Oenning, *'Du da mitti polnischen Farben . . .': Sozialisationserfahrungen von Polen im Ruhrgebiet 1918 bis 1939* (Münster, 1991), p. 115; Christoph Kleßmann, *Polnische Bergarbeiter im Ruhrgebiet, 1870–1945* (Göttingen, 1978), pp. 177–83.

124. Wojciech Wrzesiński, 'The Union of Poles in Germany (1922–1939)', *Polish Western Affairs* 9 (1968), p. 42.

125. Kleßmann, *Polnische Bergarbeiter*, pp. 183–6.

126. Elke Gemkow, Marco Heinz and Stefan Neumann, 'Die Sorben in der Lausitz', in Heinz and Neumann, eds, *Ethnische Minderheiten in Westeuropa* (Bonn, 1996), pp. 103–13.

127. Martin Kasper, 'Sorbische Sprache und Kultur unter dem Hakenkreuz', in Karin Bott-Bodenhausen, ed., *Unterdrückte Sprachen: Sprachverbote und das Recht auf Gebrauch der Minderheitensprachen* (Frankfurt, 1996), p. 106.

128. Martin Kasper, *Geschichte der Sorben*, Vol. 3, *Von 1917 bis 1945* (Bautzen, 1976), pp. 117–204; Todd Huebner, 'Ethnicity Denied: Nazi Policy Towards Lusatian Sorbs', *German History* 6 (1988), pp. 250–77; Burleigh and Wippermann, *Racial State*, pp. 132–5.

129. Wolfgang Wippermann, *Geschichte der deutsch-polnischen Beziehungen* (Berlin, 1992), pp. 33–5; Israel Gutman, 'The Victimization of Poles', in Berenbaum, *Mosaic of Victims*, pp. 97–8; J. Noakes and G. Pridham, *Nazism, 1919–1945*, Vol. 3, *Foreign Policy, War and Racial Extermination: A Documentary Reader* (Exeter, 1988), pp. 922–96; Wolfgang Jacobmeyer, 'Die deutsch-polnischen Beziehungen in der Neuzeit als Konfliktgeschichte', in D. Storch, ed., *Polen und Deutschland: Nachbarn in Europa* (Hanover, 1996), p. 28.

[196]   130. Eliot, *Twentieth Century Book of the Dead*, p. 215.

131. Omer Bartov, *The Eastern Front, 1941–1945: German Troops and the Barbarisation of Warfare* (London, 1985); Jürgen Förster, 'The German Army and the Ideological War Against the Soviet Union', in Gerhard Hirschfeld, ed., *The Policies of Genocide: Jews and Soviet Prisoners of War in Nazi Germany* (London, 1986), pp. 15–29; Mayer, *Why?*, pp. 159–275, 313–47; Georgily A. Kumanev, 'The German Occupation Regime in Occupied Territory in the USSR (1941–1944)', in Berenbaum, *Mosaic of Victims*, pp. 128–41.

132. Johann Woydt, *Ausländische Arbeitskräfte in Deutschland: Vom Kaiserreich bis zur Bundesrepublik* (Heilbronn, 1987), p. 54; Ulrich Herbert, *A History of Foreign Labour in Germany, 1880–1980: Seasonal Workers/Forced Labourers/Guest Workers* (Ann Arbor, MI, 1990), pp. 127–31; Lothar Elsner und Joachim Lehmann, *Ausländische Arbeiter unter dem deutschen Imperialismus 1900 bis 1985* (Berlin, 1988), pp. 155–81; Karl Liedke, '. . . aber politisch unerwünscht': Arbeitskräfte aus Osteuropa im Land Braunschweig 1880 bis 1939* (Braunschweig, 1993), pp. 138–42.

133. Gordon A. Craig, *Germany, 1866–1945* (Oxford, 1981), p. 735.

134. Herbert, *History of Foreign Labour*, pp. 154, 156.

135. Edward L. Homze, *Foreign Labour in Nazi Germany* (Princeton, NJ, 1967), p. 195.

136. Jochen August, 'Die Entwicklung des Arbeitsmarkts in Deutschland in den 30er Jahren und der Masseneinsatz ausländischer Arbeitskräfte während des Zweiten Weltkrieges', *Archiv für Sozialgeschichte* 24 (1984), p. 305.

137. Thenkel Straede, 'Dänische Fremdarbeiter in Deutschland während des zweiten Weltkrieges', *Zeitgeschichte* 13 (1985–6), pp. 400–4.

138. Gerhard Hirschfeld, 'Der "freiwillige" Arbeitseinsatz niederländischer Fremdarbeiter des Zweiten Weltkrieges als nicht-nationalsozialistischen Verwaltung', in Hans Mommsen and Winfried Schulze, eds, *Vom Elend der Handarbeit: Probleme historischer Unterschichtenforschung* (Stuttgart, 1981), pp. 499–500.

139. Helga Bories-Sawala, *Franzosen im 'Reicheinsatz': Deportation, Zwangsarbeit, Alltag*, 2 Vols (Frankfurt, 1996), I, p. 220.

140. Yves Durand, 'Vichy und der "Reicheinsatz"', in Ulrich Herbert, ed., *Europa und der 'Reicheinsatz': Ausländische Zivilarbeiter, Kriegsgefangene und KZ-Häftlinge in Deutschland, 1938–1945* (Essen, 1991), p. 184.

141. Bories Sawala, *Franzosen*, pp. 247, 249, 251, 252, 253, 285, 298. See also Friedrich Didier, *Europa arbeitet in Deutschland: Sauckel mobilisiert die*

Leistungsreserven (Berlin, 1943), which, despite being a Nazi publication, contains much on the recruitment of French workers.

142. Ulrich Herbert, *Fremdarbeiter: Politik und Praxis des 'Ausländer-Einsatzes' in der Kriegwirtschaft des Dritten Reiches* 2nd edn (Bonn, 1986), pp. 67–74.

143. Jürgen Kuczynski, *300 Million Slaves and Serfs: Labour Under the Fascist New Economic Order* (London, 1942), p. 12.

144. Betrieb Rode-Stankowski, *Zwangsarbeit bei Ford: Dokumentation der 'Projektgruppe Messelager' im Verein EL-DE-Haus e.V. Köln* (Cologne, 1996), pp. 47–9.

145. Herbert, *History of Foreign Labour*, pp. 154–5; Homze, *Foreign Labour*, p. 235.

146. Istvan Csöppüs, 'Ungarische Saisonarbeiter in der Landwirtschaft des Reiches, 1937–1944', *Zeitschrift für Agrargeschichte und Agrarsozioligie* 28 (1980), pp. 38, 40.

147. See the interviews of former 'nannies' carried out by Annakatrien Mendel, *Zwangsarbeit im Kinderzimmer: 'Ostarbeiterinnen' in deutschen Familien von 1939 bis 1945* (Frankfurt am Main, 1994).

148. Hans Pfahlman, *Fremdarbeiter und Kriegsgefangene in der deutschen Kriegswirtschaft, 1939–1945* (Darmstadt, 1968), p. 128.

149. Herbert, *Fremdarbeiter*, pp. 190–2.

150. H. Weisfeld, 'Zwangsarbeit in Bremen', in Diethelm Knauf and Helga Schröder, eds, *Fremde in Bremen: Auswanderer, Zuwanderer, Zwangsarbeiter* (Bremen, 1993), pp. 119–20.

151. Sigrid Jacobeit, 'Frauen-Arbeit im faschistischen Deutschland', in Klaus Tenfelde, ed., *Arbeiter im 20. Jahrhundert* (Stuttgart, 1991), pp. 93–100.

152. Gabriele Freitag, *Zwangsarbeiter im Lipper Land: Der Einsatz von Arbeitskräften in der Landwirtschaft Lippes, 1939–1945* (Bochum, 1996), pp. 13, 25–6.

153. Heinrich Burgdorf, *et al.*, eds, *Zwangsarbeiterinnen und Kriegsgefangene in Blomberg (1939–1945)* (Bielefeld, 1996), p. 7.

154. Herbert, *History of Foreign Labour*, p. 162; Helga Bories-Sawala, *Franzosen im 'Reicheinsatz': Deportation, Zwangsarbeit, Alltag*, vol. 2 (Frankfurt, 1996), p. 94.

155. Homze, *Foreign Labour*, p. 297.

156. Jehuda L. Wallach, 'Probleme der Zwangsarbeit in der deutschen Kriegwirtschaft', *Jahrbuch des Instituts für Deutsche Geschichte* 6 (1977), pp. 483–91.

157. Helga Kohne, 'Der Weg in die Hölle von Ravensbrück', in Helga Kohne and Christoph Lane, eds, *Mariopol-Herford und Zurück: Zwangsarbeit und ihre Bewältigung nach 1945* (Bielefeld, 1995), p. 202.

[198]   158. Wladimir Lipski and Bogdan Tschaly, *Mädchen, wo seid ihr: Vierzehn ehemalige Zwangsarbeiter errinnern sich* (Zeuthen, 1995), p. 103.

159. Weisfeld, 'Zwangsarbeit in Bremen', p. 121.

160. Kuczynski, *300 Million Slaves*, p. 15; Betrieb Rode-Stankowski, *Zwangsarbeit bei Ford*, pp. 51, 108.

161. Kuczynski, ibid., p. 17.

162. Burgdorf, *et al.*, *Zwangsarbeiterinnen und Kriegsgefangene in Blomberg*, p. 25.

163. Herbert, *Fremdarbeiter*, p. 267.

164. Pavel Marković Poljan and Žanna Antonovna Zajoncćkovskaja, 'Ostarbeiter in Deutschland und daheim: Ergebnisse einer Fragebogenanalyse', *Jahrbücher zur Geschichte Osteuropas* 41 (1993), p. 555.

165. Jill Stephenson, 'Triangle: Foreign Workers, German Civilians, and the Nazi Regime: War and Society in Württemberg', *German Studies Review* 15 (1992), p. 344.

166. Karl Boland, 'Zivilarbeiter und Kriegsgefangene: Beobachtungen und Erfahrungen in Mönchengladbach und Rheydt', *Geschichte im Westen* 8 (1993), p. 41.

167. Antje Zühl, 'Zum Verhältnis der deutschen Landbevölkerung gegenüber Zwangsarbeitern und Kriegsgefangenen', in Werner Röhr, *et al.*, eds, *Fascismus und Rassismus: Kontroversen um Ideologie und Opfer* (Berlin, 1992), p. 348.

168. Eva Seeber, *Zwangsarbeiter in der faschistischen Kriegswirtschaft* (Berlin, 1964), pp. 165, 179.

169. Stephenson, 'Triangle', pp. 344–5.

170. Boland, 'Zivilarbeiter und Kriegsgefangene', pp. 52–7.

CHAPTER 6

The Age of Mass Migration: Germanies after 1945

A t the end of the Second World War Germany lay in complete ruin. Collapsed buildings dominated the skylines of the major cities. Those people living in the western parts of Hitler's former Reich faced problems of homelessness and starvation, while the Germans expelled from the eastern parts of the deceased Nazi state moved westward to compete for the same resources as their western brethren. Starvation, deprivation, humiliation and foreign rule characterized Germany during the second half of the 1940s. Immediately after the war, not only did the dreams of the Nazis and their followers lie in ruins, but the economic, social and political progress of the previous 150 years appeared to have come to nothing.

By 1949 two German nation states actually existed which pointed to a return to the situation before 1871, when Germany lay divided. Both the German Democratic Republic and the Federal Republic regarded themselves as the only legitimate German state, although, with the passage of time, each tolerated the other's existence. Nevertheless, as in the decades before 1870, those between 1949 and 1989 meant the existence of a German question in the form of a divided Germany which must, at some stage in the future, become a unitary entity. The two German states developed their own form of nationalism. While the GDR saw itself as a German socialist state, the Federal Republic put forward concepts of national identity divorced from the horrors of recent German history so that there almost developed the idea of a pride in one's country divorced from its past. *Can you divorce past?*

In one sense the Federal Republic had close connections with its Nazi and Wilhelmine predecessor. All three of these state manifestations of German nationalism possessed large numbers of minorities within their borders. In the case of the importation of foreign workers, the methods used had similarities in all three cases, although neither the *Kaiserreich* nor the Federal Republic employed the forceful methods utilized by the Nazis. Nevertheless,

[200] the economies of all three depended heavily on foreign labour as fuel for economic growth, which always benefited ethnic Germans more than it did the minorities who moved into the country to help this process. The Federal Republic also resembles the Wilhelmine and Nazi eras in the sheer numbers of people who counted themselves as minorities, especially those born abroad. The FRG became a 'country of immigration *par excellence*', surpassing even the USA in the total number of newcomers attracted after 1945, so that the 1989 West German population of 61 million contained 18 million people, or one third of the total, obtained through immigration after the Second World War.[1] The largest part of this figure actually consisted of those ethnic Germans expelled or migrating from further east after 1945, but close to a third was made up of people from southern Europe, Turkey and elsewhere. A completely different situation existed in the GDR, as this state experienced population loss, mostly to the Federal Republic, rather than gain during its forty years of existence. Both countries also continued to house small peripheral minorities in the form of Danes and Sorbs. Furthermore, in addition to the tiny numbers of Jews and Gypsies which had survived the Nazis, new ones also entered the FRG.

The post-war refugee crisis

The total defeat which followed the total war of 1939–45 meant complete humiliation for the Nazis and their supporters as foreigners, in the form of the Americans, French, British and, worst of all, Russians, now controlled their country. Those Germans who had survived Allied bullets in armed combat or Allied bombs dropped from the sky on to their homes faced extreme hardship.

The economy had practically ceased to exist, which imposed a series of pressing problems on the population. Because of the neglect of agriculture a food crisis existed which meant the continuation of rationing. Death from starvation occurred due to the fact that large sections of the population received insufficient calorie intakes.[2] At the same time, as a result of Allied bombing the major German cities had witnessed a destruction of up to 50 per cent of their built-up areas and 45 per cent of their housing stock. By 1947 industrial production stood at 44 per cent of its level in 1936.[3]

The Allied occupation meant that ethnic Germans had less control over their political destiny between 1945 and 1949 than at any other time in their modern history. As a result of agreement reached in the latter stages of the war and its immediate aftermath, France, Britain, the USA and the Soviet Union [201] carved up Nazi Germany between them and each had control of its own sector. By 1949 the three western sectors had joined together in the formation of the Federal Republic, while the Soviet zone became the German Democratic Republic.[4] Just as humiliating for ex-Nazis was the implementation of a process of denazification, which involved the trial of former leaders, the removal from any positions of power of major supporters of the regime and, perhaps worst of all, a process of re-education, which involved pointing to the evils of Nazism and the virtues of liberal democracy.[5]

The years immediately after the end of the Second World War resulted in the biggest mass migration in Germany history, involving around twenty million people moving in all directions, either away from or towards German soil. The refugees, who may all be described by the collective term of Displaced Persons (DPs), divide into three groups. The first consists of those foreign workers who still found themselves within Germany at the end of the war, most of whom made their way home as soon as possible. While the majority of journeys took place to the east, others occurred to the north, south and west. The second group of migrants consisted, surprisingly, of Jews from Poland who moved from the still potent antisemitism in that country to Germany, where Judeophobia had essentially become a spent force. The largest population movement involved the entry of ethnic Germans, who represented victims of boundary changes or vindictive eastern European regimes.

By 1945, as a consequence of Allied bombing, foreign workers and prisoners of war had begun to wander aimlessly around German cities without food or shelter. The Soviet Union had decided in October 1944 that it wanted the repatriation of all its citizens living abroad, in view of the manpower shortages which it would face at the end of the war as a consequence of the population loss it had endured. Reconstruction required every fit citizen, including those living abroad. Therefore the Yalta Treaty of 11 February 1945, signed by Stalin, Churchill and Roosevelt, provided for the repatriation of civilians and prisoners of war on both sides after liberation. The vast majority of Soviet DPs, totalling almost 5 million by March 1946, went home voluntarily, although some had been forced to return. Many wished to remain in the west for a combination of political and economic reasons. Balts did not wish to return to a 'bestial' and 'murderous' 'reign of terror' in their states which had recently been taken over by Stalin. Other Soviet citizens had more to fear from returning, as they had fought against their state. Up to 10 per cent of German prisoners brought to Britain consisted of Russians. Some Soviet DPs, who spent several years in camps situated

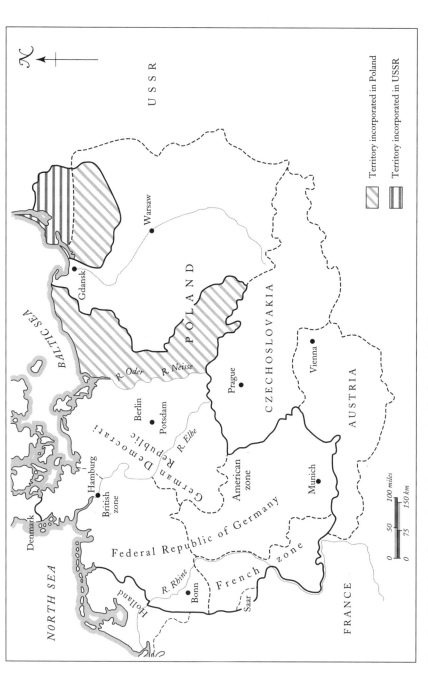

Map 5: Divided and Dismembered Germany after the Second World War.
Source: Mary Fulbrook, *A Concise History of Germany* (Cambridge: Cambridge University Press, 1990) p. 205.

throughout central Europe, looking to the west for salvation, were eventually able to secure employment in western European states. Britain acted as one of the main destinations, taking in a total of 91,151 'European Volunteer Workers' for employment in a restricted range of industries with a shortage of labour. Other European states which took in smaller numbers of Soviet and other central European DPs included France, Belgium and the Netherlands. Even those Soviet citizens who made their way home voluntarily had to face questions from their state's authorities, both within filter camps established in Germany and upon their arrival in their homeland. Inna Efomowa Kulagina recalled interviews with the KGB upon her return. She also remembered that 'our own people believed that we were enemies of the people', even though she had been forcibly transported to Germany in October 1942.[6]

At the end of the war liberated Jews made a significant proportion of the DPs who found themselves in Germany. Upon their release, about 50,000 were situated upon the territory of pre-war German borders, although, within a few weeks, because of the high death rate, this figure fell to just 30,000.[7] In Bergen-Belsen, where the number of Jews had increased from 18,000 to 60,000 in the first four months of 1945 as a result of arrivals from the east, 18,000 died in March followed by a further 9,300 during the first two weeks of April due to the dreadful living conditions which existed.[8]

By 1947 the number of Jews in Germany had actually grown to about 200,000,[9] originating mostly from Poland, which experienced serious antisemitic pogroms, which may have led to the death of as many as 1,500 Jews in the country by the summer of 1947.[10] In the summer of 1946 over 2,000 Polish Jews per week moved to the area of Greater Hesse.[11] But because of their experiences during the Second World War, the continuing existence of hostility towards them and the activities of Zionists, very few Jews had any desire to remain within Europe. Inevitably, the vast majority made their way to the newly created Jewish state of Israel. Nearly 200,000 eastern European Jews migrated to either Israel or the USA via Germany, including 120,000 who travelled through Munich.[12]

The Jews in Germany at the end of the Second World War, particularly those who had spent time in the camps, were barely alive because of the physical and psychological trauma from which they had emerged. As one contemporary observer, commenting upon the 'personality' of displaced persons, pointed out:

> The Jewish DPs show an incapacity for sustained effort and concentration. They become fatigued after a few hours' work or after a stretch of intellectual concentration. Combined with these physical and psychic effects of the harassed

[204]   life they led, have also come moral and social effects evidenced particularly in a reduced sense of social responsibility and in a diminution in the sense for private property.[13]

Nevertheless, some normality continued in the camps after liberation. In Belsen, for instance:

> From the day of liberation until 22nd June 1945, 74 marriages were solemnised, from the 22nd July 1945 to the 1st June 1947, 1,002 marriages, 362 marriages which were somehow performed before the liberation were later confirmed, making a total of 1,438.[14]

Interesting
Hopeful
Comments

At least one inmate of Belsen, Gena Turgel, married one of the British soldiers who had liberated the camp and consequently moved to England with him.[15] In December 1946 a total of 65 DP camps had existed in Germany, but these had fallen to 4 by 1 October 1950. When the International Refugee Organization closed down its office in 1952 only 12,000 Jews remained in Germany.[16]

An examination of the movement of ethnic Germans into the rump Germany, reveals that millions rather than hundreds of thousands of people became victims of the vindictive victors. Essentially, the events in central Europe at the end of the Second World War represent, along with the almost simultaneous displacement of population in the Indian sub-continent as a result of partition in 1947, the most thorough act of ethnic cleansing in human history.[17] Each event involved the removal of over ten million souls. One account of the German population displacement gave the following figures:

> By 1944–5 a total of approximately 16,500,000 Germans were living in areas affected by the mass exodus, excluding only the Soviet Union. From the end of the war to 1950 over 11,500,000 of these people had actually fled or were expelled. In 1950 more than 2,500,000 were known to have remained in or near their homes. In 1950 about 2,200,000 people were not accounted for and many of them probably perished during the exodus.[18]

Thus, while German nationals may have initiated and perpetrated some of the most brutal acts in central European history between 1940 and 1945, ethnic Germans east of the Oder–Neisse line equally became victims of dreadful inhumanity and atrocity from 1944, supported by the other truly brutal European regime of the twentieth century, the Soviet Union under Stalin, which had killed tens of millions of its 'own people'.[19]

The Germans who fled into the four zones of rump Germany at the end of the Second World War, divide into a series of groups, although some overlap exists between them. We need to remember that the vast majority left behind virtually everything they had and could never claim it back again. Often they walked hundreds of miles on foot with their families. The enduring image of Germany at the end of the war consists of lines of people streaming west-wards, often in the snow, with as much as they could carry on their backs or, if they were lucky enough, with a horse and cart packed with their posses-sions. In other cases they fled on precisely the type of goods trains used by the Nazis to transport Jews to the death camps. Once they reached safety they found themselves in a landscape of devastation where they would face home-lessness, starvation and unemployment. The ethnic Germans were victims of Stalinism, war, border changes, eastern European nationalism and post-war vindictiveness. In the same way as the Nazis had targeted the civilian popu-lations of eastern Europe, so the regimes which seized power after the Nazis had left decided to victimize men, women and children who, in many cases, had little to do with the Nazi regime. Both eastern Europeans and ethnic Germans were victims of the total war and the totalitarian regimes which dominated central Europe during the first half of the twentieth century.

Although much overlap exists between the different groups of westward-fleeing ethnic Germans, we can distinguish three. The first consists of those who simply escaped the Soviet advance into Germany, aware of the actions which the Nazis had carried out against the population of the USSR and rightly fearful of the vengeance which would occur against them. The Soviet Army had amassed on the border of East Prussia in the autumn of 1944.[20] By the end of January 1945 the area had been cut off from the rest of the Reich and the Soviets stood just 160 kilometres from Berlin.[21] Immediately upon their entry into East Prussia, Soviet forces took over the houses of Germans, raped German women and even shelled convoys of refugees with their tanks.[22]

Numerous accounts exist of the trek out of East Prussia, which began as soon as it became clear that Soviet forces would take over the province. For instance, 30 year old Edith Büchler left the village of Spullen in Schloßberg in October 1944 and travelled over 1,000 kilometres on a wagon during the following nine weeks until she reached relative safety in Lüneberg.[23] The populations of entire settlements simply fled. Werner Terpitz later recalled events in his home town of Nordenburg, south east of Danzig, once it became surrounded by Soviet troops:

> The town was endangered from beyond its borders and the people could save itself by fleeing west. A large proportion of the residents had left the location. The rural population and some inhabitants who, as arable farmers, possessed their own horses and wagons, had come together to form treks and tried to flee

southwards avoiding Danzig using rural paths. Only the first treks remained unmolested. The Russians arrived quicker than people imagined. Many of the treks became stuck on blocked roads in the ice cold. Old people and small children died.[24]

The flight of the family of sixteen year old Terpitz involved a complicated journey over land and sea, during which time members became separated and both his mother and grandfather died in Mecklenburg.[25]

The second group of ethnic Germans who fled westward at the end of the Second World War have close connections with those who moved to escape the Russian advance. They consist of those people who became victims of the border changes which moved the Russian and, consequently, Polish and German borders further to the west and potentially left up to eleven million ethnic Germans under Polish and Soviet sovereignty.[26] Even had they wanted to remain in their homelands, they could not do so because the expulsion received a legal basis following the Potsdam Conference of July and August 1945 involving Truman, Stalin and Churchill (replaced during the meeting by Clement Atlee because of the Labour Party General Election victory). When the leaders of Britain, the USA and the USSR met to decide the fate of Europe the issues they resolved included the Polish border and the fate of the Germans in eastern Europe. Article XIII of the Potsdam Protocol declared that:

> The three Governments having considered the question in all its aspects, recognize that the transfer to Germany of German populations, or elements thereof, remaining in Poland, Czechoslovakia and Hungary will have to be undertaken. They agree that any transfers that take place should be effected in an orderly and humane manner.[27]

Clearly, this did not happen, as the move from east to west of millions of people continued to result in extreme hardship and personal tragedy for many of the countless individuals involved.

As the above extract makes clear, the loss of territory as a result of the post-war settlements did not simply affect Germans in Poland and the Soviet Union, but also those in Czechoslovakia and Hungary, to which we can also add those in Romania and Yugoslavia to make up our third group of expellees. The presence of Germans in eastern Europe has a history dating back centuries but its nature had changed as a result of Hitler's expansionist policies from the later 1930s, which made the Germans a privileged group representing an invading force which inevitably caused resentment.

As a result of the annexation of the Sudetenland in 1938 the Germans in Czechoslovakia had become incorporated into the Reich, but the post-war peace settlement meant that this went back to Czech hands, with unfortunate consequences for Germans in the area. In fact the Czechoslovak President, Eduard Beneš had decided as early as 1938 that all Germans would face expulsion at the end of the Second World War, which duly happened, together with an annulment of their citizenship against a background of intense Germanophobia. Most of these deportations occurred in 1946, although they began before and continued afterwards. In this way, 800 years of German settlement in Bohemia almost came to an end. The German proportion of the population declined from 22.3 per cent in 1930 to 1.3 per cent by 1950.[28]

The number of Germans in Hungary had increased from 550,000 in 1920 to 700,000 between 1938 and 1941 because of the return of some territories lost by Hungary at the Treaty of Trianon in 1920,[29] but the Germans of Hungary suffered the same fate as similar populations in neighbouring countries after the Second World War. In 1950 around 170,000 Germans from Hungary lived in the Federal Republic, while a further 54,000 resided in the GDR.[30] Nevertheless, approximately 220,000 ethnic Germans still lived in Hungary at the start of the 1990s.[31]

The expansion of Romania at the end of the First World War, as a result of the Treaties of Trianon and Saint-Germain, created a German minority in that state, which stood at about 750,000 by 1930.[32] The German population shrank gradually during the Second World War. In 1940 the Soviet Union annexed Bessarabia and Bukovina, which meant that over 200,000 Germans left these areas by 1943; mostly for resettlement in regions taken over by the Nazis. In addition, the temporary gain of territory by Hungary meant a reduction of the German population to two-thirds of its size before 1939.[33] When the Red Army entered Romania in the late summer of 1944 more ethnic Germans fled, while those who remained faced reprisals. Nevertheless, over 350,000 Germans still resided in Romania in 1977.[34]

More than half a million Germans lived in Yugoslavia in 1921, concentrated mostly in the Voyvodina, but also focusing in the other parts of the new state, in which they had settled since the Middle Ages.[35] The association of the ethnic Germans with the Nazis meant that the military defeat of the occupying forces made evacuation of the German populations inevitable, beginning at the end of 1943. When Soviet troops approached Voyvodina in September 1944, the Germans who did not flee faced internment, a loss of citizenship and even deportation to Soviet labour camps, a process to which 100,000 people may have fallen victim,[36] in some cases staying there until the early 1950s. Just 61,000 Germans remained in Yugoslavia in 1953.[37]

The census of May 1946 gave a figure of nine million expellees in the four occupied German zones,[38] although they did not divide equally between them. At the start of 1949, 4.3 million lived in the Soviet zone of occupation, a total largely explained by its proximity to the areas which suffered population loss. The Soviet zone had taken 37.2 per cent of Germans fleeing westward, who made up 24.2 per cent of all people living there. In contrast the British zone counted 32.8 per cent of all expellees, while the American held 28.2 per cent and the French just 1.8 per cent. Consequently, they made up smaller proportions of the total populations of these zones standing at 18.1 per cent in the American one, 15.9 per cent in the area controlled by the British and 3 per cent in the French sector.[39]

A type of chain migration appears to have occurred in the move from east to west because Germans from particular areas moved to specific regions of the different zones of occupation connected to geographical proximity. This concentration was helped by the fact that the movement westward became organized by the United Nations Relief and Rehabilitation Administration which had already assisted the migration of 4.6 million people by as early as September 1945.[40] Thus East Prussians settled mostly in Lower Saxony and Schleswig-Holstein, Silesians went to Lower Saxony, Westphalia and Bavaria, while most of the Sudeten Germans moved to Bavaria.[41] The settlement occurred on an even more local level. For instance, about four fifths of expellees in Lower Saxony came from regions east of the Oder–Neisse Line, half of them from Silesia and more than half of the Silesians from the region of Breslau.[42]

The expellees moved to settlements of varying sizes. The occupying and German authorities directed them towards smaller locations because of the shortage of housing in the destroyed cities. Thus in 1949, 'of the total number of refugees in Bavaria (1,775,000), 74 per cent, or 1,200,000 are currently residing in such communities with a population of less than 4,000 inhabitants'.[43] These arrivals became a large part of the population of many small settlements in Germany. For instance, in the Westphalian village of Wewelsburg near Paderborn the number of inhabitants grew from 950 at the start of the 1930s to around 2,000 by the middle of the 1950s, when refugees made up about forty per cent of the population.[44] Similarly, the inhabitants of the town of Delmenhorst grew by more than a third from 57,330 between 1945 and 1950 due to the arrival of 17,000 refugees and expellees, although many of these subsequently made their way to towns and cities in North Rhine-Westphalia.[45] Further south, by 1950 expellees made up 17.6 per cent and 11.9 per cent of the administrative districts of [209] Heidelberg and Mannheim respectively.[46]

Clearly, in view of the devastation which already existed in the areas of Germany to which they moved, as well as the trauma of leaving behind their homeland and their possessions, the refugees had many problems, worse than those of the populations resident in the towns and villages to which they moved. Housing represented the most immediate difficulty they faced, irrespective of the size of the settlement to which they moved. A small city such as Osnabrück had lost 21,000 out of the 33,000 homes which had existed before the war due to bombing.[47] But those who moved to rural areas simply found that the housing was just not there. Consequently, radical solutions came into existence. One of these merely consisted of placing the new arrivals in all manner of camps, some of which lasted into the 1950s. In Bremerhaven 2,569 people still lived in such accommodation in October 1952.[48] In Wewelsburg, the newcomers initially moved into a former concentration camp, an SS barracks and an old people's home. In the last of these the residents initially slept on the floor and simply hung their clothes on the wall.[49] One woman who arrived from Pomerania remembered her first few days in a camp near Osnabrück which had formerly housed foreign workers:

> We did not have a bed there although we had bed linen. They had to give us covers so that we could cover ourselves up. We thought we could wash ourselves, but we could not yet. Nobody could with cold water: look, it was March, and it was cold, and we were supposed to wash ourselves with cold water. We washed our hands and then we crawled up. And then the next morning came and nobody wanted to get up.[50]

As well as placing the expellees in all manner of camps, the occupying authorities billeted people on local farmers,[51] although some natives did take in refugees voluntarily.

> But with several families trying to cook in the same kitchen, take turns in the same bathroom, and raise children of assorted age and social backgrounds under the same roof, irritations and aggravating incidents are bound to occur. It is not pleasant for anyone. It is particularly difficult for the refugee who recognizes himself as an unwanted intruder.[52]

The housing problem did not reach its full solution until the 1960s when the reconstruction of German cities destroyed during the war allowed the refugees to move into their own accommodation, although even then they tended to live in worse homes than natives.[53]

[210]   Apart from housing, the other major problem for the refugees consisted of employment. Once again, they faced similar difficulties to natives in a country devastated by war where economic activity had virtually come to a standstill, although opportunities would arise because of the loss of people of employable age during the war and the possibilities created by reconstruction. Furthermore, in the longer run the expellees provided a readily available supply of cheap labour, which facilitated the speed of the reconstruction process.[54] Some of the newcomers actually found employment fairly quickly. Many of those who moved to Wewelsburg simply replaced the foreign workers who had kept the local rural economy going during the war, although others in the village relied on government hand outs.[55] In the Soviet zone the newcomers seem to have had higher employment rates than those in the west. In December 1946 a total of 84 per cent of all the refugees worked.[56] Of the 668,153 newcomers in Brandenburg on 1 December 1945, 379,419 had employment and 132,833 of the remaining 286,734 consisted of children.[57] In Bavaria 17 per cent of employable refugees still did not have jobs in October 1948.[58] In the western sectors as a whole the newcomers had a considerably higher unemployment rate than natives. Thus, in September 1950, while they made up 14 per cent of all employable adults they formed 32 per cent of those without work.[59] Unemployment among refugees declined with economic growth in the Federal Republic during the course of the 1950s and by 1960 it had virtually disappeared.[60]

The refugees faced various other short-term problems. Poor housing combined with a lack of food and clothing to lead to malnutrition and disease.[61] As we have seen, the newcomers also faced hostility from natives in the areas in which they settled. Among the rural population around the town of Celle in Lower Saxony, stereotypes developed against the refugees which viewed them as lazy and not prepared to help in farming or wood cutting. Natives also believed that the authorities had pampered them which led to the view that the refugees had arrived badly clothed but quickly dressed better than much of the established population.[62]

Nevertheless, while short-term hostility may have existed and while the process of full integration may have taken several decades, the treatment received by the expellees differs from that meted out to all other foreign ethnic groups who moved to Germany during the nineteenth and twentieth centuries because the refugees had the right ethnicity. In this sense they resemble the exiles from East Germany and, to a lesser extent, the ethnic Germans who migrated from eastern Europe during the 1980s and 1990s. The experience of the early post-war German refugees differed significantly from that of foreign workers who would follow them from the late 1950s or the asylum seekers who began to arrive in large numbers during the 1980s. Clearly the expellees were Germans but those who followed were foreigners. Other factors such as a common language also clearly helped the expellees to integrate.

The different views towards expelled Germans compared with foreigners manifested themselves most clearly in the measures which the Federal Republic took to help the integration of the two groups. In 1947 a government office called the Amt für Fragen der Heimatvertriebenen came into existence in Frankfurt, which, two years later, moved to Bonn as the Federal Ministry for Expellees, Refugees and War Victims. In 1948 the newcomers received a Bill of Rights. Most importantly the Federal Constitution of 1949 recognized them as full citizens. A new measure in 1953, the *Bundesvertriebenengesetz*, took steps to facilitate the social and economic integration of the expellees.[63] This contrasts directly with foreign workers, as well as their offspring, who still did not have full citizenship four decades and more after some of them first arrived.

The reaction of native society at large towards the expellees also contrasts directly with attitudes towards foreigners. Although the ethnic Germans faced some initial hostility, a whole range of organizations made efforts to ameliorate their early social and economic problems and ease their integration into west German life. The churches, for instance, played a leading role in this process.[64] The expellees also received help from local charities, in the form of cash, clothing or other essentials.[65]

But the newcomers also helped themselves by establishing their own organizations, of all manner, which assisted them in a series of ways. In the first place, like the ethnic bodies opened by previous and subsequent immigrant minorities in German history they represented a way of surviving the trauma of leaving their homeland as they allowed people with similar experiences to come together and talk about the events of 1945–47 and remember the places from where they had come. Secondly, the groups set up in the Federal Republic also had the function of fighting for the rights of the expellees in a liberal democratic state. Finally, the organizations further aimed at the integration of the refugees into their new surroundings, so that some of them would disappear when the memory of their eastern homes had faded.

In fact, the expellees had started their cultural activity within the camps, largely as a reaction against their surroundings because doing nothing would inevitably have brought back the memories of life in the east and the trauma of the trek. Thus, much musical activity took place in the camps, together with the performance of theatre pieces. In addition, the expellees made lots of efforts to remember their homeland and their deceased relatives who had not managed to make the journey with them.[66]

By the beginning of the 1950s the refugees had established many organizations, following the lifting of bans on the setting up of such groupings which operated under Allied occupation. The main factors which brought people together included their place of origin, their area of settlement and the political desire to return home, although other bodies concerned themselves with activities such as occupation, singing and sport. The Landmannschaften, based on the areas of origin, also made efforts to seek out lost relatives and came together in 1949 to become the Vereinigten Ostdeutschen Landmannschaften which, in 1952 developed into the Verband der Landmannschaften. More significantly a refugee party came into existence in 1950 in the form of the Bund der Heimatvertriebenen und Entrechteten which made a major breakthrough in the Schleswig-Holstein elections of that year and managed to gain 5.9 per cent of the vote and 27 seats in the Federal Election of 1953, although by the 1960s the party had disappeared. The refugees had also established their own newspapers and participated in demonstrations against the loss of their homeland. The protests reached a high point in 1955, ten years after the expulsion.[67]

Migrants in the Federal Republic of Germany, 1949–89

Germany embarked upon its third attempt at liberal democracy in 1949, following the failures of 1848–49 and 1918–33. The durability of the Federal Republic suggests it was third time lucky. The main reason for success lies in the fact that, unlike the previous two attempts, the liberal democratic state established in 1949 had full support from the West which regarded the FRG as a key player in the Cold War. At the same time, the Federal Republic never experienced the economic crisis endured by Weimar, while the memory of the consequences of Nazism between 1942 and 1949 meant that few Germans would choose to vote for an extreme right-wing party again.

Economically, with the exception of hiccoughs in 1966–67 and 1973–74, the Federal Republic experienced almost unhindered economic growth until the problems caused by reunification during the 1990s. This growth was initially based upon the need for reconstruction, but, subsequently, continued on the basis of products manufactured since the nineteenth century including chemicals, electrical engineering and engineering, with the car acting as a leading sector. The early availability of expellees and east German refugees played a major role in the economic growth of the Federal Republic, but, following the construction of the Berlin Wall in 1961, government and industry resorted to methods employed by its Imperial and Nazi predecessors in the form of foreign labour importation.[68]

Due to the economic success of the Federal Republic the type of social problems consequent upon mass unemployment did not surface because, although joblessness began to take off during the 1970s, an advanced welfare system could deal with this and did not collapse as its Weimar predecessor had done during the 1930s. Social gradations have certainly existed in the Federal Republic, especially on the basis of occupation,[69] but, with the passage of time a more obvious schism evolved in West German society between ethnic Germans and foreigners, therefore having direct links with previous German regimes. In fact, it seems questionable whether the idea of the ethnic *Volksgemeinschaft* which circulated from the early nineteenth century and which the Nazis put into practice completely disappeared after 1945.

The Federal Constitution of 1949 very much represents a reaction against the arbitrary totalitarian state of the Nazis and contained numerous clauses aimed at preventing a return to this type of government, including a charter of fundamental rights and freedoms.[70] In fact extreme nationalist groupings have never gained representation at a national level, while the Federal Constitutional Court can ban those regarded as Neo-Nazi and a threat to the liberal order.[71] Nevertheless, while the Federal Republic may never have come anywhere near a return to Nazism and while it may be regarded as one of the freest states in the world, it remains a nation state and, consequently, practises the more subtle forms of ethnic exclusion characteristic of liberal democracies, above all the use of exclusive nationality laws.[72]

Although the Federal Republic represented a reaction against Nazism, it had difficulty in developing its own non-racist nationalism because most of the previous manifestations of this ideology had virulent anti-semitic and Slavophobic strands. Even the milder antecedents which surfaced in 1848 ultimately always revolved around the German people and created external enemies, although the threat was not racialized. The nationalism of the Federal Republic therefore became respectable because it shed its overtly racial skin and simply resembled other post-war manifestations of this belief throughout the world, meaning that an emphasis still remained on Germans as a distinct ethnic rather than racial group. Instead of focusing upon its history, which the nationalism of most states does, that of the FRG developed into an ideology

[214]   which took pride in post-war liberal values and constitutional patriotism, as well as never forgetting the horrors of the German past. For the liberal nationalists 1945 represented year zero, when the reconstructed German nation state could begin its history all over again. The extreme right certainly did not share these views as it saw Germans as victims of twentieth-century wars. Furthermore, by the 1980s and, more especially, the 1990s, following reunification, the cautious nationalism of the early post-war decades gave way to a more self-conscious belief in German values, especially in the immediate aftermath of the fall of the Berlin Wall: pride in German nationality became fashionable again, although it also had violent xenophobic manifestations.[73]

Foreign policy has perhaps represented the clearest indication of the Federal Republic's differing nationalism compared with its predecessors. Unlike either the *Kaiserreich* or the Third Reich, it has not sought to bully and walk all over its neighbours but has, instead, tried to play a key role in the evolution of a peaceful Europe in the second half of the twentieth century.[74]

The Federal Republic has had similar minority problems to its predecessors. Despite the eliminationist policies of the Nazis the established groupings did not actually disappear. Those Jews who survived the Second World War would develop into a thriving community, although on a much smaller scale than their forefathers before 1945. In addition, the Gypsies would return to Germany and face the same type of persecution which they had experienced before 1939. Furthermore, the Danes survived as an ethnic minority but increasingly assimilated into the surrounding German population, an act facilitated by the similarities between the two groups.

But the main ethnic development in the history of the Federal Republic has consisted of the arrival of millions of foreign workers and their offspring between the 1950s and the 1980s so that people born in Turkey, Yugoslavia, Italy, Spain, Greece and Portugal would become the most significant minorities in the country. While the level of exploitation differed between the newcomers who arrived in the Federal Republic and the labour migrants of the Imperial and Nazi periods, clear similarities exist. In the first place, both before and after 1945 an organized process of labour importation occurred against the background of a booming economy experiencing a labour shortage. Second, the migrants arrived on short-term contracts although, unlike those in the late nineteenth century or the Nazi period, those after 1949 would remain partly because deportation would have smacked of Nazism and partly because the economy of the Federal Republic did not undergo the sort of break caused by the end of the First and Second World Wars. The foreign workers arriving from the 1950s also, like their predecessors, moved into the most difficult jobs, although those after 1945, unlike the migrants of the *Kaiserreich* and the Nazi period who focused on agriculture in a big way, worked overwhelmingly in industry. Also like their predecessors, the arrivals after 1945 lived in poor housing, although clearly not in concentration camps. Like the late nineteenth-century Ruhr Poles the labour migrants after 1945 developed a rich ethnicity revolving around a wide variety of activities. Their importation of new religions and foods has enriched German life. However, some Germans have not appreciated this, which has meant that the post-war arrivals and their offspring have faced regular racism backed by the attitude of the state towards them as temporary migrants without civil rights.

The fundamental reason for the arrival of foreign workers in the Federal Republic lay in the strength of the economy. However, emigration also occurred from the FRG at the end of the 1940s (once the Allies lifted a ban on it designed to prevent the escape of prominent Nazis) and into the 1950s against the background of the still poor economic and social conditions. Consequently 779,700 Germans emigrated between 1946 and 1951, with 384,700 moving to the USA, 243,300 to Canada, 80,500 to Australia, while others made their way to Britain and France.[75] Although movement out of Germany declined during the course of the 1960s, it certainly did not disappear, indicated, for instance, by the fact that 215,534 Germans lived in Britain in 1991.[76]

Nevertheless, immigration rather than emigration has represented the main population movement in the history of the Federal Republic. Before the arrival of the foreign workers, and after the movement of the expellees, another group of ethnic Germans fled to the FRG in the form of citizens of the GDR. From September 1949 until the construction of the Berlin Wall, which aimed at keeping people within the country, in August 1961, at least 2.7 million people had moved out of the GDR into West Germany,[77] so that by 1960 German expellees or refugees accounted for 23.8 per cent of the population of the FRG.[78] Political and economic push and pull factors explain the emigration of people from the GDR. The refugees felt attracted to the greater freedom apparent in a western liberal democracy in which there also existed greater potential to progress economically. The Federal Republic welcomed the refugees with open arms. Under article 116 of the Federal Constitution anyone who could demonstrate German ethnic origin could enter the newly created state. Economically the newcomers from the GDR supplemented the expellees and together played a significant role in the beginnings of the German economic miracle because of the labour power they provided.[79]

The West German government did not begin to import non-German labour on a large scale until the availability of ethnic Germans began to dry up during the 1950s. This development combined with other changes to increase the need for employees, notably the continued expansion of the German economy, a reduction in the retirement age and a fall in the working week. The economic need for immigrants is indicated by continued reconstruction, a task not yet completed by the 1960s, and by annual economic growth rates ranging from 2.9 per cent to as high as 9 per cent between 1960 and 1966, falling back in 1966–67 and rising to between 3 and 8 per cent between 1968 and 1973. This demand for labour during the course of the 1960s was further heightened by a falling number of people entering the workplace due to low birth rates during the war and a lengthening of the education period.[80]

Before the 1960s, due to the availability of ethnic Germans, the Federal Republic recruited only a small number of foreigners, so that only 'about 1 per cent of the annual rate of increase in employment was accounted for by new arrivals from abroad and, out of every 1,000 employed persons, only five were foreigners'.[81] In 1955 only 80,000 foreigners lived in West Germany.[82] But by this time government, employers' organizations and trade unions had agreed upon the need to import workers because of labour shortages.

The Federal Republic's method of recruitment in many ways resembled that of its predecessors, although this German state actually sought the permission of countries which had high birth rates and unemployment from where it obtained labour by signing contracts with exporting governments. Another difference with the history of labour recruitment lies in the areas of origin of migrants. Previously they had overwhelmingly come from eastern Europe but, as countries behind the iron curtain kept in their populations for their own industrialization after 1945, the Federal Republic had to look in other directions. Consequently, it obtained foreign labourers from the Mediterranean periphery of Europe, especially Turkey, but also Yugoslavia, Italy, Greece, Spain and Portugal.

These states had social and economic characteristics diametrically opposite to those of the Federal Republic. Turkey, for instance, has had one of the highest birth rates in the world since 1945, which peaked at 44 per thousand in 1960. In 1972 the country had a population of 36.5 million, which had increased to 55 million by the end of the 1980s, when it grew at 1 million a year. The rapid population increase resulted in the presence of a large number of children, in other words dependants who could not play a full role in the economy. In the early 1970s about 40 per cent of the population was under 15, about twice the figure in industrial societies. However, between 1960

and 1970, Turkey's labour force grew by about 1.9 per cent per annum. But
economic growth, although it took place on a scale comparable with the rest
of Europe, did not expand quickly enough to keep pace with the population
increase, so that high rates of unemployment developed, which may have
reached about 5 million in the early 1970s. The readiness of Turkish governments to export population as part of a planned economic strategy also
encouraged people to move abroad. This would both ease unemployment
and bring foreign currency back to the country in the form of remittances to
families.[83] Similarly, Yugoslavia had a primarily agricultural population during the early post-war decades, with limited opportunities for urban employment. The pull of higher wages in West Germany proved the fundamental
attraction. In 1969 Yugoslav migrants in Germany could earn 318 per cent
more than they would if they had remained at home. To this we need to add
further factors causing movement, such as chain migration, as migrants came
from particular parts of Yugoslavia, and the role of the Yugoslav state, as it
was the only east European regime to allow, and even encourage, emigration
on a large scale.[84] An examination of migration from Greece to Germany
reveals similar factors operating in that country.[85]

West Germany signed its first labour importation contract with Italy in
1955. There then followed further agreements with Spain and Greece in 1960,
Turkey in 1961, Morocco in 1963, Portugal in 1964, Tunisia in 1965 and
Yugoslavia in 1968. The Federal Government actively recruited in the above
countries where the Federal Labour Office (*Bundesanstalt für Arbeit*, BfA)
established almost 400 recruitment offices. German firms who required
labour would apply to the BfA and pay a fee. The offices in the various states
in southern Europe and north Africa would interview potential migrants, screen
them for political and criminal records, carry out medical examinations, issue
contracts and transport them to the destination in which they had agreed to
work. They obtained a work permit which initially lasted for one year but
could then be renewed.

The number of foreigners in West Germany and their share of the workforce
grew dramatically from the end of the 1950s. The 95,000 aliens present
in the country in 1956 had increased to 293,000 by 1960, when they made
up 1.5 per cent of the workforce. By 1966 their numbers had reached
1.3 million. As a result of recession in 1966–67 the total had fallen to
1,089,900 by 1968, because many workers returned home and recruitment
slowed down significantly. Nevertheless, the number of migrants then increased again, reaching 2,595,000 in 1973, when their share of the labour
force stood at 11.9 per cent.[86]

Table 4:   Non-German population in the Federal Republic, 1989

Country of origin	Total	Percentage of total
EU States	1,325,400	27.4
Greece	293,649	6.1
Italy	519,548	10.7
Yugoslavia	610,499	12.5
Morocco	61,848	1.3
Portugal	74,890	1.5
Spain	126,963	2.6
Turkey	1,612,623	33.2
Tunisia	24,292	0.5
Others	1,211,220	25.0
Total	4,845,882	

Source: Klaus J. Bade, ed., *Ausländer, Aussiedler, Asyl in der Bundesrepublik Deutschland* 2nd edn (Hanover, 1992), p. 198.

The year 1973 represented a major turning point in the migration of foreign workers into West Germany. As a result of the recession caused by the oil crisis of that year the government immediately banned recruitment. The slump and consequent rise in unemployment, which would continue for decades, coincided, in the 1970s and 1980s, with the entry into the labour market of large numbers of people born during the baby boom of 1955–66, although politicians were also displeased at the fact that so-called 'guest workers' tended not only to remain for long periods, but also brought over their families to Germany, consequently adding to the social costs of the economy.[87] Furthermore, fears about the threats of foreigners to German employment and culture had also begun to circulate by this time. Despite the stop on recruitment in 1973, the number of foreigners in Germany increased dramatically over the following two decades due mostly to the migration of dependants.

During the phase of large-scale labour recruitment into Germany, the most substantial population flow into the country came from Turkey. From 1968 until 1973 the number of Turkish workers moving into Germany averaged out at about 97,053 per year: their total increased from 123,386 in January 1968 to 599,000 in December 1973. This represents only a fraction of those

who wanted to move because in September 1971 over 1.2 million Turks had
registered with local Turkish labour bureaus for employment in the Federal
Republic. The second largest number of foreign workers in the Federal
Republic in 1973 was provided by Yugoslavia, at 513,000, followed by Italy,
with 423,000. Spain, Portugal and Greece counted smaller numbers. During
the following two decades Turkey pulled far ahead of all the other states in
numbers of foreigners and their dependants.[88]

As German capitalism imported foreign workers purely as fodder to
fuel economic growth it only had an interest in the healthy and the fit,
which meant that, in the short run at least, migrant groups in the Federal
Republic had an uneven demographic structure. During the late 1960s
children under 16 made up around 15 per cent of the foreign population,
while about 90 per cent of immigrants were under 45. An uneven sex structure also existed so that in September 1969 the Federal Republic housed
1,337,400 foreign men over 16 compared with 680,200 foreign women.[89]
In the Turkish case the percentage of women increased from 6.8 per cent
in 1960 to 26 per cent by 1975.[90] By 1981 there were 658 Turkish women
to every 1,000 Turkish men in Germany below the average for foreigners
of 666 to 1,000, with Greeks, at 836 per thousand, and Portuguese, at 832,
having the most even sex structure. The foreign population was also younger
than Germans. Thus, while 17.9 per cent of Germans were under 15, the
figure for foreigners stood at 26.3 due to family re-unification and higher
fertility rates. In 1981, while foreigners made up 7.5 per cent of the German
population, they accounted for 13 per cent of births. At the other end of the
scale only 2.1 per cent of foreigners were over 65, compared with 15.5 per
cent of Germans.[91] More striking, only 211 of the 84,415 Turks in Berlin in
1976 were over 65.[92]

Family structures have changed as a result of migration to Germany with
a decline of extended units in favour of the nuclear family.[93] In some cases
the original marriage in Turkey broke up as in the case of Fatma, who
left behind her husband and children to work in Germany, but found that
when she returned her husband was living with another woman, had
spent her remittances and also lost his job.[94] Meanwhile, the uneven male to
female ratio among immigrants in Germany has led to an increase in mixed
marriages, which represents one form of integration between foreigners and
Germans. By 1990 a total of 9.6 per cent of marriages, 39,784 out of 414,475,
involved a German and non-German partner.[95]

Immigrants to the Federal Republic of Germany were imported primarily
for the purpose of working in industry which has meant that they settled in

[220] conurbations. The largest cities contain the greatest concentrations. In 1977 Frankfurt had a foreign population of 17.1 per cent, Munich 15.4 per cent, Cologne 11.3 per cent, West Berlin 8.6 per cent and Hamburg 6.9 per cent. At the other end of the scale the more rural German state of Schleswig-Holstein had a foreign population of just 2.9 per cent.[96]

Within the cities of major concentration, immigrants have tended to focus on particular locations. In some instances this was due to initial proximity to the workplace, although the process has been further assisted by chain migration and prejudice within German neighbourhoods. One survey found that 60 per cent of Italians seeking accommodation could find somewhere to live in an immigrant neighbourhood within one month, whereas only 37.2 per cent seeking living quarters in German areas found a flat so quickly.

In Duisburg the neighbourhoods closest to steel works, which imported immigrants, tended to have the highest concentrations of foreigners. The housing policies of firms, which provided accommodation for many of the newcomers, also helped in the process of inner city concentration as did the desire of the migrants to save and send remittances to relatives in the homeland where they eventually planned to return, which meant that young males were prepared to live in poor housing to save money. The settlement patterns in Cologne closely resemble that of Duisburg in the sense that concentration took place around some of the major firms which provided accommodation for the imported workers including Ford and Deutsche Bundesbahn. In West Berlin, meanwhile, the heaviest concentration of Turks developed in Kreuzberg, one of the poorest districts of the city.[97]

Upon their first arrival in Germany most foreign workers would find themselves living in communal accommodation provided by the firms employing them, city authorities, welfare associations, or even private individuals. In 1962 about two thirds of newly arrived immigrants lived in such accommodation,[98] consisting of mass overcrowded quarters with minimum furnishing and poor cooking and sanitary provision, administered by house managers in an authoritarian manner. About one third of the buildings had been constructed before 1948 and one quarter were made of wood.[99] Conditions within some of these resembled those faced by immigrants in Germany at other times in its recent history as the following description of communal accommodation in Düsseldorf in 1967 describes:

> There are six Turkish and Greek guest workers living in a space no more than 15 square meters. The beds are stacked one on top of the other and crowded

together. All the men are already lying in the bed, although it is only 8.30 in the evening. But what else do they do in this hole? There aren't even enough chairs. In the centre of the room, under a naked light bulb dangling from a crooked wire, there is a table covered by a 'tablecloth' made of old newspaper. The floor is bare and filthy, the walls are no different. You search in vain for a picture, some curtains.[100]

In time the foreign workers of the 1960s and 1970s left such communal accommodation, especially when their families arrived, although this was a gradual process so that 34 per cent of migrants still lived in such buildings at the end of 1972. But even when they moved into the private market they inevitably found themselves in accommodation below the level of that enjoyed by Germans. In the first place their houses have been smaller, so that 84 per cent of foreign families lived in homes containing less than four rooms during the early 1970s. In North-Rhine Westphalia the living quarters of aliens were 36 per cent smaller than that of the population as a whole. In addition, accommodation for foreigners on a national scale was less likely to have conveniences and foreigners were more likely to live in older build-ings. Italians and Spaniards resided in the best conditions, followed by Greeks and, considerably worse off, Turks and North Africans. Immigrants are far less likely to own their accommodation than Germans, the figure for the former standing at just 3.5 per cent in 1965 and, in Hesse, reaching 7.9 per cent in 1987, compared with 42 per cent of Germans. Also in Hesse at this time, although the gap had narrowed between the situation of Germans and foreigners since the sixties, the former still lived in larger and newer housing, a situation reflected in the Turkish population of Düsseldorf.[101]

Immigrants in West Germany, imported as uneducated industrial fuel to stoke the fires of the German economic miracle, have laboured in manu-facturing, construction and metallurgy. Particularly during the phase before the arrival of families, foreign workers in West Germany played a large role in the expansion of the economy, because of their various advantages. In the first place, their demographic structure meant they had not cost anything to rear, as the state had not paid for their schooling. Upon first arrival foreign workers, because of their age, were at the peak of their economic activity. Furthermore, as they tended to receive lower wages, this proved beneficial to German employers. Since 1970 immigrants have always formed more than 8 per cent of the labour force[102] and, with their concentration in manual employment, it is difficult to see how the growth rates of the German economy could have been sustained since the 1950s, especially in view of the desire

[222] for social mobility of Germans. The only serious argument which questions the benefit of foreigners to the German economy suggests that rationalization and increases in efficiency would have taken place without immigration, meaning that growth rates could have been sustained, although this would still not solve the problem of who would carry out some of the most menial of tasks where working with hands is crucial.

The social structure of immigrants in Germany has always differed from that of the native population, as they have concentrated in particular areas of economic activity. Those foreigners already in the Federal Republic by the early 1960s focused upon metallurgy, construction and manufacturing, although some changes took place in the distribution between these three major areas. In 1963 the percentage of the total foreign population employed in the metal trades, manufacturing and construction stood at, respectively, 22.2, 20.1 and 11.2.[103] Despite the last figure, by this time immigrants constituted over 8 per cent of employees in the building trades, compared with 5 per cent in the metal trades and 4.43 per cent in manufacturing.[104] By the middle of the 1970s 38 per cent of foreigners worked in iron and metallurgical industries, 24 per cent in other manufacturing industries and 18 per cent in construction.[105] They have continued to play a large part in these areas and have also moved into other sectors of the economy, so that in 1980 they made up 12.9 per cent of employees in building, 20 per cent in textile production, as well as 8.5 per cent of people involved in the primary industries of agriculture, forestry and fishing.[106]

Inevitably, foreign workers tend to work in jobs which require a lower amount of skill and education. In 1972 the total proportion of immigrants in Germany working as unskilled labourers stood at 38 per cent, while the percentages for semi-skilled and skilled were 41 and 20.[107] By 1980 some change had taken place when 30 per cent of foreign males worked in skilled and supervisory employment, 42 per cent in semi-skilled and 27 per cent in unskilled, although the proportions varied from one group to another with Turks counting the highest proportion of unskilled and Yugoslavs, Spaniards and Portuguese having the largest percentages of skilled and supervisory staff.[108] Nevertheless, a significant level of promotion proved much more difficult and those who did move upwards tended to progress up just one category, from, say, unskilled to semi-skilled.[109]

> In practice, guest workers perform the most menial and dirtiest tasks. They drag tar spreaders, carry pig iron, clean toilets, and cart away the garbage of affluence. The public service departments of most West German municipalities would collapse were the guest workers to disappear overnight.[110]

Those working in factories have occupied 'places in the assembly line of mass production'.[111]

Foreigners inevitably face the worst working conditions and receive the lowest wages. In the early 1970s immigrants had an accident rate at work two and a half times higher than Germans, due both to a lack of knowledge of accident prevention rules and to the fact that they laboured in more dangerous employment.[112] Furthermore, during the 1970s 'wages for male foreign workers were more than 75 per cent, in the case of women 60 per cent below the average for comparable jobs' performed by Germans. In addition, immigrants 'continued to work more frequently than their German counterparts in piecework and on shifts'.[113]

As well as labouring in the most difficult occupations, foreigners have also experienced higher unemployment rates than Germans due to their concentration in sectors of the labour market which have seen rationalization and due to their lack of education and knowledge of German. Before the economic downturn of 1974, because of the specific recruitment of foreigners for particular jobs, they had a lower unemployment rate than Germans, but since that date a greater proportion of foreigners than Germans have been affected, reaching 11.9 per cent in 1982 when the rate for Germans stood at 7.5 per cent.[114]

This difference also applied to young people, due to discrimination and problems with language experienced by foreign children at school. In many cases the children of foreigners were at a disadvantage from the start because when they first attended school they had little or no knowledge of the language of tuition in obvious contrast to Germans, although since the middle of the 1970s individual German states have made efforts to provide language classes for such pupils. In some cases this proved counter-productive because some local governments established an apartheid style education system with children of the same nationality attending their own classes. At the secondary school level, immigrant children tended to go to the lowest level of *Hauptschule*, which limited their employment opportunities when they left. They were under-represented in *Gymnasium* or *Realschule*, which would prepare them for university or white-collar occupations. Through their school life the children of the foreign workers also experienced prejudice from their German contemporaries. Once they entered the labour market ethnic minority youths were also less likely to obtain an apprenticeship than their German counterparts, demonstrating that they have continued in the disadvantaged social position of their parents. This is further indicated by the higher unemployment rates experienced by the children of foreign workers.[115] Some of these drifted into crime, such as the Turkish rap singer Durmuş, who grew up in the underprivileged Berlin quarter of Kreuzberg. In answer to a question about how he moved into crime, he answered:

> I only need to say Kreuzberg. I grew up in an international environment with Germans, Italians, Turks and others. And when one became involved in shit, we all followed. We were only children. We didn't realize the consequences of our actions. We fell into shit without realizing. Everyone I know has a criminal record.[116]

However, some ethnic minorities have moved upwards, especially through the opening of their own small businesses. Italians have established ice cream cafés and pizza restaurants, which now exist in virtually every settlement of any significance in Germany. Greeks, Spaniards, Portuguese and Yugoslavs have also opened restaurants, often simply serving their own specialities in the traditional German *Gaststätten* which already existed. In addition, Turks have moved into the catering trade, specializing in takeaways. The size of the Turkish minority in the Federal Republic has further provided the opportunity to develop businesses aimed at this grouping, especially grocers, dry cleaners and travel agents. The number of Turkish businesses increased from 22,000 in 1985 to 35,000 in 1992.[117]

With the passage of time the migrant workers to Germany have developed into mature ethnic groupings resembling the Polish community in the Ruhr before the First World War. Linguistically, the post-war arrivals continued to use their own tongue and had a poor command of German. In the early 1970s only 7 per cent of Turks and 5 per cent of Portuguese described their command of German as 'very good'. Ten years later over fifty per cent of Turks, Spaniards and Italians still spoke bad German. Immigrants in Germany used their own language in their 'ghettos' and with their families, but conversed in German when dealing with Germans or members of other minority groups.[118]

Religion has also helped to maintain ethnic identity. Islam made its first significant appearance in West Germany as a result of the post-war labour importation, especially of Turks. By the middle of the 1990s about 1.7 million Muslims lived in the country, of whom 75 per cent consisted of Turks. Arabs and people from former Yugoslavia each counted more than 100,000 adherents of Islam. Around thirty per cent of the total Muslim population regularly practised its religion, but only 22 per cent attended mosques. About half of the Muslims in Germany were indifferent to their faith.[119] Many of those who practise their religion observe Islamic rituals and feasts. Mosques were established in Germany from the 1950s, but those connected with the foreign worker influx only began in the 1960s, often in flats; since then minarets have been constructed. By the 1990s approximately 1,200 Muslim parishes existed in Germany, of which 1,100 were Turkish. A city like Duisburg had thirty mosques in 1987. Places of worship divide along national and religious lines. Muslims have also established numerous cultural, educational and religious organizations.[120]

Ethnic groupings have also developed their own culture revolving around the establishment of all manner of associations, the written word, television and radio. In 1986 Spaniards counted about 120 local organizations with interests including schooling and youth, concerns which have also attracted the attention of Greek immigrants.[121] The size of the Turkish community in Germany has facilitated a wide range of cultural developments. Eleven newspapers existed by the early 1990s: the oldest of these, with the largest circulation, was *Hürriyet*, which sold 110,000 copies, followed by *Türkiye*, with 35,000, and *Milliyet*, selling 25,000. Since 1964 the German regional radio station, WDR, based in Cologne, has broadcast radio programmes in Turkish, which, in 1990, were listened to by 52 per cent of Turks in the city on a daily basis. Turks also watched television programmes provided for them by the regional broadcasting companies and, with the development of satellite television, many tuned in to TRT-International, a station broadcasting from Turkey for Turks settled abroad, which made a third of its programmes in Germany.[122] In addition, a high culture has developed among Turks in Germany, epitomized by the work of Emine Sevgi Özdamar, born in Malataya in eastern Anatolia in 1946 but moving to Germany as a migrant worker in 1965. After returning to Turkey, she moved back to Germany in 1976 and has produced, in German, several plays and novels, with the experience of Turks in Germany playing a major theme in her work. Özdamar represents just one prominent figure amongst many German Turks writing in German.[123] The opening to her short story, *Mutterzunge*, indicates the themes and experiences covered by her work:

I sat with my twisted tongue in the city of Berlin. In a Black café, with Arabs as guests, the stools were too high and feet were swinging. An old tired croissant sat on my plate, which I still paid for to save the waiter from embarrassment. If only I knew where I had lost my mother tongue. My mother and I spoke in our mother tongue. She said to me: 'Do you know, you speak so, you think you explain everything, but suddenly you skip over unspoken words, then you explain calmly, I skip that with you, and then I breathe in calmly.' She then said: 'You half left half your hair in Germany.'[124]

Newcomers have also participated in both their own politics and German politics. For instance, they played a large role in industrial disputes during the 1960s, the early 1970s and the aftermath of re-unification in the 1990s.[125] Turks have organized themselves across the entire political spectrum. One of the largest groupings consists of Turkish Social Democrats. The mainstream Turkish Conservative parties established the Freiheitlicher deutsch-türkischer Freundschaftsverein. In addition, parties on the extreme left and right have resorted to violence. One of the best known of these consists of the Kurdistan Communist Party (PKK) which may have counted up to 50,000 members in Germany by the 1990s. The organization has carried out bomb attacks against Turkish targets in Germany and has also organized numerous demonstrations where some protestors have set themselves alight.[126]

Although racism in the Federal Republic exploded in violent manifestations following unification in 1989, it did not spring from nowhere. The attitude of the state, especially its unwillingness to recognize foreign workers as citizens,[127] has played a crucial role in the existence of prejudice towards them. Furthermore, it was unlikely that the events of 1933–45 could suddenly become irrelevant in the attitudes of future German states and their citizens towards foreigners.

Manifestations of racism have developed against the background of negative images towards immigrants in the mass media, existing in the mainstream press, radio and television and, more crudely, in newspapers of a more extreme nature.[128] Opinion surveys from 1961–62 revealed that 83 per cent of Germans believed that each group of people had naturally inherited distinctive racial characteristics, while 65 per cent thought that even if people of all nationalities had the same life chances some races would be more successful than others.[129] Such attitudes meant that, as late as the 1970s, relations between Germans and immigrants 'during leisure time and in human association were few and far between – and almost non-existent among neighbours'. Lack of knowledge of German by the immigrants did not help their position. Derogatory names circulated widely including 'sheep thieves, camel drivers, Hottentots (North Africans), Mohameds, Caraway Turks, Mussulmen (Turks), Partisans, bear trainers (Yugoslavs), spaghetti eaters, Macaronis, lemon shakers (Italians)'.[130] These views continued in the following decades leading one 28 year old woman from Macedonia, Dana, to declare that: 'I feel that if xenophobia intensified the Germans would grind us to soap powder.' She consequently went to extreme lengths to hide her ethnicity including looking at the ground as she walked along the street so that Germans would not see her dark eyes. In addition, Dana only spoke German to her children in public.[131]

The existence of extreme right-wing groupings,[132] of both a Neo-Nazi and   [227]
nationalist nature, would have added to the insecurity felt by foreigners in
Germany. By the 1980s immigrants had become legitimate targets for racists.
For instance, in January 1989 a 19 year old member of a militant group called
the Nationalrevolutionäre Arbeiter Front faced arrest for an arson attack on
a house inhabited mostly by Turks, which had resulted in the burning of a
German and three Turks, including a child. The perpetrator stated his motive
as 'hatred of foreigners'.[133]

Migrants in the German Democratic Republic

Although the GDR did not import foreign labour on anything like the same
scale as its sister republic, it represented one of the Eastern Bloc states which
indulged most enthusiastically in this process due to the fact that it had one
of the strongest economies. But in comparison with the Federal Republic,
one of the most advanced manufacturing states in the world, the economy of
the GDR remained weak, as evidenced by the collapse in employment after
reunification due to competition from western goods.[134] The GDR had an
advanced social system which compared favourably with that which existed
in the Federal Republic and which, for instance, made advanced provision for child care and higher education.[135] Like all Eastern Bloc states, it
had social gradations according to occupation.[136]

Politically, the GDR also resembled many of its neighbours because, while
it may have preached a communist ideology, it very much represented a
nation state without free market capitalism, but with a national ideology
which stressed its citizens as Germans. It also retained some of the unpleasant
legacies of the Nazi period, such as the existence of a state controlled by one
party.[137] Its authoritarianism also had much to do with its status as a Soviet
satellite, and the power of the Stasi, which at least equalled that exercised by
the Nazi secret services.[138] On the other hand, the GDR did not have some
of the other manifestations of Nazism such as the existence of racist and
nationalist groups, although these did begin to bubble below the service in
the late 1980s. After reunification violence against foreigners would explode
in eastern Germany[139] suggesting that the GDR had a repressed racism.
Diplomatically the German Democratic Republic, like its western neighbour,
remained emasculated, representing a pawn in the Cold War conflict at the
mercy of the USSR.[140]

Compared with the Federal Republic, the GDR counted fewer ethnic groups within its borders. It had fewer Jews, fewer Gypsies and fewer foreign workers. Its most advanced ethnic group consisted of the Sorbs who developed an ethnicity richer than at any other time in their history. Although East Germany did import some foreign workers it represented a country of emigration during most of its history, losing over 20 per cent of its population, or 4.5 million people, mostly to the Federal Republic. In fact, between 1950 and the end of 1989 its inhabitants declined from 18.3 million to 16.3 million.[141]

This loss of population represented one of the reasons why the GDR began importing foreign workers, especially because of the age of most of those who left, at the peak of their economic output. This combined with economic growth from the 1960s to create an economy with serious labour shortages.[142] As in the case of the Federal Republic, the GDR imported people from states with opposite problems. Cuba, which provided nearly 10,000 foreign workers, had excess labour of between 100,000 and 150,000 when it first sent people to the GDR in the 1970s.[143] Like the Federal Republic and previous German regimes, the GDR signed contracts with states prepared to send it their own workers, although in this case it came to numerous short-term, as well as a few long-term agreements, with other Soviet Bloc states. Thus, in 1961 it signed contracts with Bulgaria, Poland and Hungary for the importation of 15,000, 10,000 and 5,000 people respectively. Poland also agreed to send people in 1971 and 1988. An agreement between Cuba and East Germany in 1978 resulted in the entry of 1,026 people. Others came from Vietnam, Mozambique, Czechoslovakia, Yugoslavia and Angola. Again following the typical German pattern, the newcomers entered the country on short-term contracts, which could often be extended.[144]

The East German politburo knew exactly what sort of migrants it wanted to import and where they should work. Cubans underwent two medical examinations before leaving home and faced another one upon landing in Berlin. If they fell ill or became pregnant they faced deportation. In 1984, for instance, 133 people, including 23 pregnant women, suffered this fate.[145] An agreement with Poland in March 1963 specified that 500 people were needed to work in the lignite industry while another contract 3 years later allowed Poles to cross the border as commuters, necessary because of the tightness of control over population movement in the Soviet Bloc.[146]

The foreign workers found employment in a variety of jobs, although, as ever, they tended to focus on manual labour, a situation partly explained by the level of education of GDR citizens, which would have meant, like their western brethren, they would have shunned such work. Those who came

from Cuba laboured in factories which produced tyres, chemical fibres, tools
and vehicles. They carried out unattractive and difficult physical work.[147] By
the end of the 1990s many of the foreign workers earned around 400 marks
per month, but, in many cases, due to agreements signed with the states in
which they originated, they could only spend a certain amount in the GDR.[148]
Although by the end of the 1980s some of the foreign workers had their own
accommodation, in the shorter term they had to endure the sort of conditions
which migrants had faced in other German states. Cubans, for instance,
resided in rooms with two or four beds and had to follow strict regulations
which, for instance, forbade visitors after 8pm.[149] In other ways the newcomers
would appear to have had their needs provided for them because of the
presence of group leaders and translators, although these would largely
have had the function of keeping up efficiency as well as, in the case of group
leaders, controlling the activities of their charges.[150]

The explosion of racial violence which occurred after unification clearly
points to the fact that foreigners in the GDR must have faced some hostility.
Their legal position, which clearly delineated them as foreigners, and their
concentration in housing specially designed for them, left natives in no
doubt about their position as outsiders. Consequently, little mixing took place
between Germans and foreigners. The latter tended to stick with members of
their own groups, so that unofficial ethnic communities developed, although,
largely due to small numbers and state control, they did not become organized in the way that those in the west did.[151] In some cases, however, marriages took place between Germans and foreigners, but this did not prevent
the continuation of hostility, as one German recalled about the experience of
his wife in a letter to the *Berliner Zeitung* just after the fall of the Berlin Wall.

> I have been married to a Bulgarian for fourteen years. I therefore know that
> hostility towards foreigners existed in the GDR. During all these years my wife
> had to endure countless instances of hostility and insult. Particularly shocking
> is the fact that these insults came mainly from young shop assistants. They were
> almost always people who were born and grew up in the GDR and who were
> taught about internationalism.[152]

More disturbing was the fact that during the second half of the 1980s potent
manifestations of racism surfaced in the form of the emergence of extreme
right-wing groups, especially skinheads,[153] who often attacked foreign
workers, especially Cubans and Mozambicans. In one instance in May 1988
youths assaulted two Mozambicans on a train and then threw one of them off
it while it was moving. Several attacks occurred in Halle carried out by a
group of four people who specialized in robbing foreigners.[154]

Table 5:   Nationality of foreigners in the GDR in 1989

Nationality	Total	Percentage of all foreigners
Vietnamese	60,100	31.4
Polish	51,700	27.1
Mozambican	15,500	8.1
Soviet	14,900	7.8
Hungarian	13,400	7.0
Cuban	8,000	4.2
Belgian	4,900	2.6
Czechoslovakian	3,200	1.7
Yugoslavian	2,100	1.1
Angolan	1,400	0.7
Others	16,000	8.3
Total	191,200	100.0

Source: A. W. Stack and S. Hussain, *Ausländer in der DDR: Ein Ruckblick* (Berlin, 1991), p. 6.

As well as workers, the GDR had also counted other groups of foreigners during its history including students and, by the end of the 1980s, asylum seekers. The largest group actually consisted of Soviet soldiers, who still totalled 580,000 people in 1990, although GDR statistics did not list them as foreigners. As in other German states foreign men outnumbered foreign women and most foreigners were young. At the end of 1989, for example, of 191,190 foreigners in the GDR 134,204 consisted of males and 56,986 of females.[155]

The rebirth of Jewish, Gypsy, Danish and Sorb communities

As well as labour migrants, both of the post-war German states also counted established minorities. While they had faced some persecution, the localized groupings of Danes and Sorbs had essentially survived the Second World War because they had not become victims of the same sort of murderous treatment meted out to either the Gypsies or, more especially, the Jews. Although some members of both these latter groups did manage to escape the Nazis, the Jewish and Gypsy communities of the post-war Germanies effectively had to rebuild themselves from scratch. Despite remorse which existed about the treatment of the Jews, antisemitism still surfaced with milder manifestations. Hostility towards Gypsies remained as strong as it had been before the Nazi period.

The 12,000 Jews living in Germany in 1952 subsequently increased, although numbers would never approach pre-war levels. The FRG contained just over 32,000 by 1989 while only 380 practising Jews actually lived in the GDR at the end of the Cold War.[156] The increase in numbers occurred largely as a result of immigration. About 15,000 of the 300,000 Jews who left Germany before the war returned.[157] Marion Ruth Thimm and her parents actually moved back to Berlin from Maine at the end of the war, then returned to the USA, before finally settling in West Berlin in 1956.[158] The rest of the increase in the Jewish populations of post-war Germany occurred mostly as a result of migration from Eastern Europe and Iran.[159]

A total of 64 Jewish communities existed by 1989. The biggest were in the cities which had contained the biggest groupings before 1933, including Berlin (6,000) and Frankfurt (4,000). Other large ones included Munich, Hamburg, Düsseldorf and Cologne.[160] In addition, some smaller communities reestablished themselves including the one in Würzburg.[161] Consequently, Jewish religious life and organizations also developed after the Second World War. Synagogues were rebuilt or newly founded and charitable bodies and social and political groupings also came into existence. There are Jewish primary schools in Munich, Frankfurt, Berlin and Düsseldorf, while Jewish newspapers have come and gone. One of the longest lasting organizations consists of the Bundesverband Jüdischer Studenten in Deutschland, established in 1960. A unitary national body also came into existence in July 1950 in Hamburg in the form of the Zentralrat der Juden in Deutschland, although, as in the period before the Nazis, German Jewry divided along religious and ethnic grounds. The pressures of assimilation resurfaced in the same form as they had existed before 1933. Thus of the 163 marriages involving Jews in 1985 only 51 consisted of Jews marrying each other.[162] The East German community remained even more secular. During the 1980s it had its own newsletter and library.[163] Some revitalization would take place after the fall of the Berlin Wall with an influx of Jews from the Soviet Union, although they also represented a group which had already become increasingly assimilated.[164]

The Federal Republic put much effort into atoning for the sins of Nazism which meant a positive attitude towards Jews and Israel, partly inherited, however, from the occupying authorities. Laws of restitution from the early 1950s meant that Germany paid financial compensation to both Israel and, eventually, survivors of the Holocaust.[165] In the middle of the 1950s the Federal Republic also gave DM 6,000 to returning Jews.[166] Most post-war Germans have had a fairly ambivalent attitude towards Jews and have generally demonstrated an unwillingness to accept responsibility for the events of the Nazi period.[167] This became clear, for instance, during the controversy over Daniel Goldhagen's book which pointed the finger of responsibility for the Holocaust at ordinary Germans.[168] Research into antisemitism has revealed that 15 per cent of the population of the Federal Republic were openly antisemitic, while for another 30 per cent hostility towards Jews lies just below the surface.[169] In contrast, a survey carried out in the former GDR immediately after its collapse revealed that 80 per cent of the population remained free of antisemitic stereotyping, and that 6 per cent formed an antisemitic hard core.[170] Hatred of Jews in the Federal Republic had potent manifestations. The Neo-Nazi groupings certainly held on to antisemitism, while Jews sometimes became victims of racial violence, most notably in 1959 and 1960. On Christmas night in 1959 Neo-Nazis, in an act harking back to the Weimar years, daubed graffiti on Jewish cemeteries, synagogues and memorials throughout the Federal Republic, most notably in the Jewish synagogue in Cologne, where two members of the German Reichs Party painted swastikas and statements such as 'Jews Out'. By the end of January 1960 the police had recorded 685 incidents of a similar nature all over West Germany, many of them provoked simply by the reporting of the first incidents and the trial of their perpetrators.[171]

Jews reached a position within Germany society which approximated to that which they had held before the rise of the Nazis. Similarly, the Gypsies returned to their previous status. This meant that, while Jews once again became a predominantly middle-class group, the Gypsies lived on the fringes of mainstream society, which affected their ability to gain compensation, as did the absence of a protecting state of the type that existed for the Jews in the form of Israel. Consequently the pre-Nazi patterns of everyday discrimination and state control established themselves again after 1945.

At the end of the war only a few hundred Gypsies who had survived the concentration camps lived in the four zones occupied by the Allies. Others subsequently arrived from the territories lost by the Germans in the East and from other eastern European states. With a high fertility rate the number of

Gypsies in the Federal Republic had reached around 50,000 during the [233] 1980s.[172] By this time most Romanies had become sedentary, with only about ten per cent travelling for the whole year, although others wandered for the summer months. During the 1960s a larger percentage of this minority still had wagons, some of them made out of wood and some with no wheels. While the average sized home in the Federal Republic housed 2.4 people the same dimensions held 4.2 Gypsies. Munich had actually provided a permanent site for Gypsies in 1959 in Kranzberger Allee in the north of the city, but this developed into a ghetto because of its lack of facilities and its location. Although school attendance had reached high levels during the 1960s, Gypsies had an illiteracy rate of 35 per cent because of discrimination both during and after the Third Reich. In the academic year 1983/4 not a single Gypsy graduated from high school in Hamburg. Around 25 per cent did not work due to their lack of education and the hostility which they faced and only 20 per cent found employment as wage labourers. The rest made a living through buying and selling goods, such as carpets and textiles.[173] During the 1970s most Gypsy children could only speak Romany until they went to school, after which they became bilingual. The taboo system, which applies to members of this ethnic group throughout the world also continued to operate and determined, for instance: relationships with the mainstream German population; female behaviour; and diet.[174]

While the continued position of Gypsies as outsiders in German society partly results from their desire to remain so, it has more to do with the attitude of the state and the populace towards them. The sort of legislation which existed in the first half of the twentieth century came into operation once again, even if the desire to exterminate Gypsies had largely disappeared. As early as 1946 Bremen issued a measure for 'the protection of the population from molestation by travellers', based on the 1926 Bavarian Law. Other areas of Germany had followed suit by the end of the 1940s. The Cologne police, for instance, issued a circular on 'Combating the Gypsy Menace', and continued to register members of the minority. During the 1950s the local authorities in both Cologne and Düsseldorf compelled those who had survived the war to return to the housing which the Nazis had established for them. In Frankfurt a meeting took place on 18 April 1975 between senior police officials with the aim of preventing Gypsies from entering the city.[175]

Unofficial hostility also existed towards Gypsies in the Federal Republic. For instance, the mass circulation newspaper *Bild* has carried articles hostile towards the minority.[176] Furthermore, researchers had not escaped from their views of the Romanies which had developed before 1945 and some of those who had worked for the Nazis continued to find university employment.[177] Even the Federal Republic's long-standing adviser on Gypsy matters, Hermann Arnold, viewed Gypsies as uncivilized, childish and irrational.[178] Nevertheless, Romanies did make moves forward in West Germany, obtaining some compensation and recognition of the wrongs carried out against them by the Nazis. This partly resulted from the emergence of their own civil rights movement.[179]

One group which had a much easier time in the Federal Republic because of its closeness to the norms of mainstream German society and the existence of an external protecting state consisted of the Danes of Schleswig, who may still count 50,000 people, with their own churches, schools and political and social organizations. A series of post-war agreements protected both this grouping and the smaller German minority on the other side of the Danish border.[180]

The main localized minority in the GDR consisted of the Sorbs, who reached the zenith of their history as an ethnic group due to the support which they received from the state. Despite the Nazi persecution, they seem to have totalled around 70,000 people during the 1970s. After the war their Lusatian homeland became a major area of lignite production.[181] The strength of their ethnicity finds support in the fact that during the 1960s and 1970s almost 2,000 books appeared in Wendish, all subsidized and usually published by the state. Common themes included resistance to the Nazis and the way of life in the Sorbian village, indicating the extent to which Sorbian historiography took off. In addition, one daily newspaper, *Nowa doba* also existed, together with several other Wendish periodicals on a less regular basis, many of them for particular interest groups. The Sorbian People's Theatre came into existence in 1948, subsequently developing into the German-Sorbian People's Theatre. The main Sorbian organization consisted of the Domowina, originally founded in 1912 and re-established in 1945, working under the Communist Party. It acted as both a cultural and political organization. The Domowina disappeared immediately after reunification to be replaced by the Sorbian National Assembly and several other cultural associations.[182]

The fall of the Berlin Wall would have dramatic effects upon all of the ethnic minorities which lived in both the GDR and the Federal Republic, especially as a result of the rebirth of potent racism in the early 1990s. The certainties of the previous four decades which had transformed the two German states into relatively tolerant republics seemed to have disappeared as the ghosts of the German past surfaced again.

Notes

1. Lutz Hoffmann, *Die unvollendete Republik: Zwischen Einwanderungsland und deutschem Nationalstaat* 2nd edn (Cologne, 1992), pp. 28–9.

2. John E. Farquharson, *The Western Allies and the Politics of Food: Agrarian Management in Postwar Germany* (Leamington Spa, 1985).

3. Richard Overy, 'The Economy of the Federal Republic Since 1949', in Klaus Larres and Panikos Panayi, eds, *The Federal Republic of Germany Since 1949: Politics, Society and Economy Before and After Unification* (London, 1996), p. 5.

4. See Lothar Kettenacker, *Germany Since 1945* (Oxford, 1997), pp. 1–52.

5. See, for instance, Constantine Fitzgibbon, *Denazification* (London, 1969).

6. Wolfgang Jacobmeyer, *Vom Zwangsarbeiter zum heimatlosen Ausländer* (Göttingen, 1985); Nicholas Bethell, *The Last Secret: Forcible Repatriation to Russia* (London, 1974); Kim Saloman, *Refugees in the Cold War: Toward a New International Refugee Regime in the Early Post-War Era* (Lund, 1991), p. 146; J. A. Tannahill, *European Volunteer Workers in Britain* (Manchester, 1958); Pavel Marković Poljan and Žanna Antonovna Zajončkovskaja, 'Ostarbeiter in Deutschland und daheim: Ergebnisse einer Fragebogenanalyse', *Jahrbücher für Geschichte Osteuropas* 41 (1993), pp. 556–61; Betrieb Rode-Stankowski, *Zwangsarbeit bei Ford: Dokumentation der 'Projektgruppe Messelager' im Verein EL-DE-Haus e.V. Köln* (Cologne, 1996), p. 58; Bernd Bonwetsch, 'Sowjetische Zwangsarbeiter vor und nach 1945: Ein doppelter Leidensweg', *Jahrbücher für Geschichte Osteuropas* 41 (1993), pp. 537–42.

7. Wolfgang Jacobmeyer, 'Jüdische Überlebende als "Displaced Persons": Untersuchungen zur Besatzungspolitik in den deutschen Westzonen und zur Zuwanderung osteuropäischer Juden 1945–1947', *Geschichte und Gesellschaft* 9 (1983), p. 421.

8. Michael Brenner, *After the Holocaust: Rebuilding Jewish Lives in Postwar Germany* (Princeton, NJ, 1997), p. 9.

9. Koppel S. Pinson, 'Jewish Life in Liberated Germany', *Jewish Social Studies* 9 (1947), p. 103.

10. Bozena Szaynok, 'The Pogrom of the Jews in Kielce, July 4, 1946', *Yad Vashem Studies* 22 (1992), pp. 199–235; Michael Checinski, 'The Kielce Pogrom: Some Unanswered Questions', *Soviet Jewish Affairs* 5 (1975), pp. 57–72.

11. Wolfgang Jacobmeyer, 'Polnische Juden in der amerikanischen Besatzungszone Deutschlands 1946–47', *Vierteljahrschrift für Zeitgeschichte* 25 (1977), p. 124.

[236]   12.   Monika Richarz, 'Juden in der Bundesrepublik und in der Deutschen Demokratischen Republik seit 1945', in M. Brumlik, D. Kiesel, C. Kugelmann and J. H. Schoeps, eds, *Jüdisches Leben in Deutschland seit 1945* (Frankfurt, 1986), p. 17.

13.   Pinson, 'Jewish Life in Liberated Germany', p. 110.

14.   Bayerische Staatsbibliothek, untitled undated pamphlet produced by 'The Central Committee of Liberated Jews in the British Zone, Germany, 1945– 47', p. 25.

15.   Gena Turgel, *I Light a Candle* (London, 1995), pp. 124–6.

16.   Richarz, 'Juden in der Bundesrepublik', p. 17.

17.   For events in India and Pakistan see Ian Talbot and Gurharpal Singh, eds, *Region and Partition: Bengal, Punjab and the Partition of the Subcontinent* (New York, 1999).

18.   Hans W. Schoenberg, *Germans from the East: A Study of Their Migration, Resettlement and Subsequent Group History Since 1945* (The Hague, 1970), p. 32.

19.   See, for instance, Evan Mawdsley, *The Stalin Years: The Soviet Union, 1929– 1953* (Manchester, 1998).

20.   Günter Böddeker, *Die Flüchtlinge: Die Vertreibung der Deutschen im Osten* 3rd edn (Berlin, 1997), p. 32.

21.   William Carr, *A History of Germany, 1815–1945* 2nd edn (London, 1979), p. 383.

22.   Böddeker, *Die Flüchtlinge*, pp. 34–44.

23.   Ronny Kabus and Anke Zühlke, *Von Ostpreußen in die Lüneburger Heide: Vertreibung und Eingliederung 1945–1953* (Lüneberg, 1995), p. 9.

24.   Werner Terpitz, *Wege aus dem Osten: Flucht und Vertreibung einer ostpreußischen Pfarrersfamilie* (Munich, 1990), p. 51.

25.   Ibid., p. 9.

26.   Theodor Schieder, ed., *The Expulsion of the German Population from the Territories East of the Oder–Neisse-Line* (Bonn, 1960), p. 6.

27.   Quoted in Alfred-Maurice de Zayas, *The German Expellees: Victims in War and Peace* (London, 1993), p. 83.

28.   Hermann Raschhofer, *Die Sudetenfrage: Ihre völkerrechtliche Entwicklung vom Ersten Weltkrieg bis zur Gegenwart* 2nd edn enlarged by Otto Kimminich (Munich, 1988), pp. 135–270; Emilia Hrabovec, 'Die Vertreibung der Deutschen und die tschechische Gesellschaft', in Robert Streibel, ed., *Flucht und Vertreibung: Zwischen Aufrechnung und Verdrängung* (Vienna, 1994), pp. 134– 57; Josef Kalvoda, 'National Minorities in Czechoslovakia, 1919–1980', in

Stephan M. Horak, ed., *Eastern European National Minorities, 1919–1980: A* [237]
Handbook (Littleton, CO, 1985), p. 123.

29. Martin L. Kovacs, 'National Minorities in Hungary, 1919–1980', in Horak, ibid., p. 164.

30. Theodor Schieder, ed., *The Fate of the Germans in Hungary* (Bonn, 1961), p. 72.

31. Minority Rights Group and TWEEC, *Minorities in Central and Eastern Europe* (London, 1993), p. 40.

32. Theodor Schieder, ed., *The Fate of the Germans in Rumania* (Bonn, 1961), p. 16.

33. Ibid., p. 54.

34. Leo Paul, 'The Stolen Revolution: Minorities in Romania After Ceauşescu', in John O'Loughlin and Hermann van der Wusten, eds, *The New Political Geography of Eastern Europe* (London, 1993), p. 146.

35. Toussaint Hočevar, 'National Minorities in Yugoslavia, 1919–1980: Linguistic Minorities from an Economic Perspective', in Horak, *Eastern European National Minorities*, p. 224.

36. Joseph B. Schechtman, 'The Elimination of the German Minorities in Southeastern Europe', *Journal of Central European Affairs* 6 (1946), pp. 161–2.

37. Hočevar, 'National Minorities in Yugoslavia', p. 229.

38. Siegfried Bethlehem, *Heimatvertreibung, DDR-Flucht, Gastarbeiterwanderung: Wanderungsströme und Wanderungspolitik in der Bundesrepublik Deutschland* (Stuttgart, 1982), p. 22.

39. Alexander von Plato and Wolfgang Meinicke, *Alte Heimat – neue Zeit: Flüchtlinge, Umgesiedelte, Vertriebene in der sowjetischen Besatzungzone und in der DDR* (Berlin, 1991), pp. 25–6.

40. Johannes-Dieter Steinert, *Migration und Politik: Westdeutschland – Europa – Übersee, 1945–1961* (Osnabrück, 1995), p. 7.

41. Schoenberg, *Germans from the East*, pp. 39–40.

42. Klaus J. Bade, Hans-Bernd Meier and Bernhard Parisius, eds, *Zeitzeugen im Interview: Flüchtlinge und Vertriebene im Raum Osnabrück nach 1945* (Osnabrück, 1997), p. 13.

43. Betty Barton, *The Problem of 12 Million Refugees in Today's Germany* (Philadelphia, 1949), p. 18.

44. Andreas Lüttig, *Fremde im Dorf: Flüchtlingsintegration im westfälischen Wewelsburg, 1945–1958* (Essen, 1993), pp. 5, 6.

45. Norbert Baha, *Wiederaufbau und Integration: Die Stadt Delmenhorst nach 1945* (Delmenhorst, 1983), pp. 1, 72.

[238]   46. Rita Müller, 'Von den Schwierigkeiten einer Bergstraßengemeinde im Umgang mit den Heimatvertriebenen: Dossenheim, 1945–1950', in C. Grosser, T. Grosse, R. Müller and S. Schrant, eds, *Flüchtlingsfrage – das Zeitproblem: Amerikanische Besatzungspolitik, deutsche Verwaltung und die Flüchtlinge in Baden-Württemberg, 1945–1949* (Mannheim, 1993), p. 200.

47. Bade, Meier and Parisius, *Zeitzeugen im Interview*, p. 15.

48. Uwe Weiher, *Die Eingliederung der Flüchtlinge und Vertriebenen in Bremerhaven, 1945–1960* (Bremerhaven, 1992), p. 54.

49. Lüttig, *Fremde im Dorf,* pp. 57, 59, 60.

50. An interview with Frau Al. quoted in Bade, Meier and Parisius, *Zeitzeugen im Interview*, p. 134.

51. Barton, *Problem of 12 Million German Refugees*, p. 24; Plato and Meinicke, *Alte Heimat*, p. 47.

52. Barton, ibid., p. 27.

53. Marion Frantzioch, *Die Vertriebenen: Hemmnisse und Wege ihrer Integration* (Berlin, 1987), pp. 203–7.

54. Hartmut Berghoff, 'Population Change and its Repercussions on the Social History of the Federal Republic', in Larres and Panayi, *Federal Republic of Germany*, pp. 45–6.

55. Lüttig, *Fremde in Dorf,* p. 53.

56. Plato and Meinicke, *Alte Heimat*, p. 66.

57. Petra Pape, 'Flüchtlinge und Vertriebene in der Provinz Mark Brandenburg: Der Ende des Krieges in der Provinz', in M. Wille, J. Hoffmann and W. Meinecke, eds, *Sie hatten alles verloren: Flüchtlinge und Vertriebene in der sowjetischen Besatzungzone Deutschlands* (Wiesbaden, 1993), p. 123.

58. Barton, *Problem of 12 Million German Refugees*, p. 28.

59. Schoenberg, *Germans from the East*, p. 52.

60. Baha, *Wiederaufbau und Integration*, p. 85.

61. Dieter Brosius and Angelika Hohenstein, *Flüchtlinge im nordöstlichen Niedersachsen, 1945–1948* (Hildesheim, 1985), pp. 22–30.

62. Rainer Schulze, 'Zuwanderung und Modernisierung: Flüchtlinge und Vertriebene im ländlichen Raum', in Klaus J. Bade, ed., *Neue Heimat im Westen: Vertriebene, Flüchtlinge, Aussiedler* (Münster, 1990), p. 84.

63. Schoenberg, *Germans from the East*, p. 37; Barton, *Problem of 12 Million German Refugees*, pp. 30–4; Frantzioch, *Die Vertriebenen*, pp. 199. 201.

64. Max Hildebert Boehm, 'Gruppenbildung und Organisationswesen', in Eugen   [239]
    Lemberg and Friedrich Edding, *et al.*, eds, *Vertriebene in Westdeutschland: Ihre
    Eingliederung und ihr Einfluss auf Gesellschaft, Wirtschaft, Politik und Geistleben*,
    Vol. 1 (Kiel, 1959), pp. 524–30.

65. Brosius and Hohenstein, *Flüchtlinge im nordöstlichen Niedersachsen*, p. 33.

66. Frantzioch, *Die Vertriebenen*, pp. 122–4.

67. Ibid., pp. 146–7; Lüttig, *Fremde im Dorf*, p. 186; Hermann Weiß, 'Die
    Organisationen der Vertriebenen und ihre Presse', in Wolfgang Benz, ed., *Die
    Vertreibung der Deutschen aus dem Osten: Ursachen, Ereignisse, Folgen* (Frankfurt am
    Main, 1995), pp. 244–64; Boehm, 'Gruppenbildung und Organisations-
    wesen', pp. 531–79; Schoenberg, *Germans from the East*, pp. 70–7; Weiher,
    Eingliederung der Flüchtlinge und Vertriebenen in Bremerhaven, pp. 59–68;
    David Childs, 'The Nationalist and Neo-Nazi Scene since 1945', in Larres
    and Panayi, *Federal Republic of Germany*, p. 212; Bundesministerium für
    Vetriebene, Flüchtlinge und Kriegsgeschädigte, *10 Jahre nach der Vertreibung:
    Äusserungen des In- und Auslandes und eine Zeittafel* (Bonn, 1956), pp. 150–3.

68. See Overy, 'Economy of the Federal Republic', pp. 3–34.

69. See, for instance, J. Fijalkowski, 'The Structure of German Society After the
    Second World War', in J. P. Payne, ed., *Germany Today: Introductory Studies*
    (London, 1971), pp. 84–110; and David Childs and Jeffrey Johnson, *West
    Germany: Politics and Society* (London, 1981), especially pp. 86–109.

70. Torsten Oppelland, 'Domestic Political Developments I: 1949–1969', in
    Larres and Panayi, *Federal Republic*, pp. 74–9.

71. See, for instance, 'Nationalist and Neo-Nazi Scene', pp. 220–9.

72. See below.

73. For concepts of national identity in the Federal Republic see: the contribu-
    tions by Peter Alter and Mary Fulbrook to John Breuilly, ed., *The State of
    Germany: The National Idea in the Making, Unmaking and Remaking of a Modern
    Nation-State* (London, 1992); and below.

74. See, for instance, Imanuel Geiss, 'The Federal Republic of Germany in Inter-
    national Politics Before and After Unification', in Larres and Panayi, *Federal
    Republic*, pp. 137–57.

75. Steinert, *Migration und Politik*, pp. 8, 38–80.

76. Klaus J. Bade, 'Transatlantic Emigration and Continental Immigration:
    The German Experience Past and Present', in Bade, ed., *Population, Labour
    and Migration in 19th- and 20th- Century Germany* (Leamington Spa, 1987),
    pp. 147–8; Panikos Panayi, 'Germans in Britain's History', in Panayi, ed.,
    Germans in Britain Since 1500 (London, 1996), p. 11.

77. Klaus J. Bade, 'Einführung: Wege in die Bundesrepublik', in Bade, *Neue Heimat im Westen*, p. 5.

78. Berghoff, 'Population Change', p. 40.

79. For a full discussion of the reasons for movement from the GDR to the Federal Republic see: Helge Heidemeyer, *Flucht und Zuwanderung aus der SBZ/DDR, 1945/1949–1961: Die Flüchtlingspolitik der Bundesrepublik Deutschland bis zum Bau der Mauer* (Düsseldorf, 1994); and Volker Ackermann, *Der 'echte' Flüchtling: Deutsche Vertriebene und Flüchtlinge aus der DDR, 1945–1961* (Osnabrück, 1995).

80. Berghoff, 'Population Change', pp. 51–9; Ulrich Herbert, *A History of Foreign Labour in Germany, 1880–1980: Seasonal Workers/Forced Labourers/Guest Workers* (Ann Arbor, MI, 1990), pp. 209–10.

81. Heinrich M. Dreyer, 'Immigration of Foreign Workers into the Federal Republic of Germany', *International Labour Review* 84 (1961), p. 1.

82. W. R. Böhning, *The Migration of Workers in the United Kingdom and the European Community* (London, 1972), p. 33.

83. See: Philip L. Martin, *The Unfinished Story: Turkish Labour Migration to Western Europe* (Geneva, 1991); Ahmet Akgündüz, 'Labour Migration from Turkey to Western Europe (1960–1974): An Analytical Review', *Capital and Class* 51 (1993), pp. 153–93; Nermin Abadan-Unat, ed., *Turkish Workers in Europe, 1960–1975: A Socio-Economic Reappraisal* (Leiden, 1976).

84. Ivo Baučić, *The Effects of Emigration from Yugoslavia and the Problems of Returning Emigrant Workers* (The Hague, 1972), pp. 1–16.

85. Athina Stavrinoudi, *Die griechische Arbeitsmigration in die Bundesrepublik Deutschland* (Berlin, 1992), pp. 13–24.

86. Berghoff, 'Population Change', p. 52; Stephen Castles, *Here for Good: Western Europe's New Ethnic Minorities* (London, 1987), p. 72; Heather Booth, *The Migration Process in Britain and West Germany* (Aldershot, 1992), p. 110; Herbert, *History of Foreign Labour*, p. 224.

87. Berghoff, ibid., pp. 59–67.

88. G. E. Völker, 'Labor Migration: Aid to the West German Economy?', in Ronald E. Krane, ed., *Manpower Mobility Across Cultural Boundaries* (Leiden, 1975), pp. 12–13, 19; Bethlehem, *Heimatvertreibung*, p. 125.

89. Stephen Castles and Godula Kosack, *Immigrant Workers and Class Structure in Western Europe* (London, 1973), p. 51.

90. Nermin Abadan-Unat, 'Implications of Migration on Emancipation and Pseudo-Emancipation of Turkish Women', *International Migration Review* 11 (1977), p. 33.

91. Castles, *Here for Good*, pp. 100–6.

[241]

92. Gabrielle Mertens and Ümal Ankipar, *Türkische Migrantenfamilien* (Bonn, 1977), p. 92.

93. Abadan-Unat, 'Implications of Migration', p. 54.

94. Ayşe Kudat, 'Structural Change in the Migrant Turkish Family', in Krane, *Manpower Mobility*, p. 82.

95. Harald Schumacher, *Einwanderungsland BRD: Warum die deutsche Wirtschaft weiter Ausländer braucht* (Düsseldorf, 1992), p. 144.

96. Bethlehem, *Heimatvertreibung*, p. 121; Hans Heinrich Blotevogel, Ursula Müller-ter Jung and Gerald Wood, 'From Itinerant Worker to Immigrant? The Geography of Guestworkers in Germany', in Russell King, ed., *Mass Migration in Europe: The Legacy and the Future* (London, 1993), p. 90.

97. Blotevogel, Jung and Wood, ibid., p. 92; John R. Clark, 'Residential Patterns and Social Integration of Turks in Cologne', in Krane, *Manpower Mobility*, p. 63; Barbara von Breitenbach, *Italiener und Spanier als Arbeitnehmer in der Bundesrepublik Deutschland* (Munich, 1982), p. 98; Faruk Şen, '1961 bis 1993: Eine kurze Geschichte der Türken in Deutschland', in Claus Leggewie and Zafer Şenocak, eds, *Deutsche Türken: Das Ende der Geduld* (Hamburg, 1993), p. 23.

98. Herbert, *History of Foreign Labour*, pp. 217–18.

99. Clemens Amelunxen, 'Foreign Workers in West Germany', in William A. Veenhoven, ed., *Case Studies in Human Rights and Fundamental Freedoms*, vol. 1 (The Hague, 1975), p. 123.

100. The above extract is from *Handelsblatt*, 16 February 1967 and is translated and quoted in Herbert, *History of Foreign Labour in Germany*, pp. 218–19.

101. Amelunxen, 'Foreign Workers in West Germany', pp. 123–4; Helga Reimann, 'Die Wohnsituation der Gastarbeiter', in Helga and Horst Reimann, eds, *Gastarbeiter* (Munich, 1976), pp. 131–48; Heinz Sautter, 'Wohnsituation ausländischer Haushalte in Hessen', in Claudia Koch-Arzberger, Klaus Böhme, Eckart Hohmann and Konrad Schact, eds, *Einwanderungsland Hessen? Daten, Fakten, Analysen* (Opladen, 1993), pp. 30–48; Günther Glebe, 'Housing and Segregation of Turks in Germany', in Şule Özüekren and Ronald van Kampen, eds, *Turks in European Cities: Housing and Urban Segregation* (Utrecht, 1997), pp. 142–3.

102. Berghoff, 'Population Change', p. 53.

103. 'Die Beschäftigung ausländischer Arbeitskräfte in Deutschland 1882 bis 1963', *Wirtschaft und Statistik* 27 (1965), p. 94.

[242]   104. Hans Stirn, 'Ausländerbeschäftigung in Deutschland in den letzten 100 Jahren', in Stirn, ed., *Ausländische Arbeiter im Betrieb* (Cologne, 1964), p. 18.

105. Amelunxen, 'Foreign Workers in West Germany', p. 115.

106. Jürgen Fijalkowski, 'Gastarbeiter als industrielle Reservarmee', *Archiv für Sozialgeschichte* 24 (1984), p. 406.

107. Gerald Kühlewind, 'The Employment of Foreign Workers in the Federal Republic of Germany and their Family and Living Conditions', *German Economic Review* 12 (1974), p. 361.

108. Castles, *Here for Good*, p. 134.

109. Ibid., pp. 137–8.

110. Amelunxen, 'Foreign Workers in West Germany', p. 119.

111. Ibid., p. 120.

112. Ibid.

113. Herbert, *History of Foreign Labour*, p. 241.

114. Castles, *Here for Good*, p. 145.

115. Thomas Faist, 'From School to Work: Public Policy and Underclass Formation Among Young Turks in Germany during the 1980s', *International Migration Review* 27 (1993), pp. 306–31; Claudia Mitulla, *Die Barriere im Kopf: Stereotype und Vorurteile bei Kindern gegenüber Ausländern* (Opladen, 1997); C. Wilpert, 'Work and the Second Generation: The Descendants of Migrant Workers in the Federal Republic of Germany', in Wilpert, ed., *Entering the Working World: Following the Descendants of Europe's Immigrant Labour Force* (Aldershot, 1988), pp. 111–49.

116. *Spiegel*, 14 April 1997.

117. Şen, '1961 bis 1993', p. 27.

118. Amelunxen, 'Foreign Workers in West Germany', pp. 121–2; Breitenbach, *Italiener und Spanier*, pp. 61–7.

119. M. Salim Abdullah, 'Muslims in Germany', in Syed S. Abedin and Ziauddin Sardar, eds, *Muslim Minorities in the West* (London, 1995), pp. 68–70.

120. Faruk Şen and Andreas Goldberg, *Türken in Deutschland: Leben zwischen zwei Kulturen* (Munich, 1994), pp. 78–108; Jørgen S. Nielsen, *Muslims in Western Europe* (Edinburgh, 1995), pp. 27–33.

121. Breitenbach, *Italiener und Spanier*, pp. 109–26; Jürgen Fijalkowski, 'Conditions of Ethnic Mobilisation: The German Case', in John Rex and Beatrice Drury, eds, *Ethnic Mobilisation in a Multi-Cultural Europe* (Aldershot, 1994), pp. 126–7.

122. Gülay Durgut, 'Tagsüber Deutschland, abends Deutschland: Türkische
Medien in Deutschland', in Leggewie and Şenocak, *Deutsche Türken*, pp. 112–
22. More generally, see Michael Darkow, Josef Eckhardt and Gerhard
Maletzke, *Massenmedien und Ausländer in der Bundesrepublik* (Frankfurt, 1985).

123. See the first four chapters of David Horrocks and Eva Kolinsky, eds, *Turkish
Culture in German Society Today* (Oxford, 1996).

124. Ermine Sergi Özdamar, *Mutterzunge* (Berlin, 1990), p. 7.

125. Mark J. Miller, *Foreign Workers in Western Europe: An Emerging Political Force*
(New York, 1981), pp. 104–13.

126. *Focus* 7, 28 June 1993; Bundesministerium des Innern, *Verfassungsschutzbericht, 1992* (Bonn, 1993), pp. 146–53.

127. See below.

128. See, for instance, Horst Reimann, 'Ausländische Arbeitnehmer und Massenmedien', in Reimann, *Gastarbeiter*, pp. 111–29.

129. Badi Panahi, *Vorurteile: Rassismus, Antisemitismus, Nationalismus in der Bundesrepublik heute* (Frankfurt, 1980), p. 268.

130. Amelunxen, 'Foreign Workers in West Germany', pp. 127–8.

131. Dagmar Burkhart-Chatzfeliader, 'Das Schicksal von vier Jugoslawinnen
im deutschen Westen: Die ewige Furcht, sich falsch zu verhalten', in
R. Italiaander, ed., *Fremde raus* (Frankfurt, 1983), p. 202.

132. For more detail see below.

133. Christopher T. Husbands, 'Militant Neo-Nazism in the Federal Republic of
Germany Since 1945', in Luciano Cheles, Ronnie Ferguson and Michalina
Vaughan, eds, *Neo-Fascism in Europe* (London, 1991), p. 99.

134. See below.

135. Jonathan Steele, *Inside East Germany: The State that Came in From the Cold*
(New York, 1977), pp. 167–98.

136. Dietrich Staritz, *Geschichte der DDR, 1949–1985* (Frankfurt am Main, 1985),
pp. 165–75.

137. See Mary Fulbrook, *Anatomy of A Dictatorship: Inside the GDR, 1949–1989*
(Oxford, 1995).

138. See David Childs and Richard Popplewell, *The Stasi: The East German Intelligence and Security Service* (London, 1967), pp. 82–6.

139. See below.

[244]

140. See, for instance, A. James McAdams, *Germany Divided: From the Wall to Reunification* (Princeton, NJ, 1993).

141. Maria and Lothar Elsner, *Zwischen Nationalismus und Internationalismus: Über Ausländer und Ausländerpolitik in der DDR, 1949–1990* (Rostock, 1994), pp. 10–11.

142. Ibid., p. 11; A. W. Stack and S. Hussain, *Ausländer in der DDR: Ein Rückblick* (Berlin, 1991), p. 11.

143. Sandra Gruner-Domic, *Kubanische Arbeitsmigration in die DDR, 1978–1989: Das Arbeitskräfteabkommen und dessen Realisierung* (Berlin, 1997), p. 5.

144. Ibid., p. 5; Stack and Hussain, *Ausländer in der DDR*, p. 6; Elsner, *Zwischen Nationalismus und Internationalismus*, p. 31; Ewa Helias, *Polnische Arbeitnehmer in der DDR und der Bundesrepublik Deutschland* (Berlin, 1992), p. 6; Dirk Jasper, 'Ausländerbeschäftigung in der DDR', in Marianne Krüger Portratz, ed., *Anderssein gab es nicht: Ausländer und Minderheiten in der DDR* (Münster, 1991), pp. 151–63.

145. Gruner-Domic, ibid., p. 42.

146. Jasper, 'Ausländerbeschäftigung', p. 155.

147. Gruner-Domic, *Kubanische Arbeitsmigration*, p. 7; Stack and Hussain, *Ausländer in der DDR*, p. 11.

148. Stack and Hussain, ibid., p. 12.

149. Gruner-Domic, *Kubanische Arbeitsmigration*, p. 37.

150. Ibid., pp. 50–4; Helias, *Polnische Arbeitnehmer*, pp. 10–12.

151. Imke Commicheau, 'Ausländer in der DDR: Die ungeliebte Minderheit', *Deutschland-Archiv* 23 (1990), pp. 1435–8; Stack and Hussain, *Ausländer in der DDR*, p. 14.

152. Quoted in Irene Runge, *Ausland DDR: Fremdenhaß* (Berlin, 1990), p. 17.

153. See below.

154. Krüger-Portratz, *Anderssein gab es nicht*, pp. 56–7.

155. Stack and Hussain, *Ausländer in der DDR*, p. 8; Elsner, *Zwischen Nationalismus und Internationalismus*, pp. 77–80.

156. Heiner Lichtenstein, 'Die Minderheit der 30,000: Juden in der Bundesrepublik', in Ludger Heid and Joachim H. Knoll, eds, *Deutsch-jüdische Geschichte im 19. und 20. Jahrhundert* (Stuttgart, 1992), p. 337.

157. Lynn Rapaport, 'The Cultural and Material Reconstruction of the Jewish Communities in the Federal Republic of Germany', *Jewish Social Studies* 49 (1987), p. 141.

158. She is interviewed in John Borneman and Jeffrey M. Peck, *Sojourners: The Return of German Jews and the Question of Identity* (London, 1995), pp. 179–96.

159. Julius H. Schoeps, 'Die Last der Geschichte: Zur Situation der Juden in der Bundesrepublik heute', in Günter Gorschenek and Stephen Reimers, eds, *Offene Wunden – brennende Fragen: Juden in Deutschland von 1938 bis heute* (Frankfurt, 1989), p. 71.

160. Ibid., pp. 70–1.

161. Brenner, *After the Holocaust*, pp. 120–1.

162. Ibid., pp. 148–50; Schoeps, 'Die Last der Geschichte', p. 73; Lichtenstein, 'Die Minderheit der 30,000', pp. 339–41.

163. Monika Richarz, 'Jews in Today's Germanies', *Leo Baeck Institute Year Book* 30 (1985), pp. 269–70.

164. See below.

165. Brenner, *After the Holocaust*, pp. 60–3.

166. Rapaport, 'Cultural and Material Reconstruction', p. 143.

167. Frank Stern, *The Whitewashing of the Yellow Badge: Antisemitism and Philosemitism in Postwar Germany* (Oxford, 1992), pp. 419–23.

168. For a discussion of Daniel Goldhagen, *Hitler's Willing Executioners: Ordinary Germans and the Holocaust* (New York, 1997), see Norman G. Finkelstein and Ruth Bettina Birn, *A Nation on Trial: The Goldhagen Thesis and Historical Truth* (New York, 1998).

169. Schoeps, 'Die Last der Geschichte', p. 82.

170. Reinhard Wittenberg, Bernhard Prosch and Martin Abraham, 'Antisemitismus in der ehemaligen DDR', *Tribune* 118 (1991), pp. 103–4.

171. Wolfgang Benz, 'Die Opfer und die Täter: Rechtsextremismus in der Bundesrepublik', in Benz, ed., *Rechtsextremismus in der Bundesrepublik: Voraussetzungen, Zusammenhänge, Wirkungen* (Frankfurt, 1984), pp. 28–31; Peter Dudek and Hans-Gerd Jaschke, *Enstehung und Entwicklung des Rechtsextremismus in der Bundesrepublik*, vol. 1 (Opladen, 1984), pp. 266–9. The extreme right is considered in more detail below.

172. Wolfgang Wippermann, *Geschichte der Sinti und Roma in Deutschland: Darstellung und Dokumente* (Berlin, 1993), p. 41; Mariele Krause, *Verfolgung durch Erziehung: Eine Untersuchung über die jahrhundertlange Kontinuität staatlicher Erziehungsmaßnahmen im Dienste der Vernichtung kultureller Identität von Roma und Sinti* (Ammersbek, 1989), p. 103; Andreas Hundsalz and Harald P. Scharf, *Soziale Situation der Sinti in der Bundesrepublik Deutschland* (Stuttgart, 1982), p. 18.

[246]   173. Hundsalz and Scharf, ibid., pp. 19, 20, 21, 69, 121; Krause, ibid., p. 105; Lukrezia Jochimsen, *Zigeuner heute: Untersuchung einer Aussenseitergruppe in einer deutschen Mittelstadt* (Stuttgart, 1963), pp. 46, 47, 53; Georg von Soest, *Zigeuner zwischen Verfolgung und Integration: Geschichte, Lebensbedingungen und Eingliederungsversuche* (Weinheim, 1979), pp. 96–105.

174. Soest, ibid., pp. 53, 55, 58.

175. Josef Bura, 'Die unbewältigte Gegenwart: "Zigeunerpolitik" und alltäglicher Rassismus in der Bundesrepublik', in Rudolf Bauer, Josef Bura and Klaus Lang, eds, *Sinti in der Bundesrepublik: Beiträge zur sozialen Lage einer verfolgten Minderheit* (Bremen, 1984), pp. 14–15; Sybil Milton, 'Persecuting the Survivors: The Continuity of "Anti-Gypsyism" in Postwar Germany and Austria', in Susan Tebbutt, ed., *Sinti und Roma: Gypsies in German-Speaking Society and Literature* (Oxford, 1998), pp. 36–7; Katrin Reemtsma, *Sinti und Roma: Geschichte, Kultur, Gegenwart* (Munich, 1996), p. 128; Wolfgang Feuerhelm, *Polizei und Zigeuner* (Stuttgart, 1987), pp. 93–4.

176. Josef Bura, 'Zur Diskriminierung der Roma heute: Aktuelle Anmerkungen zu einem alten Problem', in Holger Bader, *et al.*, eds, *Sinti und Roma: Zwischen Erfolgung und Verfolgung* (Bremen, 1981), pp. 19–23.

177. Milton, 'Persecuting the Survivors', p. 40.

178. Bura, 'Die unbewältigte Gegenwart', p. 40.

179. Yaron Matras, 'The Development of the Romani Civil Rights Movement in Germany, 1945–1996', in Tebbutt, *Sinti and Roma*, pp. 49–63; Reemstma, *Sinti und Roma*, pp. 134–5.

180. Jørgen Kühl, *The Schleswig Experience: The National Minorities in the Danish-German Border Area* (Aabenraa, 1998); J. Elklit, J. P. Noack and O. Tonsgaard, 'A National Group as a Social System: The Case of the German Minority in North Schleswig', *Journal of Intercultural Studies* 1 (1980), pp. 5–18.

181. Rudolf Urban, *Die sorbische Volksgruppe in der Lausitz, 1949 bis 1977: Ein dokumentarischer Bericht* (Marburg an der Lahn, 1980), pp. 18, 39.

182. Meic Stephens, 'The Sorbs', in G. Ashworth, ed., *World Minorities* vol. 1 (Sunbury, 1977), p. 122; Gerald Stone, *The Smallest Slavonic Nation: The Sorbs of Lusatia* (London, 1972), pp. 85–9, 172–82; Timo Meškank, 'Die sorbische Geschichtsschreibung am Scheidepunkt: Versuch einer Standortbestimmung', *Deutschland Archiv* 25 (1992), pp. 42–8; Minority Rights Group and TWEEC, eds, *Minorities in Central and Eastern Europe* (London, 1992), p. 33.

CHAPTER 7

The New Germany and its Minorities

The fall of the Berlin Wall in November 1989 and the reunification of Germany in the following year marked a significant change. For the second time in the history of central Europe the efforts of Germans to create a unitary state had resulted in success. Nevertheless, unlike the events of 1870–71, achieved by force at the hands of the Iron Chancellor Bismarck, those of 1989–90 had more to do with external events in the form of the Cold War thaw. On this occasion the responsibility for forward movement lay not in the hands of a Prussian junker but in those of a Russian Soviet career politician, Mikhail Gorbachev. If unification had taken place from above in 1871, it occurred from outside in 1990. Symbolically, this indicated the dependence of Germany upon Europe, when the latter controlled the former, unlike the late nineteenth century, when Germany attempted to impose its will upon the rest of the continent.

Germans did not remain completely passive in the events of 1989. People power in the east caused the fall of the Berlin Wall and the collapse of the regime of Erich Honecker, although the refusal of Gorbachev to back Honecker's use of force against the mass demonstrations which took place in the autumn of 1989 essentially meant the death of the GDR. Immediately after the wall had fallen, the continued existence of two German states (or three including Austria) seemed possible. Nevertheless, this idea floated around for just a short period of time. After the breaching of the Berlin Wall the populations of the two former north German states inevitably moved together in an almost Wagnerian love scene. On 3 October 1990, less than eleven months after the smashing of the Berlin Wall on 9 November 1989, east and west Germany had married each other in a ceremony of reunification.[1]

However, this would not be a wedding of equals. While the GDR may, in cultural and economic terms, have represented one of the most advanced states in the Soviet Bloc, it very much remained the junior partner compared with one of the wealthiest countries in capitalism. Rather like a rich man marrying

[248] a poor woman, the latter was simply taken over. Within a few years of unification, evidence of the existence of the GDR had faded.

The beginning of the new marriage was difficult, as the new Germany endured a series of problems. This applied to the economy, especially that of the former GDR, which essentially collapsed, because its products became useless and inefficient to produce compared with those of the old Federal Republic and the capitalist world as a whole. Consequently, the unemployment rate in the new Federal states increased from zero in 1990 to 17 per cent in January 1994. While the west German economy went into recession, the change was not as dramatic, although we should mention an increase in unemployment from 6.2 per cent in 1990 to 8.8 per cent in January 1994, as well as the negative effects on the west German economy of the bill to restructure the eastern half of Germany, which included cuts in public spending.[2] These changes provide an important background for the growth of racism in re-unified Germany, especially in the east where the economic effects of the collapse of Communism were as dramatic as those which followed the Wall Street Crash of 1929.[3] At the end of the 1990s, the economy of the reunified Germany remained less healthy than it did before reunification, with the east trailing behind.[4]

In social terms, therefore, the new German state has significant divisions between *Ossis* and *Wessis*. Thus the latter have higher living standards, and superior accommodation.[5] But German society at the end of the twentieth century actually had three clear groups in the form of *Wessis, Ossis* and *Ausländer*. The last group has limited political rights and lower standards of living than West Germans. Even within these three groups, divisions exist, not least because of the position of women.[6]

Politically the new Federal Republic has expanded in purely geographical terms. The west essentially devoured the east so that the latter's political traditions and institutions not only disappeared, but the Federal Republic began to victimize the old east German order, especially those who had worked for the Stasi, as well as attempting to hold show trials of some of the East German leaders.[7] These developments symbolized the confidence of the Federal Republic in its own legitimacy. In addition, they also indicated a decline in guilt about the Nazi period as they suggested that the Stasi and the GDR equalled the SS and the Third Reich as the bogeymen of German history. Such developments link in with the rebirth of a more confident nationalism in the early 1990s, which resembled that which had accompanied the formation of the first German nation state after 1871. Like that earlier national feeling, xenophobia and racism accompanied the new one.[8]

The diplomacy of the new Federal Republic of the 1990s was little different from the old one. Certainly, there have been no serious indications that
the ghosts of the Nazi past are about to return to steer a different course for
German diplomacy, although foreign policy has become more self-confident,
and has shaken off some of the guilt feeling before 1989. This would help to
explain the use of German troops in UN and NATO action during the 1990s.
The new reunified Germany remains absolutely central to the development
of Europe, with the largest economy and one of the largest populations. It
retains complete commitment to the European Union and to NATO.[9]

The new Germany has, however, had serious minority problems. In the
first place, the expanded state began to attract millions of people in the form
of ethnic Germans and asylum seekers as a result of its geographical position,
the collapse of Communism and provisions in the constitution. This, combined with the euphoria of reunification and the bitterness felt at the economic downturn, led to a rise in the potent manifestations of racism, in the
form of attacks upon foreigners and a growth in support for the extreme right,
which, at one time, appeared to threaten the Republic. Ultimately, the new
Germany withstood the forces of reaction, although ethnic groupings at the
end of the twentieth century remain outsiders.

Mass immigration and control

The end of the Cold War and its immediate aftermath created the potential for mass migration in Europe, much of which would head for Germany.
The vast majority of the new arrivals fell into two groups. First, asylum
seekers, attracted by a relatively liberal German asylum policy compared
with other western European states. Although the refugees came from all
over the world, the majority originated from conflicts in eastern Europe, especially Yugoslavia, for whom Germany represented the first big country they
reached. Second, the Federal Republic also managed to attract ethnic Germans, representing the residue of those people who had not become victims
of ethnic cleansing at the end of the Second World War, especially within the
USSR, which had not expelled its Germans after 1945, but also within
Poland, the Czech Republic and Hungary. The opening up of borders following the end of the Cold War, the attractions of the economic prosperity of
the west, and the ethnic-based German constitution of the Federal Republic
sent millions of *Aussiedler* towards its borders. The only other groups of any

note which made their way to the new Germany in the early years of its existence included Jews from the USSR and Poles, although both arrived in
smaller numbers than asylum seekers and ethnic Germans.

The movement towards Germany of persecuted people seeking asylum
had actually begun to take off during the 1980s, although the origins of the
migration essentially lie in Article 16 (2) of the 1949 Federal Constitution,
which stated that: 'Persons persecuted for political reasons enjoy the right of
asylum', an indication of remorse at the actions of previous German governments.[10] Nevertheless, Germany, like other European states, had also signed
the 1951 UN Convention on Refugees, which meant that she and her neighbours essentially had the same attitude to the acceptance of people fleeing
persecution. But, by the 1980s, views towards immigration had changed,
especially in Britain and France,[11] which meant that the Federal Republic
offered an obvious alternative, particularly in view of its location near many
eastern European regimes which persecuted their populations. Thus the 19,737
people seeking asylum in Germany in 1983 had increased to 57,379 by 1987.
The largest total came from Poland, although Turkey provided significant
numbers, attracted by the presence of their countrymen already in the
Federal Republic, as did Iran.[12] Nevertheless, people moved from a variety of
other locations. Amalia, for instance, fled Angola to join her husband who
had lived in Germany, also as a refugee, from 1985. As she recalled:

> I came to Germany in 1987. I had many problems in my homeland. I was a secret-
> ary in a government department. In Angola there was a civil war between the
> government and UNITA. My boss had contacts with UNITA and ended up in jail.
> I also ended up in jail.[13]

With the end of the Cold War and the fall of the Iron Curtain which had
divided Europe for four decades, nationalist conflicts which had remained
dormant under Communism began to come back to life in the eastern half of
the continent, above all in Yugoslavia. By August 1992 one in ten Yugoslavs
was a refugee, either within his or her own Yugoslav state, in a neighbouring
one, or in another European country.[14] By 1995 the UNHCR was assisting
3,700,000 people affected by the war,[15] bringing the figure close to 20 per
cent of the population of Yugoslavia which stood at 22,427,600 in 1981.[16]
Because of the presence of an already large Yugoslav population of foreign
workers in Germany, 220,000 of the 531,412 refugees who had left Yugoslavia by August 1992 moved to join their relatives and friends in that country.[17] But Yugoslavs represented only one element in the 1,689,506 people
who sought refuge in Germany between 1988 and 1995. In the peak year of

1992 a total of 438,191 people applied for asylum in the country.[18] The other
major states of origin included Romania, Poland and Turkey.[19]

The influx of over 1.5 million people into any nation state in such a short period of time would cause tension and clearly such figures and, more especially, their reporting by the press, played some role in the outbreaks of racial violence which occurred in the early 1990s. Media attention and violence eventually spurred politicians into action, resulting, most significantly, in a modification of Article 16 (2) of the Federal Constitution in 1993. This meant that people who moved from states placed on a list of safe countries, including Germany's neighbours, together with, among others Bulgaria, Romania and Hungary, could not obtain asylum. The same applied to claims based on forged or contradictory evidence. The former regulation essentially meant that asylum seekers had to fly directly from their country of origin to Germany, which meant that it became unreachable for most people.[20] The Federal Republic also began deporting failed asylum seekers, while a low rate of recognition meant that many returned home of their own accord. Nevertheless, Germany remains the most generous asylum country in Europe, receiving 104,353 applications in 1997 and 98,644 in 1998.[21]

At the same time as millions of refugees fled to the Federal Republic, so did an equally large number of ethnic Germans moving away from Eastern Europe and the Soviet Union. As in the case of the asylum seekers, the origins of the flow of ethnic Germans lie in the Constitution of 1949. Article 116/I stated that those people of German origin remaining in eastern European states, including the USSR, after the post-war settlement could move to the Federal Republic. A total of 1,573,146 *Aussiedler* had made their way to the country between 1951 and 1988. With the thawing of the Cold War and the opening up of borders, the numbers increased significantly. The figure for 1988 totalled 202,673 and reached 377,055 in the following year.[22] Between 1983 and 1992, 1,556,060 ethnic Germans moved to the Federal Republic.[23] A further two million may have been waiting to enter the country.[24] Apart from the political pull factor which existed in the form of article 116/I of the Federal Constitution, the greater economic opportunities in Germany and the presence of relatives already there also attracted people. In addition, the growth of Germanophobia in Poland and Romania, which accompanied the rise of nationalism in those states, also sent Germans away.[25] In the Soviet Union Germans faced abuse as 'fascists' for events which had taken place during the Second World War.[26]

Despite their identification with Germany, the *Aussiedler* faced some hostility in their new home because many natives simply associated them with

[252] other foreigners, due to the fact that many of them looked foreign and did not speak much German. Consequently, legislation in 1990, 1992, 1993 and 1996 attempted to cut the numbers of *Aussiedler* so that only those living in the former Soviet Union had the automatic right to admission, while those in central Europe had to prove that they faced ethnic discrimination. Thus, although 2,267,000 moved to Germany between 1988 and 1996, the figure had declined to 178,000 in 1996, 97 per cent of whom came from the former Soviet states.[27]

Another significant group to move to Germany, although on a much smaller scale, consisted of Jews, who also came from the former USSR. This migration followed a decision by the Minister Presidents of the German states to invite Russian Jews to the country and to recognize them as refugees under the 1951 Geneva Convention. By 1995 about 40,000 had arrived, of whom around 5,000 lived in Berlin.[28]

The 1990s also witnessed an increase in illegal immigration into Germany from eastern Europe. One estimate claimed that as many as 150,000 illegals may have made their way to Germany in 1992,[29] although this probably exaggerates the true situation.[30] Focusing upon Hamburg, an article in *Stern* revealed the story of Stefan, who slept in his car, queued up for a job by the harbour every morning and shaved once a week looking into a car wing-mirror.[31] Partly to counter the presence of illegals, but also to fuel the rebuilding of Berlin, the New Germany has signed contracts with some of its eastern European neighbours, a return to the exploitation of Slavs practised by the *Kaiserreich* and the Third Reich. In 1991 a total 89,340 such people worked in Germany, including 35,170 Poles.[32] In 1992 the total number of Poles in the Federal Republic stood at 285,553, which included not only those on work contracts, but also seasonal workers, commuters, students, refugees and *Aussiedler.*[33]

The rebirth of racism

The ending of the Cold War resembles the immediate post-1945 period in terms of the sheer numbers of people who moved into Germany over a short period of time. Like their predecessors, those who arrived in the late 1980s and early 1990s faced hostility. However, for a combination of reasons, the animosity of the years immediately after reunification became extremely potent, manifesting itself most obviously in a rise in support for right-wing

parties and outbursts of racist violence. The major reason for these developments lies in the fact that a large proportion of the newcomers consisted
either of foreigners, in the case of asylum seekers, or were perceived as such,
in the case of ethnic Germans, many of whom spoke poor German. At the
same time, war weariness characterized the late 1940s in Germany, whereas
nationalistic euphoria surfaced in the aftermath of reunification.

But the manifestations of potent racism in the 1990s did not spring from
nowhere. Apart from the roots in the period before 1945, we have already
seen that minorities had experienced violence in both Germanies by the end
of the 1980s.[34] Furthermore, nationalistic and Neo-Nazi groupings had
always existed in the Federal Republic and had begun to surface in the GDR
on the eve of its collapse. Even in the immediate aftermath of the Second
World War parties of the extreme right had a certain level of electoral success, in the form of the Socialist Reichs Party and the German Reichs Party,
the former of which obtained eleven per cent of the vote in elections in Lower
Saxony in 1951, but which faced a ban from the Federal Constitutional Court
in 1952.[35] The next significant group in the FRG consisted of the National
Democratic Party which came into existence in November 1964. Its programme harked back towards Nazism, calling for the restoration of pre-war
borders, a united Germany and priority for German workers in employment
over foreigners. The programme of the party opposed all foreign influences
upon Germany, especially Jewish, American and immigrant. Foreign workers
had, it claimed, led to an increase in crime, and were after German women.
In 1969, the NPD gained 1,422,010 votes in the Federal Elections, when
it secured 4.3 per cent of the poll.[36] Although this represents the highest
proportion of votes ever achieved by an extreme right grouping in Federal
elections, the NPD did not gain parliamentary representation, because of the
necessity under the Federal Constitution to obtain 5 per cent of the vote.

Despite the economic crisis of the 1970s, which caused a rise in unemployment, the 1970s 'were a dismal period for the far Right in Germany',[37] a
situation which continued for much of the 1980s. Nevertheless, at the beginning of this decade, the German far right 'was organized in 73 groups with
a membership of 20,300', of which the largest consisted of Gerhard Frey's
Deutsche Volksunion, which had surpassed the NPD as the leading extreme
right group in the country. Out of the 73 groups mentioned above neither
the NPD nor the DVU fitted into the category of Neo-Nazi and consequently
illegal groupings as classified by the Office for the Protection of the Constitution (Amt für Verfassungsschutz), although 18 (most of which counted
just a handful of members) of the 73 groups were classed in this way.[38]

Right-wing extremism had also begun to secure support in East Germany by the end of the 1980s as demonstrated in the growth of the skinhead movement and the development of some support for West German parties among East German citizens.[39] The major West German neo-Nazi organization was the Free German Workers' Party (Freiheitliche Deutsche Arbeiterpartei, FAP), established in 1979, with over 450 members by 1988 and responsible for 34 per cent of all right-wing acts of violence in 1987, but receiving just under 0.1 per cent of the vote in the 1989 European election. Other organizations came and went, as a result of facing bans.[40]

But the real breakthrough in the history of the extreme right during the 1980s came in the form of the Republikaner, founded in 1983 by Franz Schönhuber, who had served in the Waffen SS. During the 1980s and into the 1990s, the Republikaner, together with the DVU and the NPD, had a similar ideology. All three supported the collective over the individual, the collective consisting of a homogeneous nation, people or state, meaning that they were more overtly racist than the democratic parties, calling for more extreme measures to deal with the 'threats' posed by foreigners within Germany, including deportation and a tightening of the right of asylum. They blamed immigrants for unemployment and for social problems and feared that German national identity would be destroyed by foreign cultures. All three parties also advocated a move away from the guilt feeling about the Nazi past, asserting that the country should take pride in its history. Furthermore, they were hostile to the EU and wanted to see Germany return to its 1937 borders, rather than those imposed at the end of the Second World War.[41]

The Republikaner made its first breakthrough in 1989 before the fall of the Berlin Wall when it gained 7.1 per cent of the vote in the elections to the European Parliament and 7.5 per cent in the regional election in Berlin. Although it fell back to 2.1 per cent of the vote in the federal elections of 1990, its share of the electorate rocketed to 10.9 per cent in the regional election in Baden-Württemberg in 1992 and it gained 5 per cent on several other occasions. Meanwhile, the DVU obtained over 6 per cent of the vote in the regional elections in Bremen in October 1991 and in Schleswig-Holstein in April 1992. By this time the Republikaner had a membership of 25,000 while the DVU and NPD counted 11,500 and 6,100 respectively.[42]

At the same time as these events took place, Germany experienced outbreaks of racist attacks reminiscent of the events of the final years of the Weimar Republic. This violence basically took two forms. First, small-scale attacks involving fewer than twenty people, which included homicides, arsons and bombings, assault and property damage and which affected the entire country. Secondly, a small number of large-scale riots, which only affected east Germany.

The year of unification, 1990, actually represented a quiet twelve months in the incidence of racist violence, with a fall in the number of attacks carried out by right-wing extremists compared with the previous year.[43] A dramatic increase occurred in 1991 with a rise, from the previous year, from 270 to 1,483 in the number of right-wing offences – attacks against people or their property – which resulted in 3 deaths.[44] Most of the incidents took place between August and October, essentially sparked off by the most serious incident, and its reporting, which occurred in Hoyerswerda in Saxony, in the old GDR. After a build-up of hostility towards asylum seekers and foreign workers in the town during the summer a full-scale riot broke out against them between 17 and 22 September involving hundreds of local residents, together with skinheads who had made their way to the town from other locations in east Germany. The violence sparked off by Hoyerswerda reached a crescendo during the first two weeks of October 1991. Morning radio news broadcasts simply began by listing the attacks which had taken place the previous evening. Incidents took place from the North Sea to the Alps and from the French to the Polish borders with the perpetrators carrying out their activity with virtual impunity.

The large number of racist attacks during 1991 increased even further during the following year to a new height of 2,584, a rise of 74 per cent. Just as notable was the growth in the number of murders from 3 in 1991 to 17 in the following year. A riot in Rostock, also in the former GDR, and its reporting between 22 and 27 August, acted as the spark for events in 1992. Throughout September 1992 immigrants and refugees were attacked with impunity with the state apparently powerless to halt the violence. On 23 November a firebomb attack in the town of Mölln in Schleswig-Holstein resulted in the death of three Turks.

The year 1992 represents the high point in racial violence in post-war Germany. In 1993 a fifteen per cent decline in the number of assaults against asylum seekers and foreign workers and their families occurred, although the number of attacks still exceeded the total for 1991. The major incident of 1993 took place on 29 May when a firebomb attack on a Turkish house in Solingen resulted in the death of three children and two women.[45]

The beginning of the 1990s therefore resulted in a racial crisis in Germany, which led many observers to fear that the ghosts of the German past had returned to seize control of the state and resurrect the Nazi hell. Before explaining why the Federal Republic fought off the new Nazis and nationalists,

[256] we need an explanation of why the potent racism took off in the first place. A complexity of causes exists.

In the first place, it is tempting to see the spectres of German history never having faced full exorcism. It seems unlikely that they could disappear forever in view of the seismic impact of Nazism upon Germany between 1933 and 1945 and the even deeper roots which go back to the Enlightenment. The Federal Republic had accepted a share of guilt, as evidenced by its policy of *Wiedergutmachung* and the influence of the memory of the Holocaust on political culture.[46] The revulsion against Nazism, and, in fact, the whole of nineteenth-century German history, reached its height during the 1960s and 1970s, a period during which positive attitudes towards national identity focused upon post-war liberal values and constitutional patriotism, as well as the concept of never forgetting the German past. During the 1980s a series of leading political figures, above all Chancellor Helmut Kohl, together with right-wing intellectuals, began to speak about reinterpreting German history, a process in which shame about Nazism would lessen as German history began before 1933. This resulted in the *Historikerstreit*, or the fight of the historians, in which leading German academics took sides and either stressed or disputed the centrality of Nazism in German history.[47] The new concept of national identity also stressed the fact that Germans had been victims during the Second World War. The rising tide of German self-confidence received a powerful shot in the arm during the process of German reunification, especially on the night of the collapse of the Berlin Wall, 9 November, when hysterical nationalism became respectable. Reunification also allowed a move away from a focus upon Nazism as the sole evil phase in German history. Revulsion at the GDR joined it as the Stasi united with the Nazis as the bogeymen of German history. In fact, the entry of the GDR into the Federal Republic also brought in a population which had never confronted its responsibility for the events of 1933–45 and had also had little experience of foreign populations. Consequently, the early years of the 1990s resemble the period after the first unification of Germany: in both cases potent nationalism had respectability in the highest circles.

In both instances the rise of racism also had socio-economic causes. The stock market crash of 1873 played a large role in the spread of antisemitism, while the rise in unemployment in the early 1990s fed into the resentment of foreigners, especially in the east, where joblessness had not existed before 1989. Even in the west, where the major successes of the right-wing parties took place, the unemployed formed a disproportionately large part of their membership.[48]

The scale of migration into Germany offers another possible socio-economic cause for the rise in potent racism during the early 1990s. However, numbers and violence do not go together in German history as the Second World War and its immediate aftermath would confirm. Nevertheless, in the early 1990s, connected with the euphoric nationalism of these years, obsessive press and government attention focused upon the asylum seekers and ethnic Germans. Even the apparently most respectable of publications could carry articles and pictures of Germany being flooded by foreigners.[49] Such reporting made rioters feel that they could act with impunity against people not regarded as part of the national community. The asylum seekers, who bore the brunt of the attacks of the early 1990s, became scapegoats for the significant downturn in the German economy which had taken place consequent upon unification.

In the end, the new Federal Republic did not go the way of Weimar. At the Federal election of 1994 the extreme right did not make the breakthrough which it had seemed to threaten in 1991 and 1992, but which seemed less and less likely from 1993. The DVU did not field any candidates while the Republikaner gained just 1.9 per cent of the vote.[50] At the same time, while outbreaks of racist violence occurred in 1994, most notably the first arson attack on a synagogue since the Nazi period, which took place in Lübeck on 25 March,[51] the overall number of attacks fell from 2,232 in 1993 to 1,489 in 1994.[52]

Several factors explain the decline of extreme racism – in the first place, the secure structural foundations of the Federal Republic. Unlike the Weimar Republic in 1929 the FRG had had forty years to establish itself, which meant that West German citizens had accepted liberal democracy. At the same time, while the economic downturn and unemployment rates in the East may have equalled that of the early 1930s, the slow-down took place on a much more limited scale in the West. More immediate factors included the change in the constitutional provision for asylum in 1993 which helped to cut down the numbers of refugees moving to Germany and distracted press attention from them. Consequently, if the support for the extreme right represented a protest vote in 1991 and 1992, the reason for the protest had disappeared. Furthermore, the Republikaner, the only group which could have seriously threatened the established parties, suffered a schism on the eve of the 1994 Federal elections, when it dumped Schönhuber as its leader.[53]

In fact, the extreme right has made little impact on politics during the second half of the 1990s. It again failed in the 1998 General Election. The Republikaner, DVU and NPD collectively polled 1,631,822 votes or 3.8 per cent of all votes cast.[54] But Neo-Nazi and nationalist organizations continue to count significant amounts of members. In 1998, for instance, 114 groups had a collective membership of 53,600. The latter figure actually represented an increase of eleven per cent over the previous year.[55] As with other periods in the history of the Federal Republic, the second half of the 1990s may represent a relatively dormant period for the extreme right, after which it may take off electorally under favourable circumstances.

Incidents of violence carried out by the extreme right also declined in the second half of the 1990s, totalling 790 in 1997 and 708 in 1998.[56] Nevertheless, for the victims these figures offer little comfort. For instance, after a festival in the east German town of Eggesin in September 1999 skinheads beat up two Vietnamese males. These foreigners certainly stood out, as elsewhere in the old GDR, because only fifteen non-Germans lived among a population of 8,000.[57]

Germans and minorities at the end of the twentieth century

The position of minorities in Germany in 1999 therefore left a lot to be desired, although they had clearly made dramatic advances in comparison with their predecessors. Minorities in late twentieth-century Germany continued to remain outsiders, distinguished from Germans in a number of ways, in terms of legal status, economic position and ethnic differentiation.

The extent of their distance from mainstream society depended upon a series of factors, above all the ethnic group of which they formed a part. The different populations residing in contemporary Germany resemble those which have lived in the country for much of the previous two centuries. The closest to the mainstream essentially consists of ethnic Germans from further east, who will probably, in the long term, assimilate into the rest of the dominant population, although, in the shorter term, they remain distinct from it in economic and linguistic terms. Many members of the Jewish community of the 1990s, especially those who returned in the 1940s and 1950s, resemble the dominant grouping. In contrast, the most recent arrivals, speaking Russian, differ significantly. The Gypsy populations who returned after the Second World War, while they may use the same language as the dominant grouping, have great distance from it because of the continued existence of underlying prejudice towards them and their different social and economic patterns.

Table 6: Germans and minorities at the end of the twentieth century (31 December 1998) according to nationality

Nationality	Total
Germans	74,717,400
Turkish	2,110,200
Serbian/Montenegrin	719,500
Italian	612,000
Greek	363,500
Polish	283,600
Croatian	208,900
Bosnian	190,000
Austrian	185,200
American	110,700
Macedonian	46,200
Slovenian	18,400
Others	2,471,400*
Total foreigners	7,319,600*
Total German population	82,037,000

Source: www.statistik-bund.de/basis/d/bevoe/bevoetab1.htm, Statistisches Bundesamt Deutschland, 'Bevölkerung nach Geschlecht und Staatsangehörigkeit'.
* A fuller list of foreign groups in Germany can be found in Cornelia Schmalz-Jacobsen and Georg Hansen, eds, *Ethnische Minderheiten in der Bundesrepublik Deutschland* (Munich, 1995), pp. 555–7.

Meanwhile, the foreign workers and their children who moved to Germany between the 1950s and the 1980s also remain distinct from Germans in ethnic terms, as well as in their social and economic position and, above all, their legal status, especially with regard to their citizenship. Finally, those asylum seekers who arrived during the late 1980s and 1990s also differ for similar reasons to the foreign workers. The same also applies to foreign workers and illegal migrants who arrived from eastern Europe, especially Poland, during the 1980s and 1990s.

Like all German nation states, the reunified Germany remains an ethnic state, which means that, in legal terms, those who can prove their Germanness enjoy a privileged position *vis-à-vis* those who cannot. Throughout the history of the Federal Republic, people born in a part of eastern Europe who can demonstrate German antecedents have had greater rights than second, third, fourth or any generation of Turks, Greeks or Italians born on German soil. The origins of this anomaly lie in the 1913 Nationality Law, which meant that Germany possessed the same legislation in this field through *Kaiserreich*, Weimar Republic, Third Reich and Federal Republic both before and after

1989. This has essentially meant that the vast majority of foreigners and their descendants in Germany do not possess German nationality, so that, in 1999, the country contained 7.4 million foreigners.[58] Part of the problem lies in the fact that much of the non-German population wishes to retain its original citizenship and therefore have dual nationality, which has proved anathema to the German political establishment. Proposals to make this possible by the Schröder government in 1999 led to a mass petition supported by the opposition, which resulted in the abandonment of this policy. At the same time, although foreigners could obtain a German passport through naturalization before 1999, this remained a difficult process, even after the passage of legislation to make this easier in 1991, 1993 and 1995.[59] The number of naturalizations increased from 20,237 in 1990 to 37,042 in 1992 and 44,950 in 1993.[60] But a new Nationality Law did come into operation in 1999 which meant that children born in Germany from 2000 of resident foreign parents automatically assumed German nationality. Nevertheless, the measure forbade dual citizenship and did little to ease the naturalization process.[61]

Nationality law in Germany has proved a basic structural problem which has excluded foreigners and their offspring from having full civil rights in the country. For instance, it has prevented non-Germans from playing a role in the political process and means that millions of permanent residents remain disenfranchised. Furthermore, they can also not obtain employment as civil servants.[62] It would be erroneous to view nationality legislation as a particularly German form of ethnic exclusion. Some states, such as Switzerland, have always employed the same *jus solis* principle, while others, such as Britain and France, have increasingly moved away from the concept of birth in their territories as an automatic guarantee of citizenship.[63] It may be asking too much of Germany to move in the opposite direction to its neighbours, although Britain and France, in contrast, do not have the same number of foreigners because many of the migrant workers who arrived after the Second World War already possessed British or French citizenship. 'Foreigners', including the second and subsequent generations, will remain second class citizens in Germany as long as their citizenship rights differ from those of ethnic Germans, who may not even have been born on German soil, even though legislation in the 1990s has tried to curb the rights of *Aussiedler* to automatic citizenship and settlement.[64]

Germany also differs from many of its European neighbours because it has no specific anti-racist legislation, although the constitution of the reunified country forbade discrimination on the grounds of sex, birth, race and language, as well as national and social origins.[65] While constitutional and legal guarantees do not prevent discrimination, they do make racists conscious of their actions and therefore do have some effect.[66] In the case of Germany, the absence of ethnic minorities from civil service employment confounds the problem of racism. An all-German judiciary and police force make discrimination inevitable among these arms of the state. During the xenophobic disorder of the early 1990s much attention rightly focused upon the apparent powerlessness of the police to halt the violence and the leniency of judicial sentencing.[67] Since that time, examples of police racism and brutality have continued. In Bremen, for instance, the authorities put much effort into dealing with foreign criminals, which meant that everyday racism became normal among the police in this city.[68] Police dealt with asylum seekers particularly badly, as they had fewer rights than virtually anyone else. For instance, in June 1994 'Emelia Ogubuike Madu, a Nigerian whose asylum application had been rejected, was taken from Volkstedt Prison in handcuffs and leg chains to the airport in Berlin to be deported'. The pilot refused to allow him into his plane. The victim describes what happened next:

> I was still handcuffed. I was taken into an airport building and pushed into a small cell. The airport police started beating me. There were about ten of them beating me with sticks and with their hands. They were calling me 'Nigger'. I said, 'Yes my name is Nigger' to get them to stop. I was bleeding; my eyes were puffy.[69]

Nevertheless, to view foreigners in Germany simply as victims of racism does not point to the full picture. The new Germany differs fundamentally from the Third Reich. As we have seen, foreign workers have developed a rich ethnicity, which revolves around religion, language and politics.[70] In addition, many of the refugee communities which have evolved since the 1980s have also established their own organizations. In 1994, for instance, Frankfurt contained 15,438 Africans, the largest nationalities within which consisted of Moroccans (9,479) and Ethiopians and Eritreans (2,447).[71] Similarly, 11,017 Africans lived in Berlin in 1993 including (of the largest groups) 1,326 Egyptians and 1,397 Ghanaians. The 87 Ugandans held regular informal meetings. In addition, African organizations have also sprung up in Berlin including the Europa-Afrika-Kulturzentrum and the Deutsch-Afrikanische Gesellschaft.[72] On a national scale the 24,769 Ghanaians actually represent one of the largest groups of approximately 200,000 'Afro-Germans', who live throughout the country. Apart from establishing their own organizations, most notably the Ghana Union, they, together with other Afro-Germans, have opened their own businesses, including restaurants, hairdressers, grocery stores and music shops.[73] Some members of the African communities in Germany have also produced their own literature, reflecting on the racial complexities of their lives, especially after reunification, as the following poem, by May Ayim indicates:

> Borderless and brazen
> a poem against the pretense of German unity
>
> I will be African
> even if you want me to be German
> and I will be German
> even if my blackness does not suit you
> I will go
> yet another step further
> to the farthest edge
> where my sisters – where my brothers stand
> where
> our
> FREEDOM
> begins
> I will go
> yet another step further and another step and
> will return
> when I want
> if I want
> and remain
> borderless and brazen[74]

The expanding Jewish communities of the 1990s have also developed a vibrant ethnicity which has built upon that which previously re-emerged after 1945. By 1994, following the arrival of people from the former USSR, a total of 80,000 Jews may have resided in Germany.[75] Some of these, both long-established, and more recent arrivals, practised their religion, while others remained secular and developed a cultural ethnicity with tenuous links to their faith.[76]

One of the most marginalized groups in Germany during the final decade of the twentieth century actually consisted of *Aussiedler*, although their position probably remains a short-term phase after which, in the longer term, its members will become increasingly assimilated into the surrounding ethnic German majority with which they claim to have affinity. Nevertheless, during the 1990s their problems remained real enough. The first of these consisted of difficulties with the German language. A survey carried out at the start of the decade revealed that 15 per cent of those interviewed considered their German good, 25 per cent bad and 50 per cent average, although most

spoke the language at home and many used it before their arrival.[77] The
reasons for these anomalies lie in the fact that many of the Germans in eastern
Europe only spoke dialects after 1945 because of restrictions on the use of
German,[78] which meant that, when they arrived in the Federal Republic they
took courses in standard German of up to ten months, which could cost as
much as DM 21,000, payed for by the state.[79] *Aussiedler* have also suffered
high rates of unemployment largely due to the fact that more of them worked
in agricultural and manual employment in their countries of origin than the
German percentages for such occupation, meaning they could not always
automatically move into the large service sector in Germany, which also often
required native command of German. In 1993 a total of 174,000 *Aussiedler*
found themselves without work. In fact, one survey revealed that 32 per cent
of *Aussiedler* were unemployed and looking for work, while 13 per cent did
not actively seek employment. The newcomers also resided in accommodation inferior to Germans. Some have lived in camps, including former gar-
risons used by French, British and US troops who began leaving the country
after the end of the Cold War, which has meant significant ghettoization
of the *Aussiedler*. Furthermore, they have also faced hostility, some of it
from otherwise progressive-thinking members of German society who view
Aussiedler as a privileged group who should face the same restrictions on
entry as other prospective migrants to Germany. Nevertheless, much of the
animosity which they face simply comes from mainstream racists, so that they
have become victims of physical attacks.[80]

Despite the efforts of the state to integrate Germans from further east into
the mainstream population,[81] at the end of the 1990s they remain at least as
distinct as the minorities which have evolved from the labour migrants of the
1950s and 1960s. Clearly, the difference lies in time scale, and there seems
no reason to doubt that the *Aussiedler* will in the longer run, even if this takes
several decades, overtake many of the non-German ethnic populations in the
level of their integration. They most resemble the German refugees who moved
westward at the end of the Second World War.

An overall assessment of Germans and their minorities at the end of the
twentieth century would have to demonstrate some optimism, especially if
comparisons are made with the years before 1945. Of course, native ethnic
Germans remain privileged in economic and legal terms, although this
depends upon whether comparisons are made with east or west Germans,
because the latter suffer serious social problems. Furthermore, racism has
certainly not disappeared, either in its potent or milder manifestations. The
Gypsies continue to remain a particularly marginalized group.[82] But grounds

for optimism exist. For instance, one survey carried out in the early 1990s revealed that the vast majority of Germans have now accepted foreigners as neighbours.[83] Although Germany has certainly not become a multicultural society, because Germans control political and economic power, the Schröder government elected in 1998 has taken a more positive attitude towards minorities than its CDU/CSU predecessors and has introduced measures to aid integration, which have, however, sparked opposition.[84] Most importantly, immigrants have had an impact on German life and, in this sense, Germany has become multicultural. An obvious manifestation of this consists of the change in the German diet. One study revealed, for instance, that 200 tonnes of donner kebabs are sold in Germany everyday, making a total of 720 million such meals per year.[85]

Nevertheless, at the end of the twentieth century migrant workers and their families, who form the bulk of ethnic minorities in Germany, and Gypsies, continue to remain marginalized in economic and political terms. In this sense both of these groupings do not differ from minorities which reside in other European states. The nation state exists for the purpose of including those with the right ethnic credential and excluding those with the wrong ones.[86] Germany therefore practises methods of exclusion characteristic of other liberal nation states.[87]

But Germany seems different because, between 1940 and 1945 the reason for the existence of the state consisted of the creation of a racial hierarchy which meant the extermination of peoples regarded as having the wrong ethnic credentials. The fact that Nazism controlled power always poses the question of whether the ghosts of the German past will ever resurface again to seize command of the state. This seems unlikely for economic and political reasons, as well as the fact that Germany has become so integrated and central to the development of Europe since 1945. While potent racism is likely to make another appearance similar to the one of the early 1990s, it is unlikely that Germany will ever return to the ethnic hell of wartime Nazism. Nevertheless, in common with all of its neighbours, a multicultural paradise Germany certainly is not.

Notes

1. For an introduction to the unification process see, for instance, Harold James and Marla Stone, eds, *When the Wall Came Down: Reactions to German Unification* (London, 1992).

2. C. H. Flockton, 'The Federal German Economy in the Early 1990s', *German* [265]
Politics 2 (1993), pp. 311–27; *OECD Economic Surveys, 1992–1993: Germany*
(Paris, 1993); *Süddeutsche Zeitung,* 9 February 1994.

3. Richard Evans, 'Germany's Morning After', *Marxism Today* (June 1991), p. 21.

4. See Christopher Flockton, 'The German Economy Since 1989–90: Problems
and Prospects', in Klaus Larres, ed., *Germany Since Unification: The Domestic and
External Consequences* (London, 1998), pp. 63–87.

5. For a statistical outline see Alun Jones, *The New Germany: A Human Geography*
(Chichester, 1994). A good oral history of East German changes is Jürgen A. K.
Thomaneck, 'From Euphoria to Reality: Social Problems of Post-Unification',
in Derek Lewis and John R. P. Mackenzie, eds, *The New Germany: Social, Political
and Cultural Changes of Unification* (Exeter, 1995), pp. 7–30.

6. A good introduction is Eva Kolinsky, *Women in Contemporary Germany: Life,
Work and Politics* 2nd edn (Oxford, 1993).

7. Numerous books have appeared on the Stasi including, in English: John O.
Koehler, *Stasi: The Untold Story of the East German Secret Police* (Oxford, 1999);
and David Childs and Richard Popplewell, *The Stasi: The East German Intelligence
and Security Service* (Basingstoke, 1996).

8. These developments are discussed below.

9. See, for instance, Lothar Gutjahr, *German Foreign and Defence Policy After Unification* (London, 1994); Arnulf Baring, ed., *Germany's New Position in Europe: Problems and Perspectives* (Oxford, 1994); and Paul B. Stares, ed., *The New Germany
and the New Europe* (Washington, DC, 1992).

10. Wolfgang Bosswick, 'Asylum Policy in Germany', in Philip Muus, ed., *Exclusion and Inclusion of Refugees in Contemporary Europe* (Utrecht, 1997), pp. 53–4.

11. See, for instance, Panikos Panayi, *Outsiders: A History of European Minorities*
(London, 1999), pp. 150–1.

12. Barbara Marshall, '"Migration" into Germany: Asylum Seekers and Ethnic Germans', *German Politics* 1 (1992), p. 125.

13. Hidir Çelik and Almut Schubert, *30 Jahre Migration, 30 Jahre Frauen in der Fremde:
Migrantinnen der Region Köln-Bonn* (Bonn, 1995), p. 75.

14. *Observer*, 15 August 1992.

15. United Nations High Commission for Refugees, *The State of the World's Refugees*
(Oxford, 1995), p. 12.

16. Vladimir Grecic, 'Former Yugoslavia', in Solon Ardittis, ed., *The Politics of
East-West Migration* (London, 1994), p. 131.

[266]   17.   Ibid., p. 127.

18.   Bosswick, 'Asylum Policy', pp. 62–3.

19.   John Bendix and Niklaus Steiner, 'Political Asylum in Germany', *German Politics and Society* 16 (1998), p. 36.

20.   Ibid., pp. 42–3; Klaus J. Bade, *Ausländer, Aussiedler, Asyl: Eine Bestandsaufnahme* (Munich, 1994), pp. 126–7.

21.   www.unhcr.ch/world/euro/germany.htm, UNHCR Country Profiles, Germany.

22.   Klaus J. Bade, 'Aussiedler: Rückwanderer über Generationen Hinweg', in Bade, ed., *Neue Heimat im Westen: Vertriebene, Flüchtlinge, Aussiedler* (Münster, 1990), pp. 128–9.

23.   Press and Information Office of the Federal Government, Foreign Affairs Division, *Hostility Towards Foreigners in Germany: New Facts, Analyses, Arguments* (Bonn, 1993), p. 77.

24.   Jurgen Fijalkowski, 'Aggressive Nationalism, Immigration Pressure and Asylum Policy Disputes in Contemporary Germany', *International Migration Review* 27 (1993), p. 851.

25.   Gerold Dembon, Dieter Hoffmeister and Heinz Ingenhorst, *Fremde Deutsche in deutscher Fremde: Integrationsprobleme von Aussiedlern im kommunalen Raum* (Regensburg, 1994), pp. 24, 82.

26.   Klaus Brake, *Lebenserinnerungen rußlanddeutscher Einwanderer: Zeitgeschichte und Narrativik* (Hamburg, 1998), p. 347.

27.   Rainer Münz and Rainer Ohliger, 'Long-Distance Citizens and Their Immigration to Germany', in Peter Schuck and Rainer Münz, eds, *Paths to Inclusion: The Integration of Migrants in the United States and Germany* (Oxford, 1998), pp. 160, 170–2; Bade, *Ausländer, Aussiedler, Asyl*, p. 149.

28.   See: Julius H. Schoeps, Willi Jasper and Bernhard Vogt, *Russische Juden in Deutschland: Integration und Selbstbehauptung in einem fremden Land* (Weinheim, 1996); Jeroen Doomernik, *Going West: Soviet Jewish Immigrants in Berlin Since 1990* (Aldershot, 1997).

29.   *Welt am Sonntag*, 16 August 1992.

30.   Ewa Helias, *Polnische Arbeitnehmer in der DDR und der Bundesrepublik Deutschland* (Berlin, 1992), p. 21, gives a figure of 10,000 Poles in Berlin and Brandenburg in 1991.

31.   *Stern*, 7 October 1993.

32.   Helias, *Polnische Arbeitnehmer*, pp. 18–20.

33. See www.polskarada.de/psc.htm, Polish Social Council Berlin, Norbert [267]
    Cyrus, 'German Gates of Entry and Polish Migration: The Making of a Recent
    System of Labour Circulation'.

34. See above.

35. David Childs, 'The Nationalist and Neo-Nazi Scene Since 1945', in Klaus
    Larres and Panikos Panayi, eds, *The Federal Republic of Germany Since 1949:
    Politics, Society and Economy Before and After Unification* (London, 1996), p. 212.

36. Richard Stöss, *Politics Against Democracy: Right-Wing Extremism in West Germany*
    (Oxford, 1991), pp. 146–7.

37. David Childs, 'The Far Right in Germany Since 1945', in Luciano Cheles,
    Ronnie Ferguson and Michalina Vaughan, eds, *The Far Right in Western and
    Eastern Europe* (London, 1995), p. 297.

38. Childs, 'Nationalist and Neo-Nazi Scene', pp. 221–2.

39. Peter Ködderitzch and Leo A. Müller, *Rechtsextremismus in der DDR* (Göttingen,
    1990); Bernhard Schröder, *Rechte Kerle: Skinheads, Faschos, Hooligans* (Hamburg,
    1992), pp. 12–14, 29–30, 70–1, 91–2; Thomas Ammer, 'Prozesse gegen
    Skinheads in der DDR', *Deutschland Archiv* 21 (1988), pp. 804–7; Claus
    Leggewie, *Druck von Rechts: Wohin treibt die Bundesrepublik?* (Munich, 1993),
    pp. 167–8.

40. C. T. Husbands, 'Militant Neo-Nazism in the Federal Republic of Germany
    in the 1980s', in L. Cheles, R. Ferguson and M. Vaughan, eds, *Neo-Fascism in
    Europe* (London, 1991), pp. 96–7; Gerhard Paul, 'Der Schatten Hitlers verblaßt:
    Die Normalisierung des Rechtextremismus in den achtziger Jahren', in Paul,
    ed., *Hitlers Schatten verblaßt: Die Normalisierung des Rechtextremismus* (Bonn,
    1989), pp. 13–40.

41. Thomas Saalfeld, 'The Politics of National Populism: Ideology and Politics of
    the German Republican Party', *German Politics* 2 (1993), pp. 177–99; Wolfgang
    Gessenharter, 'Die Parteiprogramme der Rechtsparteien', *Sozialwissenschaftliche
    Information* 20 (1991), pp. 227–33; Lilly Weissbrod, 'Nationalism in Reunified
    Germany', *German Politics* 3 (1994), pp. 222–32.

42. Hans-Gerd Jaschke, *Die 'Republikaner': Profile einer Rechtsaußen-Partei* (Bonn,
    1993), p. 118; Bundesministerium des Innern, *Verfassungsschutzbericht, 1992*
    (Bonn, 1993), p. 36; Jürgen W. Falter, *Wer wählt rechts? Die Wähler und Anhänger
    rechtsextremistischer Parteien im vereinigten Deutschland* (Munich, 1994), p. 21.

43. Bundesministerium des Innern, *Verfassungsschutzbericht, 1990* (Bonn, 1991),
    p. 124.

44. Bundesministerium des Innern, *Verfassungsschutzbericht, 1991* (Bonn, 1992),
    p. 75.

45. For more detail on the above see Panikos Panayi, 'Racial Violence in the New Germany (1990–3)', *Contemporary European History* 3 (1994), pp. 266–74.

46. Jeffrey K. Olick and Daniel Levy, 'Collective Memory and Cultural Constraint: Holocaust Myth and Rationality in German Politics', *American Sociological Review* 62 (1997), pp. 921–36.

47. The best English account of this is Richard J. Evans, *In Hitler's Shadow: West German Historians and the Attempt to Escape from the Nazi Past* (London, 1989).

48. Panikos Panayi, 'Racial Exclusionism in the New Germany' in Larres, *Germany Since Unification*, p. 142.

49. For instance, for the debate on the lead up and during the outbreaks of violence in the autumn of 1991 see, for example: *Spiegel*, 9, 30 September 1991; *Frankfurter Rundschau*, 23 September, 7 October 1991; *Welt Am Sonntag*, 6, 13 October 1991; *Rheinischer Merkur*, 2, 9, 16 August 1991; *Stern*, 14, August 1991.

50. Falter, *Wer wählt rechts?*, p. 21.

51. See, for instance, *Frankfurter Rundschau*, 26 March 1994.

52. Bundesministerium des Innern, *Verfassungsschutzbericht 1994* (Bonn, 1995), p. 81.

53. *Searchlight*, November 1994, p. 21.

54. http://focus.de/D/DI/DIE/DIEO1/die01.htm, Focus online/Politik News/Wahlen 199 . . . ahlen 98: Bundestagswahl '98 Das Ergebnis.

55. Bundesministerium des Innern, *Verfassungsschutzbericht 1998* (Bonn, 1999), pp. 15, 16.

56. Ibid., p. 20.

57. *Spiegel*, 4 October 1999.

58. *Spiegel*, 11 January 1999, p. 26.

59. Mary Fulbrook, 'Germany for the Germans? Citizenship and Nationality in a Divided Nation', in David Cesarani and Mary Fulbrook, eds, *Citizenship, Nationality and Migration in Europe* (London, 1996), p. 102.

60. Gerald L. Neuman, 'Nationality Law in the United States and Germany: Structure and Current Problems', in Schuck and Münz, *Paths to Inclusion*, pp. 273, 274.

61. www.bmi.bund.de/staatsrecht/in_aktuelles.html, Bundesministerium des Innern, 'Das neue Staatsangehörigkeitsrecht'.

62. William A. Barbieri Jr, *Ethics of Citizenship: Immigration and Group Rights in Germany* (London, 1998), pp. 35–6.

63. See, for instance: Adrian Favell, *Philosophies of Integration: Immigrants and the Idea of Citizenship in France and Britain* (London, 1998); and Patrick Ireland, *The Policy Challenge of Ethnic Diversity: Immigrant Politics in France and Switzerland* (London, 1994).

64. Münz and Ohliger, 'Long-Distance Citizens', p. 171.

65. See Martin MacEwan, *Tackling Racism in Europe: An Examination of Anti-Discrimination Law in Practice* (Oxford, 1995).

66. Panikos Panayi, *An Ethnic History of Europe Since 1945: Nations, States and Minorities* (London, 2000), pp. 179–252.

67. Panayi, 'Racial Violence in the New Germany', pp. 278–9.

68. See: Antirassismusbüro Bremen, *'Sie behandeln uns wie Tiere': Rassismus bei Polizei und Justiz in Deutschland* (Berlin, 1997).

69. Helsinki Watch, *'Germany for Germans': Xenophobia and Racist Violence in Germany* (New York, 1995), p. 48.

70. See above.

71. Amt für multikulturelle Angelegenheiten, *Afrika in Frankfurt: Kultur und Alltag in einer deutschen Stadt* (Frankfurt, 1996), p. 87.

72. Martina Müller, *Afrikaner in Berlin* (Berlin, 1993), pp. 34, 53, 55.

73. Rose Haferkamp, 'Die ghanaische Minderheit', in Cornelia Schmalz-Jacobsen and Georg Hansen, eds, *Ethnische Minderheiten in der Bundesrepublik Deutschland* (Munich, 1995), pp. 166–78.

74. Ayim, May: 'grenzenlos und unverschämt' ('borderless and brazen'), in: *blues in Schwarz Weiss*, 3rd ed. Berlin: Orlanda, 1996: translated by May Ayim.

75. Michael Cohn, *The Jews in Germany, 1945–1993* (London, 1994), p. ix.

76. See contributions to Sander L. Gilman, ed., *Reemerging Jewish Culture in Germany: Life and Literature Since 1989* (London, 1994).

77. Dembon, Hoffmeister and Ingenhorst, *Fremde Deutsche*, pp. 70, 98.

78. See, briefly, Panayi, *Ethnic History*, pp. 110–12.

79. Barbara Malchow, Keyumars Tayebi and Ulrike Brand, *Die fremden Deutschen* (Hamburg, 1993), p. 61.

80. See two good essays on the position of *Aussiedler*: Münz and Ohliger, 'Long-Distance Citizens', especially pp. 172–84; and Manuela Westphal, 'Die fremden Deutschen: Einwanderung und Eingliederung von Aussiedlern in Niedersachsen', in Klaus J. Bade, ed., *Fremde im Land: Zuwanderung und*

Eingliederung im Raum Niedersachsen seit dem Zweiten Weltkrieg (Osnabrück, 1997), pp. 167–212.

81. See Westphal, ibid.; Münz and Ohliger, ibid.; and Maldow, Tayebi and Brand, *Die fremden Deutschen*, pp. 56–65.

82. Katrin Reemtsma, *Sinti und Roma: Geschichte, Kultur und Gegenwart* (Munich, 1996), pp. 164–79.

83. Alphons Silbermann and Francis Hüsers, *Der 'normale' Haß auf die Fremden: Eine sozialwissenschaftliche Studie zu Ausmaß und Hintergründen von Fremdenfeindlichkeit in Deutschland* (Munich, 1995), p. 23.

84. See www.bmi.bund.de/themen/in-staatsrecht2.html, Bundesministerium des Innern.

85. See Eberhard Seidel-Pielen, *Aufgespießt: Wie die Döner über Deutschland kamen* (Hamburg, 1996). For multiculturalism in Germany more generally see Claus Leggewie, ed., *Multi Kulti: Spielregeln für die Vielvölkerrepublik* (Hamburg, 1990).

86. This is the argument of Panayi, *Ethnic History*; and, *Outsiders*.

87. See Panayi, *Ethnic History*, pp. 179–252.

BIBLIOGRAPHICAL ESSAY

The following bibliography simply points to some of the most important sources on minorities in recent German history, especially those which I found most useful. A full list of material would take up several volumes. Far more information can be found in the footnotes. I have used English translations of German books when they exist.

General

For general background on the evolution of Germany during the past two centuries useful starting points include Mary Fulbrook, ed., *German History Since 1800* (London, 1997) and William Carr, *A History of Germany, 1815–1990* 4th edn (London, 1991). For the period before unification readers should consult the magisterial James J. Sheehan, *German History, 1770–1866* (Oxford, 1989). For the later nineteenth and first half of the twentieth centuries there is the equally authoritative, but now aging, Gordon A. Craig, *Germany, 1866–1945* (Oxford, 1981). For the *Kaiserreich* see the magnificent Thomas Nipperdey, *Deutsche Geschichte, 1866–1918*, 2 vols (Munich, 1990, 1992) and, more briefly but equally brilliant, Hans-Ulrich Wehler, *The German Empire, 1871–1918* (Oxford, 1991). Roger Chickering, *Imperial Germany and the Great War, 1914–1918* (Cambridge, 1998) offers a good introduction to the First World War. Standard works on the Weimar Republic include Detlev J. Peukert, *The Weimar Republic: The Crisis of Classical Modernity* (New York, 1991) and Helmut Heiber, *The Weimar Republic* (Oxford, 1993). From the point of view of the themes covered in the present book the best volume on Nazism consists of Michael Burleigh and Wolfgang Wippermann, *The Racial State: Germany, 1933–1945* (Cambridge, 1991), while, for the regime more generally, Karl Dietrich Bracher, *The German Dictatorship: The Origins, Structure and Consequences of National Socialism* (Harmondsworth, 1973) remains a classic. A useful introduction to the Federal Republic is Klaus Larres and Panikos Panayi, eds, *The Federal Republic of Germany Since 1949: Politics, Society and Economy Before and After Unification* (London, 1996), while, for the GDR, Mary Fulbrook, *Anatomy of a Dictatorship: Inside the GDR, 1949–1989* (Oxford, 1995) serves the same purpose. Klaus Larres, ed., *Germany Since Unification: The Domestic and External Consequences* (London, 1998), provides an equally good introduction to the 1990s.

Several excellent studies have appeared on the history of German nationalism and racism. The best of these include John Breuilly, ed., *The State of Germany: The National Idea in the Making, Unmaking and Remaking of a Modern Nation State* (London, 1992) and George L. Mosse, *The Crisis of German Ideology: Intellectual Origins of the Third Reich* (New York, 1981). More general works on nationalism and racism include Michael Banton, *Racial Theories* 2nd edn (Cambridge, 1998) and Eric Hobsbawm, *Nations and Nationalism Since 1870: Programme, Myth, Reality* 2nd edn (Cambridge, 1992).

The present study represents the first to examine the history of all German ethnic minorities during the nineteenth and twentieth centuries. Two other works cover a broader time period. The not very academic Bernt Egelmann, *Du Deutsch: Geschichte der Ausländer in unserem Land* (Munich, 1984), proves of limited use. In contrast there is Klaus J. Bade, ed., *Deutsche im Ausland, Fremde in Deutschland: Migration in Geschichte und Gegenwart* (Munich, 1992), which contains excellent essays, by leaders in their fields, on both Germans abroad and foreigners in Germany, as well as German returnees and expellees, although it has just one short, but useful essay on the Gypsies and does not cover the Jews.

Jews

German Jewry represents one of the most widely studied groups in modern historiography, which means that this section can only offer the briefest sample of works published. A good starting point consists of the journal devoted to this group in the form of the *Leo Baeck Institute Year Book*. An excellent bibliographical study is Trude Maurer, *Die Entwicklung der jüdischen Minderheit in Deutschland (1780–1933)* (Tübingen, 1992).

Several studies which cover the Jews over a long time period have appeared. Those which I found especially useful include the, now dated, Wanda

Kampmann, *Deutsche und Juden: Die Geschichte der Juden in Deutschland vom*
Mittelalter bis zum Beginn des Ersten Weltkrieges 3rd edn (Frankfurt, 1994). Equally
dated but still useful is H. G. Adler, *The Jews in Germany: From the Enlightenment
to National Socialism* (Notre Dame, IN, 1969). There is also Werner J. Cahnman,
German Jewry: Its History and Sociology (New Brunswick, NJ, 1989), a collection of good essays. Ruth Gay, *The Jews of Germany: A Historical Portrait* (London,
1992), now provides one of the best long-term accounts, tracing the history of German Jewry until the Holocaust. Equally useful is Ismar Elbogen
and Eleonore Sterling, *Die Geschichte der Juden in Deutschland* (Frankfurt, 1988).
Peter Freimark, Alice Jankowski and Ina S. Lorenz, eds, *Juden in Deutschland:
Emanzipation, Integration, Verfolgung und Vernichtung* (Hamburg, 1991) contains
some excellent essays. Two important books by Peter Pulzer are: *The Rise of
Political Antisemitism in Germany and Austria* (London, 1964); and *Jews and the
German State: The Political History of a Minority, 1848–1933* (Oxford, 1992).
For personal accounts students should begin with Monika Richarz, ed., *Jewish
Life in Germany: Memoirs from Three Centuries* (Bloomington, IN, 1991).

The best general studies of the emancipation period include: David Sorkin,
The Transformation of German Jewry, 1780–1840 (New York, 1987); Hans
Liebeschütz and Arnold Paucker, eds, *Das Judentum in der deutschen Umwelt,
1800–1850: Studien zur Frühgeschichte der Emanzipation* (Tübingen, 1977); and
Jacob Toury, *Soziale und politische Geschichte der Juden in Deutschland, 1848–1871:
Zwischen Revolution, Reaktion und Emanzipation* (Düsseldorf, 1977). Several
excellent local studies have appeared including: Steven M. Lowenstein, *The
Berlin Jewish Community: Enlightenment, Family and Crisis, 1770–1830* (New York,
1994); Helga Krohn, *Die Juden in Hamburg, 1800–1850: Ihre soziale, kulturelle
und politische Entwicklung während der Emanzipationszeit* (Frankfurt am Main,
1967); and James F. Harris, *The People Speak! Antisemitism and Emancipation in
Nineteenth Century Bavaria* (Ann Arbor, MI, 1994). Those interested specifically in antisemitism in the emancipation period should begin with
Eleonore Sterling, *Er ist wie Du: Aus der Frühgeschichte des Antisemitismus in
Deutschland (1815–1850)* (Munich, 1956) and Paul Lawrence Rose, *Revolutionary Antisemitism in Germany from Kant to Wagner* (Princeton, NJ, 1990).

Numerous volumes have appeared on Jews in the *Kaiserreich*. The best of
these include: W. E. Mosse and Arnold Paucker, eds, *Juden im Wilhelminischen
Deutschland* (Tübingen, 1976); Werner Habel, *Deutsch-jüdische Geschichte
am Ausgang des 19. Jahrhunderts* (Kastellaun, 1977); and Marion A. Kaplan,
*The Making of the Jewish Middle Class: Women, Family and Identity in Imperial
Germany* (New York, 1991). For eastern European Jews the standard work is
Jack Wertheimer, *Unwelcome Strangers: East European Jews in Imperial Germany*

[274] (Oxford, 1987). Many of the best works on Imperial antisemitism have appeared in English including: Paul W. Massing, *Rehearsal for Destruction: A Study of Political Anti-Semitism in Imperial Germany* (New York, 1949); and Richard S. Levy, *The Downfall of Anti-Semitic Political Parties in Imperial Germany* (New Haven, CT, 1975).

The most important studies of Jews and antisemitism in the Weimar Republic include: Walter Grab and Julius H. Schoeps, eds, *Juden in der Weimarer Republik* (Stuttgart, 1986); Donald L. Niewyk, *The Jews in Weimar Germany* (Baton Rouge, LO, 1980); Anthony Kaukers, *German Politics and the Jews: Düsseldorf and Nuremberg, 1910–1933* (Oxford, 1996); and Trude Maurer, *Ostjuden in Deutschland, 1918–1933* (Hamburg, 1986).

Since the Holocaust became an accepted area of historical study during the 1970s, thousands of books have appeared on the subject. Important starting points include: Raul Hilberg, *The Destruction of the European Jews* 3 vols (London, 1985); Lucy Dawidowicz, *The War Against the Jews, 1933–45* (Harmondsworth, 1990); Arno J. Meyer, *Why Did the Heavens Not Darken: The Final Solution in History* (London, 1988); Klaus P. Fischer, *The History of an Obsession: German Judeophobia and the Holocaust* (London, 1998). The best studies of German Jewry under the Nazis include: Arnold Paucker, ed., *Die Juden im nationalsozialistischen Deutschland* (Tübingen, 1986); Avraham Barkai, *From Boycott to Annihilation: The Economic Struggle of German Jews, 1933–1943* (London, 1989); Wolfgang Benz, ed., *Die Juden in Deutschland, 1933–1945: Leben unter nationalsozialistischer Herrschaft* 3rd edn (Munich, 1993); and Marion A. Kaplan, *Between Dignity and Despair: Jewish Life in Nazi Germany* (New York, 1998). Numerous local studies have appeared, the best of which include: Henry R. Huttenbach, *The Destruction of the Jewish Community of Worms, 1933–1945: A Study of the Holocaust Experience in Germany* (New York, 1981); Dieter Goetz, *Juden in Oldenburg, 1930–1938* (Oldenburg, 1988); and Peter Juk and Martina Sellmeyer, *Stationen auf dem Weg nach Auschwitz: Entrechtung, Vertreibung, Vernichtung: Juden in Osnabrück* (Bramsche, 1989). For a deeply moving account of the experiences of one German Jewish child, readers should try to get hold of Hannele Zürndorfer, *The Ninth of November* (London, 1983).

The German Jews who survived the Holocaust, as well as those who returned at various times after 1945, have also received much attention. Good starting points include: Michael Brenner, *After the Holocaust: Rebuilding Jewish Lives in Postwar Germany* (Princeton, NJ, 1997); M. Brumlik, D. Kiesel, C. Kugelmann and J. H. Schoeps, eds, *Jüdisches Leben in Deutschland seit 1945* (Frankfurt, 1986); and Monika Richarz, 'Jews in Today's Germanies', *Leo Baeck Institute Year Book* 30 (1985). For arrivals after 1989 see: Julius H. Schoeps,

Willi Jasper and Bernhard Vogt, *Russische Juden in Deutschland: Integration und Selbstbehauptung in einem fremden Land* (Weinheim, 1996); and Jeroen Doomernik, *Going West: Soviet Jewish Immigrants in Berlin Since 1990* (Aldershot, 1997).

Gypsies

Gypsies in Germany have received much attention from German authors, but little from English ones. A starting point is Joachim S. Hohmann, *Neue deutsche Zigeunerbibliographie* (Frankfurt am Main, 1992). Several long-term perspectives have appeared, the most important of which include: Joachim S. Hohmann, *Geschichte der Zigeunerverfolgung in Deutschland*, 3rd edn (Frankfurt, 1988); Wolfgang Wippermann, *Geschichte der Sinti und Roma in Deutschland: Darstellung und Dokumente* (Berlin, 1993); Karin Reemstma, *Sinti und Roma: Geschichte, Kultur, Gegenwart* (Munich, 1996); Rainer Hehemann, *Die 'Bekämpfung des Zigeunerwesens' im Wilhelminischen Deutschland und in der Weimarer Republik, 1871–1933* (Frankfurt, 1933); Michael Schenk, *Rassismus gegen Sinti und Roma: Zur Kontinuität der Zigeunerverfolgung innerhalb der deutschen Gesellschaft von der Weimarer Republik bis in die Gegenwart* (Frankfurt, 1994); Georg von Soest, *Zigeuner zwischen Verfolgung und Integration: Geschichte, Lebensbedingungen und Eingliederungsversuche* (Weinheim, 1979); and Susan Tebbutt, ed., *Sinti and Roma: Gypsies in German-Speaking Society and Literature* (Oxford, 1998). Some excellent studies have appeared on the Nazi persecution of the Gypsies. The best of these consist of: Donald Kenrick and Grattan Puxon, *The Destiny of Europe's Gypsies* (London, 1972); and Michael Zimmermann, *Rassenutopie und Genozid: Die nationalsozialistische 'Lösung der Zigeunerfrage'* (Hamburg, 1996). Two good local studies of Gyspies under the Nazis are: Eva von Hase-Malik and Doris Kreuzkamp, *Du kriegst auch einen schönen Wohnwagen: Zwangslager für Sinti und Roma während des Nationalsozialismus in Frankfurt am Main* (Frankfurt, 1990); and Ludwig Eiber, Eva Strauß and Michael Krausnick, *'Ich wußte, es wird schlimm': Die Verfolgung der Sinti und Roma in München, 1933–1945* (Munich, 1993).

Localized minorities

Several important English and German volumes have appeared on Prussian Poles. The starting point remains the brilliant Martin Broszat, *Zweihundert*

[276] *Jahre deutsche Polenpolitk* 2nd edn (Frankfurt, 1972). Almost as useful is Wolfgang Wipperman, *Geschichte der deutsch-polnischen Beziehungen* (Berlin, 1992). There is also the extremely well researched William W. Hagen, *Germans, Poles and Jews: The Nationality Conflict in the Prussian East, 1772–1914* (Chicago, 1980). The same praise applies to Richard Blanke, *Prussian Poland in the German Empire (1871–1900)* (Boulder, CO, 1981). Students should also consult Harry Kenneth Rosenthal, *German and Pole: National Conflict and Modern Myth* (Gainesville, FL, 1976). Harald von Riekhoff, *German-Polish Relations, 1918–1933* (Baltimore, MD, 1971) covers the Weimar Republic.

The standard German histories of Schleswig-Holstein include Ulrich Lange, ed., *Geschichte Schleswig-Holsteins: Von den Anfängen bis zur Gegenwart* (Neumünster, 1996), pp. 459–85; and Otto Brandt, *Geschichte Schleswig-Holsteins* 7th edn revised by Wilhelm Klüver (Kiel, 1976). For the Sorbs see: the five-volume *Geschichte der Sorben* published between 1974 and 1979; and Gerald Stone, *The Smallest Slavonic Nation: The Sorbs of Lusatia* (London, 1972).

Migrants

Foreign workers and their offspring have received enormous amounts of attention. The starting point must be the work of Klaus J. Bade, whose most important book in this context consists of the collection of essays he edited entitled *Auswanderer – Wanderarbeiter – Gastarbeiter: Bevölkerung, Arbeitsmarkt und Wanderung in Deutschand seit der Mitte des 19. Jahrhunderts* 2 vols (Ostfildern, 1984). In English he has edited *Population, Labour and Migration in 19th- and 20th- Century Germany* (Leamington Spa, 1987). Ulrich Herbert, *A History of Foreign Labour in Germany, 1880–1980: Seasonal Workers/ Forced Workers/Guest Workers* (Ann Arbor, MI, 1990), has produced an equally useful work covering a long time span. Johann Woydt, *Ausländische Arbeitskräfte in Deutschland: Vom Kaiserreich zur Bundesrepublik* (Heilbronn, 1987), and Lothar Elsner and Joachim Lehmann, *Ausländische Arbeiter unter dem deutschen Imperialismus, 1900 bis 1985* (Berlin, 1988), have also taken a long-term perspective in order to demonstrate the historical continuities in labour importation.

Much has appeared on the *Kaiserreich.* Some high-quality empirical studies exist on Ruhr Poles, the best of which is Christoph Kleßmann, *Polnische Bergarbeiter im Ruhrgebiet, 1870–1945* (Göttingen, 1978). Nevertheless, readers should also consult: Hans Ulrich-Wehler, 'Die Polen im Ruhrgebiet bis

1918', in idem, ed., *Moderne deutsche Sozialgeschichte* (Cologne, 1966); Krystyna
Murzynowska, *Die polnischen Erwerbswanderer im Ruhrgebiet während der Jahre
1880–1914* (Dortmund, 1979); Valentina-Maria Stefanski, *Zum Prozeß der
Emanzipation und Integration von Außenseitern: Polnische Arbeitsmigranten im
Ruhrgebiet* (Dortmund, 1984); and Richard Charles Murphy, 'Polish In-
Migration in Bottrop, 1891–1933: An Ethnic Minority in a German
Industrial City' (University of Iowa PhD thesis, 1977).

Foreign migrants in the *Kaiserreich* have received significant attention. For
Poles and other eastern Europeans see, for instance: Anton Knoke, *Ausländische
Arbeiter in Deutschland* (Leipzig, 1911); Johannes Nichtweiß, *Die ausländischen
Saisonarbeiter in der Landwirtschaft der östlichen und mittleren Gebiete des Deutschen
Reiches: Ein Beitrag zur Geschichte der preussisch-deutschen Politik von 1890–1914*
(Berlin, 1959); Karl Liedke, *'. . . aber politisch unerwünscht': Arbeitskräfte aus
Osteuropa im Land Braunschweig 1880 bis 1939* (Brunswick, 1993); Karl Marten
Barfuss, *'Gastarbeiter' in Nordwestdeutschland, 1884–1918* (Bremen, 1986); and
Kathrin Roller, *Frauenmigration und Ausländerpolitik im Deutschen Kaiserreich:
Politische Arbeitsmigrantinnen in Preußen* (Berlin, 1994). Some excellent studies
now exist on Italian workers before the First World War, especially Adolf
Wennemann, *Arbeit im Norden: Italiener im Rheinland und Westfalen des späten
19. und frühen 20. Jahrhunderts* (Osnabrück, 1997), and René Del Fabbro,
*Transalpini: Italienische Arbeitswanderung nach Süddeutschland im Kaiserreich, 1870–
1918* (Osnabrück, 1996).

Because of the absence of foreign workers under the Weimar Republic
relatively little has appeared on them. The best specific article consists of Klaus
J. Bade, 'Arbeitsmarkt, Bevölkerung und Wanderung in der Weimarer
Republik', in Michael Stürmer, ed., *Die Weimarer Republik* (Königstein im
Taunus, 1985). An excellent volume on the experience of Ruhr Poles is Ralf
Karl Oenning, *'Du da mitti polnischen Farben . . .': Sozialisationerfahrungen von
Polen im Ruhrgebiet 1918 bis 1939* (Münster, 1991).

An enormous amount of attention has focused upon the Nazi exploitation of foreign workers, especially during the Second World War. The best
of the general studies include: Eva Seeber, *Zwangsarbeiter in der faschistischen
Kriegswirtschaft* (Berlin, 1964); Edward L. Homze, *Foreign Labour in Nazi Germany* (Princeton, NJ, 1967); Hans Pfahlman, *Fremdarbeiter und Kriegsgefangene
in der deutschen Kriegswirtschaft, 1939–1945* (Darmstadt, 1968); Ulrich Herbert,
Hitler's Foreign Workers: Enforced Labour in Germany under the Third Reich (Cambridge, 1997); and Ulrich Herbert, ed., *Europa und der 'Reicheinsatz': Ausländische
Zivilarbeiter, Kriegsgefangene und KZ-Häftlinge in Deutschland, 1938–1945* (Essen,
1991). In addition, specific national minorities and German locations have

[278] also received attention including, in the former category, Helga Bories-Sawala, *Franzosen im 'Reicheinsatz': Deportation, Zwangsarbeit, Alltag*, 2 vols (Frankfurt, 1996) and, in the latter, Gabriele Freitag, *Zwangsarbeiter im Lipper Land: Der Einsatz von Arbeitskräften in der Landwirtschaft Lippes, 1939–1945* (Bochum, 1996), and Heinrich Burgdorf, *et al.*, eds, *Zwangsarbeiterinnen und Kriegsgefangene in Blomberg (1939–1945)* (Bielefeld, 1996). The standard work on foreign workers at the end of the war is Wolfgang Jacobmeyer, *Vom Zwangsarbeiter zum heimatlosen Ausländer* (Göttingen, 1985).

Both social scientists and historians have examined the new migrants in the Federal Republic. Two books by Klaus J. Bade offer a useful starting point in the form of *Ausländer, Aussiedler, Asyl: Eine Bestandsaufnahme* (Munich, 1994), and, ed., *Fremde im Land: Zuwanderung und Eingliederung im Raum Niedersachsen seit dem Zweiten Weltkrieg* (Osnabrück, 1997). See also Helga and Horst Reimann, eds, *Gastarbeiter* (Munich, 1976). Good articles include: 'Population Change and its Repercussions on the Social History of the Federal Republic', in Klaus Larres and Panikos Panayi, eds, *The Federal Republic of Germany Since 1949: Politics, Society and Economy Before and After Unification* (London, 1996); and Clemens Amelunxen, 'Foreign Workers in West Germany', in William A. Veenhoven, ed., *Case Studies in Human Rights and Fundamental Freedoms*, vol. 1 (The Hague, 1975). Three important books which have appeared on Turks are: Claus Leggewie and Zafer Şenocak, eds, *Deutsche Türken: Das Ende der Geduld* (Hamburg, 1993); Faruk Şen and Andreas Goldberg, *Türken in Deutschland: Leben zwischen zwei Kulturen* (Munich, 1994); and David Horrocks and Eva Kolinsky, eds, *Turkish Culture in German Society Today* (Oxford, 1996). See also Barbara von Breitenbach, *Italiener und Spanier als Arbeitnehmer in der Bundesrepublik Deutschland* (Munich, 1982).

Foreign workers in the GDR have also received much attention, despite their relatively small numbers. The most important works include: A. W. Stack and S. Hussain, *Ausländer in der DDR: Ein Rückblick* (Berlin, 1991); Maria and Lothar Elsner, *Zwischen Nationalismus und Internationalismus: Über Ausländer und Ausländerpolitik in der DDR, 1949–1990* (Rostock, 1994); and, more specifically, Sandra Gruner-Domic, *Kubanische Arbeitsmigration in die DDR, 1978–1989: Das Arbeitskäfteabkommen und dessen Realisierung* (Berlin, 1997).

A good starting point for the period after unification is the two articles I have written: 'Racial Violence in the New Germany (1990-3)', *Contemporary European History* 3 (1994); and 'Racial Exclusionism in the New Germany', in Klaus Larres, ed., *Germany Since Unification* (London, 1998). The journal *German Politics* also published numerous articles on the rise of racism and nationalism. See also the excellent relevant essays in Peter Schuck and Rainer

Münz, eds, *Paths to Inclusion: The Integration of Migrants in the United States and* *Germany* (Oxford, 1998). Those wishing to keep right up to date should consult the website of the German Ministry of the Interior at www.bmi.bund.de, which also has links to all manner of minority organizations.

German refugees and migrants

Post-war refugees have received much attention from German authors, some of it translated. The best starting point consists of the volumes edited by Theodor Schieder including: *The Expulsion of the German Population from the Territories East of the Oder–Neisse-Line* (Bonn, 1960); *The Fate of the Germans in Hungary* (Bonn, 1961); and *The Fate of the Germans in Rumania* (Bonn, 1961). Just as important are Eugen Lemberg and Friedrich Edding, *et al.*, eds, *Vertriebene in Westdeutschland: Ihre Eingliederung und ihr Einfluss auf Gesellschaft, Wirtschaft, Politik und Geistleben*, 3 vols (Kiel, 1959). Excellent local studies include: Klaus J. Bade, Hans-Bernd Meier and Bernhard Parisius, eds, *Zeitzeugen im Interview: Flüchtlinge und Vertriebene im Raum Osnabrück nach 1945* (Osnabrück, 1997); Andreas Lüttig, *Fremde im Dorf: Flüchtlingsintegration im westfälischen Wewelsburg, 1945–1958* (Essen, 1993); Norbert Baha, *Wiederaufbau und Integration: Die Stadt Delmenhorst nach 1945* (Delmenhorst, 1983); and Uwe Weiher, *Die Eingliederung der Flüchtlinge und Vertriebenen in Bremerhaven, 1945–1960* (Bremerhaven, 1992). For migration from the GDR to the Federal Republic see: Helge Heidemeyer, *Flucht und Zuwanderung aus der SBZ/DDR, 1945/1949–1961: Die Flüchtlingspolitik der Bundesrepublik Deutschland bis zum Bau der Mauer* (Düsseldorf, 1994); and Volker Ackermann, *Der 'echte' Flüchtling: Deutsche Vertriebene und Flüchtlinge aus der DDR, 1945–1961* (Osnabrück, 1995).

Klaus J. Bade, ed., *Neue Heimat im Westen: Vertriebene, Flüchtlinge, Aussiedler* (Münster, 1990) covers ethnic German migration to the Federal Republic throughout its history before 1990. Good studies of the *Aussiedler* of the 1990s include: Barbara Malchow, Keyumars Tayebi and Ulrike Brand, *Die fremden Deutschen* (Hamburg, 1993); Gerold Dembon, Dieter Hoffmeister and Heinz Ingenhorst, *Fremde Deutsche in deutscher Fremde: Integrationsprobleme von Aussiedlern im kommunalen Raum* (Regensburg, 1994); and Klaus Brake, *Lebenserinnerungen rußlanddeutscher Einwanderer: Zeitgeschichte und Narrativik* (Hamburg, 1998).

INDEX